THE EAST EUROPEAN ECONOMIES IN THE 1970s

Butterworths Studies in International Political Economy will present new work, from a multinational stable of authors, on major issues, theoretical and practical, in the international political economy.

General Editor

Susan Strange, Professor of International Relations, London School of Economics and Political Science, England

Consulting Editors

Ladd Hollist, Director, Program for International Political Economy Research, University of Southern California, USA

Karl Kaiser, Director, Research Institute of the German Society for Foreign Affairs, Bonn, and Professor of Political Science, University of Cologne, West Germany

William Leohr, Graduate School of International Studies, University of Denver, USA

Joseph Nye, Professor of Government, Harvard University, USA

Already Published

The Political Economy of New and Old Industrial Countries

Forthcoming Titles

France in the Troubled World Economy
War, Trade and Regime Formation
Japan and Western Europe: Conflict and Cooperation
Defence, Technology and International Integration
International Political Economy – A Text
Economic Issues and Political Conflict: US – Latin American Relations

The East European Economies in the 1970s

Edited by
Alec Nove
Department of International Economic Studies, University of
Glasgow
Hans-Hermann Höhmann
Gertraud Seidenstecher
Federal Institute for East European and International Studies,
Cologne

Butterworths
London Boston Durban Sydney Toronto Wellington

First published 1982

© Butterworth & Co (Publishers) Ltd 1982

British Library Cataloguing in Publication Data

The East European economies in the 1970s.
   (Butterworths studies in international
   political economy)
   1. Europe, Eastern – Economic policy
   I. *Nove*, Alec   II. Höhmann, Hans-Hermann
   III. Seidenstecher, Gertraud
   330.947   HC244

   ISBN 0-408-10762-6

Photoset by Butterworths Litho Preparation Department
Printed in England by Robert Hartnoll Ltd., Bodmin, Cornwall

Acknowledgements

This book originated in a project sponsored by the Federal Institute for East European and International Studies, Cologne, Federal Republic of Germany. The publishers gratefully acknowledge the cooperation of the Institute in the preparation of this volume.

They also wish to thank Dr. Roger Clarke, University of Glasgow, who translated the chapters originally written in German, read the proofs of the entire book, and was a constant source of help and advice during its preparation.

Foreword

The aim of the present volume is to present a balance sheet of the development of economic policy in Eastern Europe in the 1970s. Individual country studies compare and contrast both the aims of economic development and the results of the growth process and also the instruments employed in economic policy. The volume is a sequel to a collection of analyses which appeared in the early 1970s and was similarly a product of Anglo-German cooperation*. Whereas at that time the purpose was to analyse the causes of economic reforms in Eastern Europe and to present the basic concepts of the reforms and evaluate the initial experience of the 'new economic systems', the present volume examines what has happened during the past decade after the fundamental changes in economic policy which occurred in the 1960s. We find that almost everywhere the original wave of reform enthusiasm has declined considerably but that this neither meant a return to the pre-reform situation nor can be equated with a general halt to institutional changes. On the contrary, the 1970s also brought numerous changes. But comprehensive new reform projects gave way to a strategy of gradual further development of the respective economic systems while their basic character was preserved. This 'process of reconstruction within the system' has also led to increasing differentiation of aims, institutions and instruments of economic policy between individual countries.

The aim of the present volume is to trace this process of differentiation. It includes studies of the European members of the Council for Mutual Economic Assistance and also Yugoslavia and Albania. The introductory summary attempts to draw up an overall balance sheet. The editors are very happy that they succeeded in attracting well-known specialists on Eastern Europe from the English- and German-speaking areas for this joint volume. They would also like to thank the Bundesinstitut für ostwissenschaftliche und internationale Studien in Cologne for financial support for the work.

Hans-Hermann Höhmann

---

* *Die Wirtschaftsordnungen Osteuropas im Wandel*, ed. Hans-Hermann Höhmann, Michael C. Kaser and Karl C. Thalheim, 2 vols., Freiburg im Breisgau, 1972. An updated English edition appeared in 1975 under the title *The New Economic Systems of Eastern Europe*, London and Berkeley, California.

Contributors

Włodzimierz Brus

Born 1921 in Płock (Poland); educated in Warsaw, USSR (MA in Economic Planning), Warsaw (PhD in Economics); Associate Professor of Political Economy at the Central School of Planning, Warsaw (1949–1954); Professor at the University of Warsaw (1954–1968; dismissed in March 1968 for political reasons); Head of the Department of Political Economy at the Institute of Social Sciences (attached to the Central Committee of the Polish United Workers' Party 1950–1956); Director of the Research Bureau of the Polish Planning Commission (1956–1958); Vice-chairman of the (advisory) Economic Council (1957–1963); since 1972 in the United Kingdom: Visiting Fellow, University of Glasgow; Senior Research Fellow St Antony's College, Oxford; University Lecturer and Fellow of Wolfson College, Oxford. *General Problems of Functioning of the Socialist Economy* (first edition 1961, published in nine languages, English edition 1972 under the title *The Market in a Socialist Economy*); *Economics and Politics of Socialism* (1972) published in five languages; *Socialist Ownership and Political Systems* (1975) published in seven languages.

George R. Feiwel

Born 1929 in Cracow, Poland; Associate Professor, Faculty of Commerce, University of Alberta (1962–1966); Associate, Harvard University, Russian Research Center (summer 1966, 1967 and 1971); Honorary Research Associate, Harvard University, Department of Economics; since 1966 University of Tennessee Alumni Distinguished Service Professor and Professor of Economics. *Economics of Socialist Enterprise* (New York, 1965); *Soviet Quest for Economic Efficiency* (New York, 1967, 1972); *New Economic Patterns in Czechoslovakia* (New York, 1968); *Industrialization and Planning under Polish Socialism*, 2 volumes (New York, 1971); *Essays on Planning in Eastern Europe* (Naples, 1973); *Growth and Reforms in Centrally Planned Economies* (New York, 1977); *Intellectual Capital of Michal Kalecki* (1975); *Paul Samuelson and Neoclassical Economics* (ed.) (New York, 1981, to be published).

Hans-Hermann Höhmann

Born 1933 in Cassel; studied general economics at Marburg and Berlin Universities; economics diploma (1956), special diploma for Soviet and East European studies (1959), PhD (1978); since 1962 Senior Researcher, Federal Institute for East European and International Studies, Cologne. *Wirtschaftsreformen in Osteuropa* (ed. with K. C. Thalheim) (Cologne, 1968); *Wandlungen im sozialistischen Wirtschaftssystem? Modell und Wirklichkeit osteuropäischer Wirtschaftsreformen* (Bonn, 1970); *Die Wirtschaft Osteuropas zu Beginn der 70er Jahre, Rückblick und Ausblick* (ed.) (Stuttgart, 1972); *Umweltschutz und ökonomisches System in Osteuropa* (with G. Seidenstecher and Th. Vajna) (Stuttgart, 1973); *The New Economic Systems of Eastern Europe* (ed. with M. C. Kaser and K. C. Thalheim) (London and Cologne, 1975); *Die Wirtschaft Osteuropas und der VR China 1970–1980, Bilanz und Perspektiven* (ed.) (Stuttgart and Cologne, 1978); *Partizipation und Wirtschaftsplanung in Osteuropa und der VR China* (ed. (Stuttgart and Cologne, 1980).

Michael Kaser

Born 1926 in London; read economics at Cambridge and served in the Foreign Office (1947–1951) and United Nations Economic Commission for Europe, Geneva (1951–1963), concurrently (1959–1963) teaching part-time at the Graduate Institute of International Studies; Reader in Economics at Oxford University and Fellow of St Antony's College. *Comecon: Integration Problems of the Planned Economies* (London, 1965, 1967); *Soviet Economics* (with J. Zieliński) (London, 1970); *Planning in East Europe* (London, 1970); *Health Care in the Soviet Union and Eastern Europe* (London, 1976).

H. G. Jiří Kosta

Born in 1921 in Prague; taught political economy at high schools in Prague (1956–1962); research at the Economic Institute of the Czechoslovak Academy of Sciences (1963–1968) and at the Austrian Institute for Economic Research in Vienna (1969); since 1970 Professor of Economics, specialization Socialist Economic Systems, at Frankfurt University. *Der technologische Fortschritt in Österreich und in der Tschechoslowakei* (with H. Kramer and J. Sláma) (Vienna and New York, 1971); *Sozialistische Planwirtschaft*, (Opladen, 1974); *VR China. Ökonomisches System und wirtschaftliche Entwicklung* (with J. Meyer) (Frankfurt and Cologne, 1976); *Abriß der sozialökonomischen Entwicklung der Tschechoslowakei 1945 –1977* (Frankfurt, 1978).

Manfred Melzer

Born 1934 in Berlin; studied general economics at Berlin and Bristol universities; economics diploma (1961), PhD (1979); since 1962 Senior Research Associate at the German Institute of Economic Research (Berlin); additional: since 1972 Lecturer in GDR economics at Technical University Berlin. *Handbook of the Economy of the German Democratic Republic* (one of some co-authors) (Westmead, 1978); *Economic Reform in East German Industry* (with G. Leptin) (Oxford, 1978); *Anlagevermögen, Produktion und Beschäftigung der Industrie im Gebiet der DDR von 1936 bis 1978 sowie Schätzung des künftigen Angebotspotentials* (Berlin, 1980); *The Industrial Enterprise in Eastern Europe* (one of some co-authors) (Eastbourne, 1981).

Alec Nove

Born 1915 in Petrograd; studied at the London School of Economics; after war service (British Army) and a period as a civil servant taught at the University of London (1958–1963), and then as Professor at the University of Glasgow. *The Soviet Economic System* (London, 1977); *Stalinism and After* (1975); *Efficiency Criteria for Nationalized Industries* (1973); *Economic History of the USSR* (1969); *Political Economy and Soviet Socialism* (1979), *Was Stalin really Necessary?* (1963).

Adi Schnytzer

Born 1947 in Regensburg; read chemistry and economics at Monash University Melbourne (1965–1972); completed PhD at Oxford University (1978); since 1980 Lecturer in Economics School of Social and Industrial Administration, Griffith University Brisbane. *The Albanian Economy* (Oxford, 1982, to be published).

Fred Singleton

Born 1926 in Hull, Yorkshire; read geography and history at Leeds (1947–1951), post-graduate studies in Helsinki; formerly Chairman, Post-Graduate School of Yugoslav Studies, University of Bradford, 1971–1981; Hon. Visiting Senior Research Fellow in Yugoslav Studies. *Background to Eastern Europe* (Oxford, 1969); *Industrial Revolution in Yorkshire* (Clapham, 1970); *Yugoslavia: the Country and its People* (London, 1970); *Twentieth Century Yugoslavia* (London, 1976); *Environmental Misuse in USSR* (New York, 1976); *The Just Society* (Nottingham, 1977); *Regional Economic Inequalities in Yugoslavia* (Bradford, 1979).

Iancu Spigler

Born in 1936 in Burdujeni, Bukovina, Romania; presently British citizen and Israeli citizenship; read economics at Oxford, also post-graduate research at the Hebrew University, and degree at Bucharest University; formerly Senior Associate Member of St Antony's College, Oxford, Shell Research Fellow at Reading University, and Senior Research Associate at Birmingham University; on the staff of Barclays Bank International preparing assessments of the centrally planned economies. *Economic Reform in Romanian Industry* (Oxford and London, 1971); *Direct Western Investment in East Europe* (Oxford, 1975).

Thomas Vajna

Born 1943 in Budapest; studied economics at Cologne and Vienna Universities; staff member of the Institute of German Economy (IW), Cologne. *Die Reform der ungarischen Wirtschaftspolitik* (Dissertation) 1969.

Contents

Acknowledgements v
Foreword vii
Contributors ix

1 *Economic reform in the 1970s – policy with no
  alternative Hans-Hermann Höhmann* 1
  1.1 The road to reform 1
  1.2 The retreat from reform 5
  1.3 Why no more extensive reform? 9

2 *USSR: economic policy and methods after 1970 Alec Nove* 17
  2.1 Survey of policy, methods and performance in the last
      decade 17
  2.2 Fundamental defects of the centralized planning system 25
  2.3 New attempts at reform 36

3 *The GDR – economic policy caught between pressure for
  efficiency and lack of ideas Manfred Melzer* 45
  3.1 From indirect steering to direct control 45
  3.2 Aims, methods and instruments of recentralization 49
  3.3 Between excessive bureaucracy and lack of efficiency 68

4 *Aims, methods and political determinants of the economic
  policy of Poland 1970–1980 Włodzimierz Brus* 91
  4.1 Introduction 91
  4.2 Development 1971–1975 94
  4.3 Factors of development in 1971–1975 98
  4.4 Growing tensions in the economy 104
  4.5 Economic reform 108
  4.6 1976–1980: plans and results 122

5 *Aims and methods of economic policy in Czechoslovakia
  1970–1978 Jiri Kosta* 139
  5.1 The aims of economic policy in the 1970s 139
  5.2 Ways and means of economic policy in the 1970s 155
  5.3 Economic growth and efficiency 167
  5.4 Conclusion 175

6 *Problems and trends in the development of the Hungarian new economic mechanism: a balance sheet of the 1970s* *Thomas Vajna* 180
6.1 Centralization, decentralization, recentralization – a survey of the changes in the Hungarian economic order 180
6.2 Problems of functioning and revisions of instruments in the 1970s 182
6.3 Ten years of the new economic mechanism – an attempt at a balance sheet 203
6.4 Revision of strategy for the 1980s 207

7 *Economic development and planning in Bulgaria in the 1970s* *George R. Feiwel* 215
7.1 Aspects of economic development at the threshold of the 1970s 216
7.2 Performance in the 1970s 218
7.3 Technical progress and foreign trade 223
7.4 Agriculture 225
7.5 Living standards and conditions 227
7.6 The system of planning and management 232
7.7 Impetus for and resistance to change 238
7.8 Statistical appendix 242

8 *Economic reform in Romania in the 1970s* *Michael Kaser and Iancu Spigler* 253
8.1 Publications on the Romanian system 253
8.2 The period between reforms, 1972–1978 254
8.3 The 'new economic mechanism' and its implementation, 1978–1980 264

9 *Objectives and methods of economic policies in Yugoslavia, 1970–1980* *Fred Singleton* 280
9.1 Introduction 280
9.2 The economic objectives of the Yugoslav revolution 282
9.3 The Yugoslav economy in the 1970s 284
9.4 Prospects for the future 312

10 *The economic system of Albania in the 1970s: developments and problems* *Michael Kaser and Adi Schnytzer* 315
10.1 Conservative radicalism 315
10.2 Genesis of the present system 316
10.3 The adaptations of 1970 321
10.4 Incentives 325
10.5 Agricultural organisation 330
10.6 Sharp disputes on economic policy, 1974–1976 331

Index 343

Economic reform in the 1970s – policy with no alternative

Hans-Herman Höhmann

1.1 The road to reform

For long periods of East European economic development the system of central administrative economic planning showed itself to be a suitable instrument for economic development of a 'catching up' type. The centralization of economic policy decisions in the political leadership and the strict hierarchy of administration enforced the concentration of resources at crucial points of development, enabled economic growth to be pushed forward in the manner of a campaign and permitted rapid transformation of the economic structure in the shape of industrialization based on the heavy industry and raw material sectors. Yet when in the course of the late 1950s and early 1960s the economic structure of the countries of Eastern Europe changed, when it became more mature and more complex, the efficacy of planning declined. The complexity of the economy increased more rapidly than did the capacity of the central administrative economic system to cope with this growing complexity in the planning process.

As a result of this, the USSR and a number of other East European countries had to accept a distinct fall in growth and loss of efficiency in their economies (Höhmann, 1972, 1978). These phenomena were particularly marked in Czechoslovakia and the GDR – two countries whose comparatively mature economic structure had always made the application of the system of central planning seem questionable on economic grounds. In addition to the increasing complexity of the economic structure there was the growing shortage of labour. This meant that growth of output had to be based more and more on productivity increases and the previous extensive growth process replaced by intensification. For this task, too, the central administrative planning system proved increasingly inappropriate.

Since the mid-1950s, and more so in the 1960s, the functional weaknesses of the traditional socialist planning system were discussed with growing openness in Eastern Europe and proposals for reform multiplied. Moscow gave the green light, and in the years 1963 to 1965 most of the communist governments put forward reform concepts, the gradual implementation of which was begun soon afterwards (Thalheim and Höhmann, 1968; Höhmann, Kaser and Thalheim, 1975).

What has become of this economic policy initiative of the 1960s? What driving forces and constraints govern the process of economic policy change in Eastern Europe at present and for the foreseeable future? To sum up the individual analyses and conclusions brought together in this volume, this opening chapter attempts to draw up a balance sheet of the reforms hitherto and to determine their future tendencies and limits.

Among the economic reforms of the 1960s two models can be distinguished which stand out in differing degrees of contrast to the traditional central administrative planning system: a conservative model, in which the range and depth of reform are limited, which can be designated a 'relaxed, rationalized administratively planned economy', and a more farreaching model, which was based on comprehensive use of market relations and consequently should be called a 'socialist market economy'. The limited reform model was the predominant one from the start, and only the Czechoslovak, Hungarian and, earlier, Yugoslav reforms were oriented towards market economy conceptions. The model of the 'relaxed, rationalized administratively planned economy' characterized the economic reforms in the USSR, the GDR, Poland, Bulgaria, Romania, tentatively in Albania and – after the ending of the 'Prague spring' phase of reform – in Czechoslovakia too. Of course, there were and are differences between these countries in respect of the scope of their reforms and many institutional details – such as the structure of the planning and administrative organs, the plan indicators and forms of incentives, the 'systems of economic levers' and the forms of enterprise amalgamations – yet with regard to the foundations and the principles of functioning of the reforms a farreaching similarity could be observed (Höhmann, Kaser and Thalheim, 1975; Bornstein, 1973, 1977).

All the reforms based on this model aimed from the outset at changes and improvements within the existing central administrative planning system, but not at a change of system. The essential features of the traditional planned economic system were to be retained: supra-enterprise administrative economic planning oriented towards the goals of the political leadership with scarcity signals conveyed through plan balances, priority of imperative (directive) over contractual guidance of the production and distribution activities of enterprises (associations) and plan fulfilment as the criterion of enterprise success.

Rationalization of the traditional system meant, for one thing, the search for more efficient management structures above enterprise level. These included the return to the branch principle of management of enterprises, which was expected above all to lead to successful technical progress. Second, we should note the introduction of a new, intermediate administrative level between the central organs of the economic leadership and the plan executants or enterprises in the shape of the so-called 'associations'. Such associations were created in all East European countries as amalgamations of enterprises, as 'socialist corporations'. Examples which can be mentioned are the industrial associations and production associations in the USSR, the 'associations of nationalized enterprises' (*VVB*) and the combines in the GDR, the 'large economic organizations' (*WOG*) in Poland and the industrial 'centrals' in Romania. The purpose of the formation of associations was both the simplification of planning and management by means of a reduction in the number of bodies to be coordinated (the aim 'from above') and also the utilization of the advantages of large-scale production to raise output and productivity (the aim 'from below').

The catchword 'rationalization' covers numerous other attempts to improve planning methods. These include efforts to achieve better coordination of five-year and annual plans, the use of mathematical planning models for forecasting and for plan and control figures, the introduction of electronic data processing, the development of feedback mechanisms in the information system and many others.

The catchword 'relaxation' applies primarily to changes in the sphere of planning and steering of enterprises (associations). The scope for autonomous enterprise decisions was widened; the group of plan indicators compulsorily prescribed for enterprises 'from above' through their superior management organs was reduced; inter-enterprise contractual relations were to acquire greater significance; plan indicators were established which were intended to promote greater concentration by enterprises on the quality of their products and the assortment desired by their customers; enterprises' room for financial manoeuvre was extended; larger bonus funds were made available for 'material incentives'; new wholesale prices were set; and the system of 'economic levers' to influence enterprises indirectly was enlarged. 'Economic levers' in the socialist countries mean primarily price and financial policy instruments, which are designed to induce enterprises to achieve the desired plan targets with the highest possible quality and at the lowest possible cost. The purpose of the relaxation which was sought was not to make enterprise decisionmaking processes independent as in the market economy pattern. Both the contracts concluded between the enterprises and the 'economic levers' were intended to supplement the plan, but certainly not to replace it. The purpose of the relaxation was to relieve supra-enterprise economic planning of the burden of detailed steering which was at the same time impossible and unneccessary. This was intended to restore the control of the enterprises by the central organs of the political and economic leadership that had in many respects been lost. In this reform model decentralization was thus conceived as a component of 'system-preserving reform', and was not designed to prepare the way for transition to a market economy.

The second reform model, however, did extend to such a transition to fundamentally market economy steering: this was the reform concept of the 'Prague spring', the concept which underlay the Hungarian economic reform of 1968 and which had earlier been applied in Yugoslavia in combination with the 'workers' self-management' typical of that country. The starting point of the reformers, as once formulated by Ota Šik, was that 'without making use of the market mechanism within a new conception of socialist planning' no further progress in economic policy was possible (Šik, 1967, p. 53).

Here, 'making use of the market mechanism' meant:

(1) Farreaching elimination of obligatory target planning of enterprise activity by superior authorities, or, in other words, widespread relaxation of the 'directive character' of planning;
(2) The abolition of direct allocation of means of production and establishment of a market for intermediate products, machinery and equipment (= elimination of the traditional system of 'material–technical supply');
(3) A relaxation of the state foreign trade monopoly and the creation of direct price links between domestic and foreign markets in order to deepen the international division of labour and to make use of the impetus to higher performance offered by international competition;
(4) The gradual decentralization of price setting in order to provide enterprises with economically meaningful yardsticks for autonomous decisions;
(5) The measurement of enterprise success by profit earned and no longer by the degree of plan fulfilment.

'A new conception of socialist planning' meant that state economic policy should concentrate on the implementation of long-term development goals and national economic proportions. These included, above all, the determination of the amount and structure of investments, which were also to remain even more centralized. In order to implement its economic policy objectives the state was to rely more than before on indirect means of monetary and financial policy, yet – at least for a transitional period – direct intervention in the enterprise decisionmaking process was also to be possible. The socialist order of property ownership was to be preserved. This and the marked state interventionism distinguish the market economy reform model in Eastern Europe clearly from Western forms of market economy. The steering model of the Yugoslav, Czechoslovak and Hungarian reformers can therefore rightly be characterized as a *socialist* market economy.

In the second stage of the economic reform in Czechoslovakia there was the additional characteristic that the transfer of decisionmaking powers to the enterprise level was to be linked with the extension of participation in the shape of the so-called 'workers' councils' (Kosta, 1980). These were bodies like the supervisory councils in the Federal Republic of Germany, in which workers were represented but in which there were also representatives of the enterprise management and state organs and the banks. It was the democratization of the social power structure, which was associated with the workers' councils, which above all made the 'Prague spring' so dangerous for the communist rulers.

1.2 The retreat from reform

What has become of the new orientation of economic policy in the 1960s and early 1970s? After fifteen years a balance sheet shows that in the past decade everywhere in Eastern Europe a more or less marked retreat from the reforms set in. It is true that at present there are again some signs of a serious search for greater efficiency in the steering system, associated with new reform measures. The pressure in the direction of reform increased after the 1976–1980 quinquennium, which nowhere produced very favourable results. The most recent events in Poland, too, are leading to reconsideration of economic policy questions. Nevertheless, it is doubtful whether a new initiative for reforms to change the system is imminent, so the meagre balance sheet of the reforms of the 1960s which we have set out may remain valid for some time yet.

While Hungary's 'New Economic Mechanism' in essence stood the test and was maintained, despite some restriction, the model of the 'relaxed, rationalized planned economy', in the version chosen in the 1960s, turned out not to function as efficiently as had been hoped. In all the countries in which this model had been adopted, therefore, modifications and restrictions of the reform soon occurred, so that there were more and more new 'reforms of the reform', which are discussed in detail in the individual contributions to this volume. In some countries, such as the USSR, the scope created by the reform for decisionmaking at lower administrative levels and at the level of the enterprise could not be fully used even temporarily. The economic administration resisted the loss of functions decreed for it and in practice continued very much in the style of the old management procedure, partly also because the management methods of the central economic leadership *vis-à-vis* the administration had not changed. In other countries, such as the GDR, on the other hand, a greater degree of decentralization took place, at least for a time – in the actual NES phase – before the economic policy points were set for an about-turn at the beginning of the 1970s (Leptin, 1968, 1975).

It was above all the lack of internal consistency in the reforms which meant that many of their individual elements did not have a chance to work or caused them soon to lose their effect. Thus the emigre Polish economist J. G. Zielinski, himself an active participant in the reform movement and later one of its leading observers, wrote:

> We did not envisage the possibility that, instead of the profit motive changing the TES [traditional economic system], the TES would change

or 'neutralize' the profit motive, which is what happened in practice (Zielinski, 1978, p. 7).

The weakness of the economic reforms of the 1960s (as of subsequent reform policy) is partly attributable to the fact that no theory had been created which could contribute to the elucidation of the problems of functioning of partially decentralized planning systems and could determine the minimum of consistent reform measures necessary to ensure stability of the system and an improvement in its functioning (Höhmann, 1980b; Zielinski, 1978). If the essence of the reform lay in combining central economic planning with broader scope for enterprise decisionmaking, an analysis of the interrelations between enterprises or associations and the economic management authorities, on the one hand, and of the horizontal coordination process of enterprises among themselves, on the other, was bound to be of great significance. For many reasons, such an analysis was, at best, only tentatively tackled. Yet there were differences here between one country and another. The development of theories of economic policy adequate for reforms certainly proceeded further in Poland, Hungary and Czechoslovakia than in the USSR, Bulgaria and Romania.

However, the significance of particular experiments which preceded the reform was overestimated. The fact that the results of such experiments, owing to a number of subjective and objective factors, could only be transferred to the whole economy to a limited extent was largely overlooked. The objective factors include the choice for most experiments of enterprises which were efficient in any case, the special conditions provided for experimental enterprises in many instances and the more efficient administrative supervision with a limited number of experimental enterprises. The subjective factors may include the special motivation of managers in experimental enterprises who know they are performing a special task.

The limited results of the economic reforms are not surprising: the changes which the reforms and the economic policy measures of subsequent years brought about did indeed affect the concrete institutional shape of economic planning and administration, but not the mechanism of functioning of the central administrative system. Because the basic structure of the traditional model, both at supra-enterprise and enterprise level, was retained, the economic process and all the problems of functioning connected with it were only peripherally altered. The troubles of the old system, which the reforms were supposed to abolish, were only partially eliminated, often just shifted and sometimes even exacerbated.

Deterioration of economic performance occurred above all because of the failure to accompany decentralization with provision of economically meaningful yardsticks for decentralized decisionmaking by enterprises. In particular, contradictions appeared between the greater decisionmaking freedoms of enterprises and the capacity of price systems. The rigid and mostly obsolete price structures gave enterprises only poor information about the relationships between requirements and costs in the economy. Enterprises then made wrong decisions and recentralization was the logical consequence. The Soviet economist V. V. Novozhilov once described these interconnections clearly: 'If prices do not provide the information necessary for economic decisions, then the missing information must be given in the form of an administrative instruction' (Novozhilov, 1966, p. 328).

In this situation the political leadership in Eastern Europe faced the alternatives of either going further with decentralization, creating a genuine market economy steering system and, for this purpose, a flexible, market-based price system too, or recentralizing again and seeking the way out in improvement of administrative organization and modernization of planning techniques. Except for Hungary and Yugoslavia, all the East European countries chose the road leading back to more centralism. Yet this retreat from reform occurred in differing degrees and at different times in individual countries. In the USSR the retreat was less drastic than in the GDR because the reform there was less marked in the first place. In the GDR the retreat took the form of gradual recentralization measures. In Poland there was a series of repeated attempts at reform, 'half-turns' followed again and again by setbacks and continuously deteriorating performance: 'The paradox of the Polish situation in 1975 and thereafter was that when the economy had growing difficulties to combat . . . and urgently needed the possibility of using resources better, the economic mechanism was in a state of disarray' (Brus, 1978, p. 45). Brus considers it possible that the conception of gradual reform contributed to this setback. First, a partial and gradual introduction of reform seemed to make fewer conceptual and institutional preparations necessary, which indeed affects the quality of the proposed solutions; second, the lack of harmonization of the new regulations on planning, allocation procedures and the award of bonuses, etc., which existed side by side with the old ones, was unavoidable; third – since the old system was in no way abolished – it was easier to retreat at the first hurdle, especially with all the political mistrust of protracted reforms (Brus, 1978, pp. 44f.).

Beside the internal inconsistencies of the limited reforms, new economic difficulties also affected the recentralization we have described. In the course of the 1970s disruptions of development occurred again and again, and were reflected above all in declining growth rates, inadequate increases in productivity and imbalances in both the domestic economy and external economic relations (steeply rising indebtedness). These troubles hit political leaderships which continued to pursue ambitious goals and were not willing to grant their economies the pause for breath needed for thoroughgoing reform. The pressure on the economy increased, there was a shortage of reserves which could be used to overcome the bottlenecks which occurred, and the consequence was recentralization of the economic decisionmaking process. In the USSR, for example, the start of recentralization fell in 1969, when the growth of industrial production had registered a new low point. In the GDR, too, numerous bottlenecks showed up in 1969 and 1970. Cornelsen described the consequences:

> Enterprises' scope for decisionmaking and the powers of the *VVB* and other intermediate bodies were restricted, direct state management was increased, the number of plan indicators prescribed for enterprises was raised and the indirect steering system was modified: the 'New Economic System' phase had come to an end (Cornelsen, 1978, p. 60).

Finally, world economic and political factors also affected the process of economic reform in Eastern Europe. If detente and the opening up of the East European economies to the world economy had favoured the trend towards reform, then tensions in foreign policy and disruptions of the world economy were and are bound to have a retarding effect on reform.

Thus the steep increases in oil prices affected many East European countries and the process of economic reform from two sides: from the West the danger of imported inflation made for greater centralism in price policy. This applies, for instance, to Poland, where there had been an attempt in the course of the economic reforms to create a connection between domestic and world market prices. From the East the higher prices for Soviet oil enforced concentration of economic resources on ensuring the increment in output needed to pay for Soviet oil.

It is not improbable that the present aggravation of the foreign policy situation – exemplified by the Soviet troops in Afghanistan – will have new centralizing effects, at least on Soviet economic planning. For one thing, foreign policy tension means more pressure on economic resources because of the rising demands for armaments. Tension also limits the leadership's reserves for manoeuvre and inclines it to meet economic difficulties with stricter direction rather than risky reforms.

Does the retreat from reform that we have outlined now mean a complete return to the *status quo ante*, to the economic systems of the early 1960s? Not at all. A number of changes in economic system and policy have been retained and are indeed likely to be irreversible.

Thus the planning systems of Eastern Europe today, despite all the retardation of the reforms, represent a more modern, more relaxed form of planned economy than the initial Stalinist model. Organization has been improved, new planning processes have been developed and in enterprise planning, too, many absurdities have been overcome.

Nevertheless, all these changes have not altered the basic character of the central administrative economic system. Only Hungary is an exception today, if we leave out Yugoslavia, which took the road to an economic system of its own as early as the 1950s (and Poland, where it is still not clear what the economic mechanism will be in the future). The third country with a market economy conception of reform, Czechoslovakia, had to fall into line with the conservative course of economic policy prescribed by the USSR soon after 1968:

> This survey of the management structure, the planning instruments and price and wage problems has made it clear that the means employed to implement economic policy in Czechoslovakia in the 1970s have been *those of a central administrative planning system.* All the same, compared with the pre-reform period the strictly centralized planning by means of administratively set compulsory indicators, which was the feature of that time, has given way to *greater use of commodity–money instruments* (Kosta, 1979, p. 2).

Even in Hungary we certainly cannot speak of an uninterrupted transformation to a socialist market economy (Gado, 1976; Nove, 1977, pp.290ff.; Vajna, 1978, pp. 175ff.). The Hungarian economic leaderships tried rather to steer a course of cautious reform, and above all to avoid the political risks of the Czechoslovak reform process. This was expressed in the cautious formulation that the 'New Economic Mechanism' was to create an 'integral combination of planned central steering of the economy with an active role for the market on the basis of socialist ownership of the means of production' (Csapo, in Vajna, 1978, p. 175), and thus not to lead to a new economic system. The image of a reform bearing the stamp of a market economy always remained obligatory, however, and soon movements towards a real change of system appeared. The role of the market as the instrument of short- and long-term coordination of the production and distribution processes expanded substantially. Right from the first phase of the reform, the system of plan indicators prescribed from above was fundamentally restricted.

Today direct plan instructons are given only for a small percentage of the volume of industrial production; for example, for some exports (primarily in order to be able to meet the demands of economic cooperation with the USSR) and products for state civilian and military requirements. In some fields of production, in which deficiencies in supply had arisen, the traditional system of material–technical suply was maintained. State influence on investment policy also remained relatively strong. Yet in this field, too, steps were taken towards greater decentralization. In the area of price policy a careful decentralization was undertaken, although here, as with foreign trade, certain phenomena of recentralization also appeared. The latter, however, were not designed as fundamental changes of course but were rather to serve to adapt the 'New Economic Mechanism' to changed social and economic (principally external economic) conditions.

1.3 Why no more extensive reform?

The limited nature of the reforms carried out so far, on the one hand, and the persistent economic difficulties in Eastern Europe, on the other, prompt the question: What are the limits which really thoroughgoing reforms – reforms leading to market steering mechanisms – always still encounter? At the moment it looks as if there were no alternative to the course of pragmatic but essentially conservative economic policy pursued since the beginning of the 1970s. True, the unsatisfactory economic situation in all East European countries prompts the search for new reform concepts. Yet there are weighty factors which block farreaching reforms – except possibly in Poland – for the foreseeable future (Bornstein, 1977; Burks, 1973; Höhmann, 1979).

Decisive above all else here are the manifold fears of the communist leadership (Bornstein, 1977). First, there is fear of loss of political control over the society they rule. The traditional administrative planning system was introduced in the East European countries from the start as a means of securing the regime. The subordination of broad sections of society to the instructions of the party and state apparatus and the widespread abolition of private ownership of the means of production decisively restricted the scope for political democracy and social participation and thus stabilized the role of the communist party, or of its leadership. To give up the system of economic planning by obligatory targets would at the same time be to give up a substantial part of the power and control exercised by the communist party. Furthermore, the experiences of the 'Prague spring' have shown how easily a comprehensive economic reform can spill over into other spheres of society and place the substance of the communist power system in question. Kosta concludes:

> Czechoslovak economic policy in the late 1970s continued to display the stamp of the tension between the requirements of economic growth and efficiency on the one hand and the political interests of the regime on the other. Whilst economic efficiency demands more decentralization, flexibility and openness to foreign trade, the continued existence of the power monopoly of the functionaries in the bureaucracy requires the maintenance of centralistic authoritarian decisionmaking structures and a certain isolation of the domestic economy from the outside world. (Kosta, 1979, p. 3)

For the Soviet Union the problem of internal political control has another aspect which should not be underestimated – that of nationalities policy. The central administrative planning and steering system, in its present form of economic administration through hierarchically constructed branch ministries, is the most effective and at the same time the most silent medium of Russian hegemonial policy within the USSR. The institution of the central ministry, directed from Moscow, with subordinate administrative offices, enterprises and associations throughout the country allows Russification to be pursued, so to say, within the framework of the internal personnel policy of the authorities. A socialist market economy, on the other hand, would inevitably bring local – and thus also national – elements more into play. Also, according to all international experience, a market economy could enlarge the gap in wealth between poor and rich regions of the USSR, something which has a substantial political explosive force and would endanger the position of the USSR as a unitary superpower.

In addition to fear of loss of political control there is fear of a loss of economic influence (Bornstein, 1973). The striving for rapid economic growth and the securing of a broad economic basis for armaments has always been at the centre of communist economic policy. It is true that everywhere in Eastern Europe today consumption enjoys higher priority than earlier, yet the transition to market economy steering systems involves the risk for the political leadership that the personal goals of consumers would gain precedence over the growth and armaments policy goals of the government.

Furthermore, the Soviet leadership has good reasons to assume that the underdevelopment of the economy of Siberia can more easily be overcome with the instruments of central economic steering than with any form of 'Socialist market economy'. The solution of this development problem is of great economic and geostrategic importance for the USSR today, and is outlined by the catchwords 'raw materials and energy supplies' and 'Soviet–Chinese conflict'. A market economy reform would probably delay the rapid economic development of Siberia considerably. Only if high subsidies could be paid would market-oriented enterprises be ready to invest there under the unfavourable conditions involving high costs of production. A prerequisite for such subsidies, however, is an effective state budget, which presumably could only be created over a period of time.

In another respect, too, the risk involved in a comprehensive reform, in the sense of a transition to market economic steering, is much greater in the USSR than in the smaller and structurally more balanced economies of Eastern Europe. The fact that the Soviet Union was developed for decades with a planned steering system and without regard for market demand and cost structures imposes high readjustment risks on any farreaching reform. For the superpower Soviet Union, which can only live up to its international role by straining all its economic forces, the danger of at least temporary economic setbacks is too great to make the Soviet leadership gamble on the possible but uncertain future success of reform. This is especially true at a time when the new foreign policy tensions resulting from the Soviet invasion of Afghanistan are presumably bringing increased armaments burdens on the economy and when the economic consequences of the Polish events cannot be foreseen.

Finally, in all Eastern European economies market economy reforms would involve a threat to political stability. A market economy cannot function without flexible prices. The inflationary pressure which exists today, in the producer goods sector as well as on the consumer goods market, would change from repressed or concealed inflation to open inflation to a much greater extent than at present. The economic and political risks of such a development go without saying. Also, a transition to a market economy would probably bring about at least a temporary unemployment problem: for ideological reasons alone this is scarcely an acceptable prospect for socialist systems.

A thoroughgoing market economy reform would threaten the Soviet leadership with loss of control in external as well as domestic policy. From the foreign policy point of view the administrative planned economy is the most important instrument of integration policy within the 'Council for Mutual Economic Assistance', and thus serves at the same time as a means of Soviet hegemony policy. The administrative planned economy ensures three things in this context: first, a considerable part of the economic potential of the smaller CMEA countries is tied to the USSR through bilateral plan coordination. Second, in this way the USSR can profit from technical progress in the more developed CMEA countries, notably the GDR and Czechoslovakia. This, in turn, is of particular importance at a time when foreign policy tensions are threatening to obstruct the West–East transfer of modern technology for which the Soviet side is striving. Third, and lastly, interstate plan coordination in Eastern Europe enables the USSR to plan a large part of its international economic relations. The transition to a socialist market economy in the CMEA countries, with the associated possibility of a freer choice of trading partners on Western markets, would endanger the economic and, furthermore, the foreign policy dominance of the USSR in Eastern Europe.

Ideological conceptions also still restrict the scope of the communist leaderships in Eastern Europe to carry out reforms. True, in the course of the evolution of reforms since the mid-1960s a whole series of traditional ideological notions was either abandoned or revised. As the world socialist movement shows, Marxism as a fundamental ideological concept is today capable of widely varying interpretations and can, as for example in Yugoslavia, be combined with a market economy steering system. All the same, in most East European countries – and principally in the USSR itself – a conservative variety of Marxism–Leninism, which has not yet reached such flexibility of interpretation, prevails at present. Above all, the basic ideological postulates of the ability to plan and the harmony of economic and political development in socialist societies help to preserve the existing planning system and obstruct the development of market economy steering instruments. For recognition of the market as an authority in the direction of society involves at the same time recognition of the limits of planning as well as the possibility of conflicts on the basis of socialist property relations (Höhmann, 1979).

Finally, the increasing age of the leadership in many East European countries limits their openness to reforms. For one thing, old age is a period of life when people are more concerned with preservation than with change. In adddition, the training and experience of the ageing leadership inclines it more towards the image of the planner–engineer than of the entrepreneur. Lastly, its age restricts the leadership's time horizon: the chance of guiding the economy successfully through a long and difficult process of reform is small and the risk of disaster great. This applies especially to the Soviet leadership in view of the difficult economic situation and the unbalanced economic structure of the USSR. New basic conceptions of economic policy may well only come with a change of generation in the leadership. The institutional rigidity of communist power systems restricts rapid 'elite circulation' as do the lack of an influential public opinion and the absence of a critical and at the same time informative press. But one must be careful not to draw the wrong conclusion from this: a new, modern leadership would certainly be necessary but would not be a sufficient condition for farreaching reforms. There are many factors indicating that even more up-to-date politicians would adhere to the present restrictive course in economic policy.

However, a comprehensive economic reform encounters resistance not only from the political leadership. It also finds little favour with the groups in East European society whose social position would be affected by such a reform. This applies primarily to the administrative bureaucracy, which is bound to be anxious about its position in the event of a transition to a market economy.

It should nevertheless be emphasized that the large social groups whose social position would be affected by reform measures are not homogeneous (Nove, 1979, p. 157). Within these groups there are differences both in respect of the disadvantages to be expected and in respect of the possibility of influencing the economic policy of individual countries in their own interests and of advancing or holding back reforms. This is as true of enterprise directors and workers as it is of the functionaries in the state and party apparatus. Thus functionaries at the lower administrative levels would certainly fear market economy reforms to a greater extent than the top bureaucracy, which would retain power and influence even in the case of a more fundamental reform.

The bureaucracy fears both a loss of powers and also a loss of privileges, which ensure it substantial income advantages as well as social status. Thus the bureaucracy has preferential access to comparatively cheap consumer goods and services. It enjoys opportunities to purchase bargains for itself. It has access to restaurants where other citizens must wait in queues. It also enjoys a number of completely free benefits, like the use of an official car. This stratum of middle and upper party and state functionaries will certainly exert its influence in the political decisionmaking process against a compre-hensive reform.

Even reforms *within* the existing administrative planning system, leading to the use of new organizational forms or methods of planning without changing the basic principles of the system, often encounter resistance. Thus a distinct reluctance to introduce modern mathematical planning procedures on a broad scale may be observed among longserving administrative functionaries. For such modernization would involve the danger for administrators steeped in the old routines of being replaced by younger experts specially trained in such procedures.

Enterprise directors have conflicting attitudes towards a farreaching reform. Frequent complaints in the East European press make it clear that many managers are dissatisfied with the existing system of enterprise planning. The cause of this dissatisfaction, however, is hardly a general rejection of the traditional system, and consequently it scarcely leads to the desire to replace administrative planning by a market economy. The reasons for the enterprise directors' complaints are contradictions within the existing system rather than the system itself. The difficulty of fulfilling all the plan targets from the various authorities at the same time, the constantly changing problem of finding the optimal mix of fulfilment and non-fulfilment of plans, the frequent plan alterations, the chronic irregularity of supplies of materials and equipment – all this makes the enterprise director hope for thorough changes: changes to guarantee more stability of plans and continuity of supply with means of production, but changes *within* the existing system. Market economy reforms, on the other hand, would bring new risks for management. The market demands entrepreneurial behaviour, something to which enterprise managements, however, are unaccustomed. The market demands profitability, but this can often only be achieved with difficulty, because of relationships over which the enterprise itself has no influence. Anyone who has to run an enterprise in a remote region of the USSR under high-cost conditions will have a hard time showing a profit. So the attitude of enterprise directors to reform depends to a large extent on the economic situation of their enterprise, on the likely effects of a reform on the profit position of the enterprise and on their own capacity to display entrepreneurial initiative. Under such conditions, only dynamic personalities in management in East European enterprises are likely to belong to the ranks of the advocates of thoroughgoing reforms.

There is something else besides: the traditional planning system certainly restricted greatly the scope for enterprise decisionmaking, but on the other hand it also protected the enterprise director against too much participation 'from below', from the workers and their representative organizations in the enterprises. In a socialist society – as the examples of Yugoslavia and the 'Prague spring' show – greater decentralization of decisions could sooner or later lead to more participation, and this again restricts the management's scope for decisionmaking.

For the workers, too, a farreaching reform would not be an unmixed blessing. Certainly, the workers in East European countries as consumers are interested in a rise in the overall performance of the economy, in wage increases, in an improved supply of consumer goods, in higher quality and in a better range of choice of necessities. To this extent the main direction of thrust of reform and the interests of the population coincide. On the other hand, a market economy reform, if it is to be successful, must involve a higher degree of mobility of labour and performance-based wage differentials. This could mean loss of one's job and cuts in income. A reform which involved such disadvantages for the population would, however, come up against at least suspicion and resistance from those sections of the labour force which had particular cause to fear the effect of the reform. The labour disturbances in Poland sound a clear message here. They were directly connected with price increases and changes in the wage system, and twice they forced the leadership of the country to retreat. In Hungary, too, at the beginning of the 1970s there was dissatisfaction among broad groups in the labour force with wage differentials which indeed correspond to the principles of economic reform but were starting to change the pattern of income distribution, which traditionally aimed at more equality. Here, too, a retreat in reform policy was unavoidable.

In conclusion we can say that, despite persistent economic difficulties, Eastern Europe is holding firmly to the planned economic system. Whilst problems with growth and economic structure continue to generate numerous impulses towards reform, the limits to comprehensive reforms, on the other hand, at least in the foreseeable future, prove insurmountable. These limits are particularly narrow in the Soviet Union, but the economies of Eastern Europe, too, are neither ready nor in a position for a new economic policy initiative. Reforms in these countries encounter both internal barriers and, not least, opposition from the USSR. It is scarcely likely that the Soviet Union will allow comprehensive economic reforms in the countries of the 'Council for Mutual Economic Assistance' as long as it is not prepared for thoroughgoing changes in economic policy itself. Even the Hungarian development does not contradict this assumption, for it must not be overlooked that Hungary received the green light from Moscow for its 'New Economic Mechanism' before the 'Prague spring' made it clear how farreaching comprehensive economic reforms could be. Comprehensive reforms of the economy in Eastern Europe would not only weaken the economic and foreign policy influence of the Soviet Union there but would also question the standing of Soviet socialism as the pattern to be followed.

Yet at the time of writing (December 1980) the developments in Poland throw up many questions. A new situation has arisen there because of the strong pressure from the population for improvement in the standard of living and because of the rise of an independent trade union movement. The Polish leadership, itself still not stabilized, is in a difficult situation: it must both ensure stability and progress in the economy and carry out reforms, since the traditional planning system is heavily compromised. yet is it too early to say that the points are set clearly in the direction of market socialism, let alone workers' self-management. The USSR will exert a retarding influence. But even if in Poland changes are implemented in the economic system under pressure from the population, the fundamentally conservative trend of economic policy in the other East European countries will very probably persist and even be reinforced in order to ward off the danger of 'infection' of the political order.

Thus, all in all, economic policy in Eastern Europe today is an economic policy with no alternative. The basic adherence to the planned economic system does not, however, exclude partial changes. The unfavourable economic situation of Eastern Europe will continue to make it a field for persistent though at the same time limited experiments with economic policy.

References

Bornstein, M. (ed.) (1973). *Plan and Market, Economic Reform in Eastern Europe*. New Haven and London
—— (1977). Economic Reform in Eastern Europe. In *East European Economies Post-Helsinki*. Washington, DC
Brus, W. (1978). Ziele, Methoden und politische Determinanten der Wirtschaftspolitik Polens 1970–1976. *Berichte des Bundesinstituts fur ostwissenschaftliche und internationale Studien* No. 49. Köln
Burks, R. V. (1973). The Political Implications of Economic Reform. In Bornstein, *Plan and Market*
Cornelsen, D. (1978). In Höhmann, H.-H. (1978)
Gado, O. (1976). *The Economic Mechanism in Hungary – How it Works in 1976*. Budapest
Höhmann, H.-H. (ed.) (1972). *Die Wirtschaft Osteuropas zu Beginn der 70er Jahre*. Stuttgart – Berlin – Köln – Mainz
—— (ed.) (1978). *Die Wirtschaft Osteuropas und der VR China 1970–1980*. Stuttgart – Berlin – Köln – Mainz
—— (1979). State and Economy in Eastern Europe. In *State and Society in Contemporary Europe*. London
—— (ed.) (1980a). *Partizipation und Wirtschaftsplanung in Osteuropa und der VR China*. Stuttgart – Berlin – Köln – Mainz
—— (1980b). Veränderungen im sowjetischen Wirtschaftssystem: Triebkräfte, Dimensionen und Grenzen. *Berichte des Bundesinstituts für ostwissenschaftliche und internationale Studien* No. 37. Köln

Höhmann, H.-H., Kaser, M. C., and Thalheim, K. C. (eds) (1975). *The New Economic Systems of Eastern Europe*. London
Kosta, J. (1979). Ziele und Methoden der Wirtschaftspolitik in der Tschechoslowakei (1970–1978). *Berichte des Bundesinstituts fur ostwissenschaftliche und internationale Studien* No. 43. Köln
—— Werktätigenräte im Prager Frühling 1968. In Höhmann, *Partizipation und Wirtschaftsplanung*
Leptin, G. (1968). Das 'Neue Ökonomische System' Mitteldeutschlands. In Thalheim, K. C., and Höhmann, H.-H. (1968)
—— (1975). The German Democratic Republic. In Höhmann, Kaser and Thalheim, *New Economic Systems*
Nove, A. (1977). *The Soviet Economic System*. London
—— (1979). *Political Economy and Soviet Socialism*. London
Novozhilov, V. V. (1966). Problemy planovogo tsenoobrazovaniya i reforma upravleniya promyshlennost'ju. In *Probleme zentraler Wirtschaftsplanung* (ed. by K. Wessely). München
Thalheim, K. C., and Höhmann, H.-H. (eds) (1968). *Wirtschaftsreformen in Osteuropa*. Köln
Vajna, Th. (1978). Ungarn. In Höhmann, *Die Wirtschaft Osteuropas*
Zielinski, J. G. (1978). On System Remodelling in Poland. *Soviet Studies XXX*, No.1

USSR: economic policy and methods after 1970

Alec Nove

2.1 Survey of policy, methods and performance in the last decade

Background: the failure of the 1960s reform movement

By 1970 the reform movement had run its course, and a reaction had set in. The 'high point' of reform was reached in 1965, with the adoption of a decree which had the declared intention of increasing managerial powers and reducing considerably the number of compulsory indicators 'passed down' from the centre. Prices were recalculated on the basis of cost plus a percentage of the value of capital assets, thus supposedly corresponding to Marx's 'price of production'. A major adjustment in prices was to eliminate losses in such sectors as coal and timber. A capital charge averaging 6% was to be levied. This same decree finally eliminated the *sovnarkhozy* and restored the industrial ministries with almost the pre-*sovnarkhoz* powers, one important difference being the attempt to concentrate in *Gossnab* (the State material–technical supply committee) the function of disposal which departments of ministries formerly exercised. Most of the ministries were all-union rather than union-republican; in other words, although there was a move towards greater devolution to management, the clear intention was to centralize planning and ministerial powers in Moscow. Republican and other regional planning organs lost powers.

It soon became evident that the reforms of 1965 were internally inconsistent. Ministerial powers over 'their' enterprises were those of superiors *vis-à-vis* subordinates, and orders could be, and were, issued on a wide variety of topics supposedly within the competence of management. Elaborate schemes intended to relate managerial bonuses, and payments into various incentive funds, to profitability and sales (disposals) were ineffective, for a variety of reasons. Thus plans were anything but stable, repeatedly altered within the period of their currency. The rules governing bonuses were changed arbitrarily and frequently. While management was supposed to be encouraged to aim high, success and bonuses still depended primarily on plan *fulfilment*, which meant that it always 'paid' to try to have a modest, 'fulfillable' plan. Persistent shortages of many inputs led to a number of negative phenomena: hoarding, overapplication for material allocations, production and construction delays. It also meant that ministries and enterprises made their own supply and procurement arrangements, and unofficial *tolkachi* supplemented the supply system by semi-legal deals. The stress on the profit motive, which seemed to be a feature of the 1965 reform, was also negated by several factors: the fact that any additional profits were likely to be transferred to the budget (the 'free remainder', *svobodnyi ostatok pribyli*), the much greater stress on the fulfilment of quantitative targets, and, finally, the inherent illogicality of using profits as a guideline when prices were uninfluenced by demand or need, a point to which we will return when we consider the latest attempt to introduce reforms.

By 1970 not much was left of the additional managerial powers ostensibly granted by the 1965 reform. So the plans and policies of the decade of the 1970s were applied within the traditional system of centralized planning, with multiple obligatory targets imposed on management, and administrative allocation of inputs, a task divided three ways: between Gosplan, Gossnab and ministries. As will be argued later in detail, the inherent impossibility of efficient and effective centralization underlay many, if not most, of the problems faced by the economy.

The need to improve efficiency

Yet efficiency and effectiveness, quality and technical progress were essential, and were seen to be essential. The 24th party congress in 1971, which duly adopted the five-year plan for 1971–1975, laid great stress on these matters, since the growth targets adopted by the Congress could only be reached if there was a marked improvement in labour productivity, a more rational use of investment resources, more regard to diffusion of new technology and the reduction of waste. So did the 25th Congress in 1976. Brezhnev spoke of a 'quinquennium of effectiveness and quality', and indeed stressed the need for finding new ways of planning in an age of scientific–technical revolution. There is no shortage of quotations from Brezhnev and other top leaders which show them to have been well aware of the weaknesses which exist and of the need for fundamental change. Unfortunately it is also clear that their recipe for change is to ring the changes in the organization of central planning, plus exhortation: to urge officials to take quality into account, to enforce planned delivery obligations, to insist on balanced plans, to enforce discipline, to issue orders designed to reduce waste, to relate production more closely to need, and, in fact, to act efficiently. As we shall see, all this is easier said than done, within the centralized system.

Table 2.1 shows the principal targets of the 1971–1975 and 1976–1980 plans, and the extent to which they were fulfilled. For reasons familiar to students of Soviet statistics, the physical output data are more reliable than

Table 2.1 *The ninth and tenth five-year plans (1971–1975, 1976–1980)*

	1970	(1970 = 100) 1975 plan	1975 actual	(1975 = 100) 1980 plan	1980 actual
(a) Index Numbers					
National income[a]	100	138.6	128	126	123
Industrial production	100	147.0	143	137	124
Producer goods	100	146.3	146	140	125
Consumer goods	100	148.6	137	131	121
(b) Quantities					
Electricity (milliard kWh)	740.9	1065	1039	1380	1295
Oil[b] (million tons)	352.6	505	491	640	603
Gas (milliard m³)	197.7	320	289	435	435
Coal (million tons)	524.1	694.9	701	800	716
Steel (million tons)	115.9	146.4	141	168	148
Fertilizer[c] (million tons)	55.4	90	90.2	143	104
Motor vehicles (1000s)	916	2100	1964	2150	2199
Tractors (1000s)	458.2	575	550	590	595*
Cement (1000s)	94.3	125	122	144.5	125
Fabrics (million m²)	8850	11100	9956	12800	11700
Leather footwear (million pairs)	675.7	830	698	(n.a.)	744

* Estimated from percentage increase in the total horsepower figure

Notes: Some plan figures are midpoints of ranges
  (a) Material product (utilized)
  (b) Including gas condensate
  (c) Gross weight

Sources: Pravda, 14 December 1975, 7 March 1976 and statistical returns for the relevant years.

the index numbers. Briefly, the reason for this is not any sort of crude cheating. Index numbers are calculated, in the USSR as elsewhere, by deflating value totals (e.g. in rubles) by a price index. There are strong grounds for disbelieving the official price index, because it pays management to conceal price rises whenever possible by changing the product. For example, a machine-tool or a shirt can and do alter in design. Of course, the appearance of new products and new designs is a feature of life in all countries, and to that extent all price (and therefore volume) indices are, in fact, imprecise approximations. However, where there is strict price control, and on top of that there are aggregate value plans to fulfil, there is a powerful inducement to conceal what is really a price increase. Let me give an example. Suppose that a future British government 'froze' all prices charged in restaurants, and suppose a restaurant served beef stew and chicken at £1.50. A new dish would be introduced, say curried lamb at £2, and they would cease to serve beef stew. Price increase? Not at all, just a change in the menu . . . One can also worsen quality at the same price, or reduce quantity. None of these evasions are necessary if there is no price control to evade. But when they occur, the incidental effect is to exaggerate the volume index. That exactly this happens with Soviet machinery prices is clearly stated in a recent article (Krasovsky, 1980).

This being the case, the index figures of plan fulfilment doubtless exaggerate somewhat the rate of growth, but we do not know and cannot know by how much (to re-use the above example, *maybe* the curried lamb was of much better quality than the beef stew!). In interpreting the figures it is also important to note that the rapid expansion of military output, which is included in the index, does not appear in the physical-output series.

The 1971–1975 plan originally envisaged a more rapid increase in output of consumers' goods than of producers' goods (see *Table 2.1*), but the traditional priorities reasserted themselves in the process of fulfilment, and in the plan for 1976–1980. In fact, underfulfilment was the rule in both plan periods. In 1971–1975 coal and mineral fertilizer did relatively well, but both of these were far below target in 1980, when virtually the only items of significance to reach planned levels were natural gas and motor vehicles. Consumers' goods lagged far behind, with the output of leather footwear in 1980 still well below the original plan target for 1975. Agricultural performance was subject to the vagaries of weather, and 1975 proved to be an unfavourable year, as did 1979. Despite massive injections of capital, progress was slow, and substantial grain purchases had to be made in the capitalist world, especially in the United States.

Policy objectives in the 1970s

(a) Agriculture
Investments in agriculture were to increase both relatively and absolutely, and in fact were and are very high by any standard (*Table 2.2*). In addition,

there were increased investments in industries serving agriculture: fertilizer, agricultural machinery, etc.

Priority was to be given to land improvement, notably in the non-black-earth zones which have reliable rainfall, to the mechanization of the livestock sector and to the expansion of fodder supplies. Agricultural output

Table 2.2 *Total investments in agriculture (productive and unproductive)*

	Value (milliards of rubles)	Percentage of total investment
1970	19.4	24
1975	30.8	27
1978	34.6	27

Source: Nar. khoz. 1978, p. 346.

Table 2.3 *Labour in agriculture (thousands)*

	1970	1975	1978
State agriculture	9419	10 521	11 258
Kolkhozy	16 700	15 200	14 100

Source: Nar. khoz. 1978, pp. 261, 366.

in 1971–1975 averaged 13% higher than in the quinquennium 1966–1970; the figures for 1976–1980 will probably show a smaller rise, perhaps 10%, with livestock production hit by the consequences of the bad 1979 and 1980 harvests (and the US embargo). If one allows for weather variations there has been a slow improvement in production and in yields, but this is not proportionate to the resources which have been devoted to agriculture. The rate of return is low. Costs are high. Pay in *sovkhozy* and *kolkhozy* has increased faster than productivity, faster also than pay in urban areas, while the size of the agricultural labour force is falling but remains high.

The figures in *Table 2.3* are not strictly comparable, and include some non-agricultural work (e.g. construction by *kolkhoz* members), and exclude part of the work on private plots. The point here is not statistical precision, but the trend. Average wages in state agriculture rose by over 40% during this period (*Nar. khoz.* 1978, p. 372), while pay per day worked in *kolkhozy* rose by 34%. Since expenditures on machinery, fertilizer, fuel, etc. all rose steeply, and since the government insisted on keeping retail prices of basic foodstuffs stable, this resulted in a very large subsidy, which has now grown to at least 23 billion rubles[1]. There is also a subsidy to cover sales of industrial inputs to agriculture at a discount[2]. Thus in 1978, output was 29 billion rubles higher than in 1966, but production expenses rose by 50 billions (Glushkov, 1980, p. 11). All in all, agriculture has long ceased to be a source of accumulation for industry, and has for some years been a burden for the rest of the economy. There has been much discussion as to the causes of inefficiency in agriculture. There would probably be general agreement about the following negative factors: poor quality of machines, lack of spare parts, lack of workshops and maintenance personnel, insufficient *kompleksnost'* (i.e. frequent absence of complementary machines reducing the effectiveness of other machinery), shortage of hard-surface roads, far too few specialized lorries, and lack of effective labour incentives. This last point is linked with diseconomies of scale. Farms are big and scattered, and incentives are frequently of the wrong sort: for example, tractor drivers on piecework (area ploughed) find it 'pays' to plough shallow; the pay is not related to the ultimate result, i.e. production.

A solution is to split up the farms into small mechanized units. These were called *beznaryadnye zvenya*, literally 'teams without work assignments'. They organize their own work and are paid by results. After some apparently successful experiments this method was strongly discouraged, if not banned. However, it has recently revived, under other names. The most recent example is a major article in *Pravda* (14 July 1980), in which the autonomous unit is called *zvenyevaya beznaryadno-khozraschyotnaya sistema*. Once again, great successes are claimed, and, though there are practical as well as ideological–political obstacles to universal use of this method, it may well now spread, with beneficial results.

Policy towards private plots has fluctuated. At intervals articles appeared emphasizing the importance of private cultivation and private livestock, and deploring obstruction of these legally recognized activities (specifically mentioned in the *kolkhoz* charter). Obstruction takes such forms as non-supply of fodder for livestock, and police have sometimes stopped peasants from reaching urban markets for no good reason[3]. Higher incomes have led to increased peasant consumption of better-quality foods, and even the much-increased free market prices do not stimulate larger private marketings, all of which contributes to food shortages in towns.

(b) Consumer goods

Food shortages have, in fact, been getting steadily worse, and shortages of other consumer goods have been serious too. Despite the declared intention to increase supplies faster than incomes, the reverse has been the case, owing to the fact that, in both the five-year-plan periods of the 1970s, output has risen by much less than planned. While incomes have been held to or even slightly below planned levels, the disparity has grown. *Pravda* in an editorial (27 July 1979) noted that while 'savings deposits have almost tripled in eight years, the supply of goods and services has risen much more slowly than the incomes of the population'. One way of measuring the impact of this 'inflation à la sovietique' is the growing gap between official and free-market prices of foodstuffs. These can be calculated as follows:

Free market percentage	1965	1970	1973	1978
Food sales in actual prices	10.0	8.5	7.9	8.8
Food sales valued in state prices	7.3	5.5	4.8	4.4
Implied price index, free market (State prices = 100)	137	154	164	200

Source: Nar. khoz. 1978, p. 433.

Persistent shortages have given rise to various negative phenomena: black or grey markets, petty and not-so-petty corruption, etc. There are both macro and micro disequilibria, overall excess demand, *and* shortages of specific goods (while some others remain unsold). In the case of meat, the huge subsidy ensures that demand far exceeds supply. Poor distribution exacerbates the problem. By the end of the decade shortages became very serious. By persisting with price freezes for essentials while sharply increasing other prices (e.g. for petrol, taxis, furs, coffee, restaurant meals), the government has made things very difficult both for itself and for the consumer.

This disappointing outcome was not due to a change of policy, but rather it was the consequence of serious shortfalls in production and of delays in construction, which necessitated cuts. As a failure to supply (for example) energy or steel does greater cumulative damage to the economy than a delay in providing (say) footwear or motor-cycles, the planners understandably tend to cut the latter rather than the former.

(c) Siberia

There is no doubt that part of the difficulty in maintaining planned growth rates has arisen from the necessity to tap sources of energy, timber, ores and other materials in remote areas, notably in Siberia, at very high cost. The big effort to use Siberian resources was and is necessary, indeed overdue. The oil and gas of the Tyumen province have been brought into use with remarkable speed, a huge network of pipelines has been built. Oil and gas have been exported on a large scale. It may prove difficult to increase or even maintain oil production unless large new discoveries compensate for the exhaustion of older wells, but vigorous exploration efforts are being made in Siberia and elsewhere. The great new Baikal–Amur railway project is intended to provide access to important sources of fuel, minerals and timber in East Siberia. But while all this is rational and, in the long run, likely to be a source of strength, in the medium term this represents a further burden on an overstrained economy, and not least on transport. The overloading of the railway network is among the major causes of recent difficulties.

Reasons for poor economic performance

The 1976–1980 quinquennium has been even more difficult than its predecessor, although, as *Table 2.1* shows, the growth rate envisaged was below not only the planned but also the (lower) actual growth rates of 1971–1975. Indeed, 1979 proved to be one of the worst years of Soviet peacetime history, with considerable *falls* in the output of such important items as coal, steel, cement and fertilizer. There was also a bad grain harvest, but this has to be attributed to weather. There was some recovery in 1980, but, even so, the plan had been substantially underfulfilled in almost every particular.

Soviet economic strategy during the 1970s, until 1979, in fact included the fullest utilization of the international division of labour, both with the capitalist world and within the CMEA countries. The huge increase in oil prices which occurred in 1973 added greatly to Soviet earnings of hard currency, as also did the rise in the price of gold. The availability of credits from Western countries and from the Eurodollar market also helped the USSR to finance a deficit due to the combined effects of increased purchases of Western equipment and of Western grain. It has never been the author's view that the so-called policy of détente had primarily an economic motivation. However, there is no doubt that more trade and credits, more technology and grain, were significant by-products of this policy. West Germany emerged as by far the most important Western supplier of machinery.

The 1970s has been a period of high military expenditures, although this was not publicly stated (the defence budget altered little). The achievement of parity with the United States must have been a source of strain to the rest of the economy. Owing to its high priority, the military sector takes a high proportion of the best managers, scientists, modern equipment and skilled labour. None of this can be adequately quantified, but few can doubt that this has been an important contributory cause of the enhanced difficulties which the Soviet planning system has been facing during this decade.

Some other causes of the unsatisfactory state of affairs have been mentioned already: the cost of Siberia and the heavy spending in agriculture: the unfavourable demographic situation is also partly responsible. But there is mounting evidence of the inability of the planning mechanism itself to cope with its immense task. Imbalance, shortage and contradictory plan indicators have led to increasing frustrations, and also to the growth of unofficial and sometimes corrupt supply links. But, above all, much has gone wrong (increasingly wrong) with investment planning. Delays in construction have increased relatively as well as absolutely, as will be documented in detail later.

While it may be too 'dramatic' to speak of the disintegration of the planning system (since every source of weakness has existed in some form for many years) it does appear that these weaknesses have gradually become more serious. Efficiency is now more urgently needed, because of the exhaustion of labour reserves and the greater maturity of the industrial economy: hence much talk in official circles about the transition from 'extensive' to 'intensive' growth. In this sense, past inefficiencies are now felt to be intolerable and are subjected to severe criticism in speeches and in the press. But it seems, in addition, that imbalances, bottlenecks and shortages have actually grown worse, bringing growth rates down to minimal levels at the end of the 1970s with the five-year plan very significantly underfulfilled in virtually every respect. Despite the shortfall in the production of energy, it seems that this was not a significant bottleneck, since most of the sectors which use energy were even further behind schedule. One cannot prove or quantify this, but it is widely believed that indiscipline, diversion of resources through improper channels or for improper purposes, corrupt practices and failure of interdepartmental coordination have grown so considerably as to cause something of a crisis of confidence in the system. The coincidence of a bad harvest in 1979 with the post-Afghanistan embargo has damaged agriculture, though not so severely as was feared: the figures published in July 1980 show that livestock numbers are only slightly down, but meat and milk supplies are far below plan and even further below the level of consumer demand at present prices. Dissatisfaction continues to be expressed at all levels with the pace and diffusion of technical progress. Brezhnev himself has spoken of the need for fundamentally new methods in an age of scientific–technical revolution (Brezhnev, 1976, p. 48). In the rest of this chapter we will examine more closely the ills which the latest reforms are supposed to remedy, and consider whether these reforms are likely to achieve their object.

2.2 Fundamental defects of the centralized planning system

Before we examine the latest reform measures it is necessary to analyse briefly the causes of the problems which this reform, and previous ones too, are supposed to resolve.

Causes of inefficiency

First, let us look at some of the more notable examples of inefficiency and waste, as these are presented by Soviet critics. One example in particular concerns the construction industry. Its output is insufficiently linked to completions and too closely linked with the fulfilment of plans expressed in ruble value of work done. As many Soviet sources testify, this means that management is rewarded for spending more, using expensive materials, and is under no pressure to economize. It means also that there is insufficient incentive to complete buildings, and this is reflected in the relative as well as absolute increase in the volume of uncompleted investments. This is despite repeated campaigns and exhortations to avoid 'scattering' (*raspylenie*) of investment resources and to concentrate on key operational projects. Typically, the building programme is extended over many years, a process known in Russian as *dolgostroi*, or 'longbuild'.

An important contributory factor which explains the fall in growth rates is not only a fall in the rate of growth of investment but, in the most recent years, an actual absolute decline in the volume of investment in real terms. This is due partly to rising costs of energy (oil and gas in West Siberia require very heavy expenditures, as compared with more accessible sources previously exploited), and also to additional spending on environmental protection. But Soviet sources stress particularly the escalating costs of machinery and construction costs. Apart from the already-cited article by Krasovsky, there was also an analysis by Faltsman (1980), which showed that the cost of providing the *same* productive capacity (for producing the same items) was rising during the 1970s by between 5% and 7% per annum. He called this 'the reduction of the capacity equivalent' (*moshchnostnoi ekvivalent*), and drew attention to the fact that, since 1975, this 'exceeded the growth in capital investment', leading to 'an absolute decline in the bringing into operation of productive capacity' in many vitally important industries. This implies that the official price and volume indices for investment goods are incorrect, that the volume of completions is actually falling, due not (or not only) to construction delays or higher extraction costs but to higher prices. It would appear to follow that when Soviet planners announce that there has been an increase in the volume of investments – for instance by 4% in 1979 – they are the victims of their own incorrect price index for investment goods.

Much attention has also been paid by Soviet analysts to the consequence of planning industrial output, sales and labour productivity in terms of gross value, i.e. in terms of prices which include the value of inputs. A switch to a cheaper material, with a consequent reduction in the selling price, adversely affects the value of output in money terms, which leads to an apparent underfulfilment of the production and sales plan and an equally apparent reduction in labour productivity. A recently reported example will serve to illustrate this:

At the Melitopol compressor factory, iron rings were replaced by capron, which last for 13 000 hours instead of 3000. The price of the iron rings was 2.20 rubles, the capron ones, 0.27 rubles. In producing 500 000 such rings a year, the factory lost almost a million rubles of output. Another example: the Volzhok pipe factory has started producing new pipe of higher quality, but their weight in tons was reduced by 25%, and the price was reduced too. As a result, though producing the same quantity of pipe in metres, the economic indicators of the factory worsened: the volume of sales diminished by 7%, the productivity of labour 'fell' by 15%.

The ministry too had a plan in rubles. If it reduces plan targets for its associations and enterprises, it will be in an unenviable position: its growth and productivity figures will decline, with all the resulting consequences. (Valovoi, 1979)

There is a theoretical point to be made: as Soviet prices reflect (more or less) *cost*, and not demand, scarcity or utility, it follows that plan target expressed in these prices orientate management towards effort rather than result, and unintentionally penalize economy of effort to achieve a given result. As the Soviet economist Valovoi put it, 'use values are not counted'.

A different sort of waste is frequently stimulated by plan targets expressed in quantity, for instance tons, thousands of units or pairs, or square metres, or whatever. These orientate management to produce not the product mix required by the customer but the mix which will most easily add up to the required aggregate total. Thus a plan expressed in tons penalizes anyone who economizes on metal by opting for a less heavy variant. Furthermore, as we have seen, management will frequently be supported in its behaviour by its ministerial superiors, whose plan would also be expressed in rubles and/or tons (*Pravda*, 3 September 1979). Notoriously, targets for road transport undertakings, in terms of ton–kilometres, reward long journeys, and short hauls become 'uneconomic' from the standpoint of plan-fulfilment indicators, even when evidently in the interest of efficiency in transport. These are but a few of a multitude of examples, published over the years in the Soviet press, of how the planners' intentions are frustrated by their inability to define in a meaningful way what actually requires to be produced. As we shall see, this inability is inherent in this planning model, and is not due to stupidity, ill will or error.

Another problem familiar to students of the economy has been inconsistency of plans. This manifests itself in two different ways. Firstly, there is inconsistency arising from the division of complementary activities or products between two or more different ministries. Thus, for example, fertilizer production comes under the ministry of chemical industry while machines used to spread it in the fields are the concern of the ministry of agricultural machinery. Fertilizer production greatly outpaced the supply of the required machinery, causing waste and losses and there are many other instances of 'disproportionate' mechanizations (Tikhonov, 1977; Dobrynin, 1974). More recently still, Brezhnev has complained that large fertilizer plants had been built, but operated far below capacity for lack of necessary raw materials and gas (*Pravda*, 28 November 1979). The other form of inconsistency relates to the plan-orders which management receives: thus its production plan-target comes from one office, the allocation of the needed materials is undertaken by a number of other bodies, while still others will be determining the planned wages bill, financial plans (profits, etc.), labour productivity and other obligatory targets. Furthermore, it is extremely common for output plans to be altered several times during the period of their currency without the consequential amendments being made to other plan targets (Aganbegyan, 1973). It would be extraordinary in these circumstances if the entire plan were internally consistent and balanced. This, like so many other deficiencies and malfunctions, arises from the inevitable complexity of current planning, and the fact that the task is not and cannot be completed by the beginning of the plan year. Consequently various imbalances are discovered in the course of the year which compels changes to be made without their being coordinated with other administrative organs.

Another 'disease' requires to be mentioned here, which can be amply documented and seems to be chronic. This is the tendency to alter plans during the period of their currency to the expected level of their fulfilment by the given enterprise. The cause seems to be the desire of the ministry to be able to report that all its subordinates have fulfilled plans. Thus if in early December it seems that factory A will produce 96 and factory B 104 (plans = 100), the plans are amended to 96 and 104 respectively. This, of course, makes nonsense of repeated promises of stability in plans and plan-linked bonuses.

Fear of changes in plan, worry about supplies of needed inputs, a desire to appear to be successful, incline the management to understate their production potential, to overstate their needs for inputs and to hoard labour and materials. All this adversely affects the quality of information flows upon which the central planners and ministries must depend. Soviet critics have for many years pointed to this as a major weakness, and methods have been devised to try to overcome it. One, proposed by Liberman over twenty years ago, is to reward management for bidding high; unfortunately, Gosplan insisted that there be no bonuses if the plan was not fulfilled, and so there was insufficient incentive for taking a risk by proposing an ambitious plan. Another scheme to which much publicity was given was the so-called *vstrechnyi plan*, or 'counterplan'. The idea was this: suppose the planners determine the plan at 100; the enterprise was to be encouraged to propose a higher target, say 105, and apply for inputs accordingly. Plan-fulfilment bonuses would relate to the original 100, and so an actual output of (say) 102 would be regarded as having met the target, even though it was short of 105. This, however, did not have the desired effect, for a reason which should have been apparent: the plan target is set by higher authority on the basis of information supplied by management, in a process which has been described with some truth as 'bargaining'. If, as a result, the plan target is set at 100, and *then* the management announces that it could really produce 105, the reaction of the plan-setting organs can readily be imagined. So there have been few ambitious *vstrechnye plany*.

As well as the tendency for production plans to be inconsistent with supply and delivery plans there is also the frequent problem of the non-carrying out of delivery obligations. This takes different forms, and is due to different causes. Thus in some instances the delivery plans are simply impossible to fulfil in that they exceed the productive capacity of the producing enterprise, or assume the completion of a new workshop which is not yet operational. It is this sort of situation which incites the 'customers' to send thousands of *tolkachi* ('pushers', 'expediters') who try to persuade the producing enterprise to give priority to 'them', under conditions in which it is physically impossible to carry out all the delivery obligations. Other complaints relate to wrong specifications, or to delay. The latter is a well-known cause of the phenomenon of *shturmovshchina* ('storming'), a rush to produce at the end of the plan period, which has negative effects on quality. The problem of specifications arises out of the fact that the allocation certificates relate to aggregates: thus enterprise A is ordered to supply enterprise B with 100 tons of (say) metal goods or leather, and the details of quality and type require to be negotiated in the contract between the two enterprises; but the supplier will try to 'fit' its production and deliveries to its plan targets in tons, rubles, units, etc. So frequently what is received is not what is really wanted.

In recent years Soviet rules and regulations have laid increasing emphasis on the duty to observe terms of delivery contracts. There is provision for appeal to arbitration courts, and the power exists to reject goods which are sub-standard or of the wrong specification. However, there remains the difficulty of overcoming the consequence of chronic shortage, of the sellers' market. the attitude 'take it or leave it' prevails. The cause of shortages is the subject of a recently published book by Janos Kornai (1980): he shows why the typical situation in the East is one of supply constraint. This unavoidably weakens the position of the customer *vis-à-vis* the supplier.

Nowhere is the strain and shortage more visible than in the area of investment and construction. As mentioned earlier, building enterprises have had insufficient incentives to complete buildings. But this is only part of a deeper question: the planning organs, ministries and local authorities tend to start too many projects, despite repeated edicts forbidding them to do so. So persistent and chronic a defect must have strong roots. These seem to be based upon the pursuit of sectional interest: the most effective way to attract investment funds seems to be to have something started but uncompleted, which may help to get the necessary money and physical resources for ultimate completion. The value of unfinished construction has been rising relatively and absolutely[4]. Brezhnev said: 'Gosplan does not sufficiently resist departmentalism and localism' (*vedomstvennost' i mest-nichestvo*). Investment resources are 'diverted' (*rastaskivayutsya*)'. (Brezhnev, 1976).

Brezhnev had declared at the 25th party congress that this was to be a five-year period of 'effectiveness and quality'. Investment resources, he insisted, must be used with better effect. Quality must be improved, quality both of consumer goods and of machinery. Technical progress, new designs and reequipment were also necessary to cope with the growing shortage of labour: as many sources have been insisting, the demographic situation is such that the bulk of future growth must depend on increases in the productivity of the present labour force. Agriculture is not now a major source of new recruits for industry, and in fact the farms require an annual 'import' of millions of persons from towns and from the army to help cope with the harvest peak.

Labour productivity, however, is below expectations, and is obstructed by a number of factors. One, difficult to quantify in the absence of hard facts, is the sometimes negative attitude of the work force, which Marxists might call 'alienation', and which is partly the consequence of what could be called psychological diseconomies of scale: it is not easy to identify with the enormous conglomerate firm, USSR Inc., with its complex multi-level central bureaucracy. There are many references in the Soviet press to such matters as drunkenness, indiscipline and absenteeism. A second issue relates to the interest of the management in hoarding labour, one reason for which was touched upon already (the same reason as that which 'encourages' it to hoard materials), to which must be added the responsibility of ensuring alternative employment for displaced personnel. Brezhnev mentioned another reason: to keep extra labour in case some is mobilized for outside campaigns, such as help with the harvest (*Pravda*, 28 November 1979). It is interesting to note that the so-called Shchekino experiment was facilitated by the fact that this chemical plant was expanding, and so displaced workers could be transferred to the new workshops. The Shchekino experiment was intended to encourage management and labour to reduce the workforce, by allowing a major part of the savings on wages to be shared among those who remained. However, this practice has not spread widely, probably because the planners have introduced a number of conditions and limitations, and it is significant that the reform decree published in July 1979 (of which much more in a moment) does not mention Shchekino at all, although a watered-down version may emerge from the changed rules concerning the planning of the wages fund (see below).

Reluctance to innovate

A more important question is that of labour-saving technology, and of the frustrations imposed by the system on those who sincerely desire to diffuse technical progress. Those certainly include the party leadership and the chief planners. It is worth examining in a little detail what these frustrations are[5].

All, in fact, arise from one common cause: the fact that, in most cases, the centre does not and cannot know precisely what needs doing. Where the centre *does* know, as when, for instance, a new technique is developed in a central research institute or purchased abroad, it can issue instructions to incorporate the new equipment or process, or a whole factory complex, in the plan, as was done with the Volga car plant and the Kama lorry complex. But in the economy as a whole, new designs and technological initiatives and adaptations depend greatly on managerial decisions. This applies to the decisions of management regarding both the *use* of technology and its *production*. Let us look at the causes of this situation, which have been quite widely and openly discussed in the Soviet Union.

The first cause is the question of *risk*. Anything new involves risk. Even if the innovation succeeds in the end, its introduction is frequently (in all economies) attended by growing pains, by a learning process, in the course of which cost estimates are exceeded and production is temporarily slowed down. In the Soviet case, this means the non-fulfilment of current plans, and therefore financial difficulties and possible reprimands. This is not adequately compensated by the rewards for success, which, so to speak, will be incorporated in the plan. The very notion of rewarding management for taking risks is foreign to the system (though rewards are paid to inventors). So there are insufficient incentives to counterbalance managerial attitudes of risk-aversion.

Second, to innovate on one's own initiative usually requires some changes to be made in the supply, production and investment plans, otherwise the necessary resources will not be available. It takes time and effort to persuade various departments to agree to this, and the consequences to one's plan-fulfilment in the future are unpredictable.

Third, in production decisions relating to new kinds of machinery and equipment it is a highly complex matter to reconcile the specific needs of the *user* with the success indicators written into the *output* plan. Incredible as it may seem, a manager responsible for producing chemical machinery reported that, if he made the modifications required by his customers, his plan *in tons*(!) and in rubles would be seriously underfulfilled (*Pravda*, 11 February 1978). Of course, Soviet planners know that the quality of machinery and equipment is in the end to be determined by its effectiveness in use, but how is this to be reflected in output targets which are determined by the ministry in charge of their production? Many decrees and declarations bear witness to the sincere desire of the leadership to encourage innovation and the production of good-quality modern machinery. But an order to produce it is imprecise, it takes the form of not concretely definable exhortation. When what is really needed is often known by the *user* enterprise how can one incorporate a comprehensible order in a central plan-instruction?

Another weakness relates to spare parts and components. A large volume can be filled by published complaints concerning non-delivery of spares or the non-arrival of ordered components. One cause for this has been that output and delivery targets in physical terms often relate to what is called *vazhneishaya produktsiya*, the most important items: a tractor, for instance, is 'most important', but a carburettor may not be so listed. Another is that, under the conventional gross output–value measure, a part that is in a completed machine is 'worth' more than a part supplied to an outside customer as such.

Over-complexity of centralized planning

All these deficiencies must be well known to the student of Soviet-type economies, and to some readers this must seem like going over familiar ground. Yet it is justified to list them because it facilitates understanding of a very important point: that all, or almost all, these weaknesses stem from a single source: the over-complexity of centralized planning, the sheer impossibility of coping with the informational and decisionmaking tasks which the model concentrates at the centre.

There are produced in the USSR 12 million different items (in fully disaggregated detail, separately defined and priced) (*Voprosy ekonomiki*, No. 12, 1977, p. 5) and there are 48,000 plan 'positions' (i.e. for which output plans are issued by a ministry or other planning agency). This, needless to say, does *not* mean that no plans are made for 11 952 000 items! The bulk of them are planned in aggregated units, and one can see from these figures that the *average* plan 'position' covers about 250 sub-items. In practice this can vary from none (electricity) to literally thousands. It is, of course, totally out of the question to try to plan from the centre in fully disaggregated detail. But even 48 000 plan 'positions' involve a huge amount of calculation: the production figures must not only be internally consistent in an input–output sense (since most items are inputs for other branches of the economy), but must be divided up between thousands of productive units in a network of output and material supply relationships. All of these, in turn, must be related to financial, labour-productivity, wages and other plan targets, disaggregated to enterprise level. The investment plan, too, must be converted into detailed instructions to building organizations, to those who produce, deliver and install the necessary machinery, to design offices, etc. There is also the dimension of republican and regional planning. Then there is the vital factor of time: the 1980 annual plan had to be ready by 1980, but the detailed task of formulating it could not be begun until a few months before the end of 1979.

It appears that there is hardly a single *systemic* weakness that is not related directly or indirectly to the consequences of these facts, and that, consequently, *no reform can succeed which does not take this into account.*

Planners *cannot* fulfil the tasks which the logic of the model requires them to fulfil. This places much responsibility on management, both as initiators of proposals (i.e. as suppliers of information as to what they can or could do) *and* in deciding how to fulfil aggregated and often inconsistent plan-instructions. We have left aside the question of the 'illegitimate' activities of management, though some regard these as important too, for lack of reliable information; but the occasional reported examples usually relate to semi-legal or corrupt practices designed to obtain resources needed to fulfil plans, practices rendered necessary by the malfunctioning of the supply system.

The problem of prices

But while management has important functions it lacks any criterion *other than fulfilling plan-instructions*. This is an inescapable consequence of the very nature of the Soviet planning model, of the non-existence of a developed market mechanism and of the nature of Soviet prices in both theory and practice.

Soviet wholesale (or factory) prices do not reflect scarcity, utility or opportunity cost. Since they are altered at very infrequent intervals they are seldom proportionate to costs, even if this was the basis upon which they may originally have been determined. The wide range of profitability which now exists is a consequence of cost changes over time, and is in no way intended to serve as a signal or indicator as to what is or is not most needed. At best, prices are neutral, but in practice there is frequently a conflict between profitability and need. It therefore follows that any reform based upon rewarding profitability is bound to be unsatisfactory – unless the basis of pricing is radically altered. As things are, the profit rate could be improved by altering the product mix so as to produce those items which happen to be more profitable, and these would not, except by accident, be those which the users actually wanted. Hence the view (which the writer heard expressed at a seminar in Moscow) that rewards linked to profitability should be limited to those instances in which management 'deserves' it, and any increase in profitability due to change in the product mix was 'undeserved'. It follows from such an approach that rewards should go to those who reduce costs of producing a *given* product mix, and indeed before 1965 there was an explicit obligatory cost-reduction indicator. The 1965 reform did away with it. As we shall see, it was being reintroduced, in part at least, in 1979.

The 'Kosygin' reforms of 1965 were widely misunderstood. They did not, in fact, change the essential features of the system. As far as pricing was concerned, there was a change which was incorporated in the price-revision of 1967: the introduction of a capital charge and profitability expressed as a percentage of capital assets. But these new prices retained all the defects of their predecessors, so far as their operational use was concerned. The reforms sought to reduce the number of compulsory plan indicators and thereby to increase the autonomy of management. Sales, profits and profitability (*rentabel'nost'*) were to be key elements in the formation of incentive funds, and these were all *monetary* measures. There was also a statement favouring a shift from allocation to *sale* of material inputs. However, from the first this 'reform' was contradictory and ineffective. Given the nature of prices (and therefore of profits), the planning and ministerial organs continued to issue instructions on plan-fulfilment in quantitative terms. Given the chronic shortage of material inputs, they continued to be rationed by the centre, with Gosplan, Gossnab (the material supplies committee) and ministries operating a complex system of material allocation, with its inevitable counterpart: instructions to producing enterprises as to their production and delivery obligations. Gradually the number of obligatory plan indicators increased again, sometimes by decree (e.g. when labour productivity was added to the list), sometimes by ministerial decision. By 1973, according to a survey by Aganbegyan (1973) 80% of managers reported that their superiors gave them binding orders on matters which, according to the reform decree, were within managerial competence to decide. The incentive schemes for management became more and more complex, as planners sought to deal with such problems as quality, innovation, economy of materials, production and delivery of 'most important' (*vazhneishie*) products, etc. The rules and the norms or standards relating to them were frequently changed, the bonus 'entitlements' subject to arbitrary limits. The relationship between performance and rewards, and the rules determining them, became more and more confused. The much-denounced 'gross-output' indicator (*val*) was reintroduced *de facto* as part of the measurement of labour productivity, but if any case the *sales* indicator is as 'gross' as *val*, since both include the value of inputs (the difference consists of the omission of *unsold* output from the value of sales). All the familiar defects of success indicators, analysed earlier, continued to exist, or reappeared, including the self-contradictory and inconsistent nature of multiple compulsory indicators. The adverse effect of the stress on the production and delivery of the 'most important' products has already been mentioned. The economist–journalist Valovoi has pointed out that many items not on the list of the 'most important' are in fact essential, and indeed are complementary to those which are on the list (Valovoi, 1977).

A full and well-documented survey by Gertrude Schroeder of the various changes from 1965 until 1978 has recently appeared. One can agree wholeheartedly with her words: 'The reformation of the reforms has introduced changes in working arrangements of unprecedented scope and complexity. So ceaseless has been the search for new panaceas and so numerous have been the changes in the rules, that one may advance the hypothesis that perennial administrative change is becoming part of the problem, rather than contributing to its solution' (Schroeder, 1979, p. 313).

There has been widespread discussion in the Soviet specialized press about computers and their use in planning. From the time that Kantorovich developed his ideas on programming techniques and 'objectively determined valuations', hundreds of articles and many books have appeared, with proposals mooted (or even adopted) to introduce ASU (automated management systems) (Goodman, 1979, pp. 540ff.), and to devise criteria for optimization of plans. We have described elsewhere the obstacles in the way of 'optimizing' computerized programmes (Nove, 1979). The essential point is, once again, what has been called 'the curse of scale': to collect, check and assess the information needed for computerized micro-economic management would take far too long, the number of variants which could be considered would run into an impossibly vast number of millions. It is also not possible in practice to define the overall objective, i.e. what it is that one is optimizing. All this is not to deny that the computer can, indeed does, facilitate plan-calculations. The point is only that it has not, and cannot, be a substitute for farreaching reforms, the essence of which *must* be an effective decentralization of the bulk of routine microeconomic decisionmaking.

Administrative reorganization: the introduction of associations

Among the changes initiated during the past decade is the merging of enterprises into larger units, the so-called *obedineniya*, or 'associations'. This appears to serve several objectives. First, by reducing the number of units to be planned it eases the task of the central organs. Second, it is hoped to streamline the control mechanism by reducing the number of managerial 'levels'; in some instances the *glavk* (ministerial department) is converted into an *obedinenie*, which operates on profit-and-loss accounting (*khozraschet*) basis. Some *obedineniya* are all-union, for instance the record firm *Melodiya*. Some are republican. Some, like the *Skorokhod* footwear association, group together all the factories which produce the commodity concerned in an area, in this instance north-west Russia. Some are directly linked with scientific research institutes, so as to encourage innovation. Among the objectives aimed at is to facilitate specialization *within* the *obedinenie*. At present there are still two kinds of intra-*obedinenie* organizations: in some the enterprise survives, though with more limited powers; in others, the former autonomous enterprises are reduced to the status of workshops.

With so wide a diversity of sizes and types of *obedineniya* it is dangerous to generalize, but it may be said with confidence that the basic problems of economic management remain virtually unaffected. The powers of Gosplan and of the ministries have not diminished. In those instances in which the *obedinenie* has replaced the ministerial department (*glavk*) this has changed only the labels on the doors of the same officials. Some mergers have had the effect of complicating rather than easing the task of management. Furthermore, *obedineniya* have tended to be within the 'boundaries' of a ministry, and yet many products (machines, consumer durables, components, etc.) are made by enterprises under ten or more ministries. Materials-handling equipment was made by 380 enterprises under 35 all-union and republican ministries (*Planovoe khozyaistvo*, No. 11, 1975, p. 12).

In these instances there is no way in which the *obedineniya* can take national or regional responsibility for the product in question unless ministerial demarcation lines are drastically altered, and this the ministries resist, if only because the items concerned will usually be some of many made by the production unit concerned. In brief, Soviet economists do not claim that this particular reform has made any easier the task of ensuring the more efficient operation of the planning system.

Finally, before turning to an analysis of the latest 'reform', it is necessary to examine one other aspect of the system: the weakness of regional planning. This is the inescapable consequence of centralized planning based on industrial ministries. Experience under Khrushchev of regional economic councils (*sovnarkhozy*) did indeed show that it is inefficient and impracticable to replace ministries with territorial bodies; these could not be aware either of the national problems of any specific industry or of the needs of other regions. However, when all lines of command lead to a central ministry, *regional* planning authorities, where they exist, have little real authority. Brezhnev has repeatedly complained about 'departmentalism', i.e. of the consequences of rigid boundary lines between units under different ministries. Indeed, a recent scandalous example relates to units under the *same* ministry: the Odessa railway region has 'stolen' locomotives from the Moldavia railway region to fulfil its transport plan (evidently there is a shortage of locomotives!), though both fall within the all-union Ministry of Transport (*The Times*, 28 November 1979). The regional 'complex development' problem is particularly acute in newly developed areas, notably in Siberia, where joint and coordinated activities of enterprises under different ministries are plainly indispensable. This has led to some lively discussions about the necessity of 'Territorial Production Administrations', and how these could be reconciled with the ministerial structure[6].

2.3. New attempts at reform

With this background let us now examine the decree published in July 1979, the full details of which may be found in *Ekonomicheskaya gazeta*, No. 32. Complicated as the provisions of the decree must seem, it is probably a simplification compared with the confused accretion of plan indicators which have accumulated since 1965, and which urgently needed some sort of codification.

Some elements of the decree must be seen as exhortation, or as a restatement of elementary planning principles. Thus investment plan tasks must be 'assured of the necessary material, human and financial resources'. Surely this was always to be the case! Similarly it is stated that investment plans shall be 'stable' as well as 'balanced'. Nor is there anything new about the stress on fulfilling delivery obligations, though the penalties for not doing so are increased. It is noteworthy that there is a reference to the practice of 'correcting plans downwards to the level of their actual fulfilment'; this must stop, so it is said.

Management is to be encouraged to show initiative in putting forward plans for the quinquennium, broken down by years, but this, too, is not new. Nor is the assertion that plans should be stable, coherent and consistent. This has always been the objective, and nothing in this decree suggests that the causes for instability and inconsistency have been identified and the necessary corrections made. The implication seems to be that planners should do their work better, that there be stricter discipline, etc. As we shall see, the effect of the new measures is, in fact, still further to overburden the planners, thus ensuring the continuation of deficiencies whose underlying cause is centralization itself. This the 'reform' fails to tackle: it represents another variant of the centralized 'directive' model. For this reason, in the writer's judgment, these measures will not succeed in achieving their objectives of improving the functioning of the planning system, reducing waste and enhancing efficiency (though marginal gains might be effected, especially in the construction industry), because these measures do not even begin to grapple with the fundamental problems posed by the nature of the centralized planning system itself.

Let us now examine the plan indicators which, when this decree is implemented, it will be the duty of *obedineniya* and enterprise management to carry out.

Plan indicators

One such indicator is to be *net output*, or, to be precise, *normed* net output, or normed value-added. This is to be used 'in the majority of sectors as basic in the planning of production, labour productivity and the wages fund' (*Ekonomicheskaya gazeta*, No. 33, 1979, p. 3). On the face of it, this represents a clear step forward from *val* and sales targets, as these were gross of the value of inputs, and thus encouraged management to seek expensive inputs. However, a sort of net-output indicator had been tried before, under the name of 'normed value of processing', and abandoned. Experiments in its use have been conducted, and now it is formally adopted as one of the several obligatory indicators. In our view this will not work well, for the following reasons.

It may appear relatively simple to calculate the net output of an enterprise: it consists of gross output valued at official prices, less inputs. However, this is not what is intended. There is to be a *normed* net output for each product. As Baibakov put it, 'in determining new wholesale prices there will separately be determined the norm of net output' (*Pravda*, 29 August 1979). In effect, as another article put it, for every product there will be a 'second price' determined (*Pravda*, 9 October 1979). So let us imagine an enterprise or *obedinenie*, which produces (say) fifteen separately priced items. Along with its price, each will have a normed net output calculated for it. Calculated how? Net output is equal roughly to wages plus profits. As far as can be ascertained, the wages element will represent the amount of processing work that *ought* to be devoted to the production of this item. To this will be added the notional profit, which will be represented *not* by the actual profit (if any) assignable to this particular product, but its proportionate share of the profit (actual? planned?) of the enterprise as a whole.

The separate calculation of net output by product at enterprise (or *obedinenie*) level would indeed cause difficulties: how to assign common overheads, for instance, and to avoid a situation in which needless processing is undertaken to increase net output. However, the scheme now adopted is bound to raise a whole number of problems. First and foremost is the volume of work involved. The change does nothing to ensure that what is produced conforms to user requirements. It is not clear how *growth* of *output* can be measured in such units; Valovoi advocates that it should, but he fears the consequences of retaining *val* for this purpose, so the matter remains unclear (Valovoi, 1979). Despite this, the hope is expressed that the elimination of the *val* and sales targets will eliminate the tendency to opt for dear inputs and to avoid producing spare parts. We shall see if this will be the case. One must bear in mind the existence of numerous other plan indicators, and one of them is still to be the total value of sales, which is retained 'for ministries (*obedineniya*) enterprises, to evaluate fulfilment of plan-tasks for deliveries of products in accordance with contracts', with a reduction in bonuses if this total is not reached.

Let us now turn to the other compulsory indicators (not necessarily applicable to all branches).

There will be targets for the *volume of output of the most important products*, in quantitative terms, and also the volume of *delivery* of the most important products. (*Vazhneishie* again, with its predictable consequences.) Volume is to be measured in tons, and other physical indicators, but with correction for quality. Whose task will it be to devise coefficients to convert physical units such as tons into some standard measure? How will this be accomplished? Tons as an output plan indicator have survived decades of criticism, and it seems not impossible that they will survive yet again.

Quality indicators are stressed, as they have been for many years in official declarations. It is not difficult to decide to reward quality, but how is it to be identified and measured? The imposition of minimum standards, bonuses linked with the granting of 'the state seal of quality', or the percentage of goods passed as of first quality have all been tried, with modest results, given the prevailing shortages and the absence of competition.

It should be added that, as far as consumer goods are concerned, the extent of shortage has unmistakably grown in recent years: among other sources, one can quote a *Pravda* editorial: 'Savings bank deposits have almost trebled in eight years, and the cash incomes of the population have increased much faster than the supply of goods and services' (*Pravda*, 27 July 1979)[7].

But let us return to the list of plan indicators. *Increase in labour productivity* is regarded as an essential indicator, as has been the case for ten years. But in addition we are to have limits (maximum numbers) laid down for numbers employed, *and* a target for the reduction in numbers of manual workers, i.e. those engaged in unmechanized work (*ruchnoi trud*). There is also to be a fixed *norm of wage payments per unit of net output*, presumably differentiated by sector. There is also a wages fund plan. But presumably if the labour force is reduced and net output increased it would be possible to use some of the resultant economy to increase the incomes of the remaining labour force, and in that case this could be seen as a form of the Shchekino system. However, ministerial powers to redistribute funds have been used in the past to avoid what are regarded as excessive income differentials.

Another indicator is to be the *total profit* (it seems that the profit *rate* (*rentabel'nost'*) is downgraded), and also, though in some industries only, *reduction in cost*. There is also a proposal to have a 'stable' norm for payment to the state budget out of profits, which would have the (positive) effect of ending the practice of transferring the whole profit residual ('free remainder') to the budget.

Other indicators are linked to *investment*, such as completion of new productive capacity, keeping strictly within the financial 'limit' laid down. Then there are *tasks for the introduction of new technique* (note the word 'tasks', i.e. it is assumed that the ministry of Gosplan will issue instructions).

There are also to be obligatory norms for *reduction in the use of materials*, a target explicable by the evident need to prevent waste, but one which experience shows leads to serious distortions in practice: there must frequently be instances where circumstances do not make this possible without loss of quality or durability, making it impossible to satisfy customer requirements. This indicator was condemned for just these reasons by an experienced former minister (Smelyakov, 1975, pp. 175–176).

In the much-criticised *construction industry* there is to be introduced the useful-looking indicator of the net value of work *completed*. This should finally stop construction enterprises fulfilling plans in terms of gross value of work done, whether completed or not. There are the usual declarations concerning the need to reduce the number of projects started, a greater concentration on modernization and extending capacity at existing plants. Brezhnev, too, in his speech on 27 November 1979, denounced the practice of 'scattering' investment resources, as we have seen. But this is all too familiar: will there be effective action this time? We shall see. It is evidently necessary to try.

Similarly, a useful step forward is that of designating certain ministries as 'leading' (*golovnye*) in the production of items which are made under the aegis of several ministries. It is yet to be seen how this would work in practice. Many consumer durables, for example, are made in workshops which form part of factories which may be primarily concerned with producing armaments, or steel sheet, or chemical machinery. How, then, is the 'leading' ministry to exercise its authority? Will it be possible to form trans-ministerial *obedineniya*?

There are some references in recent discussions, and also in Brezhnev's already-cited speech, to the possible creation of new kinds of complexes. The decree does speak of concentration on 'complex' tasks. An example might be a sort of agro–industrial–trade complex, with responsibility extending from the villages through transport, storage, packing materials, processing, wholesaling and retailing. These are possible adaptations or reorganizations of the centralized system. It has not happened, but it might.

The work of planning

An important part of the new decree relates to the work of the planning organs themselves. Thus they must pay more attention to regional planning, with Gosplan in particular charged with supervision of territorial production complexes, where these exist; this, while plainly desirable, could cause confusion because it will conflict with ministerial lines of responsibility (and financing). But, above all, Gosplan is charged, in consultation with producing units, with drawing up material, labour and financial balances, and then providing the management at all levels with clear five-year perspectives, on the basis of which they are to propose annual plans for the *obedineniya* and enterprises, together with long-term supply and delivery links, which, once confirmed, should be stable. Gosplan's tasks and timetable are spelled out in some detail in the decree. Thus, on the basis of the leadership's policy and priorities, Gosplan is to elaborate global long-term plans and to submit them to the Council of Ministers eighteen months before the beginning of the next quinquennium. Once approved, Gosplan sends plan 'control figures' to ministries. These work out 'control figures' to send them down to associations or enterprises. These in turn put forward on this basis their own plan for the five years, with breakdown by year. At this point they can already enter into preliminary discussions with supply organs about prospective supply/delivery contracts. The ministry assembles all these plans and they go back to Gosplan, which, after further work, must submit the now more elaborate plan to the Council of Ministers at least five months before the five-year plan is due to begin. Details of the product mix should be based on negotiated contracts. It seems to be intended to enlarge the associations' and enterprises' powers to draft their own annual counterplans (*vstrechnye plany*), though there are also to be obligatory annual plans within the quinquennium. These and some other details appear still to have to be worked out.

Management is to be given stable norms on the basis of which incentive funds will be formed: these, as before, will be three, used respectively for bonuses, welfare and capital investment. It is intended that investments financed out of the management's funds are to be included in the supply plan; this, while necessary to ensure that they can be made a reality, is the culmination of the trend to centralized control over investments, involving the virtual abolition of the category of decentralized investments. This, in turn, is the consequence of shortage of resources, and of the desire to concentrate investments on priority projects (these by definition being those initiated or specifically approved by the centre).

There is provision for the extension of the practice of long-term supply-and-delivery contracts. Like wholesale trade in inputs, this figured in the 1965 reforms, and so we have here another restatement of what was supposed already to exist. The problem remains: will these long-term contracts, even if negotiated and approved, continue to be arbitrarily altered by ministries and supply-planning organs when faced with the need to cope with any shortages that arise in the process of plan implementation? This is a sub-aspect of the general obstacles to stable plans; lack of spare capacity, inadequate reserves, 'taut' planning, plus the uncertainties and errors which are part of the imperfections of everyday life, had always had the effect of requiring frequent amendment to the production and supply plans. This received verbal recognition in the reform decree itself in that there is emphasis on the need to ensure adequate reserves to cope with the unexpected. All past experience, however, suggests that this will not happen. It is perhaps useful at this point to cite a story told by the late Professor Ely Devons, about his experience as economic adviser to the British Ministry of Aircraft Production in the Second World War. It was reported to the Minister that the flow of production was impeded by lack of spare capacity and over-taut planning, and (according to Devons) the Minister agreed that reserves were indeed necessary and should be provided, on one condition: that the output of planes did not diminish . . .

Finally, it is becoming clear that the reform of July 1979 has increased the emphasis on quantitative planning, and this in a context of greater centralization of control over production and deliveries. A *Pravda* editorial makes this clear:

Until recently, a part of the managers, in trying to increase the amount of their sales, neglected some unprofitable orders. Now production in physical terms (*v natural'nom vyrazhenii*) becomes one of the main indicators of the work of enterprises and associations. Their work will be evaluated and stimulated in relation to deliveries on the entire nomenclature of contracted output. The list of materials and manufactures centrally planned has been lengthened and will be stable for five years. On this basis some ministries listed are already drafting annual plans for their productive units in a still more detailed assortment. Thereby are created the preconditions for greater satisfaction of user requirements. (*Pravda*, 5 December 1979)

Note that these latter are seen as being incorporated in central instructions. True, the same editorial goes on to stress also the 'normed net value' indicator and to stress its advantages (as well as the hard work needed to devise for all products 'the normed price-lists of labour inputs'). But it is surely no accident that, while perhaps not secondary, it is treated second.

Assessment of the 1979 reforms

If one examines this bundle of reforms in the light of the problems which face the economy, there can be only one answer: they cannot make any serious difference to the functioning of the system, they cannot be expected to correct any of the more serious defects, because the basic causes remain untouched. Of course, improvements in this or that detailed aspect of planning or management are possible. Thus the building industry may now be better motivated to complete buildings (although they may still be prevented from doing so because of shortages of necessary inputs). But while any one error or distortion can or could be corrected or avoided, the fundamental problem remains: the planning mechanism at the centre is grossly overburdened, and a study of the latest proposals shows that the effect must be to overburden the planners still further. Imbalances, contradictions and inconsistencies arise not through lack of skill, or ill will, but, to repeat, are consequences of the 'curse of scale'. The innumerable interconnections, complementarities and qualitative indicators (quality of machinery and equipment as well as of consumers' goods) must escape the attention of the centre, and, if some of them are given special attention, this must be at the expense of others. Priority has meaning only in the context of numerically predominant non-priority.

Let us recall the two instances already referred to (p. 27), both concerning the chemical fertilizer industry. Each illustrated the lack of complementary inputs, these being required in the one case for the effective *use* of the fertilizer, the other (cited by Brezhnev) being needed actually to *produce* the fertilizer. Were these errors avoidable? In principle, of course, the answer must be 'yes'. The Politbureau could have appointed a senior member of the apparatus to oversee these matters, with powers to give orders to the several ministries concerned, and to make it clear to everyone, from the railways to the financial committees, that the decisions taken must be carried out, regardless of other calls on resources. This works quite well in the defence industries, for instance. It *can* only work in a few selected instances. Let us take these examples and analyse briefly what went wrong. One unit in the planning system, aware of the genuine need for more fertilizer, planned investments designed to expand production. It could not be the responsibility of *this* unit to plan the output of bags, machinery to spread fertilizer, means of transport, feedstock, fuel, and the inputs required to produce and transport these inputs. Those whose responsibility it was had other tasks too, unrelated to fertilizer. The capacity of those senior enough to oversee and to coordinate is necessarily limited, and if their time and effort were devoted to fertilizer they would omit some other part of their inherently impossible task.

Yet fertilizer is comparatively an important item. Consider some other examples cited in Brezhnev's speech: lack of 'the simplest medicines, soap, detergents, toothbrushes and toothpaste, needles, babies' diapers . . .' (Brezhnev, 1976). These, he said, 'for some reason are considered minor items' (*melochi*). Those responsible for them would not hold senior rank or have much power to mobilize the needed resources. Let us recall that, for anything to be done, one needs three things: information, motivation and means. We have no grounds for supposing that the official in the ministry of light industry responsible for planning the production of toothbrushes lacks motivation, and he (or she) may well know that more are needed. But the material and financial means are controlled by other (and probably more senior) officials, who have other calls on their attention and, no doubt, do not forget that they must ensure the supply of (and for) the 'most important' (*vazhneishie*) items, a list on which toothbrushes, diapers, etc. are unlikely to figure.

What is the remedy? It can *only* be in the direction of freeing management from tight central control, leaving it free, or at least much freer, to purchase inputs and to make its current production programme conform to (indeed be based on) the requirements of customers, users, of the goods or services concerned. In other words, the principles underlying the Hungarian reform of 1968 will have to be applied in some form. This is not the place to analyse the complex reasons why such a solution has been rejected. It cannot be denied that it carries risks with it, especially as no-one is accustomed to any system other than the present one, and both party–state officialdom and the beneficiaries of present priorities must be expected to resist change in this direction. The question is: how much muddle and inefficiency will the leadership be prepared to tolerate before deciding to impose fundamental reform on a reluctant bureaucracy?

One cannot but agree with Gertrude Schroeder who, before the most recent reforms were announced, wrote the following:

> So long as present working arrangements continue to yield modest, even if declining, increments in annual output, the leaders as well as the led will probably prefer to put up with the familiar deficiencies of the system, rather than to embark on untried and ideologically distasteful paths with unknown payoffs and certain disruptive consequences. (Schroeder, 1979)

The question is: for how long will there be modest, if declining, increments to annual output? Will a new leadership be less cautiously conservative? The present indications are that the emphasis will continue to be on discipline rather than on change.

Notes

1. This covers the difference between procurement prices (and other state expenditures) and the income from retail sales in respect of livestock products. Garbuzov, the Finance Minister, stated that this subsidy would equal 100 billion rubles in the five years 1976–1980, and there has been a further increase in procurement prices since then.
2. 4 billion rubles in 1980, according to Glushkov (1980, p. 10).
3. This still happens. Several cases are referred to by Voronin (1980, p. 123).
4. Unfinished construction as a percentage of total investment rose from 69% in 1965 to 75% in 1975 and to 85% in 1977 (Khachaturov, 1979).
5. For a full and well-documented account see Berliner (1976).
6. There is a long discussion on this in *Voprosy ekonomiki*, No. 8, 1978.
7. Note the words 'much faster'! Surely Portes (1977) is wrong in asserting that there is no macro disequilibrium between demand and supply!

References

Aganbegyan, A. *Pravda*, 12 November 1973

Berliner, J. (1976). *The Innovation Decision in Soviet Industry*. Cambridge, Mass.

Brezhnev, L. I. (1976). Report to the 25th party congress. *Materialy XXV s"ezda KPSS*. Moscow

Dobrynin, V. (1974). *Voprosy ekonomiki*, No. 11

Ekonomicheskaya gazeta, No. 32, 1979; No. 33, 1979

Faltsman, V. (1980). *Voprosy ekonomiki*, No. 8

Glushkov, N. (1980). *Planovoe khozyaistvo*, No. 1

Goodman, S. E. (1979). In *Soviet Economy in Time of Change*. Joint Economic Committee, US Congress

Khachaturov, T. *Pravda*, 29 August 1979

Kornai, J. (1980). *The Economics of Shortage*, Stockholm

Krasovsky, V. (1980). *Voprosy ekonomiki*, No. 1

Nove, A. (1970). Some developments in East European economic thought. In *Political Economy and Soviet Socialism* (ed. by A. Nove). London

Planovoe khozyaistvo, No. 11, 1975

Portes, R. (1977). *Economica*, May

Pravda, 11 February 1978; 27 July 1979; 29 August 1979; 3 September 1979; 9 October 1979; 28 November 1979; 5 December 1979; 11 July 1980

Schroeder, G. (1979). The Soviet economy on a treadmill of 'reform'. In *Soviet Economy in a Time of Change*. Joint Economic Committee, US Congress

Smelyakov, N. (1975). *S chego nachinaetsya rodina*, Memoirs. Moscow

The Times, 28 November 1979

Tikhonov, V. (1977). *Voprosy ekonomiki*, No. 10

Valovoi, D. (1977). *Pravda*, 10, 11 and 12 November

——(1979). *Pravda*, 3 September

Voprosy ekonomiki, No. 12, 1977; No. 8, 1978

Voronin, V. (1980). *Voprosy ekonomiki*, No. 6

The GDR – economic policy caught between pressure for efficiency and lack of ideas

Manfred Melzer

3.1 From indirect steering to direct control

In the autumn of 1970 the economic leaders of the GDR found themselves facing a momentous dilemma; should they continue to develop the then-current reforms, from which a powerful impetus to increase economic efficiency in the use of all factors of production had been expected, or should they terminate them? Did there, in fact, exist any measures within the framework of the reform course which could enable the mounting difficulties to be overcome and which could be adopted in the short term? Or were there compelling reasons which made the return to stronger centralization, and with it to the disadvantages of earlier periods, seem the lesser evil? An answer to these questions is probably more pressing than ever at present since it appears that, contrary to the prevailing doctrine, some aspects of the reforms are again secretly favoured in some quarters in the GDR.

Weaknesses of an ambitious reform

At the beginning of the 1970s the *SED* leadership could not fail to see that the 'New Economic System of Planning and Management' (NES)[1] on which it had resolved in 1963, and which had been introduced in numerous individual steps over the next few years, was not functioning as had been expected. It had neither succeeded in achieving an optimal combination of central planning and indirect steering of enterprises by monetary means – as had been envisaged – nor could numerous imperfections in the instruments be overcome. The crucial defect proved to be the contradiction between the fundamental 'principle that enterprises earn their own resources' with the profit incentives based on it, on the one hand, and the state's conceptions of the aggregate structure of the economy on the other. Enterprises used the scope they were granted to make their own investment decisions to carry out those projects which, with the existing relative prices, appeared most efficient to them, but which diverged substantially from the politically desired goals.

It soon became clear that the economic leadership could not implement the structure of development it wished with monetary steering instruments alone, simply because prices neither reflected the existing and changing state goals nor could have been adjusted to do so even approximately. A solution was sought, therefore, in expansion of the remaining framework of physical plan targets in the form of the concept of 'structure-determining tasks' elaborated in 1968 ('Beschluss . . .', 1968). This programme of priority sectors was in operation in 1969 and 1970 both for branches of the economy which were important for growth and also for political goals (Rüger, 1969), which were coupled with a series of compulsory plan indicators, and it was hoped that it would yield some outstandingly successful growth rates[2], so that it became the object of the propaganda slogan 'overtaking without catching up'. The high risk involved in a policy of this kind, which suspended the NES regulations for a significant sector of production, was completely overlooked: the establishment of priorities inevitably meant the downgrading of production not enjoying priority status, which substantially exacerbated the already inadequate flexibility of the reform system to respond to disturbances.

The NES model – as first became apparent in practice – showed certain serious imperfections and even contradictions in its set of instruments, which did not allow the 'economic levers' to operate together systematically. On the one hand, even as the reform was introduced, distinct obstacles appeared: enterprise directors had first to start to 'think like entrepreneurs', bank staff had to be retrained, obscurities concerning the powers and decisionmaking rights of the *VEB* and *VVB* brought about continuous conflicts. In addition there were imbalances and friction caused by uneven introduction of the reform measures. On the other hand, weaknesses and in some cases substantial defects appeared in the individual instruments, which doubtless contributed to the failure of the GDR reform experiment.

Despite the great trouble which had been taken with the three stages of the industrial price review (1964–1967) (*Wochenbericht*, No. 32, 1964; No. 22, 1965; Tönjes, 1967), the price structure existing in the GDR at the beginning of the 1970s was anything but satisfactory (Melzer, 1969). In particular, the prices set in the price review, which were supposed to be based on costs, took only insufficient account of capital costs because they included depreciation but not interest on capital. Furthermore, neither the scarcity of factors of production nor the urgency of demand was taken into account, and flexibility in response to change in demand was extremely small. In addition, the consequence of the principle that consumer goods prices had to remain unchanged and were therefore excluded from cost-based pricing, was that the review gave rise to economically incorrect price ratios[3]. Beside this, the effect of price changes induced by the price review and introduced subsequently was that the official gross capital stock valuations based on 1962 prices no longer corresponded to actual replacement costs. The consequence of this was that the capital charge based on the gross value of all enterprise fixed and working capital no longer provided a uniform basis of assessment; depreciation, too, was wrongly estimated[4].

Even worse than these deficiencies were the effects of the inability to solve the problem of price flexibility in the GDR price system. Instruments for changing prices had been developed which were supposed to bring about price reductions with the passage of time, but price increases still occurred[5].

The measures to bring about changes in prices played a key role in the NES as conceived, in that the introduction of the 'capital-related type of price' depended on their effectiveness. With this type of price the economically necessary expenditure of capital was supposed to be taken into account in prices[6], yet without permitting price increases. This, however, required substantial reductions in processing and material costs – that is, in existing prices – particularly in capital-intensive branches, which in turn could not be secured because of the failure of the measures to make prices decline.

Without prices of this type the *capital charge*[7] could not be met by capital-intensive branches, or at least not without severely restricting enterprise fund formation. Thus the charge was unable to perform satisfactorily its allotted functions of (1) effectively promoting the planned investment and rational utilisation of productive capital and (2) ensuring supervision of the actual investment and utilisation of productive capital (Goldschmidt and Langner, 1965, p. 28).

Since the price system was not harmonized with the structural policy goals the *deduction from net profit*, which was set at widely differentiated but constant rates for lengthy periods, also failed to achieve the state's objectives. Short-term changes in the rates of deduction were ruled out, if only because they were supposed to provide guidelines for the enterprises.

The setting of maximum rates for the formation of the *bonus fund* (700–800 marks per employee in 1969 and 1970) could operate as an obstacle rather than an incentive to performance in successful enterprises: reserves of performance were revealed only to the extent necessary to attain precisely the profit which would guarantee the maximum rates of bonus. This meant conscious restraint of possible higher performance.

The defects mentioned make it clear that the 'economic levers' were not adequately refined[8]: they did not really permit precise and rapidly effective action in respect of specific and possibly even changing partial goals. It was also hard to put changes in partial goals into effect with direct planning, as plan revisions frequently disrupted the existing coordination of individual goals and thus often created shortages in unexpected places. We see here one of the most fundamental weaknesses of the NES: like indirect steering, direct planning too — because of the ponderous nature of the planning and balancing process was also only effective if employed well in advance. The consequence of this was that changes and shifts in demand could not be adequately taken into consideration in the short term because plan indicators had been prescribed and materials allocated long before, and the monetary steering instruments set along firm guidelines. Furthermore, enterprises tried to break out of the 'corset' of prescribed plan indicators when they expected to improve their profit situation; even high rates of deduction from net profit had little effect on them since in any case more gross profit also meant more net profit.

The end of the NES

In view of the defects and imperfections pointed out in the system, it was particularly fatal that in 1969 and 1970, precisely the years when the reform had to prove itself (Melzer and Rüger, 1972, p. 32), a growth crisis arose: extreme weather conditions led to power cuts and transport disruptions, hit agricultural production and construction work, and caused shortages in supplies to the population, factors which affected practically all sectors of the economy because of insufficient reserves and the inability of enterprises to adapt. The priority for 'structure-determining tasks', which we have already discussed (p. 46), aggravated this further, because the consequence of neglect of other products also affected the priority sectors of production. In particular this resulted in disruptions in the investment sector[9], which meant that the basis for the achievement of future goals was narrower than anticipated. Finally the plan targets for 1970 and the conception of the 1971–1975 five-year plan had to be scaled down, which in turn affected coordination with other CMEA countries concerning specific goals.

In this situation the economic leaders of the GDR felt compelled to take rapid action, which in turn meant that the new course to be adopted had to be decided in a relatively short period of time. Theoretically it would have been possible to develop the system further towards a better solution of the problems which had arisen: for example, larger reserves and greater enterprise flexibility could have been allowed, more quickly effective steering instruments employed and, above all, the 'structure-determining tasks' restricted to an order of magnitude less susceptible to disturbance. This did not happen.

In practice it appeared impossible to the *SED* leadership to develop the system further quickly, because

(1) The concepts were lacking both for more effective instruments and for efficient changes to the measures already in use;
(2) The defects of the existing price structure, which severely impeded the effectiveness of the NES model, could not be corrected within the foreseeable future if the priority of constant consumer goods prices were to be maintained and price increases generally avoided;
(3) The problem of coordinating financial and physical planning in spite of the priority of 'structure-determining tasks' was becoming more and

more difficult, as, owing to the imperfections of the regulations, enterprises were increasingly pushing forward into 'free' – that is, not yet excluded – areas of manoeuvre in order to further their own interests; this, however, caused continuing disproportions among planned financial relations[10];

(4) The leadership was in no way willing to accept a restriction of the state's structural conception accompanied by an increase in enterprise decisionmaking and possibly by increasing disproportions which it feared could lead to a critical conflict over this programme[11].

After sharp criticism of the previous concept, which has still never been published, the 14th plenum of the Central Committee of the *SED* in December 1970 decided on important changes in planning and management in the direction of recentralization. The disadvantages of greater centralization, which it had been the aim of the NES model to combat, were assessed as smaller than the obstacles to refloating the stranded ship of reform. Enterprises' scope for decisionmaking and the powers of the *VVB* and other intermediate bodies were restricted and direct state control strengthened, the number of plan indicators prescribed for enterprises was increased and planning in physical terms extended and some of the indirect steering means were abolished or modified ('Beschluss . . .', 1970).

Since 1971 enterprises' scope for action has been persistently narrowed by making the net profit to be earned by the enterprise into a state plan indicator, transforming the net profit deduction into absolute amounts deductible from profits – differing from branch to branch – and subjecting investment to compulsory regulation through state plan targets ('Beschluss . . .', 1971). Enterprises' scope for making decisions about their own investment was thus almost completely suspended again and 'profit' as an incentive retreated into the background.

This brought the NES period to its end; the points were set for less freedom for the lower and more decisionmaking at the upper levels of management. A complete and consistent 'new' system had still to be developed.

3.2 Aims, methods and instruments of recentralization

'Chief task' and 'unity of economic and social policy'

Since there was no new theoretical concept for the change of course prepared there was no alternative but to fall back on the administrative methods of direction in use at the beginning of the 1960s, the defects of which had been very severely criticized seven years before ('Kritische Einschätzung . . .', 1963; Ulbricht, Vol. 1, pp. 19–25, 30–31, 52–55. 108–109, 170–178,

224–225, 360–361). For precisely this reason, with the end of the Ulbricht era and the takeover of the leadership by Honecker[12] it seemed urgent at least to link the new course with some leading idea. More concretely, it was also necessary – in view of the existing disproportions – to direct growth targets more towards overall consolidation of the economy, fulfilment of the tasks falling to the GDR under CMEA arrangements, and towards a politically highly advisable improvement in the previously extremely neglected consumption sector, rather than concentrate on the highest possible growth rates.

The consequences for economic policy were inevitable and consisted in essence in a reorientation towards the following three basic goals, resolved at the VIII *SED* Congress (15–19 June 1971):

(1) The source of economic growth was to be primarily allround intensification of production, i.e. increases in output would be achieved in the main through more rational use and modernization of the existing plant, while at the same time labour would be employed more efficiently;
(2) An increase in the quantity and an improvement in the quality of consumer goods provided were declared urgent priorities;
(3) An active social policy was to bring about additional transfers of income.

This reorientation was reflected in the economic policy objectives of the five-year plan for 1971–1975 which were laid down at the same time ('Direktive . . .', 1971):

> The principal task of the five-year plan consists in the further raising of the material and cultural living standard of the people on the basis of a high rate of development of socialist production, increased efficiency, scientific and technical progress and growth of labour productivity.

To this the law on the five-year plan added ('Gesetz . . .', 1971):

> The aims of the five-year plan are to increase the national wealth and to strengthen the material–technical basis of socialism as the foundation for the further improvement of the working and living conditions of the population, through better and better utilization of the advantages of the socialist social order. . . .

Thus the principal task became the major economic *leitmotiv*, though not without the clear indication that it presupposed additional mobilization of effort by the working people. This principal aim of economic policy was to be 'not a tactical but a fundamental long-term orientation derived from the basic economic law of socialism' (Honecker, 1971), and was therefore also valid for the second half of the 1970s (Manz, 1973); yet it has remained unclear to the present day which criteria of a 'socialist way of life' are theoretically to be recognized and which rejected.

In order to reduce the discrepancy between demands and the possibilities of domestic resources, greater weight had to be given to intensification. It was recognized that in the GDR a predominantly extensive increase in capital capacity can yield only small further advances in productivity because with a limited and fully employed labour force an increase in capital is reflected primarily in declining utilization. Therefore modernization of the capital stock took priority over investment in expansion (Fichtner, 1972). In the ensuing period this comprehensive conception of rationalization was further developed and put into precise form in ten specific tasks (*Neues Deutschland*, 28 October 1975) which gave prominence to improvement of capital investment with faster implementation of technical progress. The discussion about intensification continues to this day, since the requirement of achieving increases in production without expensive new construction is raising an abundance of problems (Koziolek, 1977).

Whilst the third of the basic objectives listed above, an active social policy, had played a comparatively minor role at the VIII Congress of the *SED* itself, it came back into prominence in 1972, when a comprehensive resolution set out numerous social policy measures ('Gemeinsamer Beschluss . . .', 1972). These included, in particular, pension increases, improvements in social provision, assistance for working mothers, birth grants and finally rent reductions for a specified range of persons. This programme was extended in the autumn of 1973 by measures to improve both medical care and also the working and living conditions of health and social workers ('Weitere Massnahmen . . .', 1973). Beside this, as the core of the social policy programme, an extensive housebuilding programme was adopted, envisaging the construction or modernization of 2.8–3 million homes during the period 1976 to 1990 (Junker, 1973) and absorbing not less than 200 billion marks in all.

Since these separate items added up to a noteworthy programme of important social policy improvements, it seemed expedient to give prominence to the social policy aims together with the principal task. This was all the more so as it became increasingly uncertain whether the previous priority for consumption on the expenditure side would be able to be maintained in the second half of the 1970s, in view of the necessity to end the period of restrictions on investment, the increased export demands from the other CMEA countries and the anticipated burden of dearer and dearer raw material imports.

For these reasons, if for nothing else, frantic efforts were made after the event, as it were, to create a close link between 'chief task' and 'social policy' and to make these the leading ideas of the Honecker era. Thus now:

> The important policy results of the VIII Congress include the implementation of its social policy programme. It became possible through the inseparable unity of economic and social policy – the essential element of the course on which the VIII Congress resolved. (Honecker, 1975).

This slogan of the 'unity of economic and social policy' continued to be stressed with great emphasis, for example in order to show the population of the GDR how state expenditure on education, culture and health, on income redistribution and rent subsidies and subsidies to maintain stable consumer goods prices were particular advantages of the 'socialist way of life' (Koziolek, 1975). This finally culminated in the inclusion of an important paragraph on the 'unity of economic and social policy' in the 'Programme of the *SED*' adopted at the IX Congress (18-23 May, 1976) ('Programm. . .' (1976). Directly after the IX Congress a new decision was published on wage policy, pension increases, mothers' assistance and reductions in working time for shift workers ('Gemeinsamer Beschluss . . .', 1976). Since the beginning of 1979, in accordance with the programme, 6.6 million workers have received three additional days and 1 million four to six additional days of holiday. At the end of 1979 an additional increase in pensions also came into force. The success of this course is loudly proclaimed and the greatly increased extent of subsidies and the rise in the 'social fund' are extolled as advantages (Honecker, 1978).

From a theoretical point of view the idea of 'unity of economic and social policy' has much in its favour in that it appears easier to implement in a socialist than in a market-oriented economic system. Even in the 'social market economy' the multiplicity of private economic interests directed towards profit is in clear contradiction to the social principle, so that the state continually – and often belatedly – has to overcome existing and new social deficiencies by redistribution. The idea of the socialist planned economy, on the contrary, is that it should be constructed so that social evils which would have to be compensated do not arise in the first place. Even if it has not yet been possible to create such a compassionate system, which does justice equally to humanitarian, economic and ecological points of view, in reality, at least economic and social policy should form one unity.

This idea is by no means new, but is part of the discussion of socialism. Thus, for example, over ten years ago Ulbricht (1967) declared:

> The aim of socialist production is the continuously better satisfaction of the material and spiritual needs of the members of society, the development of socialist social relations and the personality of people. . . . In socialism the whole product of society belongs to the working people. There exists no antagonistic contradiction between surplus product and necessary product, which in capitalism is the reflection of the class conflict between bourgeoisie and working class.

Meanwhile the gap between claim and reality has remained great and the increase in real capacity has been small. Thus the aims of the 1976–1980 five-year plan ('Gesetz', 1976) had to be set more cautiously in view of the existing problems and the disappointing advances in productivity during the previous five-year plan (total increase in industrial labour productivity: plan

– 35%, actual – 28%). The estimates of possible economic growth were somewhat lower than the actual rates in 1971–1975 and then important key figures in the five-year plan law were set at the lower boundary of the range given in the directives (see *Table 3.1*). So the much-emphasized leading idea of the 'unity of economic and social policy' in practice amounts to little

Table 3.1 *Indicators of the economic development of the GDR up to 1980*

| | Total increase (%) 1970–1975 | | Total increase (%) 1975–1980 | |
	Actual	Five-year plan target	Five-year plan Directives	Law
National income produced	30	27	27–30	27.9
Industrial commodity production	37	34	34–36	34.0
Industrial labour productivity[a]	28	35[b]	30–32	30.0
Foreign trade turnover[c]	48	42[d]	–	–
Imports	42	–	–	–
Exports	55	60–70[e]	50[e]	50[e]
Retail trade turnover[f]	28	22	20–22	21.5
Net money incomes of the population	27	22	20–22	21.4
Gross capital investment[g]	22	16[h]	28–31[i]	28.8[j]

(a) Gross production per worker and employee (excluding apprentices)
(b) Industrial ministries, commodity production basis
(c) Total imports and exports (including intra-German trade) excluding services, at constant prices
(d) CMEA countries only
(e) Socialist countries only
(f) At current prices
(g) Excluding general repairs and foreign participation
(h) Including foreign participation
(i) Volume for the whole period: 232–6 billion marks
(j) Volume for the whole period 1976–1980: 234 billion marks excluding foreign participation (8 billion marks)

Sources: Five-year plan 1971–1975 (*Gesetzblatt der DDR*, I, 1971, pp. 175ff.); Draft directive of IX *SED* Congress (*Neues Deutschland*, 15 January 1976, pp. 3ff); Five-year plan 1976–1980 (*Neues Deutschland*, 17 December 1976, pp. 3ff); GDR statistical yearbooks and plan fulfilment reports; *DIW* calculations.

more than 'the mutual interdependence of intensification, output increases and standard of living' (Koziolek, 1978). Its purpose is to create an incentive to performance through increases in consumption and social services, albeit only very limited increases[13].

Tasks of principal management organs

Formally the organizational structure of the managing bodies changed little with the recentralization, but in substance there was a distinct increase in the power of the higher organs. In addition it must be borne in mind that the official organizational scheme has superimposed on it the informal *SED* relations, the extent and importance of which must not be underestimated.

The highest government and administrative organ is the *Council of Ministers*, with at present 42 members. Beside the chairman, Willi Stoph (from October 1973 to October 1976 it was Horst Sindermann) and eleven deputies, it includes the heads of the specialized functional ministries, the industrial ministries, the state bank and certain other offices (e.g. the Prices Office, the State Planning Commission). On the basis of *SED* recommendations and resolutions the Council of Ministers is concerned especially with fundamental aggregate economic decisions, structural questions, problems of production and distribution, capital formation and consumption and principles of foreign economic policy. Its powers have been clearly extended since the recentralization (Gesetz . . .', 1972): for example, it is now directly responsible for regional planning, the formation of economic reserves and cooperation with other CMEA countries, and also for the preparation and execution of a substantial portion of investment plans.

The *State Planning Commission*, as the supreme statutory planning organ, has the following tasks ('Statut . . .', 1973):

(1) To work out structural policy and alternatives and to prepare basic decisions of the Council of Ministers;
(2) To put the decisions of the Council of Ministers into concrete form by transforming them into targets for annual and longer term plans;
(3) To bear responsibility for the coordination of plan figures;
(4) To direct the work of plan preparation, balancing and supervision of plan execution. In this it can also issue direct instructions to the ministries;
(5) To ensure that the economy can meet military requirements;
(6) To see to consistent plan fulfilment, smooth, balanced economic development and continuous improvement of the planning process.

The eleven *industrial ministries* are responsible for steering their branch of industry: they fulfil a dual function; on the one hand they are supposed to represent the interests of their branch *vis-à-vis* the superior bodies, on the other hand they have crucial powers to issue orders to their subordinate managing organs and enterprises. Their tasks are in essence participation in the elaboration of long-term structural conceptions by the planning commission, drawing up annual and longer-term plans in detail and coordination. The functions lost by the intermediate management levels in the course of the recentralization have primarily fallen to the ministries. Thus they have additional possibilities of intervention, especially in the field of consumer goods: they draw up 'product catalogues' for groups of commodities which are particularly important for supplying the population, they supervise the rapid commissioning of new capacity and carry out quality control. Finally, they influence capital goods producers to construct their own consumer goods departments and all major enterprises to set up their own building departments. They also promote construction of enterprise workshops to produce their own means for rationalization (Hahn, 1977).

The *associations of nationalised enterprises* (VVB) ('Verordnung . . .', 1973), on which important tasks of economic leadership devolved during the NES period, have distinctly declined in significance in the 1970s. In 1967 there were 85 of them, in the mid-1970s there were 52 and in the autumn of 1979 only 13. They are charged with coordination of the annual and longer-term plans of their subordinate enterprises (= breaking down the plan tasks prescribed by the ministries into specific enterprise targets), the implementation of structural policy measures at enterprise level and standardization within their branch. They, too, have a dual function: representation of their branch interests to superior bodies and powers to issue orders to subordinate enterprises.

Beside the *VVB* there are horizontal and vertical amalgamations of enterprises in the form of *combines*, the importance of which has increased substantially in the last few years. Recently many new combines have been formed (e.g. in the electrical and electronic industries, engineering, vehicle manufacture and in consumer-oriented branches) in order to promote the faster introduction of modern technologies and also help to solve planning problems more easily through greater participation by the heads of combines. A higher level of activity by combine directors on their own responsibility is intended to bring about improvements in specialization, balancing of intermediate goods, concentration of preparatory processes as well as more efficient investment and a higher degree of intensification (Friedrich *et al.*, 1977; Gerisch and Hofmann, 1979). Combines as a rule are subordinated directly to a ministry, although in exceptional cases they can also be under the direction of a *VVB* or a provincial organ. This illustrates that as well as management by branches there is also regional management, which is supposed to bring regional points of view to bear. The organs concerned are the provincial economic councils and the province, county, town and parish councils. The legal regulations concerning these bodies have cut down the powers of the town and parish councils in favour of the province and county councils ('Gesetz . . .', 1973).

The aggregate economic planning process and its problems

At present long-term plan conceptions have been published for the period from 1976 to 1990, and in fact even up to the year 2000. The following three five-year periods can be distinguished here:

(1) For the five years 1976–1980 detailed plan indicators are in force; their number has increased in comparison with the 1971–1975 plan. Furth-

ermore, the conception of the plan tried to establish individual years as firmly predetermined parts of the five-year plan;

(2) For the period 1981–1985 a simplified set of indicators has so far been published, which is intended to indicate the general directions of development;

(3) In respect of the third period, 1986–1990 – and to some extent beyond that date even – plan conceptions have been worked out concerning fundamental structural changes, scientific and technical developments, programmes of special importance and basic long-term goals of the CMEA Comprehensive Programme.

Long- and medium-term planning

The starting point for evolving conceptions of the long-term development of the economy is information about the level reached hitherto and basic objectives and magnitudes. A number of means help to solidify fundamental concepts into plan conceptions (*Zur langfristigen Planung . . .*', 1975, pp. 18ff.). On the one hand, aggregate and partial economic analyses – for example, in the form of structural, sectoral and cross-section analyses and studies of branches of special importance – are designed to explore the mutual interrelationship of the parts to one another and to the whole. On the other hand, forecasts of, for example, social and individual needs, population and employment trends, the growth of capacity, scientific and technical developments, the regional structure and energy and raw material requirements are used in an attempt to devise predictions about feasible and probable development possibilities (Haustein, 1970). Building on these foundations, decisions are taken about the principal directions and important tasks and specific aims, and realistic long-term plans are evolved.

From the latter the precise, detailed five-year plan is then derived. In it the concrete growth targets are planned in detail – taking account of resolutions of central organs, tasks under the CMEA Comprehensive Programme and other international agreements. The five-year plan lays down not only the desired proportions of sectors and branches and the directions of scientific and technical development but also determines strategies for the implementation of the goals. This medium-term plan, which only began to recover its importance about 1968, after the initial exclusive concentration on annual plans in the early years of the NES period, is again the centre of attention[14].

The construction of the plan is carried out as follows. After the basic proportions of the overall development of the economy are handed down by the State Planning Commission to its subordinate bodies the latter disaggregate them and again pass them down further. Enterprises and combines agree on the tasks imposed on them with their contractual partners and then send their plan bids back up to the superior organ responsible for them. After particular controversial questions are resolved, plan bids and plan information go up the entire hierarchy again to the Council of ministers, which takes decisions on fundamental discrepancies and necessary additional requirements (e.g. unanticipated imports of raw materials, intermediate goods and equipment). On this basis the State Planning Commission lays down compulsory medium-term plan targets and indicators. For the 1971–1975 five-year plan this process was still done in two stages[15], which allowed increased coordination. The subsequent restriction to only one stage probably reflects the fact that, compared with the 1971–1975 period, enterprises' opportunity to influence the plan, which was in any case small, has diminished still more, while the preparatory work expected of them has increased.

In principle, the old planning problems of 1963 have resurfaced again with the recentralization, only in 1980 their importance has become substantially greater because of the rise in the volume of output, increased product differentiation and more complicated production processes: the possibilities for solving the problems, on the other hand, have scarcely improved:

(1) The definition of overall economic goals is made considerably harder by the ignorance of relative scarcities (which at present is insurmountable in view of the problems of prices), by the discrepancies between the objective function laid down by the party leadership and that actually desired by society, by the inadequacies of the demand studies underlying the determination of long-term consumption norms (Ehrlich and Schilling, 1976) and, despite the collection of extensive statistical data, by the continued lack of specific detailed items of information, the supplementation of which by estimates is a source of considerable error. For this reason alone a meaningful ranking of goals in order of urgency is impossible.

(2) The basing of planning on forecasts raises substantial problems. Despite some good partial forecasts, combining them together poses great difficulties because of the different degree of uncertainty of their foundations and results. A number of forecasts consist purely of simple extrapolations of previous trends and in these cases the forecast technical parameters are frequently hard to translate into economic parameters. In particular, calculations which work back from the level of scientific and technical development estimated for some future point in time to the intervening individual years prove useless for assessing concrete alternatives to be adopted now (Schürer, 1972).

(3) The mathematical models used as aids in planning, which are intended to simulate the effects to be expected from alternative basic decisions (taking into account the mutual interdependence of partial goals) and to show up existing limits and achieve an accommodation between goals and possibilities, remain extremely imperfect. Frequently they are too highly aggregated for the problems to be solved, the available information is often in an unsuitable form for mathematical calculations – for

example, because of changes in statistical definitions – and the linear relationships built into the models are not very realistic.

(4) A fundamental problem in any calculation extending over several periods is the establishment of the price basis: on the one hand constant prices are essential in order to be able to determine real trends at all; on the other hand, however, changes in relative values with the course of time must be taken into consideration; otherwise plan values become fictitious because they diverge too far from the prices actually in force and structural proportions are not adapted to changes in relative prices. As result, various price bases are used in the GDR[16], a procedure which has the disadvantage not only of considerably increasing the difficulties of calculation and the demands on enterprise management but also of being unable to adapt real structures to anticipated future shifts in values adequately: instead of well-grounded overall price planning (Lommatzsch, 1974), planning future cost structures in advance[17], there is merely gradual adjustment of prices to some of the changes which have occurred in the structure of costs.

(5) The problem of low productivity of factors of production: despite the shortage of labour, labour is squandered because its undervaluation in relation to its scarcity obstructs sensible substitution of machinery and other equipment for labour. The situation is similar with capital; some existing capacity is underutilized, rationalization of the capital stock is neglected and the scrapping of obsolete plant frequently postponed too long. The urgently necessary savings of increasingly expensive raw materials are delayed because production performance is still principally measured by the gross value of output (Büchner *et al.*, 1978). This causes enterprises to concentrate on production not merely of goods containing a high proportion of intermediate products but on those using the dearest materials. This inevitably leads to an exaggerated, that is, false indication of performance[18].

Annual planning

The precise annual targets are laid down in the annual plan, which contains still more detail than the five-year plan. On the basis of the provisional plan fulfilment results for the previous year, which become available in January or February, the State Planning Commission first notes the discrepancies between the results achieved and the aims of the five-year plan and then takes into account new directives and particular goals handed down by the Council of Ministers in order to obtain a picture of what additional efforts will be possible and necessary the following year and/or how far corrections to the medium-term plan conceptions are required. Such adaptations to changes in circumstances are often made in annual plans without any announcement of changes in the five-year plan targets.

After basic decisions about these questions are taken and the major state tasks for individual sectors are worked out, the actual plan construction work is done during the period from April or May to October, following a precise schedule of dates which in practice is changed little from year to year ('Anordnung über den terminlichen Ablauf . . .', 1973, 1976, 1977, 1979). As well as the transmission of plan tasks from higher to lower bodies and the simultaneous detailed disaggregation of targets, a series of complicated coordination processes between the various bodies at different levels plays a major part in this work. The submission of draft plans by the lower to the higher bodies then follows in August and September. During the period from October to mid-December the State Planning Commission has the duty of carrying out the overall economic balancing, plugging the gaps which are to be expected between supply and demand for intermediate products and submitting the aggregate draft plan to the Council of Ministries.

A major problem here is whether it is preferable to start the planning process early but with only rather rough initial data or to start later on the basis of more exact data (planning for 1978, for example, did not start until July 1977), only to encounter difficulties with the coordination processes because of shortage of time. The work of planning is made substantially more difficult by the failure of higher organs to take some investment decisions until relatively late, by the frequent changes and delays in the handing down of state tasks, by failure to adhere to the prescribed schedule and by the often inadequate coordination at the various levels. The biggest problem is that while planning for the following year can take into account difficulties which developed during the preceding year, it cannot take adequate account of any which arise during the current year. The plan, then, has to be subject to current adjustments, which in turn cannot be made without substantial disruptions in particular sectors.

A further problem is that very exhaustive preparatory work is expected of enterprises and combines, in the shape of reports, tables, drafts, calculations and in filling in a multitude of forms. The plan itself also has to be drawn up in several obligatorily prescribed parts: production, sales, science and technology, capital formation (replacement of fixed assets), materials utilization, labour and labour productivity, working and living conditions, costs and finance. The following are the principal indicators used in enterprises' and combines' plans (Scherzinger, 1976; 'Anordnung über die Ausarbeitung . . .', 1979): total industrial commodity production, production sold, production of major products by quantity and value, output of finished consumer goods, supply of specialized secondary raw materials, investments, release of labour, labour productivity, capital productivity, number of employees, wages bill, exports and imports in quantity and value by areas and major product groups, export profitability by areas. In recent years there has been an increase in the importance of indicators which can be used by superior organs as 'evidence of efficiency': for example, labour productivity on the basis of enterprises' own performance (= net labour productivity), material cost intensity (ratio of material costs to commodity production), capital profitability (ratio of profit to fixed capital), total costs per 100 marks of commodity production sold, commodity production of products with official quality marks, production of new and improved products, prime cost reduction and labour saving through rationalization.

As in the Soviet Union, efforts have been made in the GDR since 1974 to induce enterprises to take on additional obligations in the 'counterplan' ('Anordnung zu den Regelungen . . .', 1974, 1977, 1978). This comprised bids made by enterprises up to the first quarter of the current plan year to exceed their state plan targets. They receive greater rewards than 'unplanned' overfulfilment through increases in the enterprises' bonus and benefits funds. Apart from the problem of the additional material balancing it necessitates, the disadvantage of the counterplan is that it cannot fulfil its intended function of overcoming enterprises' efforts to secure easy plans: enterprises try to make up their draft plans in advance in a way that leaves them scope for counterplan obligations, the more so as they have to take into account that today's above-plan performance will become tomorrow's prescribed plan target for them. This may have been the reason why at the end of August 1979 the 'order on work with counterplans' was suddenly suspended (*Gesetzblatt . . .*', No. 27, 1979, p. 247). In place of the old regulation the State Planning Commission introduced an 'Order to stimulate bids to exceed state tasks for the elaboration of the uniform plan proposal for the national economic plan for 1980' ('Anordnung zur Stimulierung . . .', 1979). As before, bids to exceed state plan targets receive increased bonuses.

Balancing

In order to ensure supplies of intermediate products, planning is accompanied by a comprehensive balancing process for these goods ('Verordnung über die Material . . .', 1971; 'Anordnung über die Nomenklatur . . .', 1971, 1975). Some 4700 balances matching supplies and requirements for materials, equipment and consumer goods are drawn up; in this way almost the whole of production (including imports) is covered. Since the recentralization the number of items balanced has increased, central allocation of quotas has been extended; there has been a shift of the balancing function to higher levels of economic management. At present 300 balances for priority items in the state plan are worked out by the State Planning Commission, 500 balances are drawn up by the Ministries and 3900 by *VVB*, combines and enterprises (Strauss *et al.*, 1973, p. 249). The 800 balances drawn up by central bodies account for 60–65% of GDR industrial commodity production (*Volkswirtschaftsplanung*, 1975, p. 163).

Beside the traditional drawing up of balances for individual items, the balancing process also employs input–output tables, both for special subsectors and for the whole economy. They are intended to show the interdependencies between sectors, branches and product groups and to enable optimal solutions to be reached by calculating the different possible variants.

The task of determining all the inputs at the various stages of production as well as planning output and its composition causes a multitude of problems. The magnitudes involved are frequently mutually interdependent, meaning that for every individual balance magnitudes have to be assumed in order to start the task even though they will not be decided until the balances are completed. Consequently, numerous provisional decisions are necessary which then have to be revised again and again, and these changes in turn substantially affect subsequent balance decisions. This makes the interconnections between the balances the crucial problem. Furthermore, where disproportions are found the balancing organs are reluctant to balance them by adjusting the supply side because the secondary effects of changes in production are immense. They prefer therefore to make adjustments on the utilization side, mostly in the form of tightening of material use norms, to the detriment of the enterprises (Schilling and Steeger, 1971).

Furthermore, serious problems arise in the calculation of variants on the basis of rough balances, which are supposed to register the basic proportions of all principal directions of development of the whole economy: on the one hand, wrong estimates by the central bodies are particularly damaging since they cannot be corrected by intermediate and lower planning bodies, or only with great difficulty. On the other hand, the input–output tables used to ascertain the basic proportions exhibit two serious defects: (1) they are too highly aggregated[19], so that the possible margin of error is very large; (2) the planning and balancing of future developments relies on input coefficients from the past; yet these coefficients change with scientific and technical progress, so that today even the direction of changes over the next fifteen years often cannot be predicted.

Indirect monetary steering today

Of the indirect steering instruments used in the NES period only the capital charge ('Verordnung uber die Produktionsfondsabgabe . . .', 1971) and part of the funds formed by *VEB* and *VVB* have continued in operation unchanged since the recentralization. The predominant part of the funds has been modified and a new fund, the performance fund, introduced in addition. The measures to make prices change have been dropped completely, the further introduction of the 'capital-related' type of price suspended and the deduction from net profit has been changed and the banking system reformed as well.

Profit, profit utilization and cost planning

In the years 1971–1972 the profit to be earned by the enterprise became a compulsory plan indicator and thus a fixed component of financial planning; since 1973 it has been an accounting indicator derived indirectly from other indicators. If profit exceeds the planned amount half of the extra profit goes to the state budget[20] and the rest may only be used for a rather restricted range of possibilities[21]. If the planned profit level is not achieved – as a rule the consequence of increased costs or failure to fulfil production targets – the result is financial difficulties for the enterprise, as it cannot form its funds according to plan, nor finance the anticipated investments: it may have only limited recourse to bridging credits, which are in any case expensive.

In view of the increased incidence of financial problems in enterprises, since 1973 the enterprise which fails to reach its planned profit may reduce its deduction from net profit by 50% of the shortfall from planned profit (1971: 0%; 1972: 30%). If the actual profit does not even reach the diminished deduction, the amount of deduction payable is reduced to the latter. Since 1976 cost increases which have been caused by price rises on raw materials may be partly covered by reductions in the deduction from net profit, until corresponding new prices are set for the finished products.

With the help of the fund formation rules, resources of the *VVB*, the combines and the *VEB* financed out of profits, and partly also out of costs, are tied up for specified purposes and must be utilized in accordance with precise legal regulations. In the *VVB* (and in the head enterprises of combines) the profit fund hitherto comprised the deductions from the net profits of the constituent enterprises, a part of which went to the state budget: the remainder was redistributed within the *VVB* (or combine) and used to finance the reserve fund, the advertising fund or the 'disposable fund' for paying bonuses for special performance ('Finanzierungsrichtlinie . . .', 1975). Now there is a definite measure of centralization of net profit within the combine in the 'account for deductions of centralized net profit'[22] and – beside the reserve, advertising and 'disposables' funds – a certain centralization of funds in general (e.g. investment fund, science and technology fund, performance fund) ('Finanzierungsrichtlinie . . .', 1979). It is significant that the general director of the combine enjoys a series of possibilities for redistribution of the resources of the various funds.

In addition, strict regulations exist governing the use of resources for investments, which are designed to ensure that they are only used for planned investments. The major enterprise funds are the investment fund, the science and technology fund, the bonus fund and the performance fund. The latter two are intended to offer the workforce an incentive for higher performance; their importance has increased in the last few years.

The bonus fund, which is planned as an absolute sum and formed out of shares in profit ('Verordnung über die Planung . . .', 1972, 1973) is intended to increase the interest of the workforce by means of bonuses for special performance and the end-of-year bonus. This fund is linked to the fulfilment of the commodity production and net profit indicators; increases in the bonus fund above the planned level depend on fulfilment of additional targets determined precisely in advance. To the extent that counterplan proposals are submitted by enterprises by the first quarter of the plan year, the planned bonus fund is to be increased by 2.5% (formerly 1.5%) for exceeding the commodity production indicator by 1% and by 0.8% (formerly 0.5%) for exceeding the planned net profit by 1%, but only to the extent of the actual overfulfilment subsequently achieved[23]. The maximum allocation amounts to 900 marks per employee (plus the 150 marks from counterplan proposals); in 1972 the actual average amount was 650 marks, in 1975 it was 764 marks and in 1978 811 marks.

The performance fund ('Anordnung über die Planung . . .', 1975, 1978), created in 1972, is designed to induce the workforce to achieve additional performance beyond the plan figures. Parts of net profit go into this fund when increases in labour productivity in excess of the plan and laid down in the counterplan are achieved, when specific material use is reduced below the level planned in the preceding year, when improvements in quality and reductions in rejects are achieved and when new products are introduced. The use of the performance fund, which requires the agreement of the enterprise trade union leaders, is for the following purposes: improvement of the working and living conditions of the workforce[24], rationalization measures financed from enterprise reserves and central trade union organization projects (construction of holiday villages and sanatoria). The annual allocation to the performance fund is probably at present about 200 marks per employee.

The outline of profit planning and utilization (fund formation) given here shows that since the recentralization profit has been devalued from an incentive for new initiatives by the enterprise to a state target to ensure the financial side of the enterprise's operations. At the same time as a multitude of physical targets are prescribed, the system of indirect steering is now also intended to exert pressure on the enterprise for performance improvements in the sense of closer plan implementation. This dual pressure through physical targets on the one hand and financial restrictions on the other can only be evaded by the enterprise by means of cost reductions.

For this reason, since 1974 enterprises have been required to plan reductions in prime costs in advance, as part of their defined cost planning ('Anordnung über die Finanzplanung . . .', 1973). They are to plan their costs in advance in terms of the kinds, places and bearers of costs, based on calculation of the necessary inputs, and also to show the anticipated revenues and rates of profit on each product. In doing this they are obliged to set the planned costs for the year lower than for the preceding year and to give a detailed breakdown of the planned cost savings in terms of rationalization measures introduced and kinds of costs. Enterprises must observe prescribed norms here (e.g. for use of materials, for overhead costs). The objective of this detailed cost planning is more efficient use of resources, the uncovering of intra-enterprise reserves and the collection of better data for comparison of enterprises. In addition, the controlling bodies hope to obtain information about intended or possible independent actions by enterprises which are not in line with central goals before they have been commenced.

The result is that instead of inducing enterprises to take initiatives, the indirect monetary steering system exerts pressure for fulfilment of the planned tasks and the achievement of cost reductions. It is true that a tendency is generated for the performance of weaker enterprises to be brought up to the level of better ones, as there is no incentive for successful enterprises to make increased efforts. Such an incentive would only be possible through increased enterprise decisionmaking rights – i.e. through limited decentralization – which the authorities, however, are unwilling to grant. Consequently, as a kind of substitute solution, there has been a shift of incentives towards the labour factor. A substantial part of the modifications to the incentive system since 1972 has concentrated on giving individual workers and enterprise workforces collectively increased fund allocations in return for taking on additional tasks, if possible announced in advance. Yet distinct limits to the stimulation function of the performance fund can be seen in the onesided possibilities of utilization of the fund's resources – with the exception, however, of the subsidy for workers to build their own homes. Furthermore, after some time – even with the best will on their part – the workers' ability to increase performance and achieve continuing large advances in labour productivity out of reserves without additional capital, through changes in work organization, avoidance of downtime, reduction of rejects and improvement of quality, is likely to be exhausted. The situation is similar with the bonus fund: successful enterprises – with the complete agreement of their workforces – will only use their reserves of performance to the extent needed just to attain the maximum bonus per employee. In addition, the linking of allocations to the bonus fund to the degree of fulfilment of net profit and commodity production plans causes concentration on a onesided product range oriented to these indicators rather than to the requirements of the population.

Price setting and price problems
The recentralization affected the price system in the GDR particularly severely, as the measures to make a prices change were suspended (*Gesetzblatt . . .*, II, No. 67, 1972, p. 761), the setting of 'capital-related' prices was interrupted[25] and a general price freeze was introduced, which initially was to last until 1975 but was then extended to 1980. For new and improved products a very extensive and bureaucratic process of price setting

was established, which gave the decisive influence to major central organs (e.g. the Council of Ministers and the Prices Office) ('Beschluss über Massnahmen . . .', 1971; 'Beschluss über die Bestätigung . . .', 1971). A new calculation guideline was laid down for these complicated methods of confirmation and introduction of prices ('Anordnung über die zentrale . . .', 1972) and at the same time the multiplicity of widely differing price decrees of previous years was suspended ('Anordnung Nr. Pr. 99 . . .', 1973). The new regulations called for exact evidence of costs and observation of prescribed norms for manufacturing and overhead costs. They stipulated that the price rise allowed on a new product had to be less than the improvement in quality; an additional profit was granted in the price for three years.

Thus up to 1975 the following three groups of prices in principle existed side by side: for a large proportion of products the prices established in the 1967 industrial price reform – on the basis of costs at that time – applied, there was a group of products for which 'capital-related' prices existed and a further group of new or improved products for which prices based on costs in the year in which production commenced (although not as a rule 'capital-related' prices) were used. Consumer goods prices also had to be fitted into the three groups, and here there was additional price differentiation for reasons of economic and social policy: thus for years the prices of a number of basic foodstuffs (e.g. bread, potatoes, fish, meat, bakery products) as well as children's clothing and some services (e.g. rents, public transport fares) had been held down by means of subsidies. Products in great demand, on the other hand, like cars and television sets, bore high production taxes. Prices here are performing a certain distribution function[26].

With this lack of uniformity in price setting it is not surprising that substantial price distortions arose and increased from year to year with shifts in costs not taken into account in the fixed price system. They bring about lossmaking production and impede necessary innovations or guide them in wrong directions. 'One form in which this appears is the preservation of old techniques and technologies, the inadequate level of scrapping of obsolete capital and the insufficient efforts to release labour' (Hoss and Schilling, 1972) – unsolved problems which remain to this day at the centre of the debate about intensification.

On top of these domestic price problems came the worldwide increase in the cost of energy. Although internal and foreign trade prices are fundamentally separate from each other in the GDR, the authorities had to decide whether and in what manner the increased cost of raw material imports and also the deterioration in the geological conditions of domestic brown coal production should be reflected in domestic prices. Since a straightforward subsidy with no change in prices would have given no impetus to savings of materials, from 1 January 1976 higher prices were

established for raw materials and raw material intensive products ('Anordnung Nr. Pr. 125 . . .', 1975) and from 1 January 1977 new prices were
brought in for semi-finished products, spare parts and some finished
products[27] ('Anordnung Nr. Pr. 210 . . .', 1976). On 1 January 1978
further price revisions were introduced for special chemical products,
machinery and equipment and for additional spare parts ('Anordnung Nr.
Pr. 249 . . .', 1977; 'Anordnung Nr. Pr. 250 . . .', 1977); at the end of July
1978 price setting for means of rationalization was changed ('Anordnung
Nr. Pr. 285 . . .', 1978). Finally, from 1 January 1979 new prices have been
in force for new construction and installation work and for finished
products ('Anordnung Nr. Pr. 249/1 . . .', 1978; 'Anordnung Nr. Pr.
250/1 . . .', 1978; 'Anordnung Nr. Pr. 211/1 . . .', 1978). In January 1979
freight rates were altered and at the end of March new prices were set for old
parts and reconditioned spare parts ('Anordnung Nr. 8 . . .', 1979; 'Anordnung Nr. Pr. 284 . . .', 1979).

On account of the political decision to hold consumer goods prices
constant, these price increases were not allowed to affect consumers, and
they were similarly designed to leave agriculture and handicrafts untouched.
The cost increases which they caused to producers of consumer goods and of
products the use of which as substitutes it was intended to stimulate, as well
as to industrial customers who had not yet been allowed to raise the prices of
their final products, were covered by a price equalization fund ('Anordnung
über die Planung der finanziellen . . .', 1975; 'Anordnung über die Planung
und Bildung von Preisausgleichsfonds . . .', 1975; 'Anordnung über die
Zuführung . . .', 1975; 'Anordnung Nr. 2 . . .', 1976; 'Zweite Durchführungsbestimmung . . .', 1978), through changes in taxes or cuts in
deductions from net profit and through enterprises' efforts to raise productivity. The problem here remains, since these price revisions must continue
in the future, especially because the price of imported energy has meanwhile
risen again. The trouble is that the timing of price revisions always lags
considerably behind the increase in the cost of imports.

Thus renewed price revisions were decided for 1 January 1980 for a large
part of those raw materials and other inputs, the prices of which had already
been increased at the beginning of 1976. The level of the new prices was
supposed to be based on the cost situation at the beginning of 1979. As well
as major raw materials and fuels, some new building and installation work
and building repairs and building materials prices were changed (*Gesetzblatt*
. . ., I, No. 15 and 16, 1979, pp. 120ff.; 131ff.; 'Anordnung Nr. Pr. 211/3
. . .', 1979; 'Anordnung Nr. Pr. 211/2 . . .'; 'Anordnung Nr. Pr. 251/1
. . .', 1979; 'Anordnung Nr. Pr. 121/1 . . .', 1979; 'Anordnung Nr. Pr. 212
. . .', 1979; 'Anordnung Nr. Pr. 219 . . .', 1979) as were investment prices
('Anordnung Nr. 3 . . .', 1979; 'Anordnung Nr. Pr. 250/2 . . .', 1979).

As the 1976 raw material prices had failed to bring about savings of
materials, and enterprises continued the production of obsolete products as

before instead of striving to innovate, further new regulations were put into effect in the middle of 1976 for the short term ('Beschluss über die Bildung . . .', 1976): under these, the enterprise which achieved cost reductions could keep the enterprise price of the product constant until 1980, which means that savings of materials no longer have a negative effect on plan accounting but are rewarded by extra profits. For new or improved products prices are now set according to the so-called price–performance ratio, that is, in relation to the improvement in use value *vis-à-vis* comparable products[28]. Since this was a departure from purely cost-based price setting, the 1972 calculation guideline had to be abandoned and replaced by a new one ('Anordnung über die zentrale . . .', 1976). As this central state calculation guideline cannot take account of either the existing above-enterprise cost norms or the differences between specific branches (e.g. in profit calculation), additional special calculation guidelines had to be drawn up ('Anordnung über die Inkraftsetzung . . .', 1977, 1978).

Besides the increase in the administrative costs involved, the new price-setting procedure gives rise to problems particularly because in view of the regulations on the utilization of profit the incentive for enterprises to develop new products is small and objective yardsticks for measuring use value are frequently lacking. The last point means that inadequate valuation of expenditure was offset by corresponding inadequate valuation of use value.

Thus price problems have been further aggravated, as, in addition to the three incompatible groups of prices already discussed, there is now a fourth group: prices which have been set on the basis of the price–performance ratio for goods of which some display only apparent or overvalued improvements in use value.

Banking and credit

The banking reform carried out in the NES period (Lang and Ruban, 1968) had made the banks into independent but noncompeting institutions which followed the 'principle of economic accountability'. In the middle of 1974 there was another reorganization: in order to secure stricter control over the banking apparatus the important Industry and Trade Bank was organizationally incorporated into the State Bank.

The duties of the State Bank comprise currency emission, foreign exchange control, conduct of accounts for the state budget and participation in the preparation of aggregate economic plan decisions. The branches of the Industry and Trade Bank, which number more than forty, not only conduct the accounts of enterprises and *VVB*, grant credits and operate the payments and clearing system, but they also supervise and inspect the implementation of, in particular, the tasks laid down in the investment plan[29]. The other banks, which operate in their respective sectors, are the *Bank for Agriculture and the Food Industry*, the *Cooperative Bank for Handicrafts and Trades*, the *German Foreign Trade Bank Co.* and the *German Trade Bank Co.*, which also plays an important role in foreign trade.

Credits are granted basically in accordance with the credit plan adopted by the Council of Ministers, which is designed to promote output of products included in the production plan. In order to avoid enterprises preferring lines of activity which were highly efficient but contrary to the plan, the banks' rights of supervision over intra-enterprise processes – quite irrespective of the source of finance – were substantially strengthened. They take part in the planning process, comment on draft plans, carry out inspections in cooperation with other supervising bodies[30], report on the results of their inspections and impose punitive interest rates or refuse credit in cases of severe contravention of the plan.

Whilst investment credits are tied to observance of specified data (e.g. technical performance, investment expenditure, completion times of projects and recoupment period, proportion of own investment and profitability criteria), fulfilment of material use norms and sound payment dates apply to credits for working capital. As a rule, credits are granted for five years at an interest rate of 5%, although for rationalization measures the minimum rate is 1.8%, and where the plan is contravened rates amount to 8–10%.

3.3 Between excessive bureaucracy and lack of efficiency

Weaknesses of the present system

Since the economic leadership in the GDR itself regarded the recentralization model created in the first half of the 1970s as not efficient enough, it adopted further new planning regulations for the 1976–1980 quinquennium ('Anordnung über die Ordnung . . .'; 'Anordnung über die Rahmenrichtlinien . . .') which have largely been taken into consideration in the above account. With these new regulations the following improvements were sought:

(1) Standardization of modes of procedure and clarity of planning methods and powers were intended to make both enterprise and aggregate economic planning easier to supervise and to counteract the dangerous tendency to excessive direction (Leptin and Melzer, 1975).

(2) An attempt was made to break down the tasks set for the five-year plan period into precise annual plan figures in advance.

(3) The problem of the inefficiency of the economy was to be met with 'effeciency planning' (Mätzig and Neumann, 1975; Ritzschke and Steeger, 1975; *Effektivität* . . ., 1975, p. 51). In view of the already limited meaningfulness of profit as a yardstick of enterprise performance because of price distortions, better information was expected from the establishment of several supplementary indicators[31].

(4) To overcome the deficiencies in the use of capital (too little scrapping of old plant and too low utilization of new plant, poor preparation and execution of investment projects, often with a backward technological level) an attempt was made to construct a complex capital planning procedure[32] which would meet the demands of this sphere of planning (*Volkswirtschaftsplanung*, 1975).

(5) To promote further intensification, the State Planning Commission drew up a 'Directive on socialist rationalization' which laid down major scientific and technical tasks and critical points for specific sectors, which the enterprises were to amplify through their own ideas (*Die Wirtschaft*, Nos 15 and 23, 1975). In addition, in order to improve the harmonization of scientific and technical development with investment, the ministries drew up coordination plans (*Die Wirtschaft*, No. 20, 1975; *Presseinformationen* . . ., No. 103, 1976), which were supposed to link the plans for science and technology to the other parts of the plan.

At first sight these attempts at improvement seemed interesting, but in practice they proved unsuccessful:

(a) Instead of more easily supervised and standardized planning, excessive bureaucracy has increased substantially because improvements – where actually achieved – have been more than offset by more precise and therefore more extensive plan accounting (Wahl, 1975).

(b) The 'efficiency planning' was unable to overcome inefficiency because with severe price distortions there can be no sound measure of efficiency even with a multiplicity of indicators expressed in value terms.

(c) The attempt to conceive the respective annual plans as precisely fixed components of the current five-year plan led to considerable planning difficulties, if only because of the price changes which occurred after 1975. Furthermore, some of the growth targets originally planned – e.g. for the chemical industry, machine tools and also consumer goods branches – had to be reduced in the annual plans.

(d) The problem of supplying the right consumer goods to meet demand was not solved.

(e) Despite numerous efforts at intensification, the problem of enterprises' unwillingness to innovate was not overcome. With the rules in force on the use of profits there was no strong incentive for innovation and risktaking. But the state has no alternative solutions available; entrepreneurial initiative cannot be planned nor replaced by complicated regulations.

(f) Numerous deficiencies in the use of capital became more and more clear:
(i) Although enterprises have had data on capacity at their disposal for years (Garscha, 1973, pp. 77–81) and since 1976 have been obliged to draw up plans for its utilization, planning of capacity could only

be done very imperfectly hitherto because differing production conditions could not be taken sufficiently into account and, with extensive product ranges, capacity could not be determined in real units (Hülsenberg and Gallenmüller, p. 50).

(ii) Despite various attempts, no functional concept of 'complex capital planning' was successfully established because this requires the solution of complicated problems (Melzer, 1977): on the one hand decisions must be taken about the proportions of closely interrelated forms of capital reproduction (scrapping, maintenance, rationalization and expansion)[33]. On the other hand substantial problems arise from the fact that relations over time and interconnections with other branches must be taken into account, as a consequence of which over 70% of the annual volume of investment is already tied up by decisions made in previous periods (Kratsch *et al.*, 1975, p. 90); furthermore, decisions on future investments should take into consideration the priority of intensification, which can only be planned with difficulty.

(iii) The marked obsolescence of the capital stock in the GDR, which swallows up high repair costs, is also a handicap ('Zur Altersstruktur . . .', 1977); not enough scrapping is done to counter this because as a rule plan tasks require that old capital also be used.

(iv) Investment was going increasingly into unplanned investment projects, which should not have happened[34]; similarly cost increases became more and more marked[35]. In practice there is still, as always, insufficient coordination of the preparation and execution of investments, which is reflected particularly in failure to complete projects within the times scheduled, even though these are in any case relatively long. The reasons given for this (Kiermeyer, Ruhle and Werner, 1976) are late starting of preparatory work, insufficient cooperation by other sectors of the economy in the planning process, inadequate designing capacity, too little preliminary scientific and technical trial and too small annual balance allocations (materials quotas) for approved projects.

These difficulties show that the expectations which the GDR economic leadership held concerning its attempts at improvement and stricter control of planning have not been fulfilled. The chief reason is probably that the changes introduced for the second half of the 1970s are formal rather than fundamental: increases in performance were supposed to be achieved by more exact, precise formal planning processes rather than by real attempts to solve problems of substance – evidently the relevant ideas for this are lacking. Rules and complicated legal regulations cannot solve the economic problems of determining objectives, deciding structure, selecting priorities and coordinating the performance of the various sectors. This is reflected in the two quintessential weaknesses of the present system, the inadequate flexibility to adapt to external disturbances or internal shifts in demand and the inefficiency of the GDR economy: with comparatively high inputs of labour, capital and raw materials only relatively low productivity is achieved, specific energy and materials consumption is in general too high and growth rates have been distinctly faltering in recent years ('Aussenwirt-schaftliche Belastungen . . .', 1980).

This is undoubtedly connected with the main economic problem of the GDR, the increased foreign trade burden. Since the middle of the 1970s the GDR, which is poor in raw materials, has faced substantial rises in the world market prices of raw materials without being able to put up the price of the commodities it exports to the same extent ('Handel DDR – USSR . . .', 1980; 'Innerdeutscher Handel . . .', 1980; 'DDR – Aussenhandel . . .', 1979). The current cost increases and the continuing price rises to be expected have further exacerbated the situation (Honecker, 1979). Increasing exports has therefore become the major task of planning and development, even at the price of diminished growth of domestic expenditure (and with opportunities for growth which are in any case reduced).

On the threshold of new changes?

The difficulties and problems we have indicated mean that renewed changes in the planning system can certainly be expected. Hopes that the NES regulations could revive and the interrupted reforms be continued are hardly likely to be fulfilled, all the same, because of the weaknesses and contradictions of the NES model pointed out at the beginning of this chapter.

Any attempt at greater decentralization and revival of the role of profit as the enterprise motive force, beside the creation of advantages for the enterprise in return for cost reductions and increases in performance, has two prerequisites; more tolerance on the part of the central authorities towards enterprises' own directions of development and solution of the prices problem. Both present problems: the first demands a rethink by the economic leadership, for which it is probably no more ready today than at the beginning of the 1970s; the second requires a fundamental price reform and revaluation of capital assets, in order to eliminate the existing price distortions and to allow an improvement in the measurement of efficiency and an increase in the efficiency of all factors of production.

But a price reform which in any case, purely for reasons of time, could not be carried out until the beginning of the next five-year plan period, is evidently not envisaged at the beginning of the 1980s, because, as has already been discussed elsewhere (Beyer *et al.*, 1980),

(i)   Numerous uncertainties exist in respect of future raw material prices both on the world market and within the CMEA;

(ii) Substantial price rises would be necessary to adjust them to actual cost levels including capital costs (and not only for raw materials);

(iii) This would mean that the politically desired maintenance of the stability of the level of consumer goods prices would no longer be possible.

Of these reasons the third is doubtless of decisive importance.

Without price reform (including revaluation of capital) and continuing future flexibility of prices there can be no fundamental reform promising any great success. The model of decentralization, while retaining the existing price distortions, can probably be as good as ruled out because it would scarcely overcome the inefficiency hurdle but at the same time would cause new divergences between the direction of development determined by the state and by enterprises. At present, therefore, only limited, partial solutions are possible – in other words 'substitute models'. Their scope is narrowly confined between, on the one hand, continuation of the previous course in the form of the unpromising strengthening of regulations, and on the other hand experimentation with partial increases in decisionmaking powers for some intermediate leadership bodies. The theoretical discussions conducted in the GDR, at any rate, keep within this limited framework (Melzer and Scherzinger, 1978).

Discussions and recent attempts to improve the system

More efficient use of capital

In order to achieve more economical use of the available productive resources ('Ausgewählte Probleme . . .', 1977), a complicated theoretical 'model of complex capital planning', designed for electronic data processing, was developed and put up for discussion by the Higher Economic School (Brossmann, 1977). It starts by ascertaining the precise quantity, structure, age, technical level and degree of wear and tear of the present capital stock (including taking account of necessary scrapping and maintenance). It then attempts to compare this stock with the future stock required for implementation of the production targets in the medium-term plan. The optimization model, which is based on a multitude of indicators, constraints, stability conditions and efficiency criteria, should then determine how the future stock can best be developed from the one existing at present.

Despite the use of numerous efficiency indicators, however, only limited 'relative' improvements in the use of capital can be achieved with this model – which requires much complicated planning work (Melzer, 1978) – because it still takes too little account of problems peculiar to individual enterprises and specific branches; nor is it likely to solve the problem of coordination of the ratios of maintenance, scrapping, replacement and expansion determined at enterprise level with the aggregate resources available in the economy[36].

The model was also unable to provide any appropriate criteria for determining that distribution of investment between sectors and branches which would best achieve the medium- and long-term goals (Kratsch *et al.*, 1975, pp. 92–93). In addition there are the manifold problems of speeding up scientific and technical progress, which are hardly likely to be.solved by regulations (Nick, 1977), although great hopes are still placed on the stimulating effect of prices based on the price–performance ratio (Bösche and Matho, 1977).

In the extensive discussion on intensification it is emphasized again and again that 'modernization of the existing machinery and plant' often 'can give equal or greater return than new investment' (Zschau and Hempel, 1978). Enterprises are urged 'to pursue capital-saving and material-saving ways of raising labour productivity' ('Grundfragen . . .', 1978). If one considers that, for example, over 70% of production costs in industry consist of expenditure on materials and that over half of all labour employed in the productive sectors is used on the production and transport of energy and raw and other materials (Heinrichs, 1978), the opportunities for rationalization which exist here become clear. With reference to these reserves and the possibilities for economies in maintenance through increased scrapping ('Zweite wissenschaftliche Konferenz . . .', 1978), a state plan for 'socialist rationalization' was introduced from 1979 (*Neues Deutschland*, 24 April 1978). It is designed to bring about a thorough rationalization process, laying down aggregate, branch and regional priorities, naming specific projects, ranking them in order of importance, ensuring necessary deliveries of materials and semi-finished goods and giving prominence to the performance which can be achieved with improved technologies (*Gesetzblatt . . .* I, No. 17, 1978). The crucial new feature in this plan is that all rationalization tasks which are important for the economy as a whole are brought together and their execution put under central supervision.

The two new decrees on investment, which are directed at the preparation of investment projects ('Verordnung über die Vorbereitung . . .', 1978; 'Verordnung über die Planung, Vorbereitung . . .', 1978) are intended to promote better implementation of state targets, to prevent unplanned investment and to avoid cost overruns. The hope is that they will simplify the preparation of rationalization measures and make that of expansion projects (including follow-up investments) more precise (Tarnick, 1978; Drasdo and Frenske, 1978). In particular, they stipulate not only that the national economic need for the project must be proved, that it must be shown that the existing capacity is fully utilized, and that the location must be justified, but they also demand discussion of whether expansion or renewal is most appropriate and whether completion (including of all equipment needed) within the scheduled time can be guaranteed[37].

Despite these stricter regulations on investment, it was already clear during 1979 that the controls were not sufficient, that construction work was still dispersed among too many projects, construction times were excessive, not enough rationalization was taking place and the coordination of building and equipping projects was inadequate. A resolution by the economic leadership ('Gemeinsamer Beschluss . . .', 1979) criticized these deficiencies, called for concentration on major complexes, and decided to establish a national list of projects ranked by importance and time sequence. The number of projects to be started in the 1980 annual plan was cut from 450 to 250 (Mittag, 1979). Unplanned projects are to be consistently blocked, unfinished investment reduced ('Anordnung über die Erfassung . . .', 1979) and construction times shortened.

The planning of major and, furthermore, well-prepared rationalization projects and the concentration on important and especially productive investments will certainly bring noticeable progress. But the call to save labour, raw materials and capital simultaneously demands such a high degree of innovation and technical progress from enterprises that it simply cannot be achieved with the given planning instruments. Even the drive for enterprises to produce their own means of rationalization (Gössel, Paust and Wedler, 1977; Wenzel, 1979) and the success of the 'innovator movement' among workers (Beau, 1978) cannot afford relief here.

Improved consumer goods planning

In order to meet better the increased demands of consumers in respect of assortment, quality and fashion an unpublished decision of the Council of Ministers ('Massnahmen . . .', 1977) introduced so-called assortment and fashion conceptions; they came into operation for the first time in the 1978 plan. On the basis of centrally approved trends in fashion the necessary production of inputs is arranged and the consequent demands on the available machine capacity are worked out (Bernheier and Wolf, *Der Handel*, 1978). The assortment conceptions laid down the division into articles, price categories, qualities, sizes and delivery dates and set out the material content of the assortment; they are worked out in collaboration with the producers, the balance organs and the wholesale and retail trade organizations (Bernheier and Wolf, *Die Wirtschaft*, 1978).

Despite these attempts at improvement, these conceptions have not yet been successfully integrated fully into planning, taken into account at the right time in the balancing process, nor linked with the plans for science and technology. Furthermore, the flexibility of intermediate production stages is completely insufficient to adapt to changes in fashion, and to increase it would call for a number of prerequisites which have not been met hitherto[38]. In addition, manufacturing techniques for the final products would have to be much more flexible, which, however, would demand a substantial expansion of finishing capacity (Liehmann, 1978).

The problem is, in particular, that the fashion conceptions are not yet precise enough to allow the necessary expenditure to be ascertained, nor compliance with given price and cost data and desired cost savings to be determined (Liehmann, 1978). But these would be essential factors for full incorporation of these conceptions – worked out a year to a year and a half earlier – in the corresponding annual plan. In view of the continuing price revision which can now be expected, this problem seems hardly soluble.

Hitherto, gaps in requirements were actually aggravated by too low sanctions for infringement of controls. In order to counter this, it was laid down in 1978 ('Verordnung zur Sicherung . . .', 1978) that sales and supply contracts were to be concluded in the plan preparation stage and that in principle goods may only be produced if their sale is guaranteed by corresponding contracts. Sanctions up to a level of 500 000 marks can be imposed for failure to adhere to the stipulations of the decree.

Performance measurement and material interest

Since gross output figures are still predominant in plan accounting, too little attention was paid hitherto to the aims of saving materials, producing to meet demand and raising quality. Instead, enterprises sought to fulfil their plans more easily by the use of material-intensive and even more costly inputs. Thus the proportion of intermediate product in the total value of gross output has risen distinctly since 1960 (Koziolek, *Einheit*, 1978). From 1960 to 1977 the share of the total social product consumed in production climbed from 55.6% to 62%, and the net ratio thus fell[39]. But if raw materials are to be saved this trend must be reversed. This, however, would require the whole of plan-accounting to be converted to net magnitudes. Consequently, the demand was first put forward in the GDR 'that the own performance indicator should be elevated to equal rank with the commodity production indicator in the assessment of performance' ('Zur Vervollkomnung', 1978), although it is pointed out that it is necessary 'to use not just one indicator but a system of indicators to record all factors in intensification'.

Just how little the previous methods of performance assessment have been directed towards intensification is shown by the following admission (Luft and Parson, 1978):

> In spite of the positive effects of setting prices for new and improved products according to the price–performance ratio, those products which contain a higher proportion of materials and subcontracted work per 100 marks of commodity production than others are still the most advantageous for enterprises in respect of fulfilment of the commodity production indicator.

To this was added ('Zu den Beziehungen . . .', 1978): 'The price–performance ratio is leading to a rise in the industrial price level,' although reduction was planned, related to performance. 'Price reductions on obsolete products are hardly applied.' Intensification measures, for example, successful rationalization, technological improvements and labour savings have no effect on 'commodity production', whilst they change 'own performance' in a positive direction. Therefore this is said to be the indicator to develop (Donda, 1978).

There was further criticism that the dependence of the bonus fund on overfulfilment of the commodity production indicator directs the material interest of the enterprise workforce primarily towards quantitative increases in production but neglects the satisfaction of requirements and quality (Schilling, 1978). Failure to meet contracts and excessive stocks are also frequently the consequence of the priority of the commodity production indicator ('Fragen der weiteren Vervollkommnung . . .', 1977).

As we have already mentioned, at the beginning of 1979 the indicator 'final product' came into operation for combines in order both to stimulate a reduction in material consumption and to prevent commodity production being inflated by transactions within the combine. But recently the objection has been raised against this indicator 'that final product, too, can be increased by inefficient subcontracting outside the combine without thereby really raising the distributable final product' (Lange, 1980). It was also pointed out that when both the final product and the commodity production indicators are used, those enterprises in a combine which actually reduce their use of materials suffer a disadvantage in plan-accounting in that their commodity production falls, although the final product of the whole combine rises (Lange, 1980). Evidently these deficiencies may have been the reason why the GDR Council of Ministers has now decided to adopt the two indicators 'net production'[40] and 'basic material costs per 100 marks of commodity production', with effect from March 1980, as an important step towards improving the assessment of performance (*Die Wirtschaft*, No. 3, 1980). The hope is that this will not only give a truer indication of the economic performance of enterprises and combines but also a better reflection of the relationship of performance to costs (Beyer and Schmidt, 'Bessere Kriterien . . .', 1980).

This doubtless very significant innovation is certainly designed to eliminate a number of the defects we have depicted. Yet whether it will be fully effective depends on how far the whole plan-accounting system is successfully transferred to 'net accounting' by the beginning of the new five-year plan, and this would be an enormous undertaking. Consequently, we may well feel doubts here, too. Evidently gross and net magnitudes are to continue to be used side by side in planning, for it was explicitly pointed out that net production 'represents only one, albeit an important criterion within the system of indicators for the comprehensive asessment of the performance of combines and enterprises' (Beyer and Schmidt, 'Bessere Kriterien . . .', 1980). Furthermore, even this new indicator cannot ascertain whether the production sold was in accordance with contract and met requirements. Thus there is also a proposal to use an indicator of 'production in accordance with requirements' (Beyer and Schmidt, 'Intensivierung . . .', 1980).

Beside this, timid moves to bring about further changes in the management and planning system in the direction of stronger incentives may be observed. Thus the East Berlin economist Harry Nick (1978) points out that the technological lag of the GDR behind Western industrial countries – which is particularly striking in the production processes used and in the organization of production – cannot be overcome merely by strengthening the plan for science and technology, but only by increasing the material interest of enterprises in economic progress. For this, however, 'substantial further development of management, planning and economic stimulation in the socialist economy as a whole' is needed (Nick, 1978). It should be directed especially towards strengthening the qualitative factors, as the previous concentration on quantitative growth had inevitably led to 'tensions in the material interconnections of production' and 'failure of supply to match demand'. Nick's extremely cautiously formulated advocacy of improvements in price setting, of an increase in the role of profit and of further improvement of economic accounting makes one sense how very conscious people in the GDR are of the extremely narrow scope of possible improvements to the sysem at present and how much adherence to the limits imposed is regretted.

Increased formation of combines to generate more lasting rationalization

Beside the discussion of the problems of efficiency, technological innovation, intensification of the use of capital and labour, economy of materials and questions of energy and raw materials which has been going on for years now, at the economic conference held by the GDR Academy of Sciences in June 1977 problems of increasing the decisionmaking powers of intermediate management levels came into prominence. The question was raised 'how the management system must be constructed in order to ensure a high level of efficiency in production, to focus the behaviour of managers and workforce, of every individual member of society, towards a more efficient economy, an economy in which efficiency rises more quickly than use of resources' ('22. Tagung . . .', 1977). Although no-one was either willing or able to give an unequivocal answer to this question, nevertheless cautious experimentation with partial decentralization of decisions in the sphere of combines was advocated.

Meanwhile there was exhaustive propaganda in the economic literature in the GDR for the formation of combines ('Stellung . . .', 1977; Friedrich, 1978; Mittag, 'Zielstrebige . . .', 1978; Hartmann, 1978), in Honecker's words 'at present the most essential step in the improvement of management and planning' ('Aus dem Bericht . . .', 1978), because 'the combine brings together the decisive stages of the reproduction process – from research and development through the design and construction of means of rationalization to the actual production, including the supply of inputs which determine the quality of the product, and then to the sale of products at home and abroad' (Mittag, 'Vorzüge . . .', 1978).

Specifically, it is hoped that the combines will help to achieve the following (Melzer, Scherzinger and Schwartau, 1979):

(1) Acceleration of scientific and technical progress through applied research centralized in the combine;
(2) More efficient investment through improved preparation and quicker adjustment to the requirements of rationalization;
(3) Progress with intensification through better coordination and increased utilization of available capacity with efficient division of labour;
(4) A better solution of supply problems, in particular through the affiliation of enterprises concerned;
(5) Production of needed goods of attractive quality through centralized sales departments, more market research and flexible response to change in demand;
(6) An increase in exports through the affiliation of foreign trade enterprises.

At the same time the reduction in the number of levels of management in the economy (from the previous three to the present two) by the abolition of the *VVB* should create shorter and more effective channels for the flow of information. The affiliation of supplier enterprises and the concentration of capacity are also designed to bring about more effective coordination of overlapping branches and to develop greater flexibility in planning and management. The central organs hope to be able to facilitate the work of planning and management, and at the same time to improve its results, by carrying out plan coordination and the harmonization processes with better organized combines and delegating a part of their plan disaggregation and balancing tasks to the combine level. The combines are expected to cooperate better with the ministries above them as well as – through the general director – to generate a certain harmonization of central with selected enterprise objectives. General directors are thus supposed to bring about efficient coordination of all the partial planning carried out in the combine, to produce comprehensive harmonization of state goals with real production possibilities and to construct a better internal organization – e.g. by greater concentration of preparatory processes, sales-oriented activities and direct production (Hofmann, 1979). Thus the general director has a crucial role to play: he is supposed to be part-minister, part-entrepreneur in one person.

From the autumn of 1979 to the beginning of 1980 the number of combines in industry and construction directly subordinated to ministries rose from 109 to 129 – in 1975 it had been only 43. Today they cover about

90% of those employed in centrally directed industry and construction (Mittag, 'Sozialistische Planwirtschaft . . .', 1979). On average the combines employ about 27 000 people each.

Although the previous planning methods, the central allocation system for resources and the predominantly centralized planning have not been fundamentally altered, the restructuring which has been carried out has had a positive effect on the combines' scope for decisionmaking (Melzer and Erdmann, 1979):

(1) The widespread elimination of the *VVB* brought the transfer of decision-making powers from the former intermediate management level to the production level, including the management bodies of the combines.
(2) The mere expansion in size and the affiliation of extra-branch enterprises has increased the decisionmaking scope of the new or reorganized combines in comparison with the previous *VVB*.
(3) Additional rights concerning the internal structure of the combines, e.g. to transfer plant between enterprises, have clearly extended the decision-making scope of the head of the combine at the expense of the individual enterprises.
(4) The increased participation of general directors with the responsible minister in coordination processes has caused a distinct growth in the power of the combines.

The detailed regulations are set out in the new decree on combines ('Verordnung über die volkseigenen Kombinate . . .', 1979). What is particularly interesting is that the general director can both change the functions and tasks of individual enterprises or transfer them to other enterprises and can also form new sections in enterprises or shift plant and production to other enterprises. Similarly, he may centralize activities such as research, investment, sales, market research and accounting. Beside planning and balancing tasks, the general director also takes over other state functions – price setting, standardization and tasks involved in socialist economic integration.

Honecker's formulation, that the ministries should now concentrate only on 'major questions' (*Neues Deutschland*, 12 February 1979) is always open to new interpretations of what are 'major questions', as is admitted even in the GDR literature (Kühnau, 1979). Thus it must be assumed that in future the ministers will still have farreaching rights of intervention on important specific problems down to enterprise level.

Although it should certainly be possible to achieve substantial gains in productivity within the combine by restructuring of units, rearrangement of production and reconstruction of whole enterprises or parts of enterprises ('Komplexe Rekonstruktion . . .', 1979), it remains questionable whether they will provide the 'clear impetus to rationalization' expected by the economic leadership. This requires a high degree of readiness to innovate on the part of general directors as well as the ability to break down bureaucratic obstructions and to reach numerous compromises with the minister concerning objectives; it also requires adequate motivation on the part of the general directors to achieve both continuous improvements in operating efficiency and a real fusion of the enterprises in the combine. The increasingly monopolistic position of combines on the one hand, and the great difficulty in determining the optimal size of enterprises – in view of the distortions in the price system – on the other, are likely to lead to obstacles even where there are general directors with great capacity for initiative: the inter-enterprise efficiency comparisons which would in turn be a prerequisite for more nearly optimal use of factors of production either cannot or will not be made.

Outlook

The discussions to which we have drawn attention and the new measures already introduced to improve the economic mechanism of the GDR indicate that revolutionary reforms can scarcely be expected in the 'order on planning for 1981 to 1985'. The previous course remains basically unchanged. Beside the aims of further polishing the existing planning methods[41], priority is likely to be given to attempts to step up intensification, to improve rationalization, to perfect the measurement of performance, to raise exports and to speed up technological progress. It is here that great things are expected from the combines. Although after initial losses due to friction some progress can certainly be expected from the latter, it is still most unlikely that they will suffice to make up fully for the increased gap between recent problems and the possibilities for solving them. The economic leadership of the GDR sees itself confronted with continually declining scope for decisions on aggregate growth and distribution: with the deterioration in the country's terms of trade it must make great efforts to export to pay for the considerably dearer raw materials which have to be imported, and domestically it is compelled to have regard for the population's income and consumption aspirations if it wants to obtain the full potential performance of the labour force. With an inevitable decline in the aggregate economic growth rate over the next five years, restriction of the growth of domestic expenditure can scarcely be avoided, after allowing for the foreign trade burden. If the expansion of investment were cut back, the negative effects on growth could only be offset by continuous successful intensification and substantially greater advances in productivity. With the existing methods of planning and management, however, they cannot be initiated to a sufficient extent. What remains, then, is only a certain restriction of consumption, both through price rises for consumer goods as well as by means of product changes and through shifts in supply to the considerably dearer 'quality' and 'delicacy' shops.

The economic leadership can only find an honest way out by a change of direction towards more fundamental reform concepts. The maintenance of a certain priority for gross values in plan-accounting, the unsatisfactory price adjustment of the data showing higher plan fulfilment, the imposition of concealed – and thus not measurable – increases in consumer goods prices on the consumer[42], and finally the maintenance of an inadequate system with completely distorted relative prices are no long-term solution.

Notes

1. The specific measures of the NES model will not be described here; the interested reader is referred to the following references: DIW, 1971, pp. 56–92; Leptin, 1968, pp. 102–130; Beyer, 1967, pp. 357–393; Ulbricht, 1968; Krol, 1972.

2. The individual targets of the structural programme were not published, and Günter Mittag called for 'the strictest state discipline in the preservation of secrets' in respect of them, because 'the class enemy is devoting particular efforts to ascertaining the structure of the development policy envisaged' (*Neues Deutschland*, 27 October 1968, pp. 3–4)

3. The maintenance of unchanged consumer goods prices, some of which were excessively high, led, for example – despite high state deductions – to a relatively high rate of profit on these products, whilst capital-intensive products of other sectors showed extremely low profit rates because of the inadequte allowance for capital costs.

4. This was promptly pointed out in the GDR itself (*Wirtschaftswissenschaft*, No. 10, 1968, p. 1699).

5. Under the system of industrial price regulations enterprises saw no adequate incentive for price reductions: when they achieved cost savings it seemed more advantageous to them to show formal cost calculations at the previous level than an increase in net profit because in this way they could finance their own development goals inconspicuously, whereas after deduction of net profits tax and allocations to specific enterprise funds only a small part of a rise in profits was left for their own investment projects. A similar situation existed in the case of progressive price reductions on new and improved products: it did not suit successful enterprises to reveal even part of their reserves when prices for new products were being set, since there was no real threat from foreign competition on the domestic market. They sought to avoid the price reductions prescribed after specified intervals of time with evidence of cost increases on intermediate products and by further product changes. They allowed production of existing products to cease before the period of steeper price reductions began at all. Cheap goods disappeared from the product range and were replaced by dearer new products, so that instead of price reductions there were continuous price increases by means of product changes (Beyer *et al.*, 1977).

6. The necessary expenditure of capital was measured by the capital employed by the most efficient enterprises and was to be the sole basis for the profit margin to be included in prices, which was not to exceed 18% of the capital expenditure.

7. An interest charge on capital, payable out of profit.

8. For a detailed critique of the instruments used in the NES see Leptin and Melzer (1978, pp. 115ff.).

9. In the investment sector there were increasing delays in completion of numerous projects and sharp rises in costs. New plants lagged behind the level of performance envisaged and the rate of utilization did not come up to expectations because adequate training of operating personnel had been neglected (Willi Stoph, 1970).

10. The 'profit' which was desired as a stimulus to performance in many cases operated as the financial basis for independent enterprise actions in precisely those directions which were not wanted by the central authorities.

11. The absolute priority of the implementation of the state's conceptions was clearly expounded at the time by a department head in the State Planning Commission (Hübner, 1971).

12. Ulbricht gave up the post of first secretary of the *SED* Central Committee in favour of Honecker on 3 May 1971.
13. Thus it was also reported that clear guiding principles were to be used in party work, such as 'We can only consume what we have first earned' and 'A rise in the standard of living requires a rise in the standard of performance' (*Neues Deutschland*, 14 March 1978, p. 3).
14. Thus the *SED* party programme says: 'On the basis of agreements with the USSR and the other fraternal socialist countries the five-year plans are to develop into the chief instrument for the management of economic activity' ('Programm . . .', 1976, p. 5).
15. For a precise account of the plan construction process at that time, see Mitz-scherling *et al.* (1974, pp. 52ff.).
16. The long-term state orientation figures up to 1990 are based on 1973 prices, the 1976–1980 five-year plan on the other hand was based on 1975 'constant plan prices' (CPP 75). State plan targets are given in the prices of the preceding year, while enterprises' and intermediate management levels' plans are in prices of the current year ('Fragen . . .', 1974).
17. Some theoretical models have been developed for this purpose (Ambrée and Mann, 1971, p. 153; Pieplow, 681ff.).
18. To remedy this, since 1 January 1979 combines directly subordinated to ministries have planned and calculated their performance in terms of the so-called end-product of the branch for which they are responsible. It consists of the industrial commodity production of a combine less deliveries of intermediate inputs between enterprises in the combine (Hoss, 1979).
19. Attempts to disaggregate the tables more were abandoned because of the great amount of work involved. The 1972 balances had covered 164 product groups compared with 27 in 1959; for 1977, however, the number was said to be only 118 (*Statistische Praxis* No. 1, 1977).
20. 'Impermissible' profits obtained by manipulating prices must be surrendered in full to the state budget.
21. Such profits may go into the bonus fund, be used for working capital, be paid into the Young Socialists' account or the performance fund. This is used to finance, in particular, improvements in work organization (especially in looking after shift workers) and the often not very

efficient production of means of rationalization (from the enterprise's own reserves).
22. From this, both the deductions from net profit of the enterprises in the combine and those of the combine itself are paid to the state, and resources are also redistributed within the combine.
23. Bonus allocations from counterplan proposals are restricted to a maximum of 150 marks per employee; they are financed out of additional profits.
24. E.g. improvements in provisions for shift workers, general cultural and social measures and assistance for enterprise employees in building their own homes or in rebuilding or extension of housing.
25. At the time just one third of industrial output had been transferred to this type of price (*Die Wirtschaft* No. 14, 1969, p. 10).
26. In 1975, for example, with a total expenditure of 90 billion marks by the population on goods and services (including rents), around 14 billion marks was paid out by the state budget in subsidies.
27. This was the only way in which it was believed that the aim of obtaining two-thirds of the energy required for the increment in output up to 1980 by economies could be achieved.
28. For details and criticism of this price-setting procedure see Melzer, (1977).
29. This supervision presents no difficulties since enterprises are obliged to have their accounts with the branch of the bank responsible for them (and this applies to their funds, too) and to make all payments to other enterprises through bank transfers rather than in cash. Any cash receipts must be paid into the bank without delay and cash withdrawals are made only for wages payments.
30. Here we should mention the chief accountant of the enterprise, who is directly subordinate to the Ministry of Finance, and the 'Workers' and Peasants' Inspectorate' (*ABI*), which enjoys numerous powers.
31. For example, prime cost and prime cost reduction, labour productivity (on the basis of the enterprise's own performance), release of labour, material cost intensity, capital productivity, capital profitability, proportion of rationalization measures in investment, quality standards.

32. By this is meant future-oriented, aggregate calculation of the capacity and state of the capital stock, including investments, maintenance and scrapping. Enterprises are required to draw up annual plans for major items like capital stock and capacity, maintenance, scrapping, a plan for the preparation of investments and the actual investment plan.

33. This is made considerably harder because the shortage of labour in the GDR dictates restriction of expansion in favour of rationalization, but the proportions of the two depend in turn on the extent to which technical progress is achieved and labour thereby released through laboursaving rationalization to man additional capacity.

34. Thus at the end of May 1978 Günter Mittag had to say that 'it generates noticeable disturbances in the economy when, for example, this year alone investments running into billions are carried out outside the plan'. The reason he gives is that often initially a small investment outlay is proposed, which is expanded again and again after the implementation of the project has been started (Mittag, 1978).

35. GDR scholars point out cases 'in which up to 50% of the price demanded was shown by a qualified price check to be excessive'. The explanation they offer is that 'the main factors pushing up investment prices are clearly to be sought on the investment construction sites, in management, coordination, transport, storage, site organization, work scheduling and installation. The gains in productivity achieved in the enterprises of the engineering, electrical and other branches of industry are often nullified here' (Matterne and Tannhäuser, 1978, pp. 220, 268).

36. On the subject of 'complex capital analysis' the GDR scholars had to admit: 'Obstacles which emerge in practice often include inability to carry out, and insufficient insight into the usefulness of, systematic analysis, as well as lack of coordination between levels of analysis and levels of decisionmaking.' They added: 'Such calculations are complicated by the restricted meaningfulness of value categories and raise the problem of the undervaluation of capital assets' ('Die höhere Effektivität . . .', 1978).

37. If a cost increase of more than 10% emerges during the preparation stage, a new application for approval of the project must be made and at the same time a lower-capacity variant corresponding to the previously approved cost must be submitted.

38. For the textile industry, for example, the following demands were made: production of more equipment for ancillary processes in textile engineering, rapid adaptation by spinners and weavers to new fashionable patterns, the creation of so-called reserve capacity, which would be relieved of the capital charge (Trautloft, 1978).

39. In the basic materials industry the decline in the net ratio is much more serious than in the economy as a whole.

40. 'Net production' equals industrial commodity production minus productive consumption (including externally supplied productive services). Unlike 'own performance', 'net production' measures performance without auxilliary materials and depreciation.

41. In general, for example, increased use is to be made of mathematical methods with electronic data processing in the various planning processes, although there is awareness of the problems of mathematical models, the hope is to solve them by improving the models (Friedrich, 'Der Beitrag . . .', 1978). In addition, five-year plans are increasingly to be drawn up for enterprises in future and – just as previously with annual planning – to be worked out in several compulsory parts (Finger, Füger and Palaschewski, 1977).

42. Apparently the economic leadership is now also prepared to allow open increases in the prices of consumer goods – although not for products which are basic necessities. For other goods, when prices are set for new or improved products with higher use value the increased costs are to be taken fully into account (Honecker, 1979).

References

Ambree, K. and Mann, H. (1971). *Das Preissystem in der sozialistischen Industrie*. East Berlin

Anordnung Nr. 3 über die bildung der Industriepreise für Investitionsleistungen und für den Export von Anlagen durch General- und Hauptauftragnehmer. *Gesetzblatt der DDR*, I, No. 19, 1979, pp. 165ff.

Anordnung Nr. 8 über Gebührentarife des Verkehrswesens. *Gesetzblatt der DDR*, I, No. 4, 1979, p. 47

Anordnung Nr. Pr. 99 zur Aufhebung preisrechtlicher Bestimmungen. *Gesetzblatt der DDR*, I, No. 2, 1973, pp. 9ff.

Anordnung Nr. Pr. 121/1 über die Preise für bautechnische Projektierungsleistungen. *Gesetzblatt der DDR*, I, No. 19, 1979, p. 167

Anordnung Nr. Pr. 125 bis 139. *Gesetzblatt der DDR*, I. No. 22, 1975, pp.369ff.

Anordnung Nr. Pr. 210 über Abnehmerbereiche von Erzeugnissen und Leistungen, für deren Industriepreise am I. Januar 1977 neue Anordnungen in Kraft treten. *Gesetzblatt der DDR*, I, No. 18, 1976, pp. 264ff.

Anordnung Nr. Pr. 211/1 über die Preise für Neubauleistungen. *Gesetzblatt der DDR*, I, No. 34, 1978, p. 376

Anordnung Nr. Pr. 211/2 über die Preise für Neubauleistungen. *Sonderdruck des Gesetzblattes der DDR*, No. 995/1

Anordnung Nr. Pr. 211/3 über die Preise für Neubauleistungen. *Gesetzblatt der DDR*, I, No. 16, 1979, p. 136

Anordnung Nr. Pr. 212 über die Preise für Baureparaturen. *Gesetzblatt der DDR*, I, No. 19, 1979, pp. 172ff.

Anordnung Nr. Pr. 219 über die Preise für Bitumen – und Teermischzuschlagstoffe und – Betone. *Gesetzblatt der DDR*, I No. 19, 1979, pp. 176f.

Anordnung Nr. Pr. 249 über der Geltungsbereich von Preiskarteiblättern bei planmässigen Industriepreisänderungen zum I. Januar 1978. *Gesetzblatt der DDR*, I, No.14, 1977, pp. 153f.

Anordnung Nr. Pr. 249/1 über den Geltungsbereich von preiskarteiblättern bei planmässigen Industriepreisänderungen zum 1. Januar 1978, und Anordnung Nr. 250/1 über die Zuordnung zu Abnehmerbereichen der Anordnungen, die im Rahmen planmässiger Industriepreisänderungen in Kraft treten. *Gesetzblatt der DDR*, I, No. 15, 1978, pp. 182f.

Anordnung Nr. Pr. 250 über die Zuordnung zu Abnehmerbereichen der Anordnungen die im Rahmen planmässiger Industriepreisänderungen in Kraft treten. *Gesetzblatt der DDR*, I, No. 14, 1977, pp. 154ff.

Anordnung Nr. Pr. 250/2 über die Zuordnung zu Abnehmerbereichen der Anordnungen, die im Rahmen planmässiger Industriepreisänderungen in kraft treten. *Gesetzblatt der DDR*, I, No. 25, 1979, pp. 235ff.

Anordnung Nr. Pr. 251/1 über die Preisbildung für Montageleistungen. *Gesetzblatt der DDR*, I, No. 19, 1979, p. 167

Anordnung Nr. Pr. 284 über die Bildung der Preise für Altteile und aufgearbeitete sowie wiederverwendungsfähige Ersatzteile und Baugruppen von Erzeugnissen der metalverarbeitenden Industrie. *Gesetzblatt der DDR*, I, No. 8, 1979, pp. 73f.

Anordnung Nr. Pr. 285 über die Preisbildung zur Förderung der Produktion von Rationalisierungsmitteln. *Gesetzblatt der DDR*, I, No. 23, 1978, pp. 263ff.

Anordnung über den terminlichen Ablauf der Ausarbeitung des Volkswirtschaftsplanes und des Staatshaushaltsplanes 1974. *Gesetzblatt der DDR*, I, No. 59, 1973, pp. 189ff; similar orders are in *Gesetzblatt . . .*, I, No. 17, 1976, pp. 229ff; No. 19, 1977, pp. 233ff. and No. 26, 1979, pp. 239ff.

Anordnung über die Ausarbeitung des Volkswirtschaftsplanes und Staatshaushaltsplanes 1980. *Sonderdruck des Gesetzblattes der DDR*, No.1011, 1979

Anordnung über die Erfassung der unvolldeten Investitionen. *Gesetzblatt der DDR*, I, No. 42, 1979, pp. 393f.

Anordnung über die Finanzplanung in den volkseigenen Betrieben und Kombinaten. *Gesetzblatt der DDR*, I, No. 6, 1973, pp. 70ff.

Anordnung über die Inkraftsetzung und Herausgabe der speziellen Kalkulationsrichtlinien für den Bereich des Ministeriums für Elektrotechnik und Elektronik. *Gesetzblatt der DDR*, I, No. 2, 1978, p. 48

Anordnung über die Inkraftsetzung und Herausgabe von speziellen Kalkulationsrichtlinien für den Bereich des Ministeriums für Bauwesen; and the two supplementary orders, *Gesetzblatt der DDR*, I, No. 25, 1977, p. 315; No. 16, 1978, p. 191; No. 39, 1978, p. 423

Anordnung über die Nomenklatur für die Planung, Bilanzierung und Abrechnung von Material, Ausrüstungen und Konsumgütern zur Ausarbeitung und Durchführung der Volkswirtschaftspläne ab 1972 – Bilanzverzeichnis. *Gesetzblatt der DDR: Sonderdruck*, No. 688, 1971; also the corresponding order for 1976–80 in *Gesetzblatt der DDR; Sonderdruck*, No. 688/6, 1975

Anordnung über die Ordnung der Planung der Volkswirtschaft der DDR 1976 bis 1980. *Gesetzblatt der DDR, Sonderdruck*, No. 775a

Anordnung über die Planung, Bildung und Verwendung des Leistungsfonds der volkseigenen Betriebe. *Gesetzblatt der DDR*, I, No. 23, 1975, pp. 416ff; also the corresponding 'Anordnung No. 2', *Gesetzblatt . . .*, I, No. 22, 1978, p. 249

Anordnung über die Planung der finanziellen Auswirkungen aus planmässigen Industriepreisänderungen per 1, Januar 1976. *Gesetzblatt der DDR*, I, No. 23, 1975, pp. 419ff.

Anordnung über die Planung und Bildung von Preisausgleichsfonds im Zusammenhang mit der Ausarbeitung und Durchführung des Volkswirtschaftsplanes und Staatshaushaltsplanes 1976. *Gesetzblatt der DDR*, I, No. 23, 1975, pp. 422ff.

Anordnung über die Rahmenrichtlinien für die Jahresplanung der Betriebe und Kombinate der Industrie und des Bauwesens – Rahmenrichtlinie. *Gesetzblatt der DDR, Sonderdruck*, No. 780

Anordnung über die zentrale staatliche Kalkulationsrichtlinie zur Bildung von Industriepreisen. *Gesetzblatt der DDR*, II, No. 67, 1972, pp. 741ff.

Anordnung über die zentrale staatliche Kalkulationsrichtlinie zur Bildung von Industriepreisen. *Gesetzblatt der DDR*, I, No. 24, 1976, pp. 321ff.

Anordnung über die Zuführung und Abführung von Preisdifferenzen im Zusammenhang mit planmässigen Industriepreisänderungen. *Gesetzblatt der DDR*, I, No. 27, 1976, pp. 373f.

Anordnung zu den Regelungen für die Arbeit mit Gegenplänen in den Betrieben und Kombinaten zur Erfüllung und Überbietung des Volkswirtschaftsplanes 1974. *Gesetzblatt der DDR*, I, No. 1, 1974, pp. 1ff. Also corresponding orders in *Gesetzblatt . . .*, I, No. 26, 1974, pp. 261ff.; No. 63, 1974, pp. 583ff.; No. 1, 1977, pp. 4ff.; No. 2, 1978, pp. 37ff.

Anordnung zur Stimulierung der überbietung der staatlichen Aufgaben für die Ausarbeitung des einheitlichen Planvorschlages zum Volkswirtschaftsplan 1980. *Gesetzblatt der DDR*, I, No. 27, 1979, pp. 247ff.

Aus dem Bericht des Politbüros an die 8. Tagung des ZK der SED. *Neues Deutschland*, 25 May 1978, p. 4

Ausgewählte Probleme der Grundfondswirtschaft in der Diskussion. *Wirtschaftswissenschaft*, No. 2, 1977, pp. 265ff.

Aussenwirtschaftliche Belastungen mindern Wachstumschancen – Zur Lage der DDR–Wirtschaft an der Jahreswende 1979/80. In *Wochenbericht des DIW* (ed. by D. Cornelsen), No. 6, 1980

Beau, I. (1978). Intensivierung im Blickpunkt des Wettbewerbs. *Einheit*, No. 4, pp. 377ff.

Bernheier, K., and Wolf, A. (1978). Wichtige Planungsgrundlagen weiter qualifizieren. *Der Handel*, No. 2, p. 88

Bernheier, K., and Wolf, A. (1978). Modisch und ökonomisch. *Die Wirtschaft*, No. 2, p. 11

Beschluss über die Bestätigung der Verbraucherpreise für Konsumgüter nach staatlichen nomenklaturen und zur Erhöhung der Verantwortung des Amtes für Preise. *Gesetzblatt der DDR*, II, No. 77, 1971, pp. 674ff.

Beschluss über die Bildung der Industriepreise zur Durchführung des Beschlusses zur Leistungsbewertung der Betriebe und Kombinate. *Gesetzblatt der DDR*, I, No. 24, 1976, pp. 317ff.

Beschluss über die Durchführung des ökonomischen Systems des Sozialismus im Jahre 1971. *Gesetzblatt der DDR*. II, No. 100, 1970, pp. 731ff.

Beschluss über die Grundsatzregelung für komplexe Massnahmen zur weiteren Gestaltung des ökonomischen Systems des Sozialismus in der Planung und Wirtschaftsführung für die Jahre 1969 und 1970. *Gesetzblatt der DDR*, II, No. 66, 1968, pp. 433ff.

Beschluss über die Planung und Leitung des Prozesses der Reproduktion der Grundfonds. *Gesetzblatt der DDR*, II, No. 1, 1971, pp. 1ff.

Beschluss über Massnahmen auf dem Gebiet der Leitung, Planung und Entwicklung der Industriepreise. *Gesetzblatt der DDR*, II, No. 77, 1971, pp. 669ff.

Beyer, A. (1967). Die Diskussion um das Neue Ökonomische System in Mitteldeutschland'. *Ordo-Jahrbuch*

Beyer, A., Erdmann, K., Lauterbach, G. and Melzer, M. (1977). Aktuelle Probleme des Preissystems in der DDR. *Analysen und Berichte aus Gesellschaft und Wissenschaft*, Erlangen, No. 5, pp. 116–122

Beyer, A., Erdmann, K., Lauterbach, G. and Melzer, M. (1980). Preisprobleme in der DDR. *Analysen und Berichte*, Erlangen, No. 1, p. 140

Beyer, H.-J. and Schmidt, H. (1980). Intensivierung unter veränderten Bedingungen. *Die Wirtschaft*, No. 2, p. 28

—— (1980). Bessere Kriterien der Leistungsbewertung. *Die Wirtschaft*, No. 3, p. 22

Bösche, J. and Matho, F. (1977). Zur Förderung des wissenschaftlichtechnischen Fortschritts durch den Preis. *Wirtschaftswissenschaft*, No. 9, pp. 1324ff.

Brossmann, K.-U. (1977). *Komplexe Grundfondsplanung*. East Berlin

Büchner, H., Hoss, P., Oelschlägel, W. and Düsterwald, M. (1978). Wachstum des Endprodukts – wichtiges Leistungskriterium sozialistischen Wirtschaftens. *Wirtschaftswissenschaft*, No. 10, pp. 1168ff.

DDR-Aussenhandel: Importrestriktionen bei unzureichendem Exportvermögen – 1978 erneute Presssteigerungen und geringeres Defizit. In *Wochenbericht des DIW* (Ed. by Horst Lambrecht), No. 47, 1979

Die höhere Effektivität der Grunfonds und der Investitionen – ein Erfordernis der Intensivierung der Produktion (Conference report). (1978). *Wirtschaftswissenschaft*, No. 5, p. 607

Die Wirtschaft, No. 14, 1969, p. 10; No. 15, 1975, supplement pp. 3–4; No. 20, 1975, supplement; No. 23, 1975; No. 3, 1980.

Direktive des VIII Parteitags der SED zum Fünfjahrplan für die Entwicklung der Volkswirtschaft der DDR 1971 bis 1975. *Neues Deutschland*, 23 June 1971, special supplement, p. 5

DIW (ed.) (1971). *DDR-Wirtschaft – eine Bestandsaufnahme*. Frankfurt am Main

Donda, A. (1978) Nutzen und Aufwand – besser erfassen, analysieren und planen. *Statistische Praxis*, No. 4, p. 150

Drasdo, O. and Frenske, E. (1978). Zur Verordnung über die Planung, Vorbereitung und Durchführung von Folgeinvestitionen. *Wirtschaftsrecht*, No. 4, pp. 207ff.

Effektivität in der sozialistischen Volkswirtschaft. (1975). Collective authorship from GDR, USSR, Czechoslovakia, East Berlin

Ehrlich, H. and Schilling, G. (1976). Die Bedeutung einer bedarfsgerechten Produktion für Intensivierung und Erhöhung der Effektivität der Volkswirtschaft und einige sich daraus ergebende Konsequenzen für Leitung, Planung und ökonomische Stimulierung. *Wirtschaftswissenschaft*, No. 2, p. 200

Fichtner, K. (1972). Höhere Effektivität des Reproduktionsprozesses durch intensive Nutzung der Grundfonds. *Die Wirtschaft*, No. 31, pp. 3ff.

Finanzierungsrichtlinie für die volkseigene Wirtschaft. *Gesetzblatt der DDR*, I, No. 23, 1975, pp. 408ff. Also the corresponding guideline in *Gesetzblatt* I, No. 28, 1979, pp. 253ff.

Finger, H., Füger, M. and Polaschewski, E. (1977). Planung und ökonomische Stimulierung im Betrieb. *Wirtschaftswissenschaft*, No. 5, p. 718

Fragen der Weiterentwicklung der Preise und der Bewertung volkswirtschaftlicher Ressourcen als wichtige Voraussetzung für die Einheit von materieller und finanzieller Planung (Thesen). Group authorship led by F. Matho and A. Muschter (1974). *Wirtschaftswissenschaft*, No. 5, pp. 660ff.

Fragen der weiteren Vervollkommnung der wirtshaftlichen Rechnungsführung. (1977). *Wirtschaftswissenschaft*, No. 8, p. 1220

Friedrich, G. (1978a). Der Beitrag mathematischer Methoden zur Vervollkommnung der Entscheidungen in der Wirtschaftspraxis. *Wirtschaftswissenschaft*, No. 3, pp. 257ff.

—— (1978b). Kombinate – moderne Form der Leitung unserer Industrie. *Einheit*, No. 6, pp. 623ff.

Friedrich, G., Gerisch, R., Haberland, F. and Hummel, L. (1977). Zur weiteren Vervollkommnung der Leitung, Planung und ökonomischen Stimulierung der gesellschaftlichen Produktion. Die Entwicklung und Festigung der Kombinate in der sozialistischen Industrie (Thesen). *Wirtschaftswissenschaft*, No. 8, pp. 1121ff.

Garscha, J. (1973). *Planung im Betrieb*. East Berlin, pp. 77–81

Gemeinsamer Beschluss des ZK der SED, des Bundesvorstandes des FDGB und des Ministerrates der DDR über sozialpolitische Massnahmen in Durchführung der auf dem VIII Parteitag beschlossenen Hauptaufgabe des Fünfjahrplanes. *Neues Deutschland*, 28 April 1972, pp. 3–4

Gemeinsamer Beschluss des ZK der SED, des Bundesvorstandes des FDGB und Ministrrates der DDR über die weitere planmässige Verbesserung der Arbeits – und

Lebensbedingungen der Werktätigen im Zeitraum 1976 bis 1980. *Neues Deutschland*, 29/30 May, 1976, p. 1

Gemeinsamer Beschluss des Politbüros, des Zentralkomitees der SED und des Ministerrats über die Erhöhung der Effektivität der Investitionen zur weiteren Stärkung der ökonomischen Leistungsfähigkeit der DDR. *Neues Deutschland* 10/11 November 1979, p. 3

Gerisch, R. and Hofmann, W. (1979). Aufgaben und Probleme der Entwicklung in der Kombinaten zur Erhöhung des volkswirtschaftlichen Effektivität. *Wirtschaftswissenschaft*, No. 2, pp. 129ff.

Gesetzblatt der DDR, II, No. 67, 1972, p. 761; I, No. 17, 1978, pp. 198ff.; I, No. 15 and 16, 1979, pp. 120ff., 131ff.; I, No. 27, 1979, p. 247

Gesetz über den Fünfjahrplan für die Entwicklung der Volkswirtschaft der DDR 1971–1975. *Gesetzblatt der DDR*, I, No. 10, 1971, p. 175

Gesetz über den Fünfjahrplan für die Entwicklung der Volkswirtschaft der DDR 1976–1980. *Gesetzblatt der DDR*, I, No. 46, 1976, pp. 519ff.

Gesetz über den Ministerrat der DDR. *Gesetzblatt der DDR*, I, No. 16, 1972, pp. 253ff.

Gesetz über die örtlichen Volksvertretungen und ihre Organe in der DDR. *Gesetzblatt der DDR*, I, No. 32, 1973, pp. 313ff.

Gössel, A., Paust, R. and Wedler, M. (1977). Eigenproduktion von Rationalisierungsmitteln – Gebot volkswirtschaftlicher Verantwortung. *Einheit*, No. 8, pp. 938ff.

Grundfragen der Theorie der Effektivität und der Intensivierungsfaktoren der erweiterten Reproduktion (Conference report). *Wirtschaftswissenschaft*, No. 8, 1978, p. 989

Hahn, H. (1977). Rationalisierung und Rekonstruktion aus eigener Kraft. *Einheit*, No. 5, pp. 577ff.

Handel DDR – UdSSR im Zeichen verminderten Wachstums. Eds J. Bethkenhagen and H. Lambrecht, *Wochenbericht des DIW*, No. 7, 1980

Hartmann, K. (1978). Grosse Verantwortung der Kombinate. *Die Wirtschaft*, No. 9, p. 5

Haustein, H.-D. (1970). *Prognoseverfahren in der sozialistischen Wirtschaft*. East Berlin

Heinrichs, W. (1978). Hauptwege zur Steigerung der Arbeitsproduktivität für weitere Erhöhung des materiellen und kulturellen Lebensniveaus des Volkes. *Wirtschaftswissenschaft*, No. 8, p. 904

Hofman, W. (1979). Zentralisierung von Funktionen im Kombinat. *Die Wirtschaft*, No. 10, p. 16

Honecker, E. (1971). Final speech to 4th plenum of central committee of *SED*. *Neues Deutschland*, 18 December 1971

—— (1978). Zur Durchführung der Parteiwahlen 1975/1976. 15th plenum of the central committee of the *SED*, *Neues Deutschland*, 4/5 October 1975, p. 4

—— (1978). Die Aufgaben der Partei bei der weiteren Verwirklichung der Beschluss des IX Parteitages der SED. *Neues Deutschland*, 18/19 February 1978, pp 3ff.

—— (1979). Aus dem Bericht des Politbüros an die 11. Tagung des ZK der SED. *Neues Deutschland*, 14 December 1979, p. 5

Hoss, P. (1979). Was ist Endprodukt – wie wird es geplant? *Die Wirtschaft*, No. 1, p. 18

Hoss, P. and Schilling, G. (1972). Die inhaltlichen Fragen der Einheit von materieller und finanzieller Planung. *Wirtschaftswissenschaft*, No. 5, p. 667

Hübner, H.-W. (1971). Wie erreichen wir eine höhere Stabilität des Volkswirtschaftsplanes 1971? *Die Wirtschaft*, No. 4, pp. 4f.

Hülsenberg, F. and Gallenmüller, O. (1978). *Planung und Analyse der Kapazität im Betrieb*. East Berlin

Innerdeutschen Handel 1979: Preissteigerungen verdecken Rückgang des Handelsvolumens (Ed. H. Lambrecht). *Wochenbericht des DIW*, Nos. 9–10, 1980

Junker, W. (Minister of Construction) (1973). Das Wohnungsbauprogramm der DDR für die Jahre 1976 bis 1990. *Neues Deutschland*, 4 October 1973, pp. 5ff.

Kiermeyer, J., Ruhle, P. and Werner, R. (1976). Wie wirkt die Planungsordnung der Volkswirtschaft auf die Stabilisierung des Investitionsprozesses? *Chemische Technik*, No. 7, pp. 385ff.

Komplexe Rekonstruktion im Betrieb. *Die Wirtschaft*, No. 3, 199, p. 14

Koziolek, H. (1975). Wirtschaftswachstum und Sozialprogramm. *Neues Deutschland*, 19 October 1975, p. 10

—— (1977). Intensivierung – Wesensmerkmal der Wirtschaft der entwickelten sozialistischen Gesellschaft. *Einheit*, No. 3, pp. 274ff.

—— (1978). Bedürfnisse des Menschen – Massstab unserer Wirtschaft. *Neues Deutschland*, 4/5 March 1978, p. 3

—— (1978). Nationaleinkommen – Wachstum – Wohlstand. *Einheit*, Nos. 7–8, p. 774

Krutsch, O. et al. (1975). *Zur Entwicklung der Verteilungsstrukturen der Investitionen auf die Bereiche und Zweige der Volkswirtschaft.* East Berlin

Kritische Einschätzung der bisherigen Praxis der Planung und Leitung der Volkswirtschaft. *Gesetzblatt der DDR*, II, No. 64, 1963, pp. 482ff.

Krol, G.-J. (1972). *Die Wirtschaftsreformen in der DDR und ihre Ursachen.* Tübingen

Kühnau, K.-H. (1979). Zentrale Leitung und Eigenverantwortung – Vereinigung von Leitung und Initiative. *Staat und Recht*, No. 1, p. 13

Lang, S.-M., and Ruban, M. E. (1968). Veränderungen im Bankensystem der DDR. *Vierteljahreshefte zur Wirtschaftsforschung des DIW*, No. 3, pp. 397ff.

Lange, U. (1980). Zur Vervollkommnung der Leistungsbewertung der Betriebe und Kombinate. *Wirtschaftswissenschaft*, No. 3, pp. 338–9

Leptin, G. (1968). Das 'Neue Ökonomische System' Mitteldeutschlands. In *Wirtschaftsreformen in Osteuropa*, (ed. by C. Thalheim and H.-H. Höhmann) Cologne

Leptin, G. and Melzer, M. (1975). Die Wirtschaftsreformen in der DDR-Industrie – Rezentralisierung ohne Konzept. *Deutschlandarchiv*, No. 12, pp. 1282–3

—— (1978). *Economic Reform in East German Industry*, in the Series Economic Reforms in East European Industry (ed. by A. Nove and J. G. Zielinski). London and New York

Liehmann, P. (1978). Bedarf – Leistung – Menge und Qualität. *Die Wirtschaft*, No. 6, p. 5

Lommatzsch, K. (1974). Gesetzmässigkeiten der Preisentwicklung – eine Grundlage für eine begründete Preisplanung. *Wirtschaftswissenschaft*, No. 5, pp. 667ff.

Luft, H. and Parson, H. (1978). Zur Vervollkommnung der Planung und Leistungsbewertung. *Die Wirtschaft*, No. 2, p. 17

Manz, G. (1973). Bedürfnisse und Bedarf der Bevölkerung als Ausgangspunkt der Planung. *Wirtschaftswissenschaft*, No. 3, p. 697

Massnahmen zur Weiterentwicklung der Produktion modischer Bekleidungs – und Schuherzeugnisse sowie Lederwaren für die Versorgung der Bevölkerung. *Die Wirtschaft*, No. 3, 1977, p. 14

Matterne, K. and Tannhäuser, S. (1978). *Die Grundmittelwirtschaft in der sozialistischen Industrie der DDR.* East Berlin

Mätzig, K. and Neumann, C. (1975). Die Vervollkommnung der Planung und der wirtschaftlichen Rechnungsführung in sozialistischen Industriebetrieben. *Wirtschaftswissenschaft*, No. 8, pp. 1238ff.

Melzer, M. (1969). Preispolitik und Preisbildungsprobleme in der DDR. *Vierteljahreshefte zur Wirtschaftsforschung*, DIW, Berlin, No. 3, pp. 313ff.

—— (1977). Preisplanung und Preispolitik in der DDR. *Vierteljahreshefte zur Wirtschaftsforschung des DIW*, No. 1, pp. 59ff.

—— (1979). Investitionsplanung der DDR im Zeichen der Intensivierung. *Vierteljahreshefte zur Wirtschaftsforschung des DIW*, No. 4, pp. 237ff.

—— (1978). Bemühungen um effektiveren Kapitaleinsatz in der Volkswirtschaft der DDR. *FS-Analysen der Forschungsstelle für gesamtdeutsche wirtschaftliche und soziale Fragen*, No. 6, pp. 41–2

Melzer, M. and Erdmann, K. (1979). Probleme der Kombinatsbildung in der DDR – volkswirtschaftliche und betriebswirtschaftliche Aspekte. *FS – Analysen der Forschungsstelle für gesamtdeutsche wirtschaftliche und soziale Fragen*, No. 8, pp 37–38

Melzer, M. and Rüger, A. (1972). Wirtschaftssysteme (III). Die Folgen der Rezentralisierung für den volkseigenen Betrieb. *Wirtschaftswoche*, No. 6, 'Kontaktstudium', p. 32

Melzer, M. and Scherzinger, A. (1978). Wirtschaftssystem der DDR im Umbau? – Wirtschaftsführung toleriert verstärkte Diskussionen. *Vierteljahreshefte zur Wirtschaftsforschung des DIW*, No. 4, pp. 379ff.

Melzer, M., Scherzinger, A. and Schwartau, C. (1979). Wird das Wirtschaftssystem der DDR durch vermehrte Kombinatsbildung effizienter? *Vierteljahreshefte zur Wirtschaftsforschung des DIW*, No. 4, pp. 365ff.

Mittag, G. (1978). Beschlüsse des IX Parteitages werden konsequent verwirklicht. *Neues Deutschland*, 27/28 May 1978, p. 3

—— (1978). Vorzüge des Sozialismus für höhere Effektivität nutzen. *Neues Deutschland*, 26/27 August 1978, p. 3

—— (1978). Zielstrebige Verwirklichung der Hauptaufgabe, *Einheit*, No. 10, pp. 789ff.

—— (1979). Mit dem Plan 1980 setzen wir die Politik zum Wohle des Volkes fort. *Neues Deutschland*, 22/23 December 1979, pp. 5f.

—— (1979). Sozialistische Planwirtschaft zum Wohle des Volkes, zur Stärkung unserer Republik. *Einheit*, Nos 9/10, p. 938

Mitzscherling, P., Lambrecht, H., Melzer, M., Otto-Arnold, Ch., Ruban, M. E., Scherzinger-Roger, A., Vortmann, H. and Wilkens, H. (1974). *System und Entwicklung der DDR-Wirtschaft, Sonderhefte des DIW*, No. 98

Neues Deutschland, 27 October 1968; 28 October 1975; 14 March 1978; 24 April 1978; 12 February 1979

Nick, H. (1977). Wissenschaftlichtechnische Revolution und Gestaltung der entwickelten sozialistischen Gesellschaft. *Einheit*, No. 12, pp. 1337ff.

—— (1978). Probleme der Vervollkommnung der gesellschaftlichen Leitung des wissenschaftlich-technischen Fortschritts. *Wirtschaftswissenschaft*, No. 4, pp. 396ff.

Pieplow, R. (1972). Zur zentralen staatlichen Planung der Ubereinstimmung materieller und finanzieller Proportionen. *Wirtschaftswissenschaft*, No. 5, pp. 681ff.

Presseinformationen der DDR, No. 103, 1976, pp. 2–3

Programm der Sozialistischen Einheitspartei Deutschlands. *Neues Deutschland*, 25 May 1976, p. 4

Ritzschke, G., and Steeger, H. (1975). Höhere Effektivität durch Effektivitätsplanung. *Einheit*, No. 3, pp. 283ff.

Rüger, A. (1969). Die Bedeutung 'strukturbestimmender Aufgaben' für die Wirtschaftsplanung und-organisation der DDR. *Sonderhefte des DIW*, No. 85

Scherzinger, A. (1976). Neue Planungsrichtlinien für Betriebe und Kombinate in der DDR. *Vierteljahreshefte zur Wirtschaftsforschung des DIW*, No. 1, pp. 50ff.

Schilling, G. (1978). Rechnungsführung und Stimulierung. *Die Wirtschaft*, No. 5, p. 15

Schilling, G., and Steeger, H. (1971). Proportionalität in unserer sozialistischen Planwirtschaft. *Einheit*, No. 5, p. 548

Schürer, G. (1972). Zur Vervollkommnung der Planung in der DDR. *Einheit*, No. 1, p. 47

Statistische Praxis, No. 1, 1977, pp. 12ff.

Statut der Staatlichen Plankommission. *Gesetzblatt der DDR*, I, No. 41, 1973, pp. 417ff

Stellung und Entwicklungstendenzen der volkseigenen Kombinate und Betriebe im Vergesellschaftungsprozess des entwickelten Sozialismus (Conference report). *Wirtschaftswissenschaft*, No. 8, 1977, pp. 1401ff.

Stoph, W. (1970). Zum Entwurf des Volkswirtschaftsplanes 1971. *Neues Deutschland*, 11 December 1970, p. 3

Strauss, C.-J., *et al.* (1973). *Die Materialwirtschaft der DDR*. East Berlin

22 Tagung des Wissenschaftlichen Rates für Wirtschaftswissenschaftliche Forschung (Conference report). *Wirtschaftswissenschaft*, No. 9, 1977, p. 1387

Tarnick, H. (1978). Zur Verordnung über die Vorbereitung von Invesititionen. *Wirtschaftrecht*, No. 4, pp. 198ff

Tönjes, H.-G. (1967). Die dritte Etappe der Industriepreisreform in Mitteldeutschland. In *Vierteljahreshefte zur Wirtschaftsforschung*, DIW, Berlin, No. 1, pp. 95ff.

Trautloft, W. (1978). Vorstufen müssen beweglicher sein. *Die Wirtschaft*, No. 6, p. 6

Ulbricht, W. (1967). Die Bedeutung des Werkes 'Das Kapital' von Karl Marx für die Schaffung des entwickelten gesellschaftlichen Systems des Sozialismus in der DDR und den Kampf gegen des staatsmonopolistische Herrschaftssystem in West-deutschland. *Neues Deutschland*, 13 September 1967, p. 5

—— (1968) *Zum ökonomischen System des Sozialismus in der DDR*, 2 vols, East Berlin

Verordnung über die Aufgabe, Rechte und Pflichten der volkseigenen Betriebe, Kombinate und VVB. *Gesetzblatt der DDR*, I, No. 15, 1973, pp. 129ff.

Verordnung über die Material-, Austrüstungs- und Konsumgüterbilanzierung – Bilanzierungsverordnung. *Gesetzblatt der DDR*, II, No. 50, 1971, pp. 377ff.

Verordnung über die Planung, Bildung und Verwendung des Prämienfonds und des Sozialfonds für volkseigene Betriebe. *Gesetzblatt der DDR*, II, No. 5, 1972, pp. 49ff.; also the 'Durchführungsbestimmungen' for this in *Gesetzblatt . . .*', II, No. 34, 1972, pp. 379ff. and I, No. 46, 1973, pp. 485ff.; also the second decree of 1973 in *Gesetzblatt . . .*', I, No. 30, 1973, p. 293

Verordnung über die Planung, Vorbereitung und Durchführung von Folgeinvestitionen. *Gesetzblatt der DDR*, I, No. 23, 1978, pp. 257ff.

Verordnung über die Produktionsfondsabgabe. *Gesetzblatt der DDR*, II, No. 4, 1971, pp. 33ff.

Verordnung über die volkseigenen Kombinate, Kombinatsbetriebe und volkseigenen Betriebe. *Gesetzblatt der DDR*, I, No. 38, 1979, pp. 355ff.

Verordnung über die Vorbereitung von Investitionen. *Gesetzblatt der DDR*, I, No. 23, 1978, pp. 251ff.

Verordnung zur Sicherung der Einheit von Plan und Vertrag bei dem Abschluss und der Erfüllung von Wirtschaftsverträgen. *Gesetzblatt der DDR*, I, No. 6, 1978, pp. 85ff.

Volkswirtschaftsplanung (1975). Collective authorship under the direction of H.-H. Kinze, H. Knop and E. Seifert. East Berlin

Wahl, G. (1975). Wie wirksam ist die Rahmenrichtlinie für die Jahresplanung? *Die Wirtschaft*, No. 22, p. 11.

Weitere Massnahmen zur Durchführung des sozialpolitischen Programms des VIII Parteitages der SED. *Berliner Zeitung*, 27 September 1973, p. 3

Wenzel, M. (1979). Die Eigenproduktion von Rationalisierungsmitteln – Beitrag zur vertieften Intensivierung der Industrieproduktion. *Wirtschaftswissenschaft*, No. 8, pp. 932ff.

Wirtschaftswissenschaft (1968). Berlin (East), No. 10

Wochenbericht des DIW (1965). Berlin, No. 32, 1964; No. 22

Zschau, U. and Hempel, W. (1978). Wege zur effektiveren Grundfondsreproduktion. *Die Wirtschaft*, No. 5, p. 3

Zu den Beziehungen zwischen Wert, Gebrauchswert und Preis im entwickelten Sozialismus (Conference report). *Wirtschaftswissenschaft*, No. 10, 1978, p. 248

Zur Altersstruktur des industriellen Anlagevermögens in der DDR. *Wochenbericht des DIW* (ed. by M. Melzer), No. 37, 1977

Zur langfristigen Planung des volkswirtschaftlichen Reproduktionsprozess (1975). Collective authorship. East Berlin

Zur Vervollkommnung von Planung und Leistungsbewertung. (Conference report). *Wirtschaftswissenschaft*, No. 5, 1978, p. 603

Zweite Durchführungsbestimmung zur Verordnung über produktgebundene Abgaben und Subventionen – 2. PADB Preisausgleichszuführungen und Preisausgleichsabführungen. *Gesetzblatt der DDR*, I, No. 3, 1978, pp. 54ff.

Zweite wissenschaftliche Konferenz ›Instandhaltung‹. *Wirtschaftswissenschaft*, No. 7, 1978, p. 852

Aims, methods and political determinants of the economic policy of Poland 1970–1980

Włodzimierz Brus

4.1. Introduction

As has been rightly noted in a preceding volume on East European economies (Machowski and Zwass, 1972) the economic life of Poland in the 1970s has become to a considerable extent determined by the direct and indirect effects of the workers' revolt in December 1970. In a broader sense this is true for the second half of the 1971–1980 decade as well.

The simple lesson driven home by the December 1970 events and their aftermath was that of the impossibility of continuing economic development at the expense of the consumer interest of the population – both in terms of the overall level of personal incomes and in terms of many aspects of social welfare. At first the new leadership of the PUWP showed itself far from sufficiently aware of the enormity of the problems it had to face: token concessions only – mainly in the form of special allowances for the very lowest income groups – were promised by Edward Gierek in his inaugural address on 21 December 1970 and in other official statements of the first few weeks after Władysław Gomułka's downfall; the return to the 'old' (i.e. pre-13 December) prices was ruled out as impossible for lack of resources and as being at variance with the aims of changing the structure of consumption. Very soon, however, the ruling elite was given forcefully to understand that changes in economic policy – at least from the point of view mentioned above – must be much more profound. Tensions in main industrial centres persisted, time and again erupting into strikes. One – a strike of textile workers, mostly women, in Lódź – finally compelled the government to retreat on prices: food prices were brought back to the pre-13 December level without annulment of the 'compensating' cuts in prices of some industrial consumer goods. Together with the rescission of the system of economic incentives which was to operate from 1 January 1971 (the Gomulka–Jaszczuk reform blueprint) putting severe restrictions on growth of nominal wages and salaries, this was the single most important step signalling the growing awareness of a need for a major redress. The continuing pressure throughout 1971 (and later) undoubtedly contributed to the consolidation of this awareness, which was soon expressed in the decision to abandon the (almost ready) plan for 1971–1975 prepared according to the 'old' guidelines, and to produce a new five-year plan. The latter took some time (the new guidelines were formally adopted at the VI Congress of the Polish United Workers' Party in December 1971, and the plan itself by the Sejm in June 1972), but the very decision to change the plan and a number of steps taken concomitantly gave a rather clear indication of the new direction[1].

The main targets of the 1971–1975 plan compared with the actual data for the 1966–1970 period looked as in *Table 4.1*.

Table 4.1 *The 1971–1975 plan*

| | Average annual rates of growth | |
	1966–1970 (actual)	1971–1975 (plan)
National income[a]	6.0	7.0
Real incomes per capita[b]	5.5	6.7
Real wages per employee	2.1	3.4
Gross investment in fixed assets[c]	8.1	7.7
Industrial production	4.9	5.4
Employment in industry	3.3	2.9
Productivity in industry	4.9	5.4
Fixed assets in industry	7.7	8.2
Gross agricultural production	2.9[c]	3.5–3.9[d]
Exports	9.8	9.2
Imports	9.0	9.7

Notes: (a) Net material product; (b) Sum of money incomes plus money social benefits divided by population; (c) Related to the average of the preceding five-year period; (d) Related to 1970.

Sources: Official Polish statistical material and surveys by B. Askanas, H. Askanas and F. Levcik of the Wiener Institut für Internationale Wirtschaftsvergleiche, Reprint-Serie Nr. 22 and 26 (*Monatsberichte des Österreichischen Institutes für Wirtschaftsforschung*, Wien, Nos. 3 and 12, 1976).

In the light of subsequent developments (which will be discussed later) these figures indicated both the desire to emphasize the improvement in the standard of living and the cautiousness which still prevailed in the first post-Gomulka period; the planned increases in real wages were far from spectacular, and the modest progress could hardly promise to lift Poland out of the last place she occupied in this respect among East European countries by 1970[2]. It was also significant that this time – unlike the economic policy switch in the mid-1950s – the gains in consumption were not to be achieved at the expense of investment; the planners learned the lesson of the adverse consequences of an abrupt cancellation of a development programme (among other things inducing a persisting cyclical movement) and on the whole preferred rather to extrapolate past trends with even a slight increase in the share of investment in national income. Apart from some changes in sectoral allocation of investments compared with pre-1971 blueprints, an important feature was the first indication of the change in foreign trade policy; imports were to grow faster than exports, albeit by a rather small margin.

It would, however, be pointless to go into a more detailed analysis of the 1971–1975 plan. The plan was soon drastically overhauled in all respects, giving way to the 'new strategy of development' consisting of a combination of a massive investment programme (aimed in the first place at extensive modernization of the capital stock) with an ambitious programme of raising personal incomes and a wide range of social benefits, of keeping prices for basic foodstuffs stable, etc. The 'new strategy' gained momentum in 1972, gradually becoming the main source of political legitimacy of the new leadership, which changed its posture from caution to overconfidence astonishingly fast. The I National Party Conference (a kind of interim congress) in October 1973 gave its formal approval to the policy and urged that it should go ahead at full speed.

We shall examine later in greater detail the factors which at the initial stage of the 1971–1975 period gave rise to the almost unqualified optimism of the 'new strategy'. Here it may be worthwhile to point out the apparent paradox of working-class pressure as the initial push: the first concessions in terms of a more generous incomes policy (almost 6% increase in real wages in 1971, greater latitude in utilization of the wage fund and its link with output) apparently produced at first a positive feedback effect on attitudes to work, and hence on industrial productivity. This initial response was understandable, particularly taking into account that during the 1961–1970 decade there was a clear downward deviation from the long-run trend rate of increase in productivity[3]: the change in policy started to release potential which otherwise would have remained hidden. To some extent a similar effect occurred in agriculture with the increase in supply of fodder and improvement of 'terms of trade' for the peasants, although the role of policy changes was difficult to assess here compared with the role of the exceptionally good weather considered decisive by some analysts. The acknowledgement of the role of increasing incomes as an active factor in economic growth was amply justified and obviously overdue in the then existing Polish conditions. The same should be said about the concept of 'import-induced growth' with purchases of modern equipment and knowhow on credit; from this point of view the programme of modernization of industry worked out under Gomulka (but then meant to be carried out under conditions of austerity) got a much better chance when the rationale of active policy both in the field of consumption and in foreign trade could be openly spelled out and put into operation. Unfortunately, correct recognition of many hitherto unused possibilities was not accompanied by proper understanding of limitations nor by the ability to distinguish between temporary and fundamental factors, the latter requiring careful and consistent grooming, among other things by appropriate institutional changes.

It would be unwarranted to maintain that the Gierek leadership followed in the footsteps of its predecessor in totally neglecting the reform of the system of functioning of the economy, but the measures taken were halfhearted, slow and subject to withdrawal at the first hurdle; and what proved to be most important – the opportunity of improving the political climate in the country, which could and should be the main gain from the tragic events of 1970 – was soon lost completely. Instead, great efforts were put into leading the country into a kind of euphoria, with sycophants among economists again declaring many vital economic interrelations as outdated and defeatist.

4.2 Development 1971–1975

The statistical record of the 1971–1975 period looked impressive indeed, compared both with the preceding quinquennium (see *Table 4.1*) and with the plan. In many respects the picture emerging from the data was the most favourable since the end of the immediate post-war reconstruction (*Table 4.2*).

In addition to the data in *Table 4.2* one should note the rapid increase in retail turnover (6.2% annually during 1966–1970, 7.4% planned for 1971–1975, and 10.3% actually reported), and a remarkable shift in growth proportions between those sectors of industry which are classified as producer goods ('group A') and consumer goods ('group B'): in the 1966–1970 period the annual rate of growth of the former was 9.4% compared with 6.6% for the latter, whereas in the 1971–1975 period the rates were practically equal (10.6% and 10.4% respectively). Within 'group A' an above-average rate of growth was recorded in engineering (higher than planned) and in the chemical industry, whereas the energy sector lagged behind the average and substantially behind planned figures; in 'group B' the food industry developed faster than planned. The only flaws in the otherwise seemingly impeccable record of *Table 4.2* were: (1) the perform-ance of agriculture, due to loss of momentum in 1974 and even an absolute drop in gross production in the following year; (2) significantly faster growth of imports compared with exports; we shall of course return to these problems later on.

The precise assessment of the true progress in the standard of living of the population is difficult both because of the general problem of aggregate index numbers (especially in measuring the change in cost of living), and because of the particular problems for an economy in which most prices are fixed but not necessarily at a market-clearing level (hence the unknown degree of availability of goods), and where the state is obviously interested

Table 4.2 *The 1971–1975 results*

| | Average annual rates of growth | | Annual rates of growth | | | | |
	1971–1975 (plan)	1971–1975 (actual)	1971	1972	1973	1974	1975
National income[a]	7.0	9.8	8.1	10.6	10.8	10.4	9.0
Real income per capita[b]	6.7	9.9	9.8	11.9	12.1	7.1	–
Real wage per employee	3.4	7.2	5.7	6.4	8.7	6.6	8.5
Gross investment in fixed assets	7.7[c]	13.9[c]	7.5	23.6	25.0	22.5	14.2
Industrial production	8.5	10.4	7.9	10.7	11.2	11.4	10.9
Employment in industry	2.9	2.8	3.1	4.6	2.8	2.4	1.5
Productivity in industry	5.4	8.1	6.0	6.8	8.6	9.3	9.7
Fixed assets in industry	8.2	9.2	5.0	8.8	9.1	12.3	11.1
Gross agricultural production	3.5–3.9[d]	3.6[d]	3.6	8.4	7.3	1.6	-2.6
Exports[e]	9.2	19.1	9.2	17.1	17.8	29.4	23.7
Imports[e]	9.7	23.6	11.9	21.4	33.1	33.4	19.6

Notes: (a), (b), (c), (d) as in *Table 4.1*; (e) in current prices in foreign currency units.

Sources: As in *Table 4.1*.

in absorbing the purchasing power of the population on the one hand, and in presenting a favourable statistical picture on the other (hence the so-called 'disguised' price rises in the shops without adequate reflection in the index numbers). The absence of independent scrutiny of the cost of living index must make one very cautious about accepting the claimed absolute results at face value. Nevertheless, there is no reason to assume that the degree of statistical distortion during 1971–1975 was significantly greater than in previous periods and in other East European countries, except perhaps Yugoslavia and Hungary, where prices usually clear the market. Thus it is reasonable to conclude that in relative terms Poland did rather well and made up the gap which separated her from other East European countries (but not much more)[4].

Despite the pegging of prices of essential foodstuffs over the whole 1971–1975 period (the pledge not to raise prices was repeated annually as a means of relaxing somewhat the continuous pressures), the official cost of living index rose by 2.4% annually (more than during 1966–1970!). The increase was particularly pronounced in 1974, to some extent as a response to the dramatic changes in world market prices, and by no means confined to industrial consumer goods and services only: food prices in 1975 were 10% higher than in 1970 (mainly because of the official registered increase of prices on the private markets, almost 37%, which was a reflection of scarcity of supply in state shops); the increase in the cost of clothing and shoes (in family budgets) was over 18% (*Rocznik Statystyczny*, 1976). The difference between price increases for food and non-food items could point to a slightly lesser impact on lower income groups, but on the whole the redistributive effect must have been negligible.

The same was probably true of differentials in nominal wages, although the evidence is extremely scarce; the net average nominal wage in the 'socialized economy' rose from 2235 złoty monthly in 1970 to 3562 złoty in 1975, i.e. by over 60%, whereas the statutory minimum wage was raised from 850 złoty to 1200 złoty, i.e. by slightly over 40%. The very fast increase in average nominal wages was to a considerable extent the result of much wider payment of increases than expected: 4.6 million employees were to be granted rises according to the plan – all 11 million employed in the 'socialized economy' received them before the quinquenium ended (*Zjazd . . .*, 1975). Employment in all sectors of the 'socialized economy' grew fast (over 3% annually, only marginally slower than during the preceding five-year period), contributing to the higher growth of income per capita than of earnings per employee. At the VII Congress a claim was made that real incomes of the peasant population grew in the same proportion as real wages; statistical data on 'real incomes' from agricultural production used for consumption and unproductive investment reported an overall increase of 4.2% annually (in 1966–1970 it was only 0.2%), and even allowing for the slight decline in the active population in private agriculture the actual figure was obviously less than that of real wages. The 1975 index of prices received by peasants for agricultural produce (1970 = 100) was 136.5 overall, 138.9 for crop products and 135.0 for animal products (*Rocznik* . . ., 1976, tables 2(122) and 13(594)). Still, in 1975 – according to the family-budgets data – the average level of consumer spending per capita was over 20% lower in peasant households than in state employee households.

Considerable steps forward were made in the field of social services, which were undoubtedly also important from the point of view of more equitable distribution. Firstly, the anachronistic distinction between manual and non-manual worker's entitlement to sickness benefits was finally abolished by 1974; second, from 1972 peasants actively engaged in agriculture and their families became covered by health insurance, and this transformed the state health system almost into a national health service[5]; many other benefits were increased or extended in time: child allowances, maternity leave, etc. The average old-age pension increased from 1144 złoty monthly in 1970 to 1545 in 1975, i.e. by much less in percentage terms than the average wage and even by less than the minimum wage.

No spectacular progress has been achieved in the important area of *housing*. The gross (without subtracting losses due to natural wastage) number of dwellings 'put to use' increased somewhat (by 21%) compared with 1966–1970 but at a rate completely inadequate for the extremely difficult housing situation: even in 1975 the gross ratio of dwellings 'put to use' to the number of new marriages did not exceed 0.8, which meant that the backlog of families without a separate dwelling was continuing to grow and the waiting times in the system of subsidized housing were getting longer (8–10 years). Negligible improvements only took place in the statutory working time: a reduction from 46 to 44.5 hours per week on average, on condition that the level of output was maintained.

Data on consumption per capita in physical terms showed some improvement both in the level and structure of consumption, though less striking than one would expect from the overall income figures. The most substantial gains were recorded in meat consumption, which (including edible offal) grew from 53 kg in 1970 to 70 kg in 1975 (over 30%), with a corresponding drop in consumption of cereals by 9% (from 131 kg to 120 kg). However, consumption of vegetables and fruit was surprisingly lower than in 1970, and not only in the terminal year 1975, which could have been a matter of chance, but consistently over the whole period. Consumption of textiles was modestly higher (cotton by 2%, wool and wool-substitutes by 25%), that of shoes even fell slightly. The item with the highest recorded rate of increase (except tea) (*Rocznik* . . ., 1976, table 12(132)) was hard liquor: from 3.3 litres (in 100° alcohol units) in 1970 to 4.6 in 1975, a rise of almost 40%.

As noted earlier, the growth in consumption was meant to be achieved not at the expense of the investment programme, but – on the contrary – at least parallel to the latter. In fact, the investment drive proved to be much stronger than gains in consumption. Gross investment outlays in constant 1971 prices were 90% higher than in the preceding quinquennium (in the socialist sector more than twice as high); per head of population the 1975 level of outlays was 220% of that of 1970. In current prices, which, of course, showed an upward trend, the increase was substantially higher. The share of accumulation (net investment plus increase in inventories) in disposable national income already exceeded the highest previous figure (1953 and 1968) in 1971 and kept climbing all the time, reaching the staggering levels of 38% and 37.8% in 1974 and 1975 respectively (in constant 1971 prices). The main bulk of this colossal – in Polish conditions – outlay went into the productive sphere (78.7%, almost 4% higher than in 1966–1970, and 1.5% higher than planned), and within the productive sphere into industry (43.8%, more or less according to plan, but over 4% higher than in 1966–1970). The share of agriculture was substantially lower than in the preceding quinquennium (13.7% versus 16.1%), but in view of the overall growth the absolute expenditure was 60% greater. The share of the non-productive sphere fell compared both with the 1966–1970 period and the plan for 1971–1975 (particularly unfortunate was the fall in the share of housing investment): again, however, in absolute terms the increase was considerable (*Rocznik . . .*, 1976, section X)[6]. Some long-delayed prestige projects judged important for political reasons (the Royal Castle, the central passenger station in Warsaw and others) were resumed and vigorously pursued, as well as several important elements of infrastructure, particularly in road-building, which was relevant from the point of view of freight transport, the development of private motoring and the desire to attract more foreign tourists. The overriding objective was, however, to expand and to modernize productive capacities, among other things in order to raise the competitiveness of Polish industrial products on world markets, and especially in the developed capitalist countries: this was to change the structure of Polish exports, to pay off the investment credits obtained from abroad and to create a more secure and up-to-date foundation for future development. By the end of 1975 the gross value of productive assets was 40% higher than in 1970; in industry – according to claims made at the VII Congress of the PUWP – over half of the fixed productive assets in use at the end of 1975 were put into operation in the course of the 1971–1975 quinquennium. It is perhaps worthwhile to note, particularly against the background of difficulties encountered at the same time elsewhere, that the investment drive was the main factor behind the creation of almost 1 900 000 new jobs in the national economy.

4.3 Factors of development in 1971–1975

In the light of the rather extraordinary picture which emerges from the above summary of results the assessment of underlying factors acquires special significance. Of course, in the framework of the present chapter the identification of the factors of development can be only limited, particularly as many 'intangible' or at least unquantifiable factors are at stake.

Let us begin with a negative statement that the difference between 1971–1975 and the previous performance in terms of national income growth cannot be traced to an increased rate of growth of employment (see *Tables 4.1* and *4.2*); only in some sectors, notably construction, was the rate of growth of employment significantly higher than during 1966–1970 (especially in 1973 and 1974, with annual increases in the range of 10%). Thus the basic direct factor must have been, and indeed was, the increase in labour productivity: overall in the material sphere (i.e. the national income-producing sphere, according to East European methodology) the index of labour productivity in 1975 (1970 = 100) was 144.5, an annual compound rate of 7.6%; the increase in overall productivity (net material product in the economy as a whole per active person in the material sphere, Y/L) contributed 90% of the overall growth of national income (index 1975:1970 = 159.4), the remaining 10% coming from the increase in employment. However, this productivity growth must have been to a considerable degree due to a very substantial increment in the capital/labour ratio, K/L, which in 1975 stood 132.9% higher than in 1970 (measured as a ratio of the mean annual value of fixed productive assets in constant 1971 prices to the mean number of active population in the productive sphere); this meant that the resulting 'productivity of fixed assets', i.e. national income/capital stock ratio $(Y/K) = (Y/L):(K/L)$ was only 108.8% in 1975 (1970 = 100), despite the massive injections of new capital, including a lot of imported equipment during the quinquennium under consideration. Of course, this was better than in 1966–1970, when Y/K did not increase at all; one should also allow for the inevitable lags, especially in the course of such rapid expansion; nevertheless, the 'x-efficiency' element of growth in this case must have been surprisingly small.

Aggregation on a national scale can be very misleading, however; let us therefore turn to a brief examination of two major sectors – industry and agriculture.

In the introductory section of this chapter we noticed the initial increase in productivity *in industry* which could be attributed (at least as a reasonable hypothesis) to a number of otherwise intangible factors such as changes in income policies, some improvement in the political climate (and expectation of further progress), first (selective) measures of reorganization of the economic system, etc. This seemed to have been reflected in faster growth of productivity (net product/labour ratio) than of the capital/labour ratio: in industry in 1972 the former increased by 6.8%, the latter by 4.9%, the resulting difference (increase in 'productivity of fixed assets') being plus 1.9%; in 1973 the analogous figures were 8.6, 6.3 and 2.3 respectively. In construction the year 1972 brought a spectacular result in the above terms:

increase in net product/labour ratio 14.1%, increase in capital/labour ratio 5.8%, increase in 'productivity of fixed assets' 7.9%. However, in the subsequent years less favourable results were recorded: in industry improvement of Y/K was only 0.9% in 1974, and in 1975 there was actually a drop of 0.4% compared with the previous year; in construction in each of the three years 1973, 1974 and 1975 productivity went up slower than the capital/labour ratio, rendering the Y/K effect lower by 3.2% in 1973, by 8.6% in 1974, and by 7.6% in 1975. Consequently in 1975 the 'productivity of fixed assets' in industry was only 4.9% higher than in 1970, and in construction it was actually 14.5% lower (*Rocznik . . .*, 1976, table 1(97))[7].

The five-year figures for agricultural production in the terms used above were much worse than in any other sector. In *Table 4.2* an average annual growth of 3.6% was shown for the 1971–1975 period (marketed production grew by over 6% per annum, also in constant 1971 prices). But these are gross figures without taking into account the material inputs needed for the increase. In net terms in constant prices Polish agricultural production in 1975 was 2.7% lower than in 1970: with the net product/labour ratio, Y/L, at 99.4% of the 1970 level (there was a slight decline in the number of people actively engaged in agriculture) and the capital labour ratio, K/L, at 129.9%, the 'productivity of fixed assets' in 1975 was only 76.8 (1970 = 100). To what extent the ratio Y/K can be taken as a yardstick of efficiency in agriculture is far from obvious, particularly in Polish conditions where peasant-type private farms prevail. Even less relevant are such ratios on an annual basis, bearing in mind the sensitivity to weather fluctuations (the degree of this sensitivity, however, is itself an indicator of the level of development). Nevertheless, it is interesting to note that the very good results in agricultural production in the first two years of the 1971–1975 quinquennium (9% and 5% respective annual increases in net agricultural production, 5.1% and 0.8% increases in Y/K over the preceding year) coincided with important policy measures favouring the peasants (sharp increase in prices paid by the state for agricultural produce, especially for animal products, abolition of compulsory deliveries of agricultural produce from 1972, reform of the land tax, greater emphasis on supply of producer goods for agriculture, extension of social security systems, etc.). On the other hand, the evident worsening of the results in each consecutive year since 1973 coincided with the reappearance of ambiguity in the official line on private agriculture, particularly as far as opportunities for expansion were concerned, both in terms of size of farm and in terms of productive equipment. Statistical data provide at least some evidence of policy fluctuations, which could have been interpreted by private peasants as signs of a return of the thinly disguised pressure for acceleration of growth of the share of socialist (primarily state) agriculture. For example sales and grants of land from the State Land Fund (which absorbs among other things land taken over from elderly peasants, fully and semi-abandoned farms, etc.) to private owners amounted to 24% of the total land distributed for permanent use in 1970, 30% in 1971, 34% in 1972, almost 39% in 1973, and then dropped dramatically to less than 18% in 1974 (a 50% fall in absolute terms) and to a mere 5.5% in 1975 (one third of the 1974 level in absolute figures) (*Rocznik* . . ., 1976, table 13(332)). Data on tractors sold to private farms show some fluctuations (an increasing trend until 1973, then a drop in 1974, then again a rise in 1975): however, the growth of the total number of tractors owned by private farms slowed down markedly from 1973 onwards. Small but very characteristic changes occurred in the ratio of the fiscal burden (actual payments) to net agricultural production in peasant farms: at first this ratio declined from 13.4% in 1970 to less than 11% in 1971, less than 9% in 1972 and 1973, and then started to climb again – 9.3% in 1974, and 10.0% in 1975. The total amount of investment credits paid out to private farmers from state sources was rising steadily until 1973, then declined in 1974 and again in 1975 (*Rocznik* . . ., 1976, tables 8(327), 90(409), and 133(432)). It is difficult to calculate the change in profitability of the main agricultural products (particularly animal products) in private farms – prices obtained by the peasants rose but costs rose much faster in the second half of the 1971–1975 period, and shortages in basic material inputs, feed grains in the first place, but also coal and other things had a serious adverse impact on peasants' attitudes.

All this is not intended either to deny the progress achieved in the first couple of years after Gomulka's downfall, or to underestimate the impact of exogenous factors (weather) on agricultural production; what seems important, however, is to see also the correlation with policies which proved unable to sustain the momentum generated in 1971–1972. As one of the participants in a round-table discussion on problems of consumption put it:

> In this particularly favourable period of our development we have failed to create lasting conditions for improvement of the level of efficiency in our economy. We failed to direct the social pressures for higher wages into a process in which higher wages are generated by raising efficiency. We have also not succeeded in sustaining the production enthusiasm observed in peasant farms between 1971 and 1973. (*Polityka*, No. 15 (9 April) 1977, p. 4).

In a situation when impressive expansion combined with substantial increases in incomes of the population could not be based on appropriate improvement in efficiency, external sources had to be brought into the picture. Indeed, one can hardly avoid the conclusion that – at least during the period under consideration – these were the main factors in the simultaneous progress on both fronts: consumption and investment.

Poland entered the 1970s decade with a relatively favourable foreign account position. Although balance of payments data are not published in Eastern Europe, there is enough indirect evidence to prove the above statement (especially with regard to the trade balance, which has a greater share in and is more directly related to the balance of payments than in industrialized Western countries). As noted in Machowski and Zwass (1972, p. 120), the cumulative Polish foreign trade deficit for the 1960–1970 decade amounted to 1413 million US dollars, out of which 284 million was with Western industrialized countries (OECD). Taking into account the Polish positive (as a rule) current balance on 'invisibles' with socialist countries, and probably also some surplus in this category with the West, the position was quite good. Even including long-term investment loans with expiry dates as far ahead in some cases as the year 2000, the total indebtedness reported was 1800 million US dollars in 1970 (Machowski and Zwass, 1972, p. 120)[8]. It is quite probable that towards the end of Gomulka's rule some hard currency reserve was created, and a great deal of effort was directed towards elimination of total indebtedness: the trade balance for 1970 with OECD countries showed a surplus of about 80 million dollars and this continued into 1971 (over 50 million dollars surplus). This in itself said nothing for the policy of Gomulka, whose unimaginative 'prudent house-holder behaviour' meant forfeiting all the advantages of wise use of credits; what was important for the new leadership, however, was the fact that they inherited a fairly clean bill of health which they could exploit. In other words, the 'reserve of past mistakes' was available in the foreign economic field as well.

Apart from this, the beginning of the 1970s brought a favourable turn in Poland's terms of trade. They remained almost perfectly stable throughout the 1960s, showed the first signs of improvement in 1970 (more than two percentage points over 1969), rose by over 4% in 1971, then by another 2.3% in 1972, making the overall 1972 index (1969 = 100) as high as 109.1 (*Rocznik . . .* 1973, table 2(518); 1976, table 2(518)).

Improved terms of trade and relative easiness of obtaining Western credits, particularly for investment goods and licences but also for industrial consumer goods and feed grains, provided the background for a radical shift in Polish foreign trade policy. True, these were the years when almost all East European countries turned to Western credits (Romania had done it earlier, and was rather backpedalling during the 1971–1975 quinquennium); however, Poland was second to none as far as the scale of the switch was concerned. The overall trade balance, which in 1970 was in deficit by only 160 million dollars, reached over 2250 million dollars annual deficit by 1975; the cumulative deficit for the five years under consideration was almost 6500 million dollars, more than 13 times as much as in the 1966–1970 period, and more than 11 times as much if the 1971 and 1973 dollar devaluations were eliminated[9].

Overall figures do not tell the whole story, however, because the trade deficit with socialist countries was relatively small (less than 190 million dollars for the period as a whole; with the USSR there was actually a surplus of around 130 million dollars), and trade with non-socialist developing countries brought a cumulative surplus of around 600 million dollars. The deficit with Western industrial countries was therefore greater than the overall one, swinging from 53.5 million dollars surplus in 1971 to almost 3000 million dollars deficit in 1975, with a cumulative deficit figure for the five years of over 6700 million dollars. In 1970 imports from Western industrial countries were around 25% of the total and equal to less than 40% of imports from socialist countries; in 1974 and 1975 imports from the West overtook imports from socialist countries, and their share in the overall value of imports was around 50%. In 1975 no more than 52% of Polish imports from the West were paid for by exports to the West; the cumulative figure for the five years was less than two thirds.

The direct impact of the net influx of foreign resources on the overall position of disposable resources can be seen from the difference between the levels and rates of growth of the so-called 'national income produced' (designated usually as 'national income' without additional qualification) and disposable national income ('national income distributed', according to the Polish statistical terminology), which includes the balance of foreign trade as the main additional item[10].

Data shown in *Table 4.3* illustrate well the important difference between the two five-year periods as far as the impact of foreign trade on disposable resources is concerned: the rate of growth of 'national income distributed' lagged behind that of national income produced during 1966–1970, and soared ahead during 1971–1975. What is more – the discrepancies were concentrated practically in the three last years of the 1971–1975 quinquennium and showed a tendency to increase not only in absolute but also in

Table 4.3 *Impact of resources from abroad on national income*

		National income of Poland Produced	Disposable ('distributed')
Average annual percentage rate of growth (in constant prices)	1966–1970	6.0	5.8
	1971–1975	9.8	12.0
Value in current prices (billion zloty)	1970	749.2	731.5
	1971	855.0	841.8
	1972	951.0	950.0
	1973	1064.8	1114.1
	1974	1209.3	1299.6
	1975	1357.0	1459.0

Source: Rocznik Statystyczny, 1976, tables 3(99), 5(101), 17(113) and 19(115).

relative terms: if we take, for example, the *increase* in total value of
consumption out of national income (in current prices) in 1973 over 1972
(77.1 billion złoty), the surplus of national income distributed over national
income produced in 1973 (49.3 billion złoty) equalled 64% of this increment; the next year the relation between these two magnitudes was 86% and
in 1975 almost 90% (increase in consumption over 1974 114 billion złoty,
surplus in disposable national income 102 billion złoty). This comparison
does not intend to convey the impression that surplus of distributed over
produced national income was the main source of increase in consumption,
but illustrates well the general point about the policy of simultaneous
growth of consumption and investment becoming increasingly dependent
on bringing in resources from abroad.

4.4. Growing tensions in the economy

The substantial influx of external resources helped greatly (some would even
say made it possible) to achieve the results reported for 1971–1975; the price
to be paid – in terms of reversing the balance of trade deficit such that
exports exceeded imports at some future date – was deferred. This, however,
did not mean that during the period under consideration the Polish economy
was temporarily free of tensions.

Usually the strains engendered by acceleration of development are
discussed in the theory of growth on the assumption of balanced foreign
trade (Kalecki, 1972, ch. 6): most of the bottlenecks tend to converge on
foreign trade which provides a unique opportunity to overcome domestic
difficulties in production of raw materials, equipment and agricultural
produce, but at the cost of an increased input/output ratio as a rule, due to
the need to find extra exports to cover the swelling import requirements (the
same applies to special promotion of import-substituting domestic production). Foreign credits obviously alleviate the situation, and make it in some
sense theoretically indefinite, because in order to detect whether an economy is or is not strained one has to consider concrete quantitative
relationships between external resources and the demand for them. This
aspect is sometimes overlooked, with discussions concentrating mainly on
the strains which present-day credits may cause in the future when the
burden of paying off and servicing the debts will grow.

In the coming years Poland will have to cope with the latter kind of
problems; but already in the 1971–1975 quinquennium overall market
disequilibria were felt painfully, and to an increasing extent as time went by.
There were several reasons for this.

To begin with, the Polish economic realities during the period under
consideration seemed not to have been determined by a thoroughly worked
out medium-term plan, in which strains and bottlenecks were well defined

and credits used in order to overcome them, but rather by a set of decisions in the course of and under the direct influence of events – as witnessed by the enormous divergence between the planned and actual rates and proportions of development, mentioned earlier; there has been an attempt to rationalize this by introducing the concept of the so-called 'open plan'. Apart from questions of internal consistency of the 'open plan' set of measures (we do not have enough material to examine this, and in any case it would go beyond the scale of this chapter), the increase in borrowing abroad must have been to a considerable degree a response to already growing bottlenecks, to failure to secure enough production for export and to find outlets corresponding to needs in terms of prices and currency areas, etc. It is clear that such situations must have closely resembled the struggle to keep trade in balance: in this case it was the constant pressure to widen the gap even more which had to be resisted or covered the hard way. Two additional factors aggravated the position in foreign economic relations: first, the change in terms of trade in 1973–1974 and, second, the rising demands for participation in Soviet raw materials investment.

As for the first, the very favourable trend of change in Polish terms of trade came to an end in 1973, when the index was 97.1 compared with the previous year's level; in 1974 and in 1975, the terms of trade remained practically stable (99.5 and 100.2 compared with the preceding year). On the whole, Poland withstood well the world market price upheaval of 1973 –1974 and the subsequent change in the principles of pricing within the CMEA; being a rather large exporter of coal and some other primary products, and making a determined effort to increase her export volume in these fields, Poland fared much better than most East European countries. The Polish terms of trade never fell below the 1970 level: in the worst year, 1974, the index (1970 = 100) was over 102. However, as in many other areas, the leadership took the initial favourable trend for granted, and was ill prepared even for a small reversal of fortunes.

The second factor – participation in some common investment projects on Soviet territory, principally in the fields of energy resources and other primary products and transport infrastructure – involved shipments of investment goods with payment (mostly in supplies of the products in question) deferred at least until the beginning of utilization of the capacities created. This is probably the most important single cause of the rather extraordinary swing in the Polish–Soviet balance of trade. Usually, as noted earlier, Poland had a negative trade balance, offset by invisible export charges, primarily for transit transport. For the five-year period 1966–1970 the cumulative negative balance was about 230 million dollars. The 1971– 1975 period, as also noted earlier, brought a switch in the other direction, rendering the cumulative Polish trade balance with the USSR positive (approximately 130 million dollars); this rather drastic change occurred in 1972 (+230 million dollars) and in 1973 (+150 million dollars). It was, of course, possible that some other factors played a part here: payment of debts incurred earlier, including perhaps the short-term emergency loan much spoken of after the December 1970 events; however, all this by itself would hardly suffice as an explanation (*Rocznik* . . ., 1970, ch. XIV; 1976, ch. XVI)[11].

On the domestic side – more closely interrelated with foreign trade than ever before – rapid acceleration on a broad front in the 'open plan' manner must have created a number of strains and disproportions. It was therefore rather surprising when at the VII congress in December 1975 one did not hear the usual complaints about deficiencies in the investment processes, most plausible when such a great number of new projects was undertaken during a short time span; on the contrary, a note of full satisfaction was included in the Congress report as far as the progress of investment projects was concerned: 'Substantial progress was achieved in the process of investment. The investment cycle [gestation period] was shortened. In 1975 the average investment cycle was 16 months shorter than in 1970 (*VII Zjad* . . ., 1975, p. 13). It could well be that relative progress was achieved, especially in view of the increased number of turnkey projects carried out by foreign firms; later statements on the topic[12] would point, however, to the then undisputedly reigning official optimism as largely responsible for these cheerful assessments. The situation in energy production was depicted in similarly rosy colours at the Congress, and next year a virtual crisis was revealed. The only sector where serious lags were acknowledged was transport. Even agriculture, despite the clearly ominous signs (15% drop in grain production compared with 1974, decline in the number of pigs, etc., later blamed on bad weather conditions) received its portion of praise, the sole negative phenomenon being the increase in world market prices of feed grain.

The sharp rise in consumer demand due to factors described above was becoming increasingly difficult to match on the supply side. The consumer market in post-war Poland was actually never in equilibrium, and certainly not at the outset of the Gierek era. Massive growth of nominal wages, peasant incomes and money benefits, while the share of accumulation in national income was pushed up to a level unknown in the past, posed an enormous problem which could not be fully satisfactorily solved. It seems almost impossible to measure aggregate levels of disequilibrium, but some indications can be gained from comparing the rate of growth of monetary incomes of the population on the one hand and that of retail sales on the other. Over the 1966–1970 period the former increased by 45% and the latter by 41.4% in current prices and by 36.2% in constant prices; over the 1971–1975 period the former increased by 90% and the latter by 77.9% in current prices and by 60.5% in constant prices (*Rocznik* . . ., 1976, table 2(122) and pp. XLVI–XLVII)[13]. The difference is visible, and can be taken as a very general indication of worsening of the overall market equilibrium, although it can also be argued that some part of the augmented excess money was legitimately (at the higher level of income) absorbed by increased voluntary savings).

However, aggregate figures never tell the main story of market disequilibria in a 'shortage economy', and they seem to have been particularly unsuitable in the Polish conditions during the second part of the 1971–1975 period, when 'partial disequilibria' on most important consumer markets made themselves forcefully felt. This was the case with the 'strategically important' (as frequently described by Polish economists) meat market: despite reported substantial increases in the retail trade network (11.5% annual rate of growth over the 1971–1975 period, in physical terms), shortages were becoming increasingly acute, and sometimes simply desperate. To a lesser extent this applied to the market for food and industrial consumer goods in general; it was periodically disrupted and continuously plagued by growing difficulties in maintaining the normal level of supply to the shops. The repeated pledge to keep the prices of staple food frozen made matters worse as time went by, but the government was politically incapable of facing up to the realities of life, at least not in an open form (disguised price rises, including rises for foodstuffs, were going on all the time, among other things by changing the product mix); when it finally decided to act in June 1976, the measures were long overdue, too steep, and presented in a most clumsy way – with the well-known result of mass workers' riots forcing the government to retreat within 24 hours.

The role of pegging the prices of basic foodstuffs ought not, however, to be exaggerated. It is true that with a different price pattern (relatively dearer food, relatively cheaper industrial consumer goods) one could expect less pressure from the growing incomes on the food market, particularly from the higher income groups with very respectable, if not even excessive levels of food consumption. But, first, relative prices are by no means the only factor influencing the structure of demand, especially in a Soviet-type economy, where availability of truly desirable goods is usually crucial; second – and not unconnected with the inability to improve supply sufficiently – prices of industrial consumer goods and services rose quite substantially over the years 1971–1975, contributing quite a lot to the disincentives to substitute industrial consumer goods and services for food in the increment in consumption[14]. During the first couple of years of the Gierek regime, the gaps in the capacity of the domestic consumer goods industry to satisfy the buyer and to absorb the rising purchasing power were filled to some degree by increased imports, including imports from the West which were highly attractive for Polish shoppers and gave returns in terms of the złoty–dollar ratio some five times higher than the average purchasing power parity. Later on, with growing strains in foreign trade, imports of this kind were severely restricted, and in some case net imports gave way to net exports despite acute shortages at home. For example, in 1971 28 million dollars worth of furniture was imported, in 1975 less than 18 million, and the overall net balance in furniture trade rose from +18 million in 1971 to +84 million in 1975; in 1972 3.8 million pairs of shoes were imported, in 1975 the figure was 2.4 million and the overall net export increased from 12.9 to 22.1 million pairs; imports of knitwear doubled in 1972 compared with 1970, but dropped below the 1970 level in 1975, etc. (*Rocznik . . .*, 1976, ch. XVI)[15].

The restrictions on consumer goods imports were, understandably enough, most drastic in the case of products from developed Western countries (except grain, for obvious reasons); items imported from the Third World were little affected and imports of cotton and cotton-substitute cloth, for example, showed a substantial increase in 1974 and 1975 (India and Pakistan being the main suppliers). An interesting phenomenon – illustrating the determination to use all means of obtaining foreign currency – was the extraordinarily rapid growth of the state valuta shops (mostly Pewex, formerly PeKao): sales in current prices (domestic, with the accounting exchange rate not given) soared from 1897 million złoty in 1970 to 15 054 million złoty in 1975, almost eight times higher. The proliferation of Pewex shops transformed them from a marginal into quite a significant factor in the overall trade turnover (and hence in Polish everyday life), which apparently led to growing misgivings, particularly as an increasing number of the most-sought goods was becoming available only (or mostly) for foreign currency[16]. Apart from its dubious image as a socialist device, the internal state foreign currency business was in a paradoxical way contributing to the increase of the 'unofficial' exchange rate between Western currencies and the złoty, despite all the inflationary losses of purchasing power in the West and several devaluations of the US dollar – the main 'standard unit' on the Polish 'currency market'; all this may be taken as an indirect indicator of the marginal złoty cost of a foreign currency unit in exports to the West.

Our discussion of tensions mounting during the 1971–1975 period should not make us forget the progress which has been achieved during these years. In the opinion of some economists tensions of this kind are the unavoidable price of strong economic growth. This writer does not accept these generalizations, and certainly not as exoneration for the inability to adopt a better balanced path of development after 1970 in Poland or to pursue consistent policies. The victims of the insufficient attention paid to the consequences of unbalanced policies once again included *economic reform*.

4.5 Economic reform

The heritage of the 1960s

Unlike the first attempts at the time of the 'Polish October' in 1956–1957, the post-December 1970 changes in the system of functioning of the Polish economy have not distinguished themselves with vision and originality which would put them in a separate category among East European countries. As for the conception of the changes, the Polish reform was an attempt to combine the elements of direct setting of binding targets and physical allocation of basic material resources with wide autonomy of economic units and somewhat greater reliance on a regulated market mechanism (parametric instruments) within the framework of central planning. Thus, the Polish variant differed in principle from the 1968 Hungarian reform and resembled in many important respects the ideas pursued in the GDR. This was even more pronounced with regard to the methods of implementation: the method of simultaneous introduction of all main instruments of the new system was rejected in favour of a gradualist approach which in the early 1970s was proclaimed as a general rule allegedly guaranteeing a smooth transition to well-tested devices fitted to the varying conditions of particular sectors.

This does not mean that the Polish reform attempt in the early 1970s was devoid of any interesting and indigenous solutions (the incentive schemes based on an ingeniously defined concept of value added deserve to be mentioned in this context), but the former pioneering spirit rather vanished. The main feature of the Polish scene in the late 1960s and in the 1970s was that endeavours to modify the system of functioning of the economy were undertaken, more often than not, in an atmosphere of political tension and instability which reflected – more strongly perhaps than elsewhere except Czechoslovakia in and around 1968 – the profound conflicts within the East European socialist system. The pressing need to raise the level of efficiency of the economy and the incapacity to meet this requirement probably had the most dramatic consequences here.

In order to understand the course and effects of the post-December developments better it seems necessary to return briefly to the late 1960s and to examine the assets and liabilities inherited by the Gierek regime in this field[17].

The 'second wave' of economic reforms (after the collapse of the previous one in the late 1950s) can be traced in Poland to the resolutions of the IV Party Congress (1964) and the IV plenary meeting of the Central Committee in July 1965. The first practical results of these general policy resolutions came in 1966, when the idea of transforming the *industrial associations* (created in 1958) into units of a more economic character was revived ('Decision . . .', 7 December 1966). According to the new rules industrial associations were to be linked with the central plan by a smaller number of direct orders (binding targets and constraints) and greater use of economic instruments; the associations in turn were to introduce similar changes into their relationship with their subordinate enterprises. The number of associations was also reduced (from 163 to 121), with a similar tendency with regard to the number of enterprises; this concentration trend was considered essential not only from the point of view of economies of scale in production and increased capacities in research and development work, but also from the point of view of facilitating central control under conditions of greater reliance on indirect methods. In this sense – as in most other East European countries – organizational concentration appeared as a counterpart to some devolution of economic decisions.

The second field in which things began to move was *foreign trade*. The general tendency was to bring closer together the industrial producers of exports and the monopolistic foreign trade corporations which were separated from industry both organizationally and economically (the so-called *Preisausgleich* – adjustment of internal prices in a way that makes the producing enterprise completely immune to external prices). The first timid step in the direction of getting industrial enterprises interested in the actual results of foreign sales of their products was the introduction in 1966 of an incentive scheme for 'export effectiveness' based on a separate system of accounting. Apart from general changes in both the principles of operation of the industrial associations and in foreign trade, special – more farreaching – solutions were to be tried out in four industrial branches ('economic experiments').

At one stage it seemed that this rather inconspicuous development would be arrested. One of the ideological sticks used to beat the students' and intellectuals' protest movement in March 1968 was the accusation of 'market deviation', accompanied by pseudo-populist attacks on the widening of income differentials purportedly aimed at by the 'marketeers'. Nevertheless, having achieved the immediate political objectives of the witch-hunting campaign, the party leadership resumed and even intensified the reforms somewhat, apparently acknowledging their indispensability for purely pragmatic reasons. The V Congress of PUWP (February 1969) proclaimed the slogan of 'transition to the stage of selective and intensive development of the economy' requiring a change in the economic system. The implementation of the 1971–1975 five-year plan, the draft of which envisaged modernization of a large part of industry and mobilization of the so-called intensive sources of growth (faster technological change as one of the main factors of increase in labour and capital-productivity, also economies of scale and better utilization of material-inputs, etc.), ought to have been started at the same time as a number of new elements were put into operation in the economic system. The main measures to be introduced from the beginning of 1971 concerned prices and incentives (and changes in the system of foreign trade which will be discussed later).

As for *prices*, from 1 January 1971 a reformed system of producer goods prices ought to have been put into operation. This included both actual changes in relative prices recalculated according to a new formula linking part of the mark-up with capital employed and new rules for price determination, with stronger emphasis on flexibility (maximum prices in some cases, contract prices for some categories of industrial equipment, more frequent adjustment of prices, etc.) and on controlled links between internal and foreign market prices. In retail turnover a drastic change of relative prices between food and industrial consumer goods was expected to bring about the desired shifts in the pattern of consumption; this change – kept secret, as usual, until the last moment – was to become the immediate reason for the December 1970 explosion.

As for *incentives*, which were to be implemented from January 1971 as well, the changes were supposed to become the backbone of the entire reform ('Nowy system . . .', 1970). The scheme intended to link the wage fund of an enterprise (and industrial association) with *improvement* of the results of its operation compared with those of the preceding year; for the salaried employees (white-collar) this link had to be direct, for the wage earners (blue-collar), indirect, i.e. in proportion to the increase for the first group. The indicators of results for the purpose of calculating the salary fund were to be divided into two groups: (a) *synthetic indicators* (reduction of production cost per unit, overall level of cost, rate of profit, overall profit – one of these, chosen individually for an association and its enterprises), and (b) *specific indicators* (rise in productivity of fixed assets, economically justified technical progress, increase in volume and profitability of exports, quality improvement, growth of labour productivity, saving in material input, fulfilment of subcontracting targets, reduction of the amount of defective products); out of this list no more than four specific indicators could be selected for a particular enterprise. In order to make them additive each indicator had been given a weight (the synthetic one 25% of the total, all specific ones together, 75%). The white-collar employees were to be entitled to an increase in their bonus fund in line with this 'weighted' assessment, out of which end-of-year bonuses could be paid above the basic (fixed) salaries. As for the wage earners, their wage fund was to increase at the same rate as the bonus fund with corrections for planned changes in employment and special targets directed at elimination of overmanning; the increases actually obtained in the wage fund were to be paid out at the end of the year as additions to normal wages earned according to the established wage rates. This system, described here in a most summary form, was extremely complicated because of the problem of comparability of indicators with preceding periods (and particularly with 1970, which was to serve as the base year), and of the need to accommodate numerous specific regulations governing wages, salaries and bonuses of various groups of employees and different categories of enterprises. The other, and main, source of unpopularity of the incentive scheme was the imposition of overall ceilings on the possible rises: theoretically, around 16% over the whole five-year period, in practice, even less, because the fund for 1970 was to remain almost frozen (the base had to be kept under strict control), and the increase due for 1971 was to be paid out only in the first quarter of 1972, when the annual results were in. By these not very sophisticated methods the party leadership intended to step up the modernization programme without unleashing inflationary forces. When on top of this (and after a decade of practically stagnating average real wages) came the increase in food prices, announced and implemented just before the peak Christmas shopping week, the explosive mixture became more than sufficient for the violent outburst of working-class discontent[18].

One of the first decisions taken after the toppling of the Gomulka regime was to abrogate the 1970 incentive scheme and – at least temporarily – to return to the old rules with some adjustments ('Decision . . .', 9 February 1971)[19]. It was stressed, however, that the new Gierek leadership intended not to stop but rather to go ahead with the reform, widening its scope and making it more consistent. In this connection some valuable disclosures about the genuine state of affairs in the system of functioning were made, including the fact that in 1970, despite formal retention of only six obligatory indicators for industrial enterprises, the real number of indicators which had in practice to be regarded by enterprises as obligatory reached in some cases 100 (Ząbkowicz, 1974, p. 25).

Unlike the incentive scheme (and, of course, the changes in retail prices), several other measures prepared under Gomulka for introduction from the beginning of 1971 were retained by the new leadership. This applied to the reform of prices of producer goods, and particularly to the reorganization of the foreign trade system, where two important moves were envisaged. The first was a break in the monopolistic position of the specialized foreign trade corporations (*centrale handlu zagranicznego*) subordinated to the Ministry of Foreign Trade; industrial ministries and associations could now get permission to organize their own foreign trade enterprises or to arrange their export business through a specialized foreign trade corporation on a commission basis. This led to a substantial increase in the direct involvement of industry in foreign trade, especially where manufacturing exports were concerned. Second – as in both Hungary and the GDR – the Preisausgleich system was to be in principle replaced by charging (import) or paying (export) the user or producer enterprises the so-called transaction price, i.e. the foreign currency price converted into złotys by a coefficient for the respective currency area (in principle three coefficients – for Western convertible currency, for the clearing area (mainly with developing countries) and for the ruble zone); the actual practice never corresponded fully to this simple rule, nevertheless the change did affect the financial interests of industrial enterprises and hence their behaviour with regard to foreign trade.

The post-December blueprint

With the incentive scheme abrogated, the above changes, as well as the general intention to make the system of functioning less rigid, to enhance the autonomy of enterprises, to strengthen the role of long- and medium term plans, etc., were left hanging in mid-air. In order to fit them into an overall concept, a special high-level commission was created as early as February 1971: the Party-Government Commission for Modernization of the System of Functioning of the Economy and the State[20]. It took the commission more than a year (until April 1972, well after the VI Congress of the party in December 1971) to present the general blueprint of the economic reform, or rather of the 'process of improvement of the system of planning and management' as it was officially put in a watered-down formulation. It was then that the idea of a comprehensive economic reform to be introduced simultaneously in all basic elements was finally rejected in favour of a strategy of gradual implementation by selected (and willing) 'large economic organizations' called 'pilot units' (*jednostki inicjujące*). The gradualist approach was to allow for careful preparation of changes and to combine some general rules with individualized solutions adapted to the conditions of particular sectors of economic activity. In 1973 27 'large economic organizations' (*WOG* in Polish) started to operate as 'pilot units'; at the end of 1974 their number grew to 62 (covering 44.7% of total industrial production and services sold, and 38.5% of total employment); and at the end of 1975 to 110 (67.7% of sales, 61.0% of employment) (*Rocznik . . .*, 1976, table 39 (242))[21].

The emphasis on the *WOG* reflected a continuation of the idea of organizational concentration referred to earlier. Three main types of *WOG* came to be distinguished. (1) *Industrial associations*, a more centralized organization, whose constituent parts (enterprises), although remaining separate legally and as accounting units, have limited economic autonomy; the association's headquarters has considerable powers, especially with regard to redistribution of resources within the association and in relations with the state (e.g. some financial flows from and to the budget are conducted centrally for the association as a whole). (2) *Associations of industrial enterprises*, where the main organizational unit is the enterprise (direct relations with the budget, possibility of direct investment borrowing from the banks, etc.), and central redistribution of resources by the headquarters is limited. Both (1) and (2) are constructed *horizontally*, i.e. they group enterprises of the same branch from the point of view of final product. (3) *Combines* – both *horizontal* and *vertical* (grouping of subsequent stages of production, from semi-fabricates, or even primary products, to the final product); in combines only the association is the legal and accounting unit, and the constituent parts have the status of *establishments* (*zakłady*).

The differences in the degree of integration notwithstanding, the state organs of economic administration (ministries) were supposed to act mainly through the *WOG*, leaving internal problems and forms of management more to the discretion of the *WOG* itself. The same was expected to apply to the planning process, which was to give wider scope to WOG plans and to rely much more on economic instruments in bringing these plans into line with the national ones. For this purpose both remuneration of employees and claims on development funds were to be linked to progress in economic performance, measured in 'synthetic' terms (see below). The interference of direct targets, constraints and physical allocation devices was to be reduced to a minimum. However, as in the GDR and other CMEA countries, except Hungary, the latter point was defined with the usual vagueness, leaving a lot to interpretation and practical expediency. According to the general rules the pilot units were under an obligation to honour the following targets and constraints, which could be imposed on them from above: deliveries of 'some' (specified) products to the domestic and foreign markets; minimum export quotas, subdivided by socialist and capitalist countries; currency quotas for imports from capitalist countries; quotas of material inputs allocated centrally (data on the number of these could not be found, but it hardly declined as far as main types of primary goods and semi-fabricates were concerned); investment of 'fundamental importance for the national economy'; research projects linked to the 'key problems' of the national research plan. It is impossible to ascertain how these potential targets and constraints were applied overall, because practice differed for different sectors and even individual pilot units; there could be no doubt, however, that the central organs made wider use of them towards the end of the 1971–1975 period. What was interesting was that in principle directive targets and constraints were to be 'disconnected' from the incentive schemes, apparently in order to avoid the old disease of hiding true capacities; in some pilot units only, the bonus for top management could be made conditional on fulfilment of a maximum of two directives.

It should be noticed that the list above did not include employment and wage fund, neither for various categories of employees nor in aggregate terms. This indeed was to be the main innovation of the Polish reform: the growth and structure of employment and the wage fund were left to the pilot unit (and the constituent enterprises) themselves and made dependent on progress achieved in terms of two indicators: *production added* (PA) and *profit* (P).

PA was regarded as the more important of the two (the main objective function), because the total remuneration fund (except bonuses for management personnel and some other strictly specified items) was made dependent on it. The theory behind the choice of PA instead of profit (as in Hungary in the original version; in the GDR the overall remuneration fund was determined in the plan) emphasized three main reasons: (1) PA as a value-added type of indicator reflected more closely the contribution to national income of labour employed in a particular unit; (2) it was less prone (than P) to fluctuation caused by changes in external conditions; (3) it promised to avoid the extremely complex and socially sensitive problem of proper weighting of the current and future interests of the staff in the distribution of profit (if P were used as the source of both additional wages and of development funds), especially difficult where no sufficient competitive pressure can be created. PA was defined basically as the difference between the value of sales and the value of material input (including inputs used for increase in inventories); however, to bring it closer to this contribution, several adjustments to the simple value-added concept had to be made: elimination of distortions caused by specific redistributive elements in prices (by subtraction of turnover tax, allowance for subsidies, etc.), inclusion of the net balance of contractual penalties paid and received, and – most important – subtraction of the repayment of investment credits (inclusive of interest). The latter element was intended to neutralize the impact on productivity of increased capital intensity (capital/labour ratio) caused by influx of resources from outside, and hence not achieved by the unit in question[22].

The wage fund (WF) was linked to PA by one of the following two formulae:

$$WF = WF_O \left(1 + R \frac{PA - PA_O}{PA_O}\right) \tag{1}$$

$$WF = PA \ \frac{WF_O}{PA_O} \ U \tag{2}$$

Where *PA* and *WF* respectively represent 'production-added' and 'wage fund' of the current year, whereas PA_O and WF_O stand for the same magnitude in the preceding year. *R* and *U* are coefficients given to the 'pilot unit' and the enterprise by the respective higher level of the economic hierarchy.

We shall not dwell on the consequences of applying one or other of these two formulae (the first – used much more widely, and therefore regarded as fundamental – linked *increments* in *WF* with *increments* in *PA*, the second operated on the basis of a changing share of *WF* in *PA*); the most important feature was the dissociation of the wage fund from annual planning targets, with the coefficients supposed to be fixed for three years (*R* in the 0.5–0.9 range, with 0.6 the most frequently used value; *U* in the 0.95–0.99 range, with 0.97 the most frequently used value). *WF* by means of formula (1) or (2) was the so-called disposable wage fund, constituting the upper limit of payments; if actual payments made throughout the year were less than *WF*, part of the surplus was to be kept as a reserve (divided between the pilot unit and the enterprise) and part distributed in various forms: if the reverse were true, the deficit would have to be covered from the reserves or (if both the enterprise and the pilot unit had insufficient reserves) from a special bank credit carrying a penal rate of interest. Where extra payments were made for at least two consecutive years (which also means sufficient reserves), the additions should be considered permanent and used for changes in wage rates.

The precise definition of profit (P) could not be conveniently derived from the above definition of PA because of some cost elements previously disregarded. Roughly, however, we could say that gross profit (P_g) would be equal to PA minus a 5% charge on the unit's own net assets, minus disposable wage fund, minus a 20% tax on wages paid. Net profit (P_n) equals P_g minus appropriations to the research fund and minus some additional repayments of credit. Part of P_n, determined by coefficient N, fixed by higher levels, again as a rule for three years, was to constitute the bonus fund for the personnel in management positions (excluded from benefiting from PA-related increases in WF); the first claim on the bonus fund (up to 10%) could go to the reserve, the rest, intended for payment of bonuses, was to be taxed on a progressive scale depending on the percentage growth over the preceding year. Thus, the rank and file was to be directly interested in growth of PA, with the management's self-interest geared to profitability, which in any case was considered too remote an objective for the rank and file; obviously, management could not remain indifferent to PA, if only for reasons of securing growth of wages, let alone for the directives upon which the bonuses could be made conditional. The general interest in profitability was to be upheld via the development fund, credited with the other part of P_n remaining after deduction of the bonus fund (in case this residuum exceeded a certain threshold it became subject to obligatory deposit reserves and taxation). Complicated rules governed the allocation of the development fund between pilot units as such and their constituent enterprises (different rules applied to different types of WOG), but the general idea was to permit relatively greater latitude in utilization (particularly for autonomous investment), and to gear an increased range of self-financing to both the wage – and the profit – aspects of the incentive scheme: both PA and P increased when development needs were self-financed to a higher degree (lower deductions for repayment of credits with interest).

A special form of interdependence was introduced between the value of exports to the West and the value of import entitlement from that area for the pilot unit in question (the so-called coefficient D); this was applied, however, to a limited number of pilot units only, for obvious reasons of the lack of the necessary correspondence between import needs and export capabilities of particular units.

The definition of PA and P established quite a strong link with the kind of market conditions faced by the enterprises. The value of sales (gross revenue) was to be measured as a rule in *current selling prices* (and not in 'factory prices' insulated from selling prices by turnover tax fixed as a difference in absolute terms); only within the pilot unit could a system of differentiated accounting prices be introduced. The value of export sales and imported inputs (except basic raw materials) was to be determined in most cases by the transaction prices. The rules for price determination had also been changed, most importantly concerning the degree of flexibility and of adjustment to market conditions[23]. General managers of associations have acquired the right to fix prices for internal turnover and for some other products (specified by the State Price Commission and according to established rules); many prices were fixed as maximum prices, i.e. with pilot units having the right to reduce them; prices of new or 'especially attractive' commodities could be determined by the producers in agreement with the purchaser (trade organization), in practice on a 'what the market would bear' basis for two years. The new guide lines emphasized much more strongly than before the need to consider utility substitution as a factor in determining price relativities, closer scrutiny of foreign prices of similar products, etc. In order to make producers more responsive to market conditions a gradual change was envisaged from the difference principle in turnover tax to rates expressed as a percentage of the selling price. The tendency to lift the role of the market found its reflection also in the regulation that comparability of PA and P from year to year (of fundamental importance in an increment-based system of incentives!) should be deemed unaffected by price changes, except in drastic cases.

It might be added that some of the regulations applied to pilot units were extended to all industry, for instance the bonus scheme for management personnel (from 1973). Efforts were also made to adjust the methods of central planning and information flows (including reports on results) to the new rules for pilot units. Some organizational changes in the banking system were carried out (rather tending to concentrate banking institutions). No general assessment could be made of the degree to which these adjustments succeeded in alleviating the inevitable conflict between partial changes and the old overall framework. From the sources mentioned one could sense that the pressure of direct target planning, imposed limits, physical allocation, etc. was felt from the very beginning and resulted in significant discrepancies between the postulated and the actual set of rules under which the pilot units had to operate.

The setback

As in other East European countries, the discrepancy between postulated and actual rules tended to be resolved in Poland by, at least partial, retreat. Although the figures referred to earlier indicated a rather fast expansion of the scope of operation of pilot units, this was accompanied as early as 1974, and particularly later, by a number of measures restricting the actual application of, or simply withdrawing, some basic elements of the new rules.

The first area of retreat was the celebrated integration of foreign trade and domestic operations: in 1974 some sort of 'balancing account' system was reintroduced for the pilot units in the chemical industry; from 1 January 1975 an extra tax on all export earnings (defined as the difference between the transaction price and the domestic selling price) was levied, cancelling out 85% of earnings due to the foreign price received. Blanket authorization of the central organs to impose direct quotas of products for export to particular markets came to be used on a wide scale, together with growing restrictions on imports (including practical cancellation of the entitlement to a foreign currency share of export earnings); direct targets and limits were again applied on a short-term basis – annual and shorter (quarterly, monthly). In December 1975 most elements of the old system of foreign trade planning were reintroduced, separating among other things the yardsticks of plan fulfilment in foreign trade operations (in foreign units of account) from those of production for export (in domestic prices). These measures were to a large extent motivated by the new situation in foreign trade after the 1973 upheaval on world markets and accelerating inflation; however, on that score, as was shown earlier, the Polish economy was affected relatively less than other East European countries, and other methods of dealing with adverse phenomena could have been contemplated (e.g. adjustment of the exchange coefficients).

Towards the end of 1974 the basic tenets of the incentive schemes became affected by corrective measures: pilot units and enterprises were judged to have accumulated excessive reserves of wage funds and were therefore subjected to additional obligatory transfers into 'ministerial reserves' unknown in the initial scheme and without any specific commitments as to the way or time of return (they were simply blocked pending the government's decision on general wage levels). In fact, pilot units were not accused of excessive wage payments in relation to their production effects measured in *PA*; on the contrary, all sources, including the report of the Central Committee to the VII Party Congress in December 1975, seemed rather pleased with the reported results. What happened was in the first place the rapid development of overall disequilibria mentioned earlier, which (1) made unexpectedly large increases in wage fund excessive even if they were within the rules, (2) opened up larger possibilities of benefiting from relaxation of the price code and planning of product mix than anticipated, (3) caused acute shortages of some materials and labour. The latter aspect had particularly disastrous consequences for the pilot units; first, they increased employment at a higher rate than industry as a whole (this was within their rights and means, and it was too early to expect any results of labour-saving investment) and were subjected to a special tax on incremental manpower (as part of the transfers mentioned above; the rate per person employed above the preceding year's average was 20 000 złotys, at that time around 50% of the average industrial wage); second, the pilot units were not exempted from a whole range of hastily imposed general restrictions, such as limits on various categories of workers, an embargo on new entrants, a campaign on 'stocktaking' of manpower reserves (April, 1975), etc.

Similar developments – undermining the new 'rules of the game' for the pilot units – took place in the field of investment. The principle of full devolution to the pilot units (or even individual enterprises in type 2 *WOG*) of decisions concerning investment for replacement and modernization – as distinct from 'developmental investment' comprising the main bulk of the total under direct central control – was hardly implemented from the very beginning, notwithstanding the availability of funds out of retained profits. Nevertheless some autonomous links between funds and pilot units' investment apparently occurred in 1974, and they immediately came to be considered disruptive. From 1975 a rigid classification of investment was introduced barring the pilot units from any autonomous investment construction work. Even more damaging to the new scheme was the provision (again from the beginning of 1975, i.e. after barely two years of operation of the first pilot units!) that when funds accumulated according to the pilot units' rules were considered (by central bodies, obviously) excessive for the units' investment needs, the 'surplus' could be used to finance central investment projects; the bank (or the budget in the case of investment in infrastructure and in services) simply reduced correspondingly the amount allocated from central sources. Another effective restriction of autonomous investment was the necessity to get physical allocation orders for most materials and equipment; with the rising overheating of the economy, these were increasingly difficult to come by, especially as the list of so-called 'priority projects' supposed to enjoy privileged status in allocation of inputs grew longer (22% of the total value of investment was under this heading in 1974, by itself a sign of the scale of disequilibrium). Finally, in 1975 a total ban on starts of new projects was announced, which, of course, did not result in practice in a genuine halt of new investment but did result in subjecting all new projects to detailed government scrutiny.

We cannot go into more detail here, but the general picture seems sufficiently clear: by the end of 1975 it was the organizational framework of *WOG* which remained in practice the main tangible element of the gradual reform; the essential features of the new rules of planning and steering the economy by parametric methods disappeared – openly or simply as a matter of fact – under the resurgent wave of familiar centralistic devices.

At the launching stage of the pilot units, a great deal of attention was devoted by the experts to the question of assessment of the solutions introduced and their variations; a whole set of yardsticks was proposed for comparing the performance of pilot units with 'ordinary' enterprises, for checking the validity of individual parameters and schemes, for determining the conditions and time sequence for extending the range of application of the new methods. It is, and always will be, very difficult to carry out such an

'audit' in a running economy, because no laboratory environment conform-
ing to the *ceteris paribus* clause can ever be created. However, in the Polish
case in the early 1970s the frustrating factors went far beyond the usual: the
'experiments' were denied any serious chance not only to prove (or
disprove) themselves, but even to be properly introduced. This was the
more ironic as one of the overriding ideas of the new rules of behaviour was
to replace the short-term scramble over indicators and resources by longer-
term normatives and incentives as necessary components of a planning
system with a broader perspective.

To a considerable degree the reform was undermined by the over-
expansionary policy of the Polish post-1970 leadership, which had to give in
to the pressure for higher incomes and did not want to reduce an
over-ambitious investment drive, but, on the contrary, stepped it up almost
to the last moment of the 1971–1975 quinquennium. As was emphasized
earlier, tensions became felt first in foreign trade (the relative deterioration
of the terms of trade in 1973–1974 was a secondary factor), spreading
rapidly despite massive borrowing which kept the economy going at a fast
pace but could not relieve the growing strains. It might well be that in such a
situation, when not only profit-conscious enterprises but the government
itself were most anxious to use the acute seller's market conditions for
skimming off purchasing power, the new rules of the game were beginning
to influence the overall equilibrium adversely. The most pertinent question
in this context is, however, whether this situation was inevitable? In the light
of our discussion in the first part of this chapter, an affirmative answer seems
hardly justified.

It could also be that the gradualist conception of reform contributed to its
setback. Firstly, partial and gradual introduction seemed to require less
conceptual and institutional preparation, which could have affected the
quality of the proposed solutions; secondly, the lack of coherence between
the new and old rules existing side by side in planning, allocation procedures, incentives, etc. must have been unavoidable; third, with the old
system by no means dismantled it was much easier to retreat at the first
hurdle, particularly with all the lingering political mistrust towards reform.
From this point of view the comparison between Poland and Hungary is
instructive and comes out in favour of the latter. The paradox of the Polish
situation around and after 1975 was that when the economy had to cope
with growing difficulties (among other things because it had to live more
within its own means) and desperately needed the ability to make better use
of resources, the economic mechanism found itself in a state of confusion.

As a matter of record, it ought to be said that both in analytical
discussions and in the practical implementation in the 1971–1975 period the
question of the interrelation between devolution of economic decision and
workers' self-management hardly occupied a place of prominence, if
mentioned at all. In any case, nothing changed in the actual position of the

moribund organs of self-management in industrial enterprises during the shortlived spell of the Polish economic reform in the first half of the 1970s.

Halfturn again

In the light of the illfated experience of the first half of the 1970s (this was at least the third failure of this kind) it might have been expected that economic reform would be abandoned for a long time, if not for good. This did not happen fully, however, which again showed how little else the government could offer as a remedy. It was clear before the end of 1975 that the overriding priority must be to bring the economy into at least some sort of equilibrium. At first, a set of purely restrictive measures of administrative character was applied, as was shown earlier (pp. 117–119). Furthermore, the failure to influence the pattern of demand by raising food prices in June 1976 intensified the administrative restrictions in many fields, including introduction of formal rationing of sugar, informal rationing of coal for the peasants, etc. The results of 1976 proved easily that, whatever the short-term effects of crude restrictions, they would not solve the real problem of restoring equilibrium: better utilization of capacity to increase exports and supplies for the domestic market. In March 1977 the government decided to revive the idea of special status for *WOG*, but not for all which had it before ('Resolution . . .', March 1977). The modified system was to apply to *WOG* subordinated to four ministries (engineering, chemical industry, heavy machinery, light industry) and only to very few beyond them. The main step back to the 1972 concept was to consist of reviving the link in *WOG* between wage fund and 'production added' (*PA*) by means of a coefficient with some degree of stability (fixed for 1977 and 1978, approximate for 1979 and 1980). The renewed attempt to 'extend the planning horizon' for enterprises, i.e. not to change the 'rules of the game' time and again and not to assess plan fulfilment over very short time spans was motivated first of all by the impediments to exports, which fared badly indeed under the harsh regime of 1975 (see above); more direct links between export performance and bonuses were also restored, as was the retention quota for foreign currency earned (albeit on a limited scale and mainly for autonomously decided imports which would result in export expansion). As far as decentralized investment out of development funds (part of net profit) was concerned, the strict central control introduced in practice in 1975 was somewhat relaxed: the government produced a list of types of investment projects, aimed at modernization of plants, which could be left to the discretion of the *WOG* and scrutinized by the banks from the viewpoint of rapid recoupment of outlays.

As can be seen, the re-reform moves of 1977 have been in themselves very cautious. But even these limited measures were circumscribed by a number of qualifications, and particularly by the new role assigned to the industrial ministries[24]. The ministry now receives strictly planned indicators concerning production and – most important – the wage fund; the coefficients for *WOG* are to be fixed *by the ministry* within the framework of its plan. In the case of unpredicted opportunities to increase market production (i.e. goods saleable to households) at the cost of additional wage outlays, the ministry may seek to conclude a special 'contract' with the Planning Commission specifying the degree of overfulfilment of the plan on either side. Apart from this, the system of progressive 'liabilities' (the term taxation was officially avoided) deducted from enterprises and *WOG* in relation to increases in the wage fund above a certain rate is also to be administered by the ministry, which has to fix the ceilings and the rates and to accumulate the proceeds in the ministerial reserve; this reserve is to be used for unforeseen wage outlays in the future or (after some time) even for increasing wage rates (in the latter case, however, only on approval by higher authorities).

At the same time as the status of the ministries was enhanced, some of them were split into smaller ones: the ministry of heavy industry was divided into the ministry of the iron and steel industry and the ministry of heavy and agricultural machinery, the ministry of mining and power was split into the ministry of mining and the ministry of power generation and atomic energy and a new ministry of materials was created, obviously reflecting the task of tightening up central balancing and physical allocation of resources. The number of deputy prime ministers, responsible for broadly defined sectors of governmental activity ('super-ministers') increased as well, exceeding the number during the Stalinist period (nine then, ten now); the economic department of the Central Committee of the party was also split into three departments. All this is a clear indication of increased reliance on administrative direction and supervision of the economy, rather incompatible with genuine autonomy of enterprises and associations. Against this background the sudden publicity given to workers' self-management[25] was clearly for propaganda purposes in a search for more effective methods of exhortation to raise productivity as well as to arrest the growth of absenteeism and the widely reported fall in quality of production.

By mid-1977 the prospects of a relevant improvement of the system of functioning of the economy looked more remote than before 1975: the political will to prepare a comprehensive and consistent reform package was nowhere in sight, and conditions for piecemeal and gradual changes were worse than ever since the economy had lost its previous momentum but had not found the badly needed balance.

4.6 1976–1980: Plans and results

The starting point

At the outset of the second half of the 1970s the social pressures engendered by the 1970 workers' revolt had not only persisted but apparently even increased. Any hopes the party leadership might have cherished with regard to political gains from the relatively better performance compared with that of Gomulka's team were shattered by the forceful rejection of the attempted increase in food prices in June 1976. In some paradoxical sense, despite a much less dramatic course of events, the political depth of this defeat of the Gierek regime could be considered comparable with that of Gomulka's. True, the scope of the attempted increase in food prices was extremely high (39% overall against 16–22% in 1970: the highest single increase in meat prices proposed in 1970 was 36%, whereas in 1976 meat prices were to go up by 69% on average, and the price of sugar was almost to double). In most other respects, however, the purely economic side of the intended measures could have seemed more acceptable for the population: the increase came after a period of relatively fast growth of real earnings and social benefits in a dynamic economy, whereas the 1970 attempt followed years of stagnation and deterioration in the standard of living; compensation was offered not in the dubious form of some cuts in prices of industrial products but in cash supplements to wages, family benefits and pensions[26]. Nevertheless, the government policies were rejected outright, in a most determined manner, and only the immediate retreat saved Poland from a repetition of the 1970 bloodbath. Moreover, this time the government faced the threat of some sort of alliance between the workers, the dissident intellectuals and the Catholic Church; this undoubtedly accounted for further forced retreats both on the economic side (from plans to reintroduce a less steep price increase to practical abandonment of the whole idea at least for two years) and on the political one (from the noisy campaign against 'wreckers and hooligans', followed by a number of stiff prison sentences, to final release of all those detained).

Any sober analysis of the situation must have led to the conclusion that the political credit of the Gierek leadership was low, and that – even in the existing international conditions – the first commandment for a government striving to secure a workable level of stability must be to 'deliver the goods', i.e. to attain a palpable improvement in the material wellbeing of the population. In other words, the message of 1976 remained by and large the same as in 1971; the objective circumstances, both economic and political, were, however, much less favourable.

Leaving aside short-term factors which, unlike in 1971–1973 (see sections 4.2 and 4.3) adversely affected the 1975–1977 economic performance, the medium-term prospects for 1976–1980 as a whole held out considerable difficulties. With reference to the economic reform discussed above one could hardly expect a substantial boost to 'x-efficiency' from this quarter; at the same time the substitution of additional labour for insufficient productivity and fluctuations in material supply became harder both because of a generally lower increase in manpower (during 1971–1975 the increment in the labour force of the national economy was 1.8 million, for 1976–1980 it was estimated at 1.1 million) and because of changes in distribution (for the first time an absolute increase in employment in individual agriculture was envisaged) which were expected to leave the state and cooperative sectors with increments only one-third of those in the preceding quinquennium (0.6 million compared with the whole 1.8 million)[27]. However, the most formidable obstacles to restoration of equilibrium with concomitant growth of real incomes had come obviously from the *external side of the balance*: the 1971–1975 pattern, with disposable growing faster than produced national income thanks to the utilization of currency reserves and a huge influx of resources from abroad, was to be sharply reversed in 1976–1980. The plan postulated an average annual rate of growth for 'national income distributed' of 4.8%, whereas the 'national income produced' was to grow by 7–7.3% per year (the corresponding figures for 1971–1975 were 12% against 9.8%). This meant that annual increments of disposable national income in the 1976–1980 quinquennium were to be two-and-a-half times smaller in percentage terms than during the preceding one. Of the roughly 7 percentage points slower growth of disposable national income (12 minus 4.8) less than a half (3.4) was to come from the slowing down of the rate of growth of national income produced, the other – larger – part was accounted for by much higher growth of exports (to 175% of the 1975 level over the whole five-year period) than imports (125.8%). However, this did not mean that in absolute terms Poland's trade was to show a surplus over the period: the cumulative exports figure was to reach 71 billion US dollars (236 billion 'valuta złoty' at the accounting rate of 0.301 dollars to 1 'valuta złoty') against 73 billion dollars of imports (242.5 billion 'valuta złoty'); the idea was to run diminishing trade deficits in the first three years and then to attain a small surplus in the last two. This could be regarded as a modest start to the repayment of debts towards the end of the quinquennium (in the first part the indebtedness would go on growing albeit at a slower rate), if it were not for the following qualifications: (1) the published foreign trade plan figures were not disaggregated between the CMEA countries and the West, where the entire debt burden was concentrated; (2) an increasing part of any surplus in trade with the West would be needed just to service the debt (by 1976 it was estimated that around 25% of Polish exports to the West was needed for this purpose); (3) Polish participation in joint investments might have required a trade surplus on balance. Of course, some offsetting factors had to be taken into account (invisibles) but on the whole the severity of resource constraints on output for domestic use was clear.

The 1976–1980 plan

Small wonder, therefore, that the 1976–1980 five-year plan took almost as long to prepare as the previous one, despite the fact that this time there was no change in political leadership: the 'guidelines' were published in the autumn of 1975 and adopted at the VII Congress of the PUWP in December 1975, but the final version – very prudent as far as the published details were concerned – was adopted only a year later (V Plenum of the Central Committee and a hasty acceptance by the Sejm in December 1976). The main problem was the extent of the rather obvious 'manoeuvre' (this was the term used) to *halt the investment drive* in order to save a larger slice of the smaller cake for consumption: the VII Congress even went as far as almost freezing investment outlays at the 1975 level, the final version had to be less radical (43% increase over the five-year period compared with the 1971–1975 quinquennium), but still the average annual increase was to be merely 2.3% against 18.3% in 1971–1975 (in constant 1971 prices). As a result the share of net investment (in fixed capital) in national income was to fall from 31.7% in 1975 to 26–27% towards the end of the period; assuming a stable share of increase in inventories (around 6%), total accumulation was expected to fall from almost 38% in 1975 to 32–33% in 1980; the crudely estimated share of gross investment in gross national income showed a similar decline. Taking into account that 25–30% of the total investment bill had to be directed to the continuation of projects started earlier, the planned expansion in new projects was relatively modest. This shift in final distribution of national income and the stronger emphasis on exports were reflected in the planned relative rates of growth of the three aggregate components of industrial end-product: for sales to the population ('market production') the 1980 index (1975 = 100) had been fixed at 157 (9.3% compound annual rate), for exports – 186 (13.2% compound annual rate) and for investment plus increase in inventories – 136.5 (6.3% compound annual rate).

The main indicators of the 1976–1980 plan compared with the 1971–1975 official record appear as in *Table 4.4*. A surprising feature of the plan was that it insisted on an almost stable index of the cost of living: the average nominal wage was to rise by 25% by 1980, which – with an increase in real wages by 16–18% over the same period – made the expected rise in the cost of living only 6–8% for five years or 1.2–1.5% annually! This might have meant either that the government had completely abandoned the idea of an open price increase in the course of the quinquennium, or (more probably) that it did not want to show its cards in advance, and the effects on both sides would be treated as 'extras'. The formula for peasant incomes for 'consumption and non-productive investment (housing)' was that they ought to grow at the same rate.

The *structure of supply* to meet the planned increase in the purchasing power of the population revealed severe strains from the very outset. As was to be expected, the emphasis was on increasing the share of industrial consumer goods at the expense of food; however, taking into consideration the imbalance on the official food market in 1975–1976 the plan stipulated a rather substantial increase in food supplies to the shops (40% in 1980

Table 4.4 *The 1976–1980 plan*

| | Annual average rates of growth | |
	1971–1975 (Actual)	1976–1980 (Plan)
National income produced	9.8	7–7.3
National income distributed	12.1	4.8
Real wage per employee	7.2	3–3.4
Employment in the national economy	2.3	1.2
Gross investment in fixed assets	18.3	2.3
Industrial production	10.4	8.2–8.5
Gross agricultural production	3.6	3.0–3.5
Export	10.7	11.8
Imports	15.2	4.7

Note: All data relate to the last year of the preceding quinquennium
(1970 and 1975); values in constant prices.

Sources: For 1971–1975, *Polish Statistical Yearbook*, 1976; for 1976–1980
plan, *Gospodarka Planowa*, No. 2/1977; *Polityka*, 51/1976 (T.
Checinski, 'Priorytety pięciolatki' (The Priorities of the
Five-Year Plan).

compared with 1975, presumably at constant prices, but this was nowhere
indicated clearly). Such real growth presented formidable problems from the
point of view of agricultural production (we shall have something to say
about this below), but, even so, it hardly promised to remove the main
thorn of the Polish consumer market, namely the shortage of meat; on this
account the plan was modest in the extreme, envisaging a mere 6.7%
increase in average per head consumption of meat, poultry and meat
products (from 70.3 kg in 1975 to 75 kg in 1980). This assumed a coefficient
of income elasticity of demand for meat of less than 0.4 (on a formal basis,
because there is no way to gauge the degree of unsatisfied demand in 1975)
whereas over the last twenty years it had never fallen below 1. Thus at the
very outset the plan pointed to a painful bottleneck.

Another persistent source of social dissatisfaction in Poland is *housing*.
The plan was to increase the number of dwellings 'put to use' by 40% (on a
1976–1980 to 1971–1975 comparison) and to reach a seemingly respectable
indicator of 10 new dwellings per 1000 inhabitants by 1980. However, even
the planned figures hardly meant the easing of the acute shortage of housing
because of the huge backlog of unsatisfied demand, which was to go on
growing until the very end of the 1976–1980 quinquennium, when the ratio
of dwellings 'put to use' to the number of new families (marriages), which
stood at below 0.8 in 1975, was expected to reach 1 (and even this had
probably not accounted for natural wastage – about 15% of the number of
dwellings 'put to use' in 1976). It was not surprising therfore that a special
plan was announced in 1977 to tackle the problem after 1980[28].

Naturally, the question arose whether the 1976–1980 plan, however modest compared with the overall official record of the preceding quinquennium, was realistic enough. One of the most obvious worries, both from the point of view of domestic consumption and of the balance of trade, was *agriculture*.

As noted in sections 4.2 and 4.3, agricultural production began to falter towards the end of the 1971–1975 period, and in 1975 its value (in constant prices) dropped below the 1974 level; particularly significant was the drop in crop production (both grains and potatoes), which made a strong impact on the number of livestock in the subsequent year: the number of cattle counted in the June 1976 census was 3% lower and the number of pigs (the main source of meat in Poland) 12% lower than a year earlier; in 1976 meat production in physical terms went down compared with 1975 by over 5%, and meat purchases by the state from the producers by almost 14%. There was a further decline in 1976, somehow arrested in the second half of 1977. Bearing in mind the shortages in domestic food supply and the rising burden of foreign trade[29], this was hardly an auspicious start to the plan which called for a 3.7–4.2% annual growth of crop production and 2.5–3.0% for animal production (the difference was intended to make up for the earlier drop in crop production and to provide for a more secure fodder base).

The adversities in agriculture were officially blamed on the weather; the role of this factor could not be denied but, as we have indicated, there was an ominous correlation between renewed pressure on private peasant farms and deteriorating production results. It was interesting to note that this pressure had clearly relented after the June 1976 workers' revolt against the increase in food prices[30]. Thus it would seem that when confronted with grave immediate threats the government resorted – as in the past – to more pragmatic policies. Whether this alone will suffice is hard to say, however, because in the long run some basic questions are involved. For example, the present structure of Polish farming is quite an obstacle to a major rise in efficiency: in 1975 81% of the total sown area was still owned by 3 060 000 individual rural households; even leaving aside the dwarf owners (those with less than 2 hectares, 27% of the total number) for the majority of whom the main source of income is outside agriculture, out of the remaining groups over 60% hold farms of less than 7 hectares total area. According to the communist 'conventional wisdom' the only avenue to agricultural progress is to amalgamate land in state farms and all kinds of cooperative farming; this is regarded by many today as gross and harmful over-simplification. It is clear, however, that economically sound development of family farming would require not only cessation of harassment of private peasants willing to expand, but a serious and *sustained* positive effort to assure profitability, to allow some private concentration of land, and encourage capital investment, to promote substantial improvements in the way of life (economic, social and cultural) and to create an overall favourable climate for choosing farming as a career by young people (Kozlowski, 1977). Needless to say, such a policy would require a revision of the still-reigning ideology; without it the post-June 1976 policy had to be regarded as merely short-term expediency with diminishing returns even in the course of its duration (people's behaviour is determined by experience, after all) and greater setbacks when the next swing comes. Under these conditions no relief could be expected for the economy from the side of agriculture.

As for *overall industrial growth*, the 1976–1980 plan was by no means overambitious – on the contrary, some analysts argued that the considerable rejuvenation of the vastly expanded productive apparatus (by 1980 72% consisted of post-1970 assets, with a substantial share of up-to-date machinery of Western provenance) should warrant a higher rate of productivity than planned (around 7.5% annually) (Gomulka . . ., note 4). In this respect the plan for industry seemed to contain some reserves. However, from the very beginning the main problem was not the overall growth of industrial production (although this should not be dismissed) but its impact on domestic equilibrium and on the balance of payments. The first aspect was linked with the ability of industry to turn out an appropriate product mix and to maintain the necessary balance between real increments to market supply and the rise in wages pressing on the demand side; the backpedalling in economic reforms might have had adverse consequences here, notwithstanding the intention to curb excessive wage payments by reintroduction of direct controls. As for the second aspect, the tough aggregate export objectives presented an especially difficult task for industry (and within industry for general and electrical engineering), whose export performance had to be well above the average to compensate for the declining share of agricultural produce and raw materials. In view of the continuing slack in Western demand for industrial imports and the rather slim prospects for a steep upturn, the task of accelerating the growth of Polish industrial exports to the West sharply seemed particularly formidable, despite the fact that some subcontracting agreements for exports were due to come into operation. Polish exports to the West were to grow at an annual rate of 16% in constant prices (against the 11.8% overall rate of growth of exports) which in the circumstances looked hardly realistic, with sharply negative consequences for the balance of payments and for the prospects of reducing the burden of debt.

The results and prospects

At the time of completing this study (May 1980) obviously no definitive results of the 1976–1980 quinquennium could be at hand. None the less the data for the 1976–1979 period plus information on the plan for 1980 are basically sufficient for a preliminary assessment; the VIII Congress of the Polish United Workers' Party (February 1980) has even provided an outline of the plan for 1981–1985, thus enabling us to put the results of the 1971–1980 decade in a broader perspective.

Sceptical attitudes to the viability of the 1976–1980 plan have proved to be more than justified. What was termed by the Polish leadership as an 'economic manoeuvre' intended to restore equilibrium while maintaining (even if somewhat reduced) the momentum of the economy turned into full-fledged and by no means orderly *retreat*.

This could be witnessed, first of all, in the area of *investment policy*. Not only did the idea of a smooth curve of investment growth, free of sudden fluctuations, which was strongly emphasized at the beginning of the 1970s, have to be abandoned, but even the objective of the 1976–1980 plan to reduce substantially the rate while maintaining at least some *increase* in investment proved unattainable. Gross investment in the national economy (in constant prices) practically stagnated in 1977 and 1978, and in 1979 dropped sharply, by 8% as compared with the preceding year; the plan for 1980 envisaged a further drop of 8%, which should leave the investment level in 1980 at approximately 92% of that in 1975[31]. The share of accumulation (net investment plus increase in stocks) dropped from over 35% of national income in 1975 to an estimated 26% in 1979, and – assuming that the plan were fulfilled – to 23% in 1980. By itself such a reduction of the burden of accumulation would be welcomed from the point of view of consumption; however, a U-turn of this magnitude must have caused great losses in unfinished projects, unutilized equipment (frequently imported for scarce foreign currency) and deeper imbalances between different sectors of the economy. Cuts 'on the run' in the late 1970s appeared as a sort of counterpart to the massive increases 'on the run' a few years earlier (the ill-fated 'open plan' discussed in section 4.4); they could, however, hardly provide compensation in terms of reduced tensions. Bottlenecks began to accumulate on a large scale, particularly as the tendency (usual in such cases) to shelter the immediate gains in production resulted in serious underinvestment in some infrastructural sectors (transport and electricity generation in the first instance). The former belonged to the few sectors with absolute reduction in investment outlays: by 1978 the overall level was only about 84% of 1975 (in constant prices) with the lion's share probably spent on the broad-gauge line from the Soviet border to the new steel-mill 'Katowice'. The electricity generating industry was still growing in terms of investment outlays, but at a reduced rate (2% only in 1978 compared with 1977). This has put both the electricity supply and transport capacity in a perilously overstrained situation, and when the 1978–1979 winter exceeded the average degree of severity, a real disaster struck, bringing the country almost to a standstill at the outset of 1979.

The realities of the reorientation in foreign trade policy proved perhaps even more painful. The increase in exports to the developed Western countries fell far below the objectives of the plan (even in current prices, let alone in real terms), and not only because of growing market difficulties but – and probably mainly – because of disappointing performance of the export sectors of the economy. This has led to a double setback: first, the balanced trade with the West envisaged for the last two years of the quinquennium (with even a small surplus) could not be achieved; second, whatever reduction in the trade deficit with the West has been attained has come predominantly through savage cuts in imports. The adverse impact of the latter on production turned out to be very severe: it has transpired that the 'import-led growth' of the first half of the 1970s was by no means due only to the import of investment goods (technology and 'know-how'), but to a considerable degree to the so-called 'current imports' of materials, semi-fabricates and spare parts which alleviated substantially the usual supply bottlenecks. Reduction, and in some cases simply stopping, of this kind of import brought about serious difficulties in utilization of already existing capacities. In this context one ought to mention the movement of the 'terms of trade': they deteriorated in 1977 in relation to the preceding years and did not recover in 1978–1979. This has been an additional factor in Poland's external economic problems; however, one should keep in mind that this was a reflection of the belated impact of world market prices on intra-CMEA prices (which concentrated the deterioration on the Eastern side of the balance), and – second – that the overall index of 'terms of trade' still remained favourable compared with 1970 (102.4 in 1978). As for the systemic factors, there were no changes which could have contributed to overcoming the mounting problems of the economy. The tendencies noted at the end of section 4.5 – towards administrative methods of management of state industry – have become stronger the greater the bottlenecks became and hence the striving for emergency measures. Some attempts at increasing flexibility were continued in the form of extension of the semi-private and private sector in small-scale trade and services (a number of state retail trade enterprises also received greater autonomy), but in the general framework of growing market disequilibria the results of this development were quite ambiguous; some observers even consider this as one of the factors contributing to the rapid spread of corruption throughout the economy.

With regard to agriculture, none of the problems mentioned at the end of the preceding section showed any clear signs of even the beginning of a solution. Socialized agriculture was further increasing its share in the total (22.4% of the gross agricultural production in 1978 compared with 14.3% in 1970), and in the production of meat the share has more than doubled, reaching 35.5% in 1978 (*Rocznik . . .*, 1979, table 1(277)), but this failed to produce the desired stable upward trend of agricultural production: the overall results for the 1976–1979 period were far behind the planned targets (see below), and the costs connected with the increased share of socialized agriculture have been very substantial.

To sum up the general evaluation of the 1976–1979 performance, one can say that the Polish economy has shown a remarkably consistent loss of dynamism (the rates of growth of national income in consecutive years were: 1976 – 6.8%, 1977 – 5%, 1978 – 3%, 1979 – *minus* 2%, the first absolute fall in national income in the post-war period!) without regaining either external or internal balance. As for the *external* position, Poland's indebtedness rose continuously throughout the second half of the 1970s, albeit at a slower rate from 1977. At the end of 1979 the total indebtedness (gross) was estimated as between 17 and 18 billion US dollars, with some 2000 million dollars interest payments alone due in 1980. The plan for 1980 envisaged a balance in trade with capitalist countries which – if achieved – should stop a further increase in indebtedness (with maturing debts and interest payments refinanced). This should mean, however, that even with the fulfilment of the planned growth of national income (1.4–1.8% above the 1979 level), the distributed national income (for 'use') will have to decline and at the end of 1980 will fall (in real terms) below the 1976 level. Any reduction of the external debt in subsequent years would mean the necessity to keep the *volume* of distributed national income below that of national income produced.

The domestic imbalances showed a marked tendency to grow, at least up to the end of 1979. Their consequences were increasingly felt not only in the field of consumer goods and services (long queues, informal price increases, flourishing black market, etc.) but also in the field of producer goods, with painful disruptions of the flow of supplies. All this has given rise to acute dissatisfaction and an increasing degree of corruption which must have had a seriously negative effect on the economy and undoubtedly contributed to the low efficiency of factor utilization both of capital and labour. The standard efficiency indicators presented in section 4.3 for the 1971–1975 period showed a marked deterioration for the years 1976–1978: with the increase of fixed assets in the production of national income ('material sphere') by 31.4%, increase in labour force by 1.7%, and increase in national income produced by 15.6% (from 1975, in constant 1977 prices), the derived 'productivity of fixed assets', i.e. the national income/capital stock ratio (Y/K), was only 0.88 of the 1975 level, and labour productivity (K/L) no more than 1.14 (i.e. an increase of 3.3% per annum – well below the assumptions of the plan and the growth of the capital/labour ratio) (*Rocznik* . . ., 1979, tables 1(89) and 2(90)). Taking into account the relatively large scale of modernization of capital equipment, the results have to be evaluated even more critically. The capacity of the Polish economy to absorb technically efficient means of production has proved well below the expectations of the protagonists of the 'import-led growth' strategy. Not only has the unreformed system of management at the industry level proved inadequate to the tasks of intensive development, but so, clearly (and perhaps mainly) has the quality of the top macro-policy decisions, unable to identify economic and social constraints and to launch the necessary structural transformations. Independent analyses of the causes of the failure, quite abundant in Poland in recent years, invariably point to the political system as the basic culprit[32].

The comparison of the results with the planned indicators for the 1976–1980 quinquennium can be presented on the basis of the four years (1976–1979) data alone or by supplementing the four-year record with the figures from the plan for 1980; the differences are negligible: nevertheless both approaches are used in *Table 4.5*.

Table 4.5 *The 1976–1980 results*

| | | *Average annual rates of growth* | |
	1976–1980 (Plan)	1976–1979 (Actual)	1976–1980 (1980 plan figures added to actual record for 1976–1979)
National income produced	7–7.3	3.1	2.8
National income distributed (disposable)	4.8	1.7	1.6
Real wage per employee	3–3.4	1.2	1.2
Employment	1.2	0.7	0.7
Gross investment in fixed assets	2.3	0.07	–1.7
Gross industrial production	8.2–8.5	5.8	5.4
Gross agricultural production	3–3.5	0.7	1.3
Exports	11.8		
in current prices		10.1	
in constant prices		6.2	
Imports	4.7		
in current prices		6.8	
in constant prices		2.2	

Sources: Plan data 1976–1980 as in *Table 4.4*.
Actual data 1976–1979 computed from '*Mały Rocznik Statystyczny (Concise Statistical Yearbook)*, 1980.
Plan data for 1980 from *Trybuna Ludu*, 3 December 1979 and *Polityka*, No. 1, 1980.

Table 4.5 seems to illustrate well the point about the 'economic manoeuvre' turning into a retreat. What is more, the plan for the 1981–1985 period, as outlined at the VIII Congress of the Polish United Workers' Party in February 1980, seems to indicate that the second part of the 1970s might be more of a rule than an exception. At least the basic indicators – as they stood at the Congress, i.e. by no means definitive – look rather similar to the 1976–1980 record: the average rate of growth of national income 3% per annum, gross industrial production between 3.7% and 4.4%, gross agricultural production between 2.3% and 2.5%, and that of real wages between 1.7% and 2.1% annually. Assuming full implementation of this plan the improvement over 1976–1980 would be very modest indeed. In a sense, taking a bird's-eye view of the quarter of a century of Polish economic development 1960–1985 one could come to the conclusion that the five years

1971–1975 constituted an exception in an otherwise not very distinguished record for a system which takes long-run growth as its main claim to superiority. *Table 4.6* illustrates the point in terms of four basic indicators, with columns 1 and 2 reflecting the actual statistical picture of the 1961–1970 decade and the 1971–1975 quinquennium respectively, and column 3 presenting a 'synthetic' projection of the 1976–1985 decade (computed from actual official figures for 1976–1979 plus plan for 1980 plus the outline of the plan for 1981–1985 approved by the VIII Congress).

Table 4.6 *Three periods in a quarter of a century of Polish economic development (1961–1985)*

	Average annual rates of growth (%)		
	1961–1970 *(Actual)*	*1971–1975* *(Actual)*	*1976–1985* *(Actual + projected)*
National income produced	6.1	9.8	2.9
Industrial production (gross)	8.5	10.4	4.8
Agricultural production (gross)	2.3	3.6	1.8*
Average real wage	1.8	7.2	1.6

* For 1981–1985 'net final production'.

Sources: As in *Table 4.5. Statistical Yearbook of Poland*, 1973; Materials of the VIII Congress of the PUWP, February 1980.

The significance of this sweeping juxtaposition of three different periods (with one of them only vaguely projected) should not be exaggerated; the conditions differed enormously, and the meaning of lower rates of growth calculated from a higher starting point achieved during the years 1971–1975 ought not to be overlooked. Whatever the setbacks, Poland's material potential has increased substantially and it must not be assumed that it will forever remain so badly used. On the other hand, the environment – in a general sense, not only from the point of view of energy resources – may become rougher in the near future than in the past, contrary to the continuous complaints of the official interpreters of the reasons for failure. It could therefore hardly be expected that the challenges of the 1980s might be more successfully met without substantial systemic changes.

It does not seem necessary to return to the main features of the Polish economy in the second half of the 1970s. We have tried to draw some conclusions in the course of the analysis itself, stressing – let us hope without bias – the conflicting sides of the picture, both in static and in dynamic terms. The most remarkable thing which emerges from this picture is not so much the difficulties (after all, which economy does not have difficulties?), but the apparent inability to combat them with purposeful, longer lasting, consistent policies of the type one would expect to find in a centrally planned economy. There are surely many reasons for this, some arising from specific circumstances not amenable to generalization. It is, however, this author's view that among the paramount causes of the phenomenon in question is the increasingly negative impact of the essentially totalitarian political system. Lack of open and free debate of macroeconomic alternatives hardly helps to find a relatively suitable course, and more often than not leads to one-sided *Wunderwaffen*, hastily swapped for another extreme after fingers have already been burned. But probably the most harmful effect of the existing political system is the widespread feeling of dissociation, the perception of the supposedly common socialist economy in 'them'-and-'us' terms. Not only does this hamper the advance of productivity in a broad sense but it narrows down dangerously the probability of a positive response to even genuine need for simple temporary patience, let alone sacrifice. It is clear that this adversely affects the chances of a 'manoeuvre' in time of difficulties, and that economic failures in turn feed political distrust.

Notes

1. Changes in plans for 1971–1975 in the direction of raising the indices of the standard of living of the population were introduced in most countries of the Soviet bloc; it is quite probable that this was a reflection of the shock which the Polish December events must have caused.

2. The index of real wages in 1970 (1960 = 100) was 146 for Romania, 143 for Bulgaria, 127 for Czechoslovakia; the USSR had 134 but this was for overall 'real income' including all kinds of social benefits. The Polish index of real wages was only 119. (Based on figures from the official statistical yearbooks of the respective countries brought together in *Kraje RWPG . . . 1972*, table 12(103).)

3. According to Stanislaw Gomulka (1976) the trend rate in Polish industry, measured in net output (value added) per employee, has been 6.1% annually; the 1961–1970 rate was 4.9%, due to several factors, but certainly with a prominent part played by severe restrictions on wages. Gomulka also made a number of valuable comments on an earlier draft of the present paper which are gratefully acknowledged here.

4. In 1975 the official index of real wages (1960 = 100) was 166 in Bulgaria, 149 in Czechoslovakia, 176 in Romania, 153 in

Hungary, 161 in the USSR (but see Note 2) and 165 in Poland. (*Rocznik . . ., 1977*, table 26(765).) Data for the GDR are not shown, as in the case of 1970 (see Note 2).

5. By 1975 almost all the population was covered by some sort of social security system (99.7%); it is surprising, however, that by 1970 this percentage was as high as 76.6, which must have meant that a large proportion of the agricultural population could become entitled before the new regulations, presumably on the strength of someone in the family employed outside the private farm.

6. All private data in constant 1971 prices.

7. There is one puzzling element in the table from which these figures are cited: the 'productivity of fixed assets' in the entire non-agricultural material sphere showed an index number of 110.4 in 1975 (1970 = 100), which would be consistent with the index for the national economy as a whole (108.8); however, the index for industry was only 104.9 and for construction it was far below 100 (85.7), which would mean that in the remaining non-agricultural sectors of material production (transport, telecommunications, trade and 'other' sectors) an enormous improvement had

taken place. There is no explanation of this puzzle (data for these sectors are not shown).

8. This figure was about 50% of annual exports in 1970.

9. Computed from data in *Rocznik . . .*, 1973, 1976. Of course, comparisons in current prices (as here) are inflated; nevertheless, the leap was enormous.

10. 'National income differs from national income distributed by the difference between imports and exports (this can be either positive or negative) and by losses of national income. The surplus of imports over exports (or *vice versa*) has been calculated as a difference in transaction prices, i.e. in valuta złotys converted into internal złotys according to the established coefficients.' (From Methodological Remarks in *Rocznik . . .*, 1976, ch. VI, p. 66.) It is impossible to say what relationship the 'established coefficients' bear to prices and hence to revenue lost (exports) or gained (imports); changes in the composition of the final bill of goods are therefore most probably not reflected. Nevertheless, the distinction between national income produced and distributed is an important indication of the direct role of surplus (or deficit) in the balance of trade (the other item – losses of net material output already produced – is usually negligible).

11. The role of investment participation as a factor strongly influencing the Soviet balance of trade with other CMEA members (in conditions when financial flows cannot be used because of inconvertibility) is discussed in Askanis, Askanis and Levcik (1976).

12. For example, the statement by the prime minister, Jaroszewicz, to the Sejm on 30 May 1977 (*Trybuna Ludu*, 31 May 1977).

13. Monetary incomes omit the (estimated) peasant money incomes spent on consumer goods because of difficulties in finding comparable data for the two periods in question: therefore the index given above represents only the growth of incomes of wage (and salary) earners plus social benefits in money. For the purposes of our comparison this seems indicative enough.

14. In the index of cost of living for an average employee family in 1975 (1970 = 100) the cost of food showed a 9.5% increase whereas the cost of clothing and shoes rose 18.3% (*Rocznik . . .*, 1976, table 4(124)).

15. It is interesting to note that in 1972 Poland had net imports of 11 000 tons of raw meat whereas in 1974 net exports were 94 000 tons.

16. The data on turnover in valuta shops almost certainly do not include many other sales for foreign currency, above all *dwellings*. There are no aggregate data on the scale of operations in this field but figures for some towns revealed in the press (*Polityka*) show a substantial share of 'valuta dwellings' (10–12% of the total or almost one-third of dwellings distributed by the general housing cooperatives).

17. In this section the author has drawn on his research undertaken in the framework of the East European Economic History Project at St Anthony's College, Oxford, funded by the British Social Science Research Council.

18. As in other similar cases the 'regulation of prices' of 13 December 1970 was presented as neutral from the point of view of distribution of income between the population and the budget (price rises for food were allegedly compensated by cuts in prices for industrial products, increases in child allowances, etc.) Despite widespread criticism (*ex post*, obviously) of the deposed Gomulka leadership the full financial balance of the ill-fated operation was never officially disclosed.

19. For an evaluation of the conception and the practical effects of the pre-1970 reform see among others Zielinski (1973, chs I and IX).

20. Under the chairmanship of Jan Szydlak (hence the name 'Szydlak Commission'), at that stage a member of the Politbureau and secretary of the Central Committee and ranking almost immediately below Gierek in the political hierarchy. The very broad terms of reference given to the commission (modernization of the economic and the *state* system) were in line with the intention then prevailing of giving the population the impression that a new era was beginning politically as well after the shameful collapse of the Gomulka regime. In fact, no genuine changes in the political system were carried out under Gierek, although some were proposed, and there was only an administrative reform, in which, however, the Szydlak Commission was not directly involved.

21. The summary description of the new rules of operation which follows is based on official documents and on commentaries contained in Sliwa (1974), Glinski (1975) and Glinski, Kierczynski and Topinski (1975).

22. Nothing is subtracted for fixed assets financed out of the unit's own resources (retained profits), although a 5% payment is charged against gross profit.

23. The formula of the basic 'normal' price (*cena wyjściowa* – literally 'point of departure price') was modified, integrating the mark-ups on fixed and working capital to 8% of the net value of assets and including the mark-up on the wage fund. To obtain the 'normal' price for a particular product the mark-ups derived from average magnitudes for the association as a whole were to be related to the *processing* costs (total costs minus cost of outside inputs) of the product in question:

$$p = k + s \times kp$$

where k is the average (branch) costs of production of the product in question, s the mark-up (percentage) and kp the processing cost of the product in question. s was to be derived from the formula:

$$s = \frac{s_1 \times C + s_2 \times V}{Kp}$$

where s is the mark-up on capital (8%), s_2 the mark-up on the wage fund (20%), C the net value of capital assets, V the wage fund and Kp the processing costs, all in the association as a whole. This concept of the 'normal' price was thought to fit into the incentive scheme based on PA.

24. 'The most essential element in the changes now being introduced is the new approach to the functions of the branch ministries. The ministry – developing and perfecting its functions as the head organ of the state administration – acquires new rights and possibilities to influence associations and enterprises economically. . . . In this way a serious step forward has been taken towards bringing together the economic and financial system and central planning' (Szydlak, 1977).

25. There was a joint session of the party Politbureau, the Presidium of the government, the Presidium of the Central Council of Trade Unions with the representatives of the 'self-management organs' (7 April 1977).

26. According to official calculations (Jaroszewicz, 1976) the 39% rise in food prices was to put the cost of living index up by 16% (the share of food in average household expenditure was over 40%) and to bring an increase in state revenue of 107 billion złotys; the net compensation was calculated at 108 billion złotys. As usual, the official figures were grossly disbelieved and the distribution of the compensation sharply criticized for its anti-egalitarian bias.

27. Unless otherwise stated all figures concerning the 1976–1980 plan are derived from the official presentation of the plan in the monthly journal *Gospodarka Planowa* (No. 2, 1977).

28. Apart from the obvious social aspects, housing policy in Poland has an interesting economic side as well. With the tendency to increase the share of private financing of both construction and running costs (the so-called 'housing cooperatives', private family houses, sales of state flats to sitting tenants, etc.) housing became an important factor in absorbing part of the purchasing power of the population, and particularly an inducement to savings, which in most cases have to be accumulated and paid in as deposits before one is even put on a formal waiting list. This convenient system of mopping up money with delivery of the goods long deferred cannot, however, be overstretched. Recent years have shown a deceleration of the rate of growth of savings in Poland (from some 24–25% annual growth in savings deposits in 1972–1974 to 16% in 1975 and less than 10% in 1976–1978), and the opening up of better prospects in housing may be considered relevant to the improvement of the precarious position in the balance of incomes and expenditure of the population.

29. Over the 1971–1975 period the balance of trade in foodstuffs (agricultural produce and products of the processing industry) brought a cumulative deficit of 2241 million valuta złotys (675 million dollars at the 1975 accounting rate of exchange) whereas over 1966–1970 there was a surplus of 1530 valuta złotys (380 million 1970 dollars).

30. In Jaroszewicz's introduction of the 'price reform' on 24 June 1976 the 'terms of trade' with the peasants were to remain unchanged (the increases in purchase prices for agricultural produce were

offset by higher prices of food sold to the peasants and of producer goods supplied to them); three weeks later the effect of the increase in prices of producer goods for agriculture was cut by half, leaving the peasants with a net gain of 12 billion złotys annually. The IV Plenum of the Central Committee (September 1976) criticized the anti-peasant discrimination in the distribution of land from the State Land fund; at the V Plenum (January 1977) figures were given showing the decline in peasants' earnings per day in livestock production, a blueprint of a pension scheme for private farmers was adopted, etc. On this subject see also Laeuen (1977).

31. Calculated from data in *Rocznik . . .*, 1979, table 1(155). Information about the 1980 plan is taken from *Trybuna Ludu* (3 December 1979) and *Polityka* (No. 1, 1980). Data for 1979 are from the Central Statistical Office report in *Trybuna Ludu* (9–10 February 1980) and from *Maly Rocznik . . .*, 1980. Most of the data related to the latter part of the 1976–1980 quinquennium come from these sources.
32. Among numerous studies published unofficially in Poland mention should be made at least of 'Uwagi . . .', (1978); Bartecki (1978); 'Doswiadczenia . . .', (1979); Kuczynski (1979).

References

Askanis, B., Askanis, H. and Levcik, F. (1976). *Die Wirtschaft in den RGW-Ländern 1976 bis 1980*, Wiener Institut für Internationale Wirtschaftsvergleiche, Reprint-Serie Nr. 22 and 26 (*Monatsberichte des Österreichischen Institutes für Wirtschaftsforschung*, Nos. 3 and 12

Bartecki, (1978). *Gospodarka na manowcach*, published unofficially in Poland; republished by Institut Literacki, Paris, 1979

Decision of the Council of Ministers No. 383, 7 December 1966

Decision of the Council of Ministers, 9 February 1971, *Monitor Polski*, No. 10, 1971, item 65

Doświadczenia i przyszłość. An attempt at a comprehensive assessment of Polish socio-economic realities based on contributions by over fifty experts from all walks of life, published unofficially in Poland, republished by Institut Literacki, Paris, 1980

Glinski, B. (ed.) (1975). *Zarys systemu funkcjonowania przemysłowych jednostek inicjujących*. Warsaw

Glinski, B., Kierczynski, T., and Topinski, A. (1975). *Zmiany w systemie zarządzania przemysłem*. Warsaw

Gomulka, S. (1976). VII Zjad PZPR: Uwagi do planu 1976–1980. *Aneks*, Vol. 11. Uppsala and London

Gospodarka Planowa, No. 2, 1977 (The 1976 –1980 plan)

Jaroszewicz, P. (1976). Speech in the Sejm on 24 June 1976, *Trybuna Ludu*, 25 June 1976

Kalecki, M. (1972). Introduction to the Theory of Growth in a Socialist Economy. In *Selected Essays on the Economic Growth of the Socialist and the Mixed Economy*. Cambridge

Kozłowski, Z. (1977). Socialism and Family Farming; the Polish Experience. *Osteuropa-Wirtschaft*, Vol. 22, No. 1 (March)

Kraje RWPG – ludność, gospodarka, kultura, Polish Statistical Office, Warsaw, 1972

Kuczynski, W. (1979). *Po Wielkim Skoku*, NOWA (The Independent Publishing House), Warsaw. (A specialist examination of the economic policies of the 1970s, published by the Society of Academic Courses – the so-called 'Flying University').

Laeuen, H. (1977). Polens Dorf in der Auflösungsperspektive der Partei. *Osteuropa*, Vol. 27, No. 2 (February)

Machowski, H. and Zwass, (1972). Polen. In *Die Wirtschaft Osteuropas zu Beginn der 70er Jahre* (ed. by Höhmann, H.-H.). Stuttgart

Maly Rocznik Statystyczny 1980. Warsaw

'Nowy system bodźców materialnego zainteresowania. Zbiór podstawowych dokumentów' (1970). Joint resolution of the Council of Ministers and the Central Council of Trade Unions of 1 July 1970. Warsaw

Polityka, No. 15 (9 April) 1977; No. 1, 1980

Resolution of the Council of Ministers of 18 March 1977, *Trybuna Ludu*, 25 April 1977

Rocznik Statystyczny, 1973; 1976; 1977; 1979. GUS, Warsaw

Sliwa, J. (ed.) (1974). *Nowy system ekonomiczno-finansowy w organizacjach przemysłowych*. Warsaw

Szydlak, J. (1977). Speech to the plenary session of the commission for modernization of the system of functioning of the economy and the state on 29 June, *Życie gospodarcze*, No. 28 (10 July) 1977

Trybuna Ludu, 3 May 1977; 31 December 1979; 9–10 February 1980

'Uwagi o sytuacji gospodarczej Polski'. Comments on the economic situation by a group of economists, with an introduction by Edward Lipinski, published unofficially in Poland, republished with contributions to the discussion from economists from Poland and abroad in *Aneks*, No. 20, (1979). London and Uppsala

Ząbkowicz, L. (1974). *O metodach zarządzania polskim przemysłem*. Warsaw

Zielinski, J. G. (1973). *Economic Reforms in Polish Industry*. London

VII Zjazd Polskiej Zjednoczonej Partii Robotniczej 8–12 grudnia 1975. Podstawowe dokumenty i materiały. Warsaw, 1975

Aims and methods of economic policy in Czechoslovakia 1970–1978

Jiri Kosta

5.1. The aims of economic policy in the 1970s

The starting point

At the beginning of the 1970s – more precisely, after the invasion by the Warsaw Pact troops in August 1968 and the subsequent changes in the party and state leadership in 1969 – the economic situation of Czechoslovakia was officially described, not without justification, as one of 'crisis'[1]. Growth was declining, the imbalance between the effective demand of the population for consumer goods and of enterprises for investment goods was reaching threatening proportions, and economic efficiency was falling everywhere. In view of this situation, the original targets of the fourth five-year plan (1966–1970) had to be replaced by short-term development goals and these in turn were only achieved by means of restrictive wage and investment policies. The corresponding growth trends are shown clearly in *Table 5.1*.

If the actual rates of economic growth (which are traditionally higher than comparable magnitudes in Western national income accounting) are relatively high for the five-year period 1966–1970, this is undoubtedly due to the preceding period of reform, above all to the years 1966 and 1968. Yet it must be assumed (precise data are not available) that, contrary to the global plan

Table 5.1 *Indicators of Czechoslovak economic growth (annual or average annual percentage change)*

	1966–1970 Plan target	Actual	1966	1967	1968	1969	1970
					Actual figures		
National income produced	4.1–4.4	6.8	9.2	5.2	8.4	6.5	5.0 (5.5)
Industrial production	5.6	6.5 (6.8)	9.2	6.8	7.3	6.6	7.5 (8.4)
Personal consumption	3.2–3.5*	5.6	5.3	3.5	11.1	7.5	1.0
Gross investment	5.6	8.3	9.6	2.8	10.4	13.1	6.1 (5.9)

* Including social consumption.

Sources: Economic Survey of Europe 1970, Part 2, Geneva–New York 1971, p. 67; figures in brackets from *Statisticka ročenka ČSSR 1973*, pp. 24–27.

fulfilment, the *structure* of production and expenditure or consumption was not achieved as planned. In other words, overfulfilment of some plan targets contrasted with bottlenecks in the supply of other goods and services.

Published party documents and the specialist press lamented not just the familiar mismatch between production and demand but a quite general lack of efficiency and, in particular, excessive costs as a result of irrational use of factors of production, as well as the reluctance of enterprises to innovate[2]. In this study of the aims and means of Czechoslovak economic policy in the 1970s we shall seek to answer the following four questions.

(1) Has Czechoslovakia succeeded in escaping from the bitterly criticized *extensive* growth path and adopting the much sought-after course of *intensive* development? This aim was frequently described in the CMEA countries as 'adoption of the scientific and technical revolution'.

(2) Has greater attention been devoted to the shortages in the sphere of *private consumption* and the traditional priority of heavy industry abandoned? In other words, has the traditional Soviet-type accumulation model been abandoned?

(3) Was the original centralized administrative *planning system* of the pre-reform period (before 1965) restored in the 1970s or have the reformers succeeded in saving some kind of decentralized market-like economic order of the Hungarian type (while, of course, renouncing their political demands)?

(4) What conclusions for the *future course* of economic policy can be drawn from the results of economic development?

In this study we shall examine thoroughly the trends to be observed in the economy and the economic policy of Czechoslovakia in relation to these four questions.

The aims of the two five-year plans (1971–1980)

As in the other countries of Eastern Europe, the planned growth rates in the 1970s were reduced in comparison with the preceding five-year plans[3]. True, the plan figures in the fifth five-year plan (1971–1975) for national income produced were exceeded (plan target: 5.1%, actual increase: 5.7%); the relatively low target of 4.9% in the 1976–1980 plan was not reached during the years 1976 to 1978, when the actual average growth was only 4.1% (see *Table 5.2*). If the provisional plan fulfilment data for 1979 are included (national income was said to have risen by 2.6–2.8% and industrial production by 3.7% over the previous year[4]) the rates of growth of output for the period 1976–1979 would be some 10% lower.

An approximate answer to the question how far an intensive growth model based on technical progress was established or implemented during the five-year plan should be indicated by the trends in factor productivity.

141

Table 5.2 *Factors and efficiency of economic growth (annual average percentage growth)*

	Productive sectors[a]				Industry			
	1966–1970 *Actual*	1971–1975 *Actual*	1976–1980 *Plan*	1976–1978 *Actual*	1966–1970 *Actual*	1971–1975 *Actual*	1976–1980 *Plan*	1976–1978 *Actual*
Output[b]	6.9	5.7	4.9	4.1	6.8	6.7	5.9	5.4
Employment	1.2	0.9	0.7	0.6	1.2	0.7	0.6	0.7
Tangible fixed capital	4.4	5.8	7.2	6.3	4.3	5.6	7.0	6.4
Labour productivity	5.6	4.8	4.2	3.5	5.5	6.0	5.3	4.7
Capital productivity[c]	2.4	-0.1	-2.1	-2.1	2.4	1.0	-1.0	-0.9
Capital intensity[d]	3.2	4.9	6.5	5.7	3.1	4.9	6.4	5.7

(a) Industry, construction, agriculture and forestry, transport, posts and communications, internal trade.
(b) In productive sectors; net material product (henceforth 'national income'): in industry; gross output.
(c) Output in relation to tangible fixed capital.
(d) Tangible fixed capital per employee.

Source: F. Levcik, *Strukturprobleme der ČSSR in den siebziger Jahren*, Reprint-serie des Wiener Institut für Internationale Wirtschaftsvergleiche, 39/1979, p. 10; *Statisticka ročenka ČSSR 1979*

The growth of labour and capital productivity in the 'productive' sectors of the economy as a whole and in industry in particular may be found in *Table 5.2.*

First we must note that, as a consequence of East European statistical methods, the labour productivity indicator, in particular, is likely to be exaggerated[5]. Yet for our purposes this magnitude is sufficiently meaningful since we are concerned here with comparison over time. Labour productivity growth as a reflection of (labour-saving) technical progress, the objective of which was supposed to be to raise productivity, declined during the 1970s in comparison with the preceding period in the productive sectors of the economy as a whole, though in industry the decline only became visible in the second half of the decade. What is particularly serious is the fact that, despite the reduced targets for 1976–1980, the planned increase in labour productivity in the three years 1976 to 1978 was not achieved (plan target for all productive sectors: 4.2%, actual growth: 3.5%, plan target in industry: 5.3%, actual growth: 4.7%). Because of the exaggeration mentioned above the real growth rate of the social product according to the 'Western' definition, and thus that of productivity too, is likely to be about 1–2% lower.

If the rise in labour productivity can in no way be favourably regarded, this applies all the more to the trend in capital productivity (the relationship of national income produced and tangible fixed capital). Whereas in the second half of the 1960s this indicator showed a positive growth rate of 2.4%, in the following decade the rates were contracting (first −0.1%, then −2.5% in the next five-year period), with the negative plan target (−2.1%) being 'fulfilled' in the three years 1976 to 1978. To guard against misunderstanding it should be said that, with high capital intensity, stagnation or even a moderate decline in capital productivity is acceptable if this is compensated by especially marked advances in labour productivity; this, however, is not the case here.

The adverse long-term trend in efficiency is also confirmed in a study published at the beginning of 1980 by members of the staff of the Economic Institute of the Czechoslovak Academy of Sciences (Vintrova, Klacek and Kupka) which is based on an internal research project[6]. According to this study, national economic efficiency (not precisely defined) showed the following annual average rates of growth: 1951–1970: 2.1%; 1971–1975: 1.1%; 1976–1978: 0.4%. The first conclusion is that Czechoslovakia failed to secure any intensification of the growth process which would indicate the achievement of scientific and technical progress.

In the reform discussions of the 1960s it was repeatedly pointed out that conquest of the extensive development pattern was closely bound up with abandonment of the accumulation-oriented industrialization model of the first two five-year plans (1949–1953 and 1956–1960) (Kosta, 1978, Ch. II). The priority expansion of heavy industry, comprising the basic materials branches and engineering, in itself requires disproportionately high inputs of factors of production of all kinds. For this reason greater concentration on the processing branches, and especially on consumer goods industries, is necessary. Such a strategy would represent a significant alleviation of the burden on the growth process and would create a better input to output ratio and thus more favourable conditions for intensification. Furthermore – this was no less weighty an argument in the reform discussions – priority for consumption should revive the moribund incentives for the labour force.

Doubtless considerations of this kind were still present in the minds of a good many Czechoslovak politicians and above all of the planning experts who formulated the development goals of the two five-year plans in the 1970s, despite the political changes after 1968. A more marked orientation towards consumption, as indicated by the 'chief aim of development' proclaimed at the XIV congress of the CP of Czechoslovakia, namely 'the raising of the standard of living' ('Smernice . . .', 1971; *Economic Survey* . . ., 1972), was certainly also based on political factors in addition to the economic aspects: the example of the Gdansk disturbances in 1970[6] (which were to be repeated once again in Poland in 1976) was frightening enough for all the leadership elites of Eastern Europe.

We must now examine how far there was in fact a turn towards more marked expansion of the consumption-oriented branches in the 1970s, both in the plans and in the actual development. The substantial economic growth which was registered in the second half of the 1960s was based on both a strong investment drive and an expansion of private consumption which was unusual for Eastern Europe (see *Table 5.3*). During the 1970s the rates of growth of consumer good production and, above all, of private consumption gradually slumped, a trend which becomes especially clear in the years 1976 to 1978 (annual growth rate: 3.5%). According to the Federal

Table 5.3 *The structure of economic development (average annual percentage growth 1966–1980)*

	1966–1970 Actual	1971–1975 Plan	1971–1975 Actual	1976–1980 Plan	1976–1980 Actual*
National income produced	9.5	5.1	5.7	4.9	4.1
Gross industrial production	6.7	6.0	6.7	5.9	5.4
of which producer goods	7.0	–	7.0	–	5.9
consumer goods	6.4	–	6.2	–	4.3
Gross capital investment	7.2	6.2	4.8	6.4–6.7	4.7
Personal consumption	5.4	5.1–5.5	4.8	–	3.5
Retail trade turnover	6.3	5.1–5.4	5.5	4.3–4.6	2.6

* 1976–1978.

Sources: *Statisticka ročenka ČSSR 1972*, p. 407; *1979*, pp. 20–23, 28–29, 137, 488; J. Kosta, *Abriss der Sozialökonomischen Entwicklung der Tschechoslowakei 1945–1977*, Frankfurt, 1978, table 45, p. 161; F. Levcik, *Strukturprobleme . . .*, p. 7.

Statistical Office's plan fulfilment report at the beginning of 1980 money incomes rose by only 0.6% in real terms in 1979 compared with 1978, while retail trade turnover was 3.6% higher. In other words the already slow growth of personal consumption also ceased in 1978. These tendencies are also reflected in the structure of utilization of national income (*Table 5.4*).

In order to be able to trace the rates of accumulation and consumption (here the share of personal consumption in national income) back over a longer period, the calculations were done on the basis of constant prices (of 1 January 1967; the relevant data were available only for 1966 to 1976). As *Table 5.4* shows, the accumulation rate rose more or less continuously from 1969 to 1977 in comparison with the reform period (1966–1968); it reached a peak in 1975 at 26%. The consumption ratio (referring to personal consumption) shows a trend of continuous decline up to 1976. The figures cited for 1977 and 1978, which are on a different price basis, indicate a turning point, which, however, would presumably not be as marked in constant prices. Finally it should be borne in mind that the rates of economic growth after 1976 were low, so that a higher consumption ratio does not represent any appreciable rise in the standard of living.

The trend revealed here is also confirmed by calculations by the Prague authors cited above (Vintrova *et al*, 1980) according to which the investment ratio (the share of gross investment in 'final social product') first fell from 20.4% in 1965 to 18.4% in 1970 and then rose to 32.8% in 1975 and 32.4% in 1978. Another indicator, called 'investment intensity' (the ratio of investment in commodity production to the growth of final social product) is said to have risen from 2.9% in 1966–1970 to 3.7% and finally to 5.1% (Vintrova *et al.*, p. 38).

Neither the targets of the two five-year plans nor the actual course of development, as we have seen, show abandonment of the accumulation model, which seemed to be starting to occur during the reform period. Of course, we can no longer observe the kind of extreme priority for heavy industry which was typical of the 1950s.

The adherence to the traditional development goals of the Soviet industrialization model – priority development of producer goods branches and the consequent inevitable lag of private consumption as well as some parts of public consumption (infrastructure) – exacerbated the already difficult situation in certain problem areas of the Czechoslovak economy such as, above all, the labour market, the supply of basic materials, the investment sphere and the foreign trade sector. These mutually interrelated problem areas will be examined individually in the following section.

Problem areas of development strategy in the 1970s

The structural change corresponding to the plan goals is dependent on the availability and mobilization of the resources of growth: (a) labour, (b) basic

Table 5.4 *Structure of utilization of national income (percentage shares)*

	1966	1967	1968	1969	1970	1971	1972	1973	1974	1975	1976	1977[a]	1978[b]
Total consumption	79.4	79.2	79.2	79.0	76.8	78.2	77.8	76.5	75.2	74.0	74.3	(75.8)	(76.3)
of which personal consumption	60.3	59.4	59.9	60.1	57.9	58.2	57.8	56.3	55.5	55.5	54.4	(55.3)	(55.8)
Accumulation	20.6	20.8	20.8	21.0	23.2	21.8	22.2	23.5	24.8	26.0	25.7	(24.2)	(23.7)

(a) On the new 1976 price base.
(b) Accumulation = growth of capital stock plus growth of inventories plus uncompleted construction.

Souces: Statisticka Ročenka ČSSR 1974, p. 166; 1976, p. 159; 1979, p. 137.

materials and (c) capital. The supply of all three is becoming noticeably scarcer in Czechoslovakia. Hence we must analyse what possibilities of overcoming this scarcity were seen and how they were used. Finally, we must examine a particular danger point in Czechoslovak economic development, foreign trade.

(a) The labour market

While in 1950 only 76% of the population of working age (according to the Czechoslovak definition this means men aged 15–60 and women aged 15–55) were in gainful employment, the proportion had risen to 95% in 1970. This means that in the 1970s, apart from students and apprentices and the sick and disabled and the armed forces, all men and almost all women (with the exception of young mothers) were in employment (Sokolowsky, 1980). The increase in the number employed from 7 033 000 in 1970 to 7 539 000 in 1977 (*Statisticka ročenka ČSSR 1977*, p. 23), that is, by about half a million in absolute terms (an annual average growth of 1%), was made possible, in view of the excess demand for labour, primarily by the growing population of working age and in addition by increased participation in the labour force by pensioners (Kosta, p. 150). The planners are also hoping to release more labour than hitherto by the mechanization of agriculture and certain branches of industry, as well as transport and communications, which should alleviate the urgent need for labour in priority sectors like mining, power generating, engineering and construction (Kosta, pp. 162ff.).

Yet up to the present the shift of labour from the production sectors to the services sector, which is typical of industrially developed economies of a similar degree of maturity, has occurred only slowly in Czechoslovakia. This is shown in *Table 5.5*, which projects the future trends in the sectoral employment structure up to 1990 on the basis of official figures. The high proportion of employment in the secondary sector (1970–1978: 47%; 1990: 49%) is a consequence of both the structural and the productivity effects. The structural effect is a result of the more or less labour intensive branch

Table 5.5 *Employment by economic sectors 1961–1990 (percentage shares)*

	Primary sector	Secondary sector	Tertiary sector
1961	24	46	30
1970	18	47	35
1978	15	47	38
1990	11	49	40

Sources: J. Kosta, Beschäftigungsstruktur und Arbeitskräftepolitik in der Tschechoslowakei, in *Arbeitsmarkt und Wirtschaftsplanung* (ed. by H.-H. Höhmann), Cologne and Frankfurt, 1977, table 7, p. 152; *Statisticka ročenka ČSSR 1979*, p. 182.

structure, the productivity effect is indicative of the degree of labour-saving technical progress.

A substantial role in the labour market is also played by other structural aspects such as the regional distribution and the matching of supply and demand for different skills. Thus efforts are made to counter regional imbalances by means of special incentives (as in the unattractive area of north-west Bohemia) (*Hospodarske noviny*, No. 3, 1979, p. 5). A much more serious problem, however, consists in the disparities in the pattern of skills. Just as in the 1950s, experts' positions are frequently occupied by unqualified personnel while some specialists are doing jobs which in no way correspond to their qualifications. This situation is a consequence of the present personnel policy, according to which criteria of ability often carry less weight than party membership and political conformity[7].

(b) Supply of basic materials

A particularly serious problem for the Czechoslovak economy in the 1970s lies in the supply of fuel and power. This is primarily attributable to three factors (Kosta, 1978, p. 165):

(1) A feature of every modern industrial economy is increasing consumption of fuel and power in the course of economic expansion. This applies all the more to Czechoslovakia, as, around the middle of the 1960s, the necessary attention was no longer devoted to the expansion of the domestic raw material base, which was primarily dependent on coal, and too much reliance was placed on future imports of crude oil and natural gas.

(2) The Soviet Union, the major fuel supplier, no longer finds it so easy as before to meet the growing demand of the Czechoslovak economy for fuel – and this will be true for the foreseeable future. This applies especially to the demand for crude oil, which in the 1950s and 1960s was imported practically exclusively from the USSR and which has since had to be imported, even if only to a minor extent, from other suppliers too.

(3) The most serious problem is that the Czechoslovak economy has been hit by the rise in world prices of raw materials, especially petroleum, after 1973. Since 1975 the level of prices charged by the Soviet Union and other CMEA suppliers to customer countries in the CMEA for basic materials has lagged only a little behind world levels.

As *Table 5.6* shows, Czechoslovak energy production in the 1960s was based predominantly on solid fuels (coal, to an increasing degree brown coal). The switch to petroleum and natural gas occurred much more slowly than in the Western industrial countries as a consequence of Czechoslovakia's dependence on imports. The rise in the price of imported raw materials, as well as capacity problems in the Soviet Union, led to only slow growth in the share of liquid and gaseous fuels (Kosta, 1978). In addition there was the delay of several years in the completion of the first

Table 5.6 *Structure of primary energy consumption in Czechoslovakia (%)*

	1965	1970	1975	1980	1985
Solid fuels	82.9	75.3	66.0	65.7	52.2
Liquid fuels	11.7	17.6	24.7	25.1	28.1
Gaseous fuels	1.5	3.5	5.5	6.0	11.9
Other fuels	3.9	3.8	3.8	3.2	7.8
of which atomic power	–	–	0.1	1.2	5.2

Source: K. Houdek, Zdroje json stale nakladnější, *Hospodarske noviny*, 16/1978, p. 3.

nuclear power station (Jaslovske Bohunice, in Slovakia), although the planning apparatus particularly favours and promotes the development of atomic energy in view of the taut energy balance and the considerable uranium deposits in Czechoslovakia. The share of nuclear energy in primary energy consumption, at 1.2% in 1980 (see *Table 5.6*), with an output of 3.5 billion kWh, which is to rise to 5.2% in 1985 (produced in 10–12 nuclear power sets with an output of about 17.5 billion kWh), indicates a major effort under the circumstances (Levcik, 1979, p. 10; *Hospodarske noviny*, No. 39, 1977, p. 8).

All measures taken hitherto have been insufficiently effective insofar as the rising demand for energy was far from being met. Although party documents and the specialist press have been sounding the alarm for many years and all possible administrative, material incentive and ideological means have been employed for the purpose of increasing the output and for reducing the consumption of fuel and power, the situation recently (the winter of 1978–1979) has become catastrophic[8]. In the most recent past power cuts at peak periods for both enterprises and households increased, the time of starting work at the beginning of the day was often postponed, leisure time events in the evenings were reduced, etc. It is clear that power generating capacity has not grown to meet the demands placed on it under exceptional circumstances such as are caused, for example, by winter weather conditions[9].

Although in the past two decades (1956–1975) Czechoslovakia succeeded in reducing energy consumption per unit of output by an annual average of 1.5%, and by as much as 3% between 1966 and 1975 – although at very high costs – the further saving of 1.5% on average per year envisaged for the 1980s by Prague economists is likely to be very hard to achieve (Vintrova *et al.*, p. 37). These efforts will also, of course, be counteracted by energy-intensive production programmes (petrochemicals, metallurgical industries, heavy engineering, the spread of motor vehicles, etc.).

(c) Investment

Investment poses increasing difficulties. This sector has always been a problem child of centralized, administratively directed economies, which has led to permanent investment cycles in the post-war development of Czechoslovakia (Goldmann and Kouba, pp. 41–82). At the stage of industrial development now reached new problems arise, which result from the growing complexity of the investment processes. In addition, foreign trade obligations and domestic development targets cause the expansion of demanding capital projects, the 'completion' of which – this has recently become a household word in the Czechoslovak specialist press – creates special problems of coordination (*Hospodarske noviny*, No. 18, 1978, p. 3; No. 37, 1978, pp. 1, 7). Not least, the increasing shift of investment into heavy industrial sectors (recently above all into equipment for nuclear power stations[10]) places excessive demands on scarce factors of production just as was the case in the 1950s (Kosta, 1978, pp. 72ff.). This not only retards the growth of consumption (see *Tables 5.3* and *5.4*) but in addition has a negative effect on overall economic growth.

In this context Levcik (1979, p. 8) rightly points out that in the reform period (1966–1968) investment in modernization was preferred and that at the time the branch structure of investment shifted away from basic materials to processing branches of industry. As *Table 5.7* shows, this led in the 1970s to an expansion of capacity in branches such as wood-processing, the paper and pulp industries, the production of building materials, the clothing industry, production of chemicals, leather goods, textiles and the printing industry. In major basic material industries (metals, fuels), on the other hand, the growth of the capital stock between 1970 and 1976 was

Table 5.7 *Increase in capital stock in Czechoslovakia by branches, 1970–1976 (%)*

	Total capital	Machinery and equipment
All industry	39.9	52.3
Wood processing	77.1	104.3
Paper and pulp	73.4	101.4
Building materials	64.1	67.9
Clothing	61.8	93.1
Chemicals	59.8	81.3
Leatherworking	54.9	75.5
Printing	54.6	52.0
Textiles	51.5	65.6
Electric power	46.0	48.3
Machinery	42.7	54.5
Foodstuffs	40.5	54.3
Glass, china and ceramics	38.3	52.5
Non-ferrous metals	31.4	41.9
Fuels	30.3	44.7
Iron and steel	18.7	22.0

Source: F. Levcik, *Strukturprobleme . . .*, p. 8.

below average. To this extent the course of the fifth five-year plan (1971–1975) was still affected by the positive impetus to growth which was released by the investment decisions of the reformers (see section 5.3).

If we examine the structure of investment built into the sixth five-year plan (see *Table 5.8*) there can be no doubt that the familiar accumulation model of the 1950s, much criticized during the reform period, has been deliberately reintroduced. This confirms what we have already said. The rate

Table 5.8 *Growth of investment by volume in the sixth five-year plan (1976–1980) (fifth five-year plan = 100)*

Whole economy	135.9
Industry and construction	146.9
of which industry	147.4
of which fuels and power	156.3
metals	175.4
engineering	159.6
chemicals	132.6
consumer goods	130.6
foodstuffs	124.2
building materials	138.7
Agriculture and forestry	104.3
Transport and communications	141.5
Housebuilding	127.6
Special projects of national committees*	136.1

* i.e. regional projects (infrastructure).

Source: Hospodarske noviny, p. 18.

of growth of investment in industry – and particularly in basic material industries and engineering – is far higher than the rate of expansion in the consumer goods and foodstuffs sectors or in housebuilding. The only plus point is that this time more was also invested in the long-neglected transport and communications sector.

In order to complete the picture of the structure of investment in the 1970s, the actual figures for the sectoral structure of investment broken down into a 'production sector' and a 'non-productive sector', as well as into buildings and equipment, should be presented (*Table 5.9*). The relevant figures show that the share of investment in the production sector rose by more than three percentge points from 69.7% in 1970 to 73.0% in 1977 and that the high proportion of buildings (61.9% in 1970) compared with technological equipment (38.1%) declined by 2.5 points over the same period. Here, too, we observe an extensive growth process rather than the sought-after intensive path of economic development. This extensive investment trend, which runs counter to the modernization of the Czechoslovak

Table 5.9 *Sectoral structure of investment in the 1970s*

	1970	1970–1977* 1975	1977*
Total investment in the economy	100.0	100.0	100.0
Production sector	69.7	71.0	73.0
Non-productive sector	30.3	29.0	27.0
Buildings	61.9	60.7	59.4
Equipment	38.1	39.3	40.6

* Provisional data.

Source: *Čisla pro Každeho*, Prague, 1978, p. 49.

economy, is one of the causes of the inadequate capacity to implement technical progress (see section 5.3).

(d) Foreign trade

The problems described in the fields of basic materials supply and investment have already suggested connections with the foreign trade sector. The rising demand for fuels cannot be met without growing imports and the exacting exports of investment goods impose a burden on the already overloaded capacity of construction, metallurgical and engineering enterprises. In spite of the high demands made on Czechoslovak foreign trade the degree of foreign trade involvement of this small, industrially developed but raw material poor country was still not particularly high in 1970: the volume of exports per inhabitant was US $142 in 1960 (USSR $26, West Germany $214) and $273 in 1970 (USSR $53, West Germany $553) (Hrncir *et al.*, 1975, p. 15). Czechoslovak economists criticized the foreign trade intensity of the economy because it was still too small.

The data presented in *Table 5.10* show that the import side is still dominated by raw materials as before, although their share of total Czechoslovak imports declined significantly between 1960 and 1978 (by 8

Table 5.10 *Commodity structure of Czechoslovak foreign trade (%)*

	Imports 1960	1978	Exports 1960	1978
Machinery and equipment	21.7	40.2	45.1	52.9
Raw materials and fuels	53.0	45.1	29.2	26.4
Agricultural products, including raw materials	22.0	8.4	5.3	3.8
Other consumer goods	3.3	6.3	20.4	16.9

Source: *Statisticka ročenka ČSSR 1973*, pp. 419, 420; *1979*, pp. 454–455.

percentage points). The share of this commodity group in Czechoslovak exports, on the other hand, declined somewhat less (by 3 percentage points). As in previous periods the foreign currency necessary to pay for the raw material imports had to be earned primarily by machinery exports (Kosta, 1978, pp. 98ff., 167f.). Here, too, the trend during the 1970s was unfavourable. The share of machinery and equipment in Czechoslovak exports rose excessively.

The exports of technology which are the result of agreements with the CMEA countries mean too heavy a burden on the development of the Czechoslovak economy (Kosta, 1978). This burden arises from the export deliveries to the Soviet Union and the other East European trading partners, because they place excessive demands on the capacity of, above all, the engineering and other producer goods industries of Czechoslovakia (see *Table 5.11*). Thus it is not surprising that insufficient human and material resources can be made available for the remaining branches of the economy, in particular for consumer goods industries, services and infrastructure.

Table 5.11 *Indicators of Czechoslovak foreign trade (shares %)*

	1965	1970	1976
Share of the CMEA in total exports	68.0	64.7	69.4
machinery and equipment in total exports	48.5	50.2	50.1
in exports to socialist countries	55.9	58.6	57.4
Western industrial countries in total imports	18.8	24.5	25.0
machinery and equipment in total imports	29.9	33.3	36.6

Sources: Statisticka ročenka ČSSR, 1968, 1972, 1977.

Table 5.11 presents data on foreign trade which are of central importance for the development of the domestic economy of Czechoslovakia. They show a high proportion of exports to the East European countries, accompanied by a substantial proportion of machinery and equipment exports from Czechoslovakia to this part of the world. This constitutes the starting point for the accumulation model which has already been discussed.

On the import side, too, machinery and equipment have become increasingly important (*Table 5.10*). With advancing technical and industrial development the Czechoslovak economy is no longer in a position to meet its growing demand for technology largely from domestic production, as used to be the case. Imports of high-grade machinery and equipment from the Western industrial countries are of increasing importance for the fulfilment of Czechoslovakia's economic plans [11]. The rise in the proportion of machinery imports from the West is in no way the consequence of political priorities, as the exports of machinery to Eastern Europe are but result primarily from hard economic necessity.

An increase in exports of consumer goods to Western countries – and this applies to exports of investment goods too – was impeded not only by certain trade barriers of a political nature (for example, the EEC regulations) but also by deficiencies in assortment, quality and customer services which were attributable to the inability of the Czechoslovak export industries and foreign trade organizations to adapt to Western markets (Kosta, 1978, p. 168).

In contrast to industry, which has presented substantial difficulties for the foreign trade sector in Czechoslovakia, the trend of agricultural production meant a reduction of the burden on foreign trade. Since 1965 the agricultural sector has registered good results (see *Table 5.17*, p. 169), which have provided substantial relief for the foreign trade balance. In 1960 the share of agricultural products in total Czechoslovak imports still amounted to some 22%, in 1965 it was 16% and in 1978 only 8.4% (*Table 5.10*). True, the share of agricultural products in exports also declined somewhat (1960: 5.3%; 1978: 3.8%), yet without significantly affecting the supply of the products concerned (beer, malt, hops, preserves, etc.) to the domestic market.

Particular problems are raised by the regional structure of Czechoslovak foreign trade (Kosta, 1978, pp. 186ff.). The figures selected in *Table 5.12*

Table 5.12 *Regional structure of Czechoslovak foreign trade, 1948–1978 (%)*

	1948	1953	1957	1963	1970	1978
Exports	100.0	100.0	100.0	100.0	100.0	100.0
Socialist countries	39.6	78.1	65.3	75.5	70.6	73.6
of which the CMEA*	32.5	71.5	56.2	70.0	64.7	68.7
Western industrial countries	44.0	14.7	20.1	15.3	20.4	18.0
Developing countries	16.4	7.2	14.6	9.2	9.0	8.4
Imports	100.0	100.0	100.0	100.0	100.0	100.0
Socialist countries	39.7	78.9	70.1	73.5	69.4	71.9
of which the CMEA*	32.5	72.5	64.4	68.8	63.8	67.9
Western industrial countries	47.3	14.8	20.7	17.2	24.5	23.2
Developing countries	13.0	6.3	9.2	9.3	6.1	4.9

* Bulgaria, GDR, Hungary, Poland, Romania, USSR; 1978 includes Cuba.

Source: I. Angelis, *ČSSR*, Prague, 1976, p. 331; *Statisticka ročenka ČSSR 1979*, p. 441.

indicate that the efforts of the Czechoslovak leadership to achieve extremely high rates of growth of trade with the CMEA countries could only be maintained temporarily and in the short term, such as in 1953 (when these countries' share was 72%) and 1963 (when it was 69–70%). After a low of 64% in 1970 a share of 68% was reached again in 1978.

Whether the goal laid down in the sixth five-year plan of priority growth of foreign trade with the East European countries compared with the West can actually be achieved remains to be seen. In any case there are two conflicting tendencies evident here. On the one hand, Czechoslovak enterprises' interest in importing technology from the West is in no way diminishing, but on the other hand imports from the West are having to be cut back because the efforts to increase exports were unsuccessful, as the figures for 1977 to 1979 show[12]. This situation is aggravating the already adverse trend of the trade balance with the West in particular (see *Table 5.13*).

Table 5.13 *Trade balance by major country groups (cumulative balance in million Kčs at current prices)*

	1970–1973	1974–1977
Total foreign trade	+3118	−15 652
Trade with the CMEA	+3388	−5906
Trade with Western industrial countries	−4196	−14 154
Trade with the remaining countries	+3926	+4408

Source: Statisticka ročenka ČSSR 1978, p. 438.

After the explosion of raw material prices in 1973 a substantial deficit ensued (*Table 5.13*). If we follow the calculations of Altmann and Slama (1979), the cumulative Czechoslovak foreign trade balance from 1950 to 1973 with the Western industrial countries amounted to a deficit of US $955m., but a surplus of $1083m. with the European CMEA countries. If we carry the cumulative balances forward to 1979 inclusive, the result is in the first case (the West) a deficit of $4579m. and in the second (CMEA) a deficit of $1056m. (these figures leave out of account the developing countries and the remaining socialist countries, with which there were cumulative surpluses of $2617m. and $966m.) (Altmann and Slama, 1979, p. 83).

The following dilemma arises: either the Czechoslovak leadership must continue to apply the brakes on imports from the West, since a larger and larger part of export earnings is being swallowed up by interest and debt repayments, in which case the plan targets seem scarcely attainable, or alternatively there must be greater opening up to the West, but then it remains questionable how the trade balance is to be corrected.

Whereas in the 1960s Czechoslovakia's trade with the CMEA countries was in balance or showed a surplus, this changed from 1974 onward (*Table 5.13*). From 1975 the Soviet Union introduced – with a certain time lag – a kind of moving rising prices based on the average world market prices of the previous five years (*Wochenbericht*, No. 17, 1975, pp. 134ff.). This has recently led to an extreme deterioration of the terms of trade, which were in any case moving against Czechoslovakia, with its CMEA partners too. According to Czechoslovak data (Kosta, 1980), the real terms of trade have deteriorated by about 20% in the course of the 1970s as a whole. In comparison with 1971 it required a one quarter greater volume of exports in 1979 to pay for the same quantity of imports. The terms of trade with the socialist countries fell by around 12% from 1970 to 1977. If the deficit is to be balanced now, more would have to be exported for the same volume of imports. It is obvious that under these conditions the contribution of foreign trade to economic growth is smaller. The Czechoslovak specialist literature logically therefore singled out foreign trade relations as the crucial problem of future economic development (*Ceskoslovenska ekonomika . . .*, 1975, pp. 59–76).

The development strategy built into the plan goals for the 1970s – to sum up section 5.1 – has set limits on the sought-after switch from the extensive to the intensive growth model because of its foreign trade (and basically foreign policy determined) orientation towards accumulation. Furthermore, the scope for the rise in the material welfare of the Czechoslovak population which was envisaged at the same time was thereby restricted. We must now examine how far the economic policy of the 1970s has contributed to the achievement of the contradictory goals – the exacting investment programme, the sought-after rise in efficiency and the simultaneous efforts to raise the standard of living.

5.2 Ways and means of economic policy in the 1970s

In this section we shall consider the following constituent elements of a planned economic system of the East European type as ways and means of economic policy:

(1) Management structure and decision makers;
(2) Planning and steering instruments (compulsory targets, commodity–money instruments;
(3) Incentive systems.

Before going into the individual elements in detail we must briefly outline the fundamental problems which came clearly to the fore in the reform debates of the 1960s and in a somewhat diluted and often ideologically veiled form are discussed to the present day. The fulfilment of exacting plan goals, the maintenance of continuous economic growth, the required rise in economic efficiency and the necessity of transition from extensive to intensive economic development demand more decentralization and flexibility and a more open economy. These points recurred again and again in works by Czechoslovak economists and experts in the 1960s too[13] (of course, there is also a minority of orthodox theorists among the economists, but they scarcely ever submit concrete proposals for reform). In what follows, and in the concluding section, we shall try to show whether and what steps in the direction of reform indicated have been taken or could possibly be taken in the future.

Management structure and decisionmakers[14]

Figure 5.1 represents the state organs of economic management (excluding the numerous partly formally and partly informally superior party institutions and bodies which are legitimized by 'the leading role of the party').

Compared with the centralistic structure of state planning and management which survived into the reform period one major change is to be observed: the federal state constitution has also affected the central level of planning and management. On the basis of the federal state structure adopted in institutional form at the end of 1968, the state planning commission and the Czech and Slovak planning commissions are responsible organs for the preparation and allocation of annual and five-year economic plans and for supervision of plan fulfilment. The *central* decision-making level also includes the federal ministries and the national branch ministries for the Czech and Slovak socialist republics (CSR and SSR) and finally the provincial national executives which bear responsibility for communal services and some kinds of infrastructure (local transport, housing, roadbuilding, schools and health, etc.).

The associations of enterprises ('vyrobni hospodarske jednotky' – 'VHJ') managed by general directorates, which are classed as the *intermediate* decisionmaking level, are organized as 'whole-branch enterprises', 'concerns' or 'trusts': whole-branch enterprises are large, highly concentrated enterprises, to which most subsidiary plants are linked. Concerns are vertically integrated associations of enterprises at different stages of production (for example, ore extraction, metal production, metalworking). Trusts are horizontally organized groups of enterprises with similar production programmes.

The individual enterprises, as the *basic units*, are subordinated either to the central authorities (ministries or provincial organs) or to the intermediate bodies (associations of enterprises). *Figure 5.1* also shows the strict separation and hierarchical organization of the agricultural and foreign trade sectors.

In comparison with the 1950s and 1960s the intermediate management level of the 'VHJ' has recently undergone a distinct strengthening, a trend similar to that to be observed in other East European countries (for example, the 'VVB' in the GDR). The Czechoslovak specialist press – presumably in agreement with the official view of the party leadership – points out the advantages of the 'concern' type of organization, which implies a relatively strict centralization and hierarchy within the association of enterprises[15].

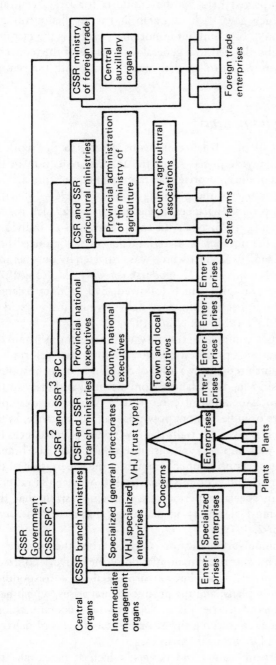

Figure 5.1 *The state management organs in the 1970s. Other central organs: Ministries of finance (CSSR, CSR, SSR); CS State Bank; Ministries of forestry and water (CSR, SSR); Ministries for labour and social security (CSSR, CSR, SSR); Ministry of transport (CSSR); Ministry of telecommunications (CSSR); Ministries of internal trade (CSR, SSR); Federal prices office; top organs of cooperative and social organizations.*

[1] *SPC = State planning commission;* [2] *CSR = Czech Socialist Republic;* [3] *SSR = Slovak Socialist Republic;* [4] *Federal ministries for fuel and power, metallurgy and engineering, technical development and investment;* [5] *Republic ministries for housebuilding, construction, industry*

Source: F. L. Altmann, Wirtschaft, in Tschechoslowakei (Länderberichte Osteuropa III), München and Vienna, 1977, p. 167.

Evidently some part is played here by the euphoria for large, centrally managed enterprises which goes back to Lenin and is recalled again and again in the Soviet Union[16]. Not without importance, lastly, is the fact that enterprises which are subordinated to a general directorate of the 'concern' type can be far more firmly controlled than was the case with the remote ministries.

Planning and steering instruments

The traditional method of plan balances remains central to the work of preparing annual and five-year plans. After the marked reduction in the number of balances, and of the enterprise plan targets and indicators derived from them, during the course of the planning reforms of 1965–1968, the number of material and product balances in the fifth five-year plan rose at first to 380 (Horalek *et al.*, 1975, p. 7). In the preparation of individual annual plans, however, the number of material balances was reduced here and there between 1971 and 1975, a fact which was criticized by one member of the Czech planning commission (*Hospodarske noviny*, No. 31, 1978, p. 4). For the sixth five-year plan which followed, 590 product balances were drawn up and the number of obligatory delivery indicators is said to have been raised by 10–15% (Horalek *et al.*, 1975, p. 7).

A measure which is not completely contrary to the general centralizing tendency is the institution, practised already before the reform, of 'management' (*gesce*), which represents a kind of delegation of the responsibility for planning and drawing up balances from a central authority to the general directorate of an association of enterprises[17]. When, for example, such a branch directorate occupies a monopoly position (for instance, in the motor vehicle industry) it is given the right to draw up the plan balances for the supply (production plus imports) and distribution (households, branch and regional organizations, export) – of course, under the supervision of the ministry and the central planning commission – and to oversee the rationalization of the plans. In specialist periodicals it is emphasized that this 'management' leads to more flexibility in planning (*Hospodarske noviny*, No. 25, 1978, p. 7; No. 2, 1979, p. 4).

The fulfilment of compulsory indicators derived from the balances is supposed to be ensured by improved manipulation of the delivery contracts between customer enterprises, which have incorporated the corresponding plan targets in their supply plans, and the producer enterprises, which have included the targets in their deliveries plans. Such contracts contain, among other things, greater detail concerning the assortment and dates of delivery of the total quantities laid down in the plan targets[18].

Beside the compulsory indicators and targets, which at times take the form of 'limits', that is, maximum and minimum quantities, the enterprises may receive orientation figures or global magnitudes (detailed targets for individual products) which leave them somewhat greater scope for decision[19]. The fulfilment of the imperative targets, and of the other plan indicators which are non-compulsory or not set in detail, is ensured by a system of monetary instruments. In so far as such forms of steering are accompanied by decentralization of enterprise decisions they are described in the East European literature, in accordance with Soviet terminology, as 'commodity–money relations'. The term 'market economy' forms of steering has been proscribed in Czechoslovakia since 1969.

The principal monetary instruments, which must now be considered, are (a) enterprises' financial resources (profit, deductions, taxes, etc.), (b) prices and (c) wages (including salaries).

(a) Enterprises' financial resources[20]

In contrast to the 'gross income' (net value added) which was introduced in the reform period as the usual success indicator, profit is now supposed to take over the function of enterprise efficiency criterion. Since, however, under the central administrative planning model the volume of output represents the priority plan fulfilment goal, profit can only have a secondary influence on enterprise decisions. Positive effects from profit are supposed to be ensured by 'normatives' which earmark part of the funds earned for bonuses and decentralized investment purposes (a steering instrument of this kind was introduced for a time in the course of an earlier Czechoslovak planning reform in 1958 and it also corresponds to similar forms of planning in the GDR).

The most important enterprise deductions or taxes in the 1970s are the 'deduction from profits', the 'capacity charge' and a 'contribution to social insurance'. At the beginning of the 1970s the rate of profits deduction was 60% (1971–1972), then it was raised to 75% (1972–1977) and then reduced to 70% (from the beginning of 1978)[21]. The capacity charge, which corresponds to the earlier charge for fixed and working capital, was calculated at the beginning of the 1970s at a rate of 5% on the basis of the purchase prices of the capital stock and since the beginning of 1978 at 3% of the book value of assets. The contribution to social insurance amounts to 20% of total wages in the current year and is thus intended to operate as a kind of payroll tax (which there previously was) (*Hospodarske noviny*, No. 46, 1977).

The three deductions described have not only a fiscal function; they are in addition expected to exert a steering effect which should contribute to rational factor allocation. The rates of deduction are set in accordance with the other macroeconomic monetary magnitudes, in particular prices, wages and turnover tax (which is not at a uniform rate but, as before the reform, differentiated by broad sectors).

The problem with this kind of enterprise accounting structure, which is supposed to bring about increases in efficiency, is not really whether there could be better steering instruments or more favourable monetary relations than those which were adopted. In the writer's view the crucial question is how far monetary forms of planning can be effective at all when they are subordinated to compulsory output indicators.

(b) Prices[22]
Price policy in the 1970s followed no clear-cut concept. At first, a decree which came into force at the beginning of 1970 froze all wholesale prices at their levels on 1 January 1969 and most retail prices at their levels on 30 June 1969. The reason for this measure was the inflationary pressure threatening both the consumer goods and the investment sectors. One of the most important indirect steering instruments of the planning system, on which the reform had relied, was thereby put out of action. True, the price freeze was presented as a temporary step; yet the economic policy makers conceded that in the longer term this measure was bound to have an adverse effect on the responsiveness of production enterprises and trade organizations to demand[23]. All the same, it must be admitted that at first the price freeze contributed to the reduction of excess demand, that is, of inflationary pressure: this occurred, however, as we have already indicated, at a much reduced level of consumption.

After the lifting of the price moratorium in 1973 there was a return to the pre-reform practice of central price setting for standard products in retail trade, though prices for 'new products' were set, according to specific rules, partly decentrally yet at the same time under strict supervision by the authorities. The available publications do not provide any clear picture of whether cost-based prices (corresponding to 'value' or 'social expenditure', as it was called) or supply and demand-related criteria (discussed using the terms 'use value' or 'innovation-stimulating') played a larger role in price setting. Presumably the criteria applied were primarily scarcity for retail prices and costs for wholesale prices (industry selling prices), as in the traditional Soviet system. At any rate, reading the Czechoslovak specialist press[24] on price problems gives one the impression that too many mutually contradictory functions and tasks were expected to be performed by prices.

The officially emphasized effort to maintain a stable retail price level could scarcely succeed under the conditions of rising costs – a consequence of the soaring prices of raw materials on world markets and the inefficiency of the domestic economy (otherwise in order to balance the financial deficits which arose either subsidies would have been necessary or public expenditure would have had to be cut or other state revenues raised).

Under these conditions it is no wonder that price rises became necessary in the retail trade sector. The increases in a variety of prices were often presented using the pretext of novelty of the goods concerned (such increases are scarcely reflected in the official price index statistics). A central increase in prices on a broad scale is undertaken with great reluctance in

Czechoslovakia because of the dangerous policital consequences, especially in the case of mass consumption goods. Yet, owing to rising costs and import prices, the economic policy makers felt compelled in July 1977, after long hesitation, to raise substantially the prices of some foodstuffs (coffee, cocoa, chocolate, etc.) and industrial products (fabrics, clothing, glass, china, among others). The price reductions introduced at the same time on other, primarily durable consumer goods (refrigerators, television sets, etc.) were far from sufficient to compensate for the loss to consumers (*Prace*, 23 July 1977, p. 1; *Listy*, No. 5, 1977, pp. 3–5).

As far as the setting of wholesale prices is concerned, there was a return to the former practice of a set of prices fixed for a long period, based on a recalculation in accordance with changes in costs. A reform of this nature was envisaged for wholesale prices right at the beginning of the 1970s, to come into effect on 1 January 1976. Prices were to be of a two-channel type related to capital (costs + margins related to capital employed and to wage costs) (Janecek, 1978, p. 38). As a result of the continuing rise in raw material prices and organizational difficulties with the review, the calculation of the new wholesale prices was delayed by a further year, so that they only came into operation at the beginning of 1977.

The completion of the review of wholesale prices has led to substantial changes in the price level and in relative prices between sectors (Janecek, 1978, p. 38). Thus the level of prices for products of basic materials industries rose by 8.4% while in manufacturing industry it declined by 6.4%. For selected raw materials, above all fuels and power, the rise in prices amounted to as much as 52% on average, making material inputs more costly for enterprises (by a total of 5 percentage points). The aim of the planners here was more economical use of basic materials, the overwhelming proportion of which had to be imported. On the other hand, prices of investment goods were substantially reduced in the course of the review, which was intended to stimulate the replacement of increasingly scarce labour by capital.

It is hard to make out how far the changes in wholesale prices reflected actual costs at the time and how far the desired effects have been achieved. In any case, even if this were so, the problem of 'correct prices' will come up again and again as production conditions and demand vary in the short term – not least because foreign trade prices can never be relied on to remain stable. The question arises whether, under these circumstances, the policy makers should not fall back on the conclusions of the reformers, who advocated a flexible price system.

(c) Wage policy[25]

The textbook formula that pay must correspond to the quantity, quality and social importance of work still applies as before; in other words, payment by performance, the principle of 'material interest', is to serve as the chief instrument to increase labour motivation.

The review of the structure of wages and salaries announced in 1971 and carried out from 1972 to 1975 sought to ensure payment for workers and employees which would be 'more exact and more justly related to performance'. The profit-sharing which had been introduced in the reform period was at first retained in somewhat modified form – though with smaller bonuses. The so-called normatives, that is, numerical relationships between plan fulfilment and bonus funds, became an additional means of stimulating earnings.

The wage scales (Brcak, 1977, pp. 61ff.) for workers were extended from eight to nine grades and the gap between grades is now 13.5%, that is about 2–4 percentage points more than in the old 1959 wage scales. The ratio of the average wage for grade 1 (4.50 Kčs) to the average for grade 9 (12.40 Kčs) now amounts to 1:2.75. This ratio is once again somewhat higher than was the case with the previous rates. The salary scale for white-collar employees in the new wage structure comprises 17 grades (directors and their deputies are not included in these grades but paid separately). Here the ratio between the lowest and the highest salary categories (excluding directors) is 1:5.1.

The corresponding catalogues of qualifications (*Hospodarske noviny*, No. 4, 1978) (at the beginning of 1948 there were 29 specialized catalogues for workers, according to occupation and branch of the economy) and the way in which workers are assigned to so-called 'personal grades' are subject to regulations which are modified according to occupation and branch of the economy and are intended to be coordinated with the other provisions of wage policy. The different wage scales take account not only of qualifications and performance but also of branch and regional planning priorities. Thus traditionally wages have always been set comparatively higher in the categories for heavy industry than for light industry and the services sector (of course, there are also substantial differentials within these sectors). The example of regional priority for north-west Bohemia has already been mentioned. The raising of wage rates for preferred activities can also be interpreted as a recognition of the scarcity aspect in so far as plan priorities (mining, remote regions, etc.) are frequently less attractive for labour, resulting in shortages.

The relative wage scales which are laid down are reflected – if not in every detail, then at least in the basic trends – in the relative real incomes in particular branches and sectors of the economy. This can be verified from the data assembled in *Table 5.14*.

Both the planned and the actual wage relativities, which differ only slightly (*Table 5.14*), indicate for the whole period from 1970 to 1980 the wage advantages of those employed in the preferred branches – mining, the metals industries – and the low wage level in the 'less valued' branches like trade and consumer goods industries.

Table 5.14 *Relationship of wages between sectors of the economy, 1970–1980*

| | Fifth five-year plan (actual figures) | | Sixth five-year plan (plan figures) | |
	1970	1975	1975	1980
Whole economy	100.0	100.0	100.0	100.0
Industry	100.8	100.9	100.7	101.1
of which fuels	139.0	133.3	135.5	137.6
power	110.1	111.1	111.6	115.0
metallurgy	113.7	116.0	117.1	116.2
heavy engineering	103.1	106.3	107.0	108.3
consumer goods[a]	89.5	88.2	88.1	87.5
Construction	111.6	109.9	110.5	110.5
Agriculture	94.2	96.7	97.3	97.6
Transport[b]	113.5	111.5	110.8	109.4
Trade and catering	90.8	89.5	89.6	89.3
Science and technology	115.9	113.5	111.8	112.0
Education	93.8	96.1	96.1	95.7
Health[c]	94.1	99.2	99.4	98.4

(a) Excluding foodstuffs
(b) Excluding communications
(c) Including social care

Source: J. Tichy, Odvetvove mzdove relace v cs. narodnim hospodarstvi, *Planovane hospodarstvi*, 6/1977, pp. 44–47.

Finally, the income differentials between workers and technical personnel in industry are of interest; in the course of the reform (1965–1968) they increased somewhat, in accordance with the watchword 'anti-levelling'. As *Table 5.15* shows, the differences have diminished somewhat during the 1970s and are now closer to the position in 1960.

There is unlikely to have been much change in comparison with the 1950s and 1960s in the extreme income privileges of the stratum of official functionaries (which are not statistically recorded). Directors' salaries, too, which in the 1950s, according to official reports, were supposed to amount

Table 5.15 *Average monthly wages and salaries in industry, 1965–1976 (Kčs)*

	1965	1968	1972	1976
(1) All categories employed*	1574	1790	2113	2412
(2) Technical personnel	1835	2159	2444	2759
(3) Workers	1529	1712	2048	2388
(2) : (3)	120.0	126.1	119.3	118.0

* Workers, technical and sales personnel, other employees.

Source: Statisticka ročenka ČSSR 1971, pp. 249, 250; 1975, pp. 249, 250.

to about three times workers' wages, but were really higher because of special bonuses, presumably retain the same relationship to the average incomes of employees as before.

In contrast to the reform concept a further difference lies in the fact that the enterprise is not responsible for pay on the basis of its own calculations (within the framework of the state incomes policy) but is told its its total wage bill from above as a compulsory limit (maximum) (*Hospodarske noviny*, No. 35, 1971; *Planovite rizeni*, 1976, pp. 140–161). In comparison with the central administrative system of planning, which prescribed the averge wage as well as the total wage bill, this means only a minor relaxation.

The total wage bill is planned in coordination with the planning of enterprise performance (production output or services turnover). In this way the allocation of financial resources for wages is linked with the fulfilment of output targets. At the beginning of 1978 the relevant decrees were tightened up and tied more closely to the planning of manpower, measures which were designed to achieve 'the maintenance of the occupation structure planned by the state, the preferential provision of labour for the priorities established, the promotion of shift working and the utilization of labour resources tied to their place of residence' (Formanek, 1978, p. 59).

Incentive systems

Wages at the prescribed rates, performance bonuses and other personal payments (e.g. compensation for lost wages, remuneration in kind, etc.) are entered in enterprise accounts as costs and are separated from the so-called 'bonus fund' (*fond odmen*). This latter is money which is taken out of the profit earned and used on the one hand for profit-sharing and on the other for special bonuses for managers, for 'victors in socialist competition' and similar purposes. In some respects this regulation is reminiscent of the reform measures of 1965–1968; the major difference compared with the earlier reform conception lies in the fact that in the Prague Spring of 1968 profit-sharing was accompanied by participation by workers and employees in enterprise decisionmaking ('workers' councils').

The dual incentive system – through wages and profit-sharing – is supposed to be linked to the trends in labour productivity and profit. The planners are here following a rule of thumb of East European planning theory according to which labour productivity should rise faster and total costs more slowly than average wages. In this connection one planner writes with satisfaction of how in the fifth five-year plan labour productivity rose by 5.8% (plan target: 4.5%) and average wages by 3.3% (plan target: 2.7–3.2%) and also the proportion of labour costs to total outlays had taken a favourable course (15.5% instead of the plan target of 16.09%) (Kutalek, 1978, pp. 68f.). The reformers had criticized this approach on the grounds that it neglects the incentive effect which a faster rise in wages may have in accelerating the growth of labour productivity.

Finally, it is interesting to see how far profit-sharing, that is, the share of bonuses in total pay, has changed in the 1970s since the reform conception and the reform development. A comparison shows that the proportion of profit bonuses amounted to about 5% in 1968 (*Statisticka ročenka 1972*, p. 82), and according to their own statements the reformers had aimed at a share of 10–15% in the following years. In contrast to this, the specialist press shows that in 1975 the share of the bonus fund in the total incomes of industrial workers amounted to only 1.7%, and 3.4% in the case of technical personnel (Kutalek, 1978, p. 72).

If we consider the wages policy of the 1970s as a whole it becomes clear that while the principle of interest in profits continued to be observed, the intended effect on efficiency, because of the linking of pay to quantitative plan indicators, is likely to have been achieved to only a limited extent, if at all.

Beside material incentive instruments non-material forms of stimulation in the shape of 'socialist competition' continue to be practised as before. Thus, for example, we read in the official statistics for 1977 that 2.3 million voluntary personal work obligations were undertaken (with a total labour force of 7.1 million people), of which 55% were fulfilled in the first half of the year (*Cisla* . . ., 1978, pp. 29, 44). This and many other announcements of successful results of socialist competition would nevertheless have had little effect when measured against the overall development of the economy (quite apart from the available personal reports from Czech and Slovak workers and employees which indicate that such attempts at motivation are not to be taken seriously).

This survey of the management structure, the planning instruments and price and wage problems has made it clear that the means employed to implement economic policy in Czechoslovakia in the 1970s have been *those of a central administrative planning system*. All the same, compared with the pre-reform period the strictly centralized planning by means of administratively set compulsory indicators, which was the feature of that time, has given way to *greater use of commodity–money instruments*.

Halfhearted attempts at reform at the beginning of the 1980s

Throughout the 1970s Czechoslovak economic policy was characterized by the juxtaposition of two tendencies; on the one hand, a clear trend towards centralization, which was to be observed particularly in the management structure, in the drawing up of plans (balancing, etc.) and in the instruments used for policy implementation in some sectors of the economy (foreign trade obligations to the CMEA, investment decisions, etc.), and on the other hand increased use of monetary instruments (normatives, efficiency indicators, etc.). When, however, at the beginning of 1978, the third year of the new five-year plan, a more decentralized steering system, relying on commodity–money instruments, was introduced 'for the purpose of experiment' in over 100 enterprises ('Komplexni experiment . . .', 1977) it was not initially clear whether this should be regarded as the prelude to a nationwide planning reform.

Under this 'complex experiment' the associations of enterprises were to receive from the central planning bodies a stable, long-term plan (set initially for three years, 1978–1980, and thereafter for the following five-year plan, 1981–1985) in physical and value terms, on the basis of which the enterprises' annual plans would be drawn up relatively autonomously in the form of 'counterplanning'. As in the earlier Czechoslovak planning reform in the late 1950s, which, however, was very shortlived (and as also in the GDR in the 1960s), 'normatives' were introduced which were intended to induce enterprises to adopt 'progressive, mobilizing' plan targets. Such normatives create a connection between the 'own performance' and 'capital profitability' indicators on the one hand and the formation of enterprise funds on the other. The greater the enterprise's own performance and capital profitability, the greater the amount which can be allocated to the enterprise funds for purposes like individual bonuses and 'limit-investments' (i.e., decentralized investments of limited size). Monetary indicators and material incentives are reflected in the sphere of wage, price, credit and currency policy.

Despite this decentralizing tendency, which is reminiscent of earlier reform attempts and discussions, a number of other elements in the experiment nevertheless indicate clearly the halfhearted nature of the measures, for instance:

(1) The restricted number of associations of enterprises taking part in the experiment, which occupy a special position *vis-à-vis* the rest of the economy;

(2) The confining of the decentralization to the level of general directorates of concerns or trusts (the so-called economic production units – 'VHJ') so that the actual enterprises remain as controlled as before;

(3) The still substantial number of compulsory indicators, even though they are less concerned with physical quantities and are more monetary- and efficiency-related than before.

In addition to individual reports on the success of the experiment in the mass media, an article (Vacha, 1979) appeared in the autumn of 1979 according to which these enterprises did better in 1977 and, particularly, 1978 than the rest of the economy operating under the traditional steering system. The comparison refers to such indicators as output, costs, profit, productivity, etc. All the same, the author points out that the enterprises selected as 'guineapigs' for the experiment had already been successful ones under the centralistic system, so that the positive results had to be treated with caution.

Beside 'success stories' the specialist press also carried complaints from general directors that the superior planning authorities still treated the gross output indicator, which was now supposed to be 'for orientation purposes', as compulsory and that production enterprises had suffered from the fact that they could not take up indirect contacts with foreign partner firms on their own responsibility (*Hospodarske noviny*, No. 30, 1978, p. 9).

At any rate, there was little in the reaction of the specialist press in 1978 and 1979 to the 'complex experiment' to suggest that these principles were to be introduced throughout the whole economy. When the party and state leadership nevertheless decided on such a reform at the beginning of 1980 ('Resolution of the presidium of the KPC and the government of the CSSR on the improvement of the system of planned management') (*Rude pravo*, 7 March 1980; *Hospodarske noviny*, No. 11–12, 1980) this 'great leap forward' was presumably explicable by the extremely bad economic performance during 1979, which gave a stimulus to the pragmatically inclined forces around the prime minister, Strougal, and the finance minister, Ler. All the same, the conception of the reform is not comparable with the 1965 Czechoslovak model (which resembled the present market economy-oriented Hungarian 'New Economic Mechanism'); the principal difference is that the 'improved' system is still based on distribution of centrally prescribed indicators to enterprises, whereas the 1965 'new' system in principle eliminated compulsory target figures of this kind (this was three years before the 'Prague Spring', which in addition to decentralization brought a radical democratization in the shape of 'workers' councils'). Under the 1965 system (as in Hungary) the enterprise was guided in the direction of the plan goals by market forces regulated by economic policy. To this extent the new course may be regarded as a step forward, in the writer's view, but it is, however, nowhere near sufficient to bring about the much-sought switch from the extensive to the intensive growth path.

Before we conclude by discussing the future prospects for economic policy, we must examine in the next section the results of economic development up to the present.

5.3 Economic growth and efficiency

It would, of course, be wrong to ascribe the results of economic development – growth rates and their relationship to the inputs employed, that is, the efficiency achieved – solely to the economic policy pursued in the period under examination. Apart from the fact that allowance would have to be made for the time lag between the implementation of measures and the effects brought about, the results will be influenced by additional factors which lie partially or wholly outside the scope of economic policy measures (for example, foreign trade and foreign policy decisions, weather conditions, sectoral or regional structures which have evolved or been inherited from the past, investment cycles initiated earlier, etc.). Nevertheless, especially in planned economic systems of the East European type, the set of economic planning and steering instruments which in this chapter we have called economic policy is a significant (co-)determinant of real economic developments.

We must therefore examine how far the goals initiated and stressed time and again by the Czechoslovak political leadership have been achieved. The goals of economic policy include, in particular, economic growth based on efficient use of factor inputs, specifically, overcoming weaknesses like high materials consumption, inadequate increases in productivity, dispersion of investment resources, rising stocks and failure to adapt to the changing structure of demand. Finally, the rise in efficiency is supposed to be positively reflected in the material living conditions of the population.

For the purpose of reviewing these goals we shall cite empirical data to enable us to formulate detailed verdicts on the rate of growth attained and the trends in efficiency achieved.

As the figures assembled in *Table 5.16* indicate, use of production inputs – raw material, and other basic materials – rose rapidly in the course of the

Table 5.16 *Economic growth and production inputs (average annual increase, %)*

	1966–1968	1969–1970	1971–1975	1976–1978
Total product (gross)	8.7	6.5	5.7	4.4
Production inputs	8.0	6.6	5.8	4.5
National product (net)*	9.8	6.5	5.7	4.1

* Identical to 'national income produced' (net material product).

Source: Statisticka ročenka ČSSR 1973, pp. 143–145; 1976, pp. 155–157; 1979, pp. 133–135.

economic growth of the reform period (1966–1968), but this was accompanied by a very much higher growth rate of national product. This economic effort could not be maintained in the following periods. Since 1969 the rate of growth of inputs use has exceeded that of national product, signalling declining efficiency. The trend was particularly unfavourable in the last three years. Overall, despite constant exhortations by the economic policy makers and planners, the goal of improved material utilization could not be achieved.

We showed in section 5.1 that the trend of labour productivity in the 1970s left something to be desired (*Table 5.2*). *Table 5.17* confirms the

Table 5.17 *Economic growth and labour productivity (average annual increase, %)*

	1966–1970	1971–1975	1976–1978
National product[a]	6.9	5.7	4.1
Industrial production[b]	6.7	6.7	5.4
Agricultural production[b]	4.8	2.6	3.0
Construction output[b]	7.9	8.4	5.9
Total productivity[c]	5.1	4.6	3.0
Productivity in industry	5.2	5.9	3.6

(a) Identical to national income produced;
(b) Gross value (branch statistics);
(c) Based on national product (excludes foreign trade and private housebuilding).

Source: Statisticka ročenka ČSSR 1976, p. 247; 1979, pp. 20–32.

picture already given of a falling trend in productivity growth. Both the volume of output of the major sectors of the economy (industry, agriculture, construction) and the corresponding labour productivity (output per employee) show a declining growth trend. This is all the more unwelcome as reserves of labour are now practically exhausted. This in turn illustrates the failure to achieve the much-sought labour-saving technical progress.

The most recent data, on 1979, indicate that the declining trend in growth is assuming threatening proportions: official statistics show the following figures for growth in 1979 compared with the preceding year: national product: 2.6–2.8%; industrial production: 3.7%; agricultural production: −3.9% (an absolute decline); construction output: 3.7% (gross figures for each sector); labour productivity in industry 2.9% and in construction 3.1% (*Hospodarske noviny*, No. 7, 1980).

What is particularly noteworthy is the fact that almost all the indicators cited show a deteriorating growth rate in the three successive periods (fourth five-year plan, fifth five-year plan, first three years of the sixth five-year plan). Taken all together, the development between 1971 and 1975 may still be regarded as relatively favourable. Before offering our reflections on the reasons for the tendencies revealed here a series of further data on efficiency will be analysed in order to supplement those already presented.

The efficiency of use of materials and employment of labour have already been examined (*Tables 5.2, 5.16, 5.17*). One further indicator relates to the efficiency of investment, which creates the conditions for future capital productivity. For this reason we must consider again the trend of capital productivity (see *Table 5.2*). After growing on average by 2.4% annually in the second half of the 1960s the rate of change dropped to −0.1% in the 1971–1975 period and to −2.1% in 1976–1978. Since investment creates the conditions for the future efficiency of capital, we must first examine how far the familiar weakness of the central administrative planning system, excessive completion times for capital investment projects, still persists.

The figures in *Table 5.18* appeared in a small book published by the Federal Statistical Office, with a critical commentary, and supplemented by additional data: in 1977 several large plants had not been commissioned at the scheduled time; the extent of overspending to complete projects had risen steeply from year to year, and so on.

Table 5.18 *Commissioning of capital capacity included in obligatory plans*

	Target	Number of projects Actual	Shortfall	Plan fulfilment (%)
1973	67	36	31	53.7
1974	56	40	16	71.4
1975	81	59	22	72.8
1976	69	45	24	62.9
1977	77	62	15	80.5

Source: Čisla pro Každeho 78, Prague, 1978, p. 51.

In section 5.1, in which the plan goals were discussed, the unfavourable structure of investment was pointed out (the priority position of heavy industry, etc.). Both the negative trend of capital productivity (*Table 5.2*) and the excessive dispersion of investment funds (*Table 5.18*) are, of course, causally connected with the prescribed structure of investment since the latter prevents a favourable input:output ratio. As a result, even recently completed plants are hardly likely to bring about any marked improvement in capital productivity in future years.

A further problem which is the object of frequent criticism is the excessive level of stocks, which tie up too many resources out of economic circulation. Acording to one expert's conclusion (Pechacek, 1977, pp. 75ff.) the situation developed not too badly in the years 1971–1973, when (for all that) the real increase in stocks was 15.6 billion Kčs greater than envisaged in the plan, whereas during the fourth five-year plan (1966–1970) the target figure was exceeded by 32.9 billion Kčs. But the trend was much worse in 1975 and 1976, when the planned rise in stocks was overshot by 20.3 billion Kčs: this he attributed to

(1) the growing difficulties in foreign trade;
(2) The expansion of cooperation and specialization in the CMEA countries, which required increasing deliveries of material-intensive products (atomic energy programme, the Orenburg pipeline, etc.);
(3) The rate of growth of capital construction.

If we look at the trend in the level of stocks over the fifth five-year plan period (1971–1975) as a whole, then – according to Pechacek (1977) – the planned figures were far from being maintained. Stocks rose by 36 billion Kčs more than the plan target and by 31 December 1975 had reached 314.5 billion Kčs (this would be almost three times the national income produced in 1975). The major reasons which he advances for this unsatisfactory trend are:

(1) Disruptions in the relations between suppliers and customers, which encourage the hoarding of stocks;
(2) Producers' reluctance to innovate, which leads to stocks of unusable products;
(3) Defects in investment construction, e.g. the increase in uncompleted plants, failure to coordinate deliveries, unsatisfactory preparation of projects, etc.;
(4) Weaknesses in planning, organization, and, blatantly, in stock management itself.

It can hardly be assumed that stock control improved substantially after 1976. The excessive stocks of basic and auxiliary materials and of finished products on the one hand and the bottlenecks in the case of other products and services on the other show the persistence of that familiar weakness of central administrative planning systems – inability to adapt to the structure of supply and demand.

A further indicator of efficiency, which illustrates the excessive level of stocks and thus also the failure to meet demand, is the 'degree of finality' of output (*Table 5.19*). This shows the proportion of final products in

Table 5.19 *Share of final products in sales of industrial production (%)*

	1971	1972	1973	1974	1975	1976	1977	1978
Total sales	100.0	100.0	100.0	100.0	100.0	100.0	100.0	100.0
Final products	35.7	36.3	36.4	36.6	36.2	36.2	35.1	35.2
of which for								
retail trade	15.7	15.6	15.6	15.6	15.4	15.0	14.8	14.6

Source: Statisticka ročenka ČSSR 1973, p. 242; 1975, p. 257; 1977, p. 337; 1979, p. 347.

industrial output. The trend in the proportion of all final products (consumer and investment goods for the domestic market less exports), and within it the proportion of goods going to retail trade (that is, to supply the population) may be seen in *Table 5.19*. The data indicate a falling trend in the degree of finality since 1974, and the retail trade share has decreased continuously, implying a relatively smaller flow of supplies to the retail network.

The aims of the efforts to raise the efficiency of the Czechoslovak economy – as we have shown – include, amongst others, improvement of the standard of living of the population. In the last part of this section we shall examine how far this aim has been successfully achieved.

Table 5.20 compares the trend in the standard of living during the 1970s with the peak years of the reform period (1967–1968). The comparison is unfavourable for the later period (1971–1975) and especially for 1976–1978. All the same, it must be admitted that in the last quarter of 1968 panic buying in reaction to the invasion by the Warsaw Pact troops inflated retail turnover and private consumption (Kosta, 1978, p. 156). The data assembled in *Table 5.20* further show that during the fifth five-year plan (1971–1975) the standard of living rose, following the 'normalization' years 1969–1970 when restrictive economic policy only allowed the level of consumption to rise slightly. Not until after 1975 did a clear turn for the worse occur.

Table 5.20 *Indicators of the standard of living I (annual average growth rates, 1970–1977)*

	1967–1968	*1969–1970*	*1971–1975*	*1976–1978*
Personal consumption	7.1	3.8	4.8	3.0
Personal consumption per head	6.8	4.0	4.2	2.3
Retail trade turnover	9.0	4.2	5.5	2.6
Real wages*	5.4	2.5	3.5	1.7

* Excluding members of agricultural production cooperatives and apprentices.

Source: *Statisticka ročenka ČSSR 1970*, pp. 24f.; *1972*, pp. 167, 407, 480; *1978*, pp. 23, 488.

Throughout the 1970s there has been criticism in the Czechoslovak specialist literature to the effect that consumer goods production and retail trade had no longer satisfied the growing demands of the economy (Kosta, 1978, pp. 162ff.). Thus, according to a report by the ministry of trade of the Czech republic in 1974, supply of 150 kinds of consumer goods had been inadequate. There were particular criticisms of the shortages of textiles, carpets, floor coverings, building materials, etc. Poor quality had led to an increase in complaints by consumers. Similar criticisms were made in subsequent years, too.

By international standards the level of private consumption in Czechoslovakia was already quite high in 1970 and had increased further by 1976 (*Table 5.21*). Yet there are still sectors which lag behind, like housing, some branches of infrastructure (transport and communications, the retail network, repair services, etc.) and foreign travel among others. Consequently the chief problem is not so much the general standard of living attained as

Table 5.21 *Indicators of the standard of living II*

	1970	1976
Consumption per head		
Meat (Kg)	71.9	81.0
Milk and dairy products (Kg)	196.2	213.6
Vegetables (Kg)	76.3	71.2
Eggs (number)	277	294
Fabrics (m)	43.4	47.8
Dresses, suits, etc. (number)	2.6	2.8
Shoes (pairs)	4.7	4.7
Electricity (Kwh)	278.8	456.8
Durable consumer goods per 100 households		
Washing machines and spin dryers	86	115
Refrigerators	56	83
Radio receivers	140	176
Television sets	79	107
Passenger cars	18	33

Source: Čisla pro Každeho 78, 1978, pp. 179–182.

the range of goods available and the unequally developed sectoral structure of both private and public consumption.

Finally, we should not overlook the fact that the growth of output and the goods and services available have been achieved by means of exhaustion of the potential labour force. The proportion of the total population gainfully employed (excluding security and military personnel and women on pregnancy leave and persons only working part-time) on 31 December 1976 was 47.3%, and the figure for women on the same date was 41.8%. (If the participation rate were calculated in the conventional way, that is, if the number actively employed were calculated as a proportion of the population of working age, the figures would be far higher than the comparable ones for other countries.) With a working week of 42 hours, overtime is also not uncommon in the major sectors of the Czechoslovak economy. These facts also explain why, despite a good standard of living, the amount of time which is necessary in order to earn consumer goods and services is rather high. The following comparison of the position of a worker in Czechoslovakia with that of his equivalent in West Germany illustrates these relationships (*Table 5.22*).

How can we sum up our study of the results of Czechoslovak economic development in the 1970s? Although a series of indicators of efficiency shows an adverse trend, in the first half of the decade the growth of output was successfully maintained, even if at a somewhat slower pace than earlier. The standard of living, too, was raised, although a number of problems in this sphere were revealed. A far less favourable picture emerges for the years

Table 5.22 *Amount of time to earn selected consumer goods and services for an industrial worker in Czechoslovakia and West Germany (1976) (in hours (°)/minutes (')*

	Mixed bread	Potatoes[a]	Pork[b]	Butter	Margarine	Sugar (refined)	Coffee	Man's shirt[c]	Man's town shoes[d]	Radio receiver	Refrigerator	Train ticket[e]	Letter post[f]
	1 Kg	5 Kg	1 Kg	1 Kg	1 Kg	1 Kg	1 Kg	1	1 pr	1	1 (1974)	50 Km	1
Czechoslovakia	12'	32'	2°18'	3°05'	1°27'	37'	12°18'	6°09'	18°05'	104°37'	136°09'	32'	3'
West Germany	12'	32'	1°03'	50'	24'	9'	2°07'	2°07'	5°23'	20°55'	48°53'	59'	3'

(a) Czechoslovakia: main crop potatoes;
(b) Czechoslovakia: roasting meat; West Germany: chops;
(c) Poplin;
(d) Box calf;
(e) Czechoslovakia; passenger train: West Germany; local transport return ticket;
(f) Internal;

Sources: Statistická ročenka ČSSR 1977, pp. 245, 341, MBWI, *Leistung in Zahlen '76*, p. 25; BIMB, *Zahlenspiegel* (Vergleich BRD – DDR), p. 27.

1976 to 1978 in respect of growth, efficiency and the continued improvement of the material living conditions of the population. In our concluding survey we shall consider the question of the causes of both the positive and the negative tendencies revealed here.

5.4 Conclusion

The first question to be answered is what factors made the maintenance of economic growth accompanied by continuing expansion of private and public consumption possible in the period from 1971 to 1975. Levcik (1979) lists four factors which should have had a favourable influence on development in the first half of the 1970s: (1) the success of agriculture, (2) the favourable structure of fixed capital established during the reform period, (3) the equilibrium created on the consumer goods market in 1970 and (4) positive effects of the trade surplus with the developing countries (*Statisticka rŏcenka 1978*, pp. 91, 172). In our view an additional factor was the few surviving elements of the preceding and largely abandoned reform policy. Specifically this concerns the following points.

In the agricultural sector the production cooperatives were for the most part freed from compulsory targets and detailed indicators at the beginning of the reform period. In addition, purchase prices of agricultural products rose more than did the prices of inputs into agriculture. Not least, these and other measures led to a substantial improvement in the incomes of cooperative farm members. In contrast to the dismantling of reform measures in industry, the advances gained in agriculture were in essence maintained after 1969. This explains the success of this sector, which registered average annual growth rates of about 3% from 1969 to 1977 without great fluctuations. As has already been shown, this led to substantial relief of the burden on foreign trade.

As a result of investment decisions taken during the reform period total industrial fixed capital increased by 40% between 1970 and 1976 (at constant prices), and the stock of machinery and equipment rose by as much as 52%. From this it may be concluded that investment in modernization enjoyed priority. In contrast to the onesided drive to develop heavy industry, especially basic materials industries, in the 1950s, in the 1970s fixed capital increased faster in manufacturing than in basic materials branches. (See also section 5.1.)

Furthermore – and this is another positive factor – the Czechoslovak leadership succeeded in implementing a price increase in retail trade in the course of 1969 (the price index for all consumer goods was said to have risen by 4.3%, for industrial products by 6.4% and for private services by 7.6%), and with the help of an extremely restrictive wage policy was able to contribute to the restoration of equilibrium in the consumer goods market.

Another favourable aspect was that trade surpluses in freely convertible currencies were earned with certain developing countries rich in raw materials (Iran, Iraq, Syria), which partly offset the deficit with Western industrial countries. It is assumed that in 1969 and 1970 additional relief for the Czechoslovak balance of payments was provided by the Soviet leadership's approval of some reduction in Czechoslovakia's armaments obligations under the Warsaw Pact and development aid to Cuba, Vietnam and certain Arab states.

Not least, it should be pointed out again that not all the positive elements of the reform were abolished. Thus in the foreign trade sector the price conversion procedure survived, which tends to assimilate the different domestic and foreign relative prices; so, too, did (admittedly small) bonuses for enterprise employees in the form of profit sharing and, finally, so did the generally more free mode of behaviour of enterprises *vis-à-vis* their superior planning bodies.

If our previous arguments are correct the positive effect of the factors mentioned could only be temporary (Levcik, 1979, p. 8). Apart from the favourable situation in agriculture, which presumably could last, the position in the other sectors is deteriorating: the structure of investment has shifted towards the familiar extensive pattern again in recent years, the terms of trade with all foreign trading partners have worsened distinctly and the equilibrium on the domestic market can only be maintained at the expense of private consumption and certain branches of infrastructure which are important to the citizen. In addition there is the evidently growing pressure from the Soviet Union and the other CMEA countries, whose demands for deliveries of investment goods are an extremely heavy burden on Czechoslovak production capacity. When we take into account the continuing deficiencies of the central directive steering mechanism – the priority of quantity over quality, of volume over efficiency, flexibility and capacity for innovation – the poor economic results of the years 1976 to 1978 are clearly explicable.

What alternatives emerge from this gloomy summary? Will future economic policy show greater readiness for reform, which in the writer's opinion is unavoidable if the present difficulties are to be overcome? This second question cannot be answered unequivocally, because the answer does not depend on economic considerations alone. Consequently we shall adhere to the following conclusion, which was formulated elsewhere a year earlier (Kosta, 1978, p. 180):

Czechoslovak economic policy in the late 1970s continued to display the stamp of the tension between the requirements of economic growth and efficiency on the one hand and the political interests of the regime on the other. Whilst economic efficiency demands more decentralisation, flexibility and openness to foreign trade, the continued existence of the power monopoly of the functionaries in the bureaucracy requires the maintenance of centralistic authoritarian decisionmaking structures and a certain isolation of the domestic economy from the outside world. Which tendency will gain the upper hand will depend on the interplay of diverse domestic and foreign economic and political factors, the influence of which is hard to foresee in detail.

Notes

1. Of course, the party leadership's attribution of the reasons for this crisis to the previous reform policy was completely false (see Husak, 1971). In reality the situation only became critical after the invasion by the Warsaw Pact troops (see Kosta, 1978, pp. 154ff.).
2. See the material for the XIV party congress in *Hospodarske noviny*, No. 21, 1971; on the February 1972 Central Committee plenum see the supplement to *Hospodarske noviny*, No. 8, 1972.
3. See the country studies in Höhmann (ed.), 1978.
4. According to the Federal Statistical Office plan fulfilment report in *Hospodarske noviny*, No. 7, 1980.
5. Following the Soviet pattern, the labour productivity indicator is calculated as the relationship of gross output and average number employed. Since gross output includes multiple counting of intermediate products the result is an exaggerated figure.
6. On this see, among others, the chapter on Poland by V. Fox in Höhmann (ed.), 1978.
7. This statement is based on information from dissident circles.
8. At least one article was devoted to this topic in each issue of the weekly paper *Hospodarske noviny* during 1977 and 1978.
9. This information is based on statements in the weekly *Hospodarske noviny* and on personal conversations with visitors to Czechoslovakia.
10. As the prime minister, Strougal, stressed at a CMEA session on 27 June 1979, on the basis of bilateral 'agreements on cooperation in the production of equipment for nuclear power stations' concluded with the Soviet Union in 1974 and 1976, 'comprehensive development of engineering and metallurgical capacity both for domestic needs and for export' is taking place in Czechoslovakia. 'This development', he continued, 'represents a fundamental structural change and is very exacting in that it restricts the possibilities of development of other branches of engineering, including those involved in the export programme to third countries.' Strougal's critical speech ws published only in the agricultural daily paper *Zemedelske noviny*, 28 June 1979; even this may have been an oversight. The share of technology imports (machinery, equipment, apparatus, vehicles) in total Czechoslovak imports from the Federal Republic of Germany amounted to more than 50% in 1976 (*Statisticka ročenka ČSSR 1977*, p. 463).
12. See the report on plan fulfilment in 1978 in *Hospodarske noviny*, No. 8, 1979 (supplement), pp. 6f. This thesis is more explicitly substantiated by Levcik (1979, p. 11), who draws the following conclusion from a statistical analysis: 'The planned export offensive to the Western industrial countries failed.' See also *Presseschau Ostwirtschaft*, No. 2, 1980, p. 13.
13. See a series of contributions in the periodical *Czechoslovak Economic Papers*, No. 16, 1976 and No. 17, 1977; also, a number of articles in the representative theoretical economic journal *Politicka ekonomie*, all volumes, clearly express the call for a reform of the planning system.
14. This sub-section to a large extent follows the discussion in Kosta (1978, pp. 172ff.).
15. This trend from horizontal ('trusts') to vertical associations of enterprises ('concerns') is comparable to the replacement of *VVB* by *Kombinate* in the GDR. See the 'discussion platform' in *Hospodarske noviny* under the heading 'K otazkam planoviteho rizeni', especially No. 37, 50, 51–52, 1977 and 5, 1978.

16. See the report of an international CMEA meeting on management problems in *Hospodarske noviny*, No. 23, 1978, p. 3.
17. 'Management' here means entrusting a particular organizational unit – the so-called 'manager' – with the direction and coordination of certain activities (e.g. sales, procurement, research) *vis-à-vis* other organizational units (*Ekonomika ceskoslovenskeho . . .*, 1960, p. 97).
18. Even the delivery contracts are an old practice, based on the Soviet pattern and in use under the central administrative planning system before the reform (*Ekonomika ceskoslovenskeho . . .*, 1960, pp. 305ff.).
19. For details of the various direct and indirect instruments see *Planovite rizeni . . .*, 1976, especially Section 3; a somewhat more general presentation may be found in a textbook on the economic policy of the KPC (*Hospodarska politika KSC*, 1977, Chs 4–12).
20. In general this sub-section follows the discussion in Kosta (1978, pp. 174ff.).
21. Law No. 133, 1969 (3 December 1969) and Law No. 168, 1969 (18 December 1969); see also *Hospodarske noviny*, No. 46, 1977, special supplement, p. 4.
22. Where no specific sources are cited the presentation of price policy follows Kosta (1978, pp. 169f., 177f.).
23. See the report by the prime minister, Strougal, at the KPC Central Committee plenum on 10 December 1970, in *Rude Pravo*, 16 December 1970.
24. See, for example, the publication by the head of the Federal Price Office, M. Sabolcik, in *Planovane Hospodarstvi*, No. 7, 1977, pp. 3ff., and *Hospodarske noviny*, No. 40, 1978, pp. 1ff.
25. Where no further sources are cited the discussion of wage policy follows Kosta (1978, pp. 175ff.).

References

Altmann, F.-L. and Slama, J. (1979. *Strukturentwicklung der tschechoslowakischen Wirtschaft und ihre Rückwirkung auf den Aussenhandel*. Munich.

Brčak, J. (1977). Rationalization of Wage Systems in Production: Experience and Problems. *Czechoslovak Economic Papers*, No. 17

Ceskoslovenska ekonomika v sedmdesatych letech (Collective authorship) (1975). Prague

Čisla pro Každeho (Annual). Prague

Czechoslovak Economic Papers, No. 16, 1976; No. 17, 1977

Economic Survey of Europe in 1971, Part 2, ECE, Geneva–New York, 1972, pp. 15–138

Ekonomika ceskoslovenskeho prumyslu (1960). Textbook, collective authorship. Prague

Formanek, K. (1978). Nova opatreni v planovani a regulace zamestnanosti a mezd. *Planovane hospodarstvi*, No. 5

Goldmann, J. and Kouba, K. (1969). *Economic Growth in Czechoslovakia*. Prague

Höhmann, H.-H. (ed.) (1978). *Die Wirtschaft Osteuropas und der VR China 1970–1980*. Stuttgart – Berlin – Köln – Mainz

Horalek, V. and Filip, V. (1975). Soustava planoviteho rizeni v 6 petiletke. No. 11

Hospodarska politika KSC. Collective authorship (1977). Prague

Hospodarske noviny, Prague, No. 21, 1971; No. 8, 1972; (supplement) No. 37, 39, 46 (supplement), 50, 51–52, 1977; No. 4 (supplement), 5, 18, 23, 25, 30, 31, 37, 40, 1978; No. 2, 3, 8 (supplement), 1979; No. 7 (supplement), 11–12 (supplement), 1980

Hrncir, M. *et al.* (1975). *Vnejsi ekonomicke vztahy a efektivnost cs. narodniho hospodarstvi*. Prague

Husak, G. (1971). Report to XIV KPC Congress, May, in *Hospodarske noviny*, No. 21, 1971

Janecek, V. (1978). K novym cenovym relacim v soustave velkoobchodnich cen. *Planovane Hospodarstvi*, No. 3

Komplexni experiment rizeni efektivnosti a kvality. Resolution of 8 December 1977 of government presidium

Kosta, J. (1978) *Abriss der sozialökonomischen Entwicklung der Tschechoslowakei*. Frankfurt

—— (1980). Zur wirtschaftlichen Zusammenarbeit mit den RGW-Ländern. *Osteuropa-Wirtschaft*, No. 3

——(1977). Beschäftigungsstruktur und Arbeitskräftepolitik in der Tschechoslovakei. In *Arbeitsmarkt und Wirtschaftsplanung* (ed. by H.-H. Höhmann).

Kutalek, Z. (1978). Poznamky k diskusi o regulaci mzdoveho vyvoje. *Planovane hospodarstvi*, No. 2

Levcik, F. (1979). *Strukturprobleme der CSSR in den siebziger Jahren*, Reprint-Serie No. 39

Listy (Journal of the Czechoslovak Socialist opposition), No. 5, 1977. Rome

Pechacek, P. (1977). Tendence ve vyvoji zasob. *Planovane hospodarstvi*, No. 9

Planovane hospodarstvi, No. 7, 1977

Planovite rizeni narodniho hospodarstvi ve svetle zaveru XV sjezdu, Prague, 1976

Prace (Czechoslovak trade union newspaper), 23 July 1977. Prague

Presseschau Ostwirtschaft, No. 2, 1980. Vienna

Rude Pravo, 16 December 1970, 7 March, 1980

Směrnice XIV sjezdu KSČ k 5 pětiletemu planu rozvoje narodniho hospodarstvi na léta 1971–1975. *Rude Pravo*, 2 June 1971 (supplement)

Sokolowsky, P. (1980). *Der Arbeitsmarkt in der Tschechoslovakei*. Dissertation. Frankfurt

Statisticka ročenka ČSSR, Prague (Annual statistical abstract)

Vacha, J. (1979). Prvni rok experimentu rizeni efektivnosti a kvality v prumyslu. *Statistika*, Nos. 8–9, pp. 345–52

Vintrova, R., Klacek, J. and Kupta, V. (1980). Ekonomicky rust v ČSSR, jeho bariery a efektivnost. *Politicka ekonomie*, No. 1, p. 32

Wochenbericht des DIW, No. 17, 1975. Berlin

Zemedelske noviny, 28 June 1979

CHAPTER 6

Problems and trends in the development of the Hungarian new economic mechanism: a balance sheet of the 1970s

Thomas Vajna

6.1 Centralization, decentralization, recentralization – a survey of the changes in the Hungarian economic order

In the past three decades the relationship between central and decentralized decisions in Hungary has perceptibly shifted several times. If we accept that, beside the question of ownership, this relationship represents the most important feature of the economic order, then the respective centralization and decentralization trends can be interpreted as changes in the fundamental conception of the political order.

In the second half of the 1940s a very rapid and intensive process of centralization took place in the Hungarian economy, as a product of developments in the social and political spheres: based on almost total nationalization of productive capital, the course of the economy was thoroughly regulated by means of central instructions. This process had already reached its peak around 1950. Further centralization tendencies were counteracted not so much by political considerations but rather by the fact that in practice there was no more potential for centralization available.

From this high level of centralization the 'minor economic reforms' of 1957 and 1964 initially brought about scarcely perceptible movements towards decentralization. In concrete terms this could be observed in the restriction of the number of compulsorily fixed plan magnitudes. The scope this created for decentralized decisions remained narrow all the same, and it was left to the initiative of the enterprise director to exploit it to the full. Only the beginnings of a system of material incentives could be recognized.

The 'major economic reform' of 1968 reduced the degree of centralization at a stroke. The relative weight of central and decentralized decisions in the 1968 reform conception can only be measured indirectly. Indications are provided by the proportion of central investment decisions, the proportion of sales going through centrally determined channels and the proportion of centrally regulated prices. On the basis of these attempts at quantification we can conclude that central and decentralized decisionmaking powers were more or less equally balanced.

It emerges unequivocally from all the declarations of intent on the introduction of the 1968 economic reform that the degree of decentralization achieved at the beginning of the reform was to be extended further. No binding declarations were made, however, about the speed of the decentralization process. The only time scale set was a vague one of around fifteen years for the transition to a market-determined price system. In so far as one can judge this at all for such a short period, the years 1969 and 1970 were indeed clearly characterized by a further decline in the centralization of economic decisions. This was accompanied by a parallel decentralization in the political bodies, among which the lower members of the hierarchy of councils were furnished with increased powers. The general trend towards decentralization was completed on the social policy plane by greater emphasis on participation within the enterprise, though this, of course, was more ideological than factual.

Then in the course of the 1970s this process came to a standstill in some spheres of economic policy and in others there was even a reversal of the trend. The tendency towards recentralization became perceptible about 1973–1974, when the economic situation of Hungary was threatened with severe disequilibrium owing to the extreme increases in the cost of raw material imports. The forms in which the recentralization showed itself were highly diverse. The clearly visible forms include the decision to put a few dozen major enterprises under direct ministerial supervision and the revision of the pronounced liberal attitude towards the independent craft enterprises. Less tangible was the change of direction in the field of price policy, where the proportion of centrally administered prices increased in many branches and yet contracted in others.

How far recentralization is politically prescribed as a trend for the coming years must initially remain an open question. The conception of economic management up to 1980 which could be derived from the last plan law provides no unequivocal indication, at any rate, of a drive to reduce decentralized decisionmaking. To be sure, the future trend of policy on the economic system depends to a great extent on whether balanced economic growth can be achieved. For the experience of recent years confirms that disturbances ultimately lead inevitably to political decisions in the direction of recentralization. Favourable results, on the other hand, create more scope for decentralization – this is the background to the most recent decisions of the Hungarian Parliament in December 1977, granting enterprises more freedom again in the operational sphere.

In what follows the trends of development since 1968 are illustrated by reference to the three major areas of economic policy – price policy, income policy and investment policy – so that a brief concluding summary of experience up to the present with the New Economic Mechanism can then be presented.

6.2 Problems of functioning and revisions of instruments in the 1970s

Price policy

The 1968 reform conception gave prices such important functions in the planning and steering of the economy that for many price policy constitutes the core of the reform (Haffner, 1972; Csikos-Nagy, 'Az uj magyar . . .', 1968).

For one thing, prices as a medium for the transmission of market impulses were intended to raise the efficiency of planning. As the amount of decentralization prescribed included the shifting of a significant part of the responsibility for planning to the individual enterprises, prices had become equally important as guidelines for macro-level and micro-level planning. In the hope that improvements in the price system would facilitate the creation of market-like conditions, prices were expected to have farreaching, allocation effects (Vajna, 1969). Nothing in this has changed in principle. When the medium-term economic policy for the fourth five-year plan (1971–1975) was adopted the reform conceptions were corroborated:

> We have demanded of the price system that it should contribute towards the efficient use of resources, the adjustment of production to meet effective demand, the expansion of output of modern products . . . (Vallus and Racz, 1970, p. 25).

The corresponding passages relating to the intentions of economic policy during the fifth five-year plan (1976–1980) are almost identical; in addition they refer to impetus for modernization of technology and a 'more efficient structure of production' (Nyul, 1977, p. 6).

For another thing, price policy was intended to be used as an independent instrument for the synchronization of individual enterprise and aggregate economic interests. Therefore economic policy reserved to itself the right to intervene directly in the price system within the framework of a set of priorities. In this way a certain mistrust in the natural allocation effect of prices came to light (Csikos-Nagy, 1969). The price system created and put into operation in this somewhat interventionist manner thus corresponded very closely to the 1968 conception of the economic order, the motto of this order being 'as much market as possible, as much plan as necessary'.

In concrete terms the mixed system of prices was reflected in the fact that at the various stages specified proportions of prices were regulated by the authorities: in industry initially 50%, in agriculture about 85% and in retail trade turnover about 75% (Csikos-Nagy, 1969). Prices were administered with differing degrees of strictness, which varied from fixed prices through maximum prices to price ranges (Haffner, 1972, p. 76). Meanwhile this list has been supplemented by contract prices. These are prices which are based on principles of calculation laid down by the state and are also established by contract between seller and buyer for lengthy periods – though subject to escalation clauses (Antal, 1976, p. 53). According to the original intention of the responsible Materials and Prices Office the proportion of administered prices was to be gradually reduced (Csikos-Nagy, 'A magyar . . .', 1968). In general this tendency only lasted until 1970–1971. *Tables 6.1* and *6.2* show that since then there has been little overall change.

Table 6.1 *The structure of producer prices, 1971 and 1976 (shares, %)*

Sectors	Officially fixed and maximum prices 1971	1976	Official price ranges 1971	1976	Free prices 1971	1976
Mining	77	76	–	–	23	24
Electricity	94	97	–	–	6	3
Metallurgical industries	85	73	1	1	14	26
Engineering	30	26	5	2	65	72
Building materials industry	30	22	–	–	70	78
Chemical industry	47	57	–	–	53	43
Light industry	21	18	3	4	76	78
Food industry	12	21	5	3	83	76
All industry	34	35	2	2	64	63
Construction	60[b]	90	–	–	40	10
Agriculture	76[b]	63	16[a]	25[a]	8	12

Notes: (a) Standard prices and guaranteed prices;
(b) 1974.

Table 6.2 *The structure of consumer prices, 1971 and 1976 (shares, %)*

Commodity groups	Officially fixed and maximum prices 1971	1976	Official price ranges 1971	1976	Free prices 1971	1976
Foodstuffs	65	62	17	17	18	21
Clothing	4	4	60	57	37	39
Household effects	44	45	10	10	46	45
Solid building materials	98	96	–	–	2	4
Products of the chemical and oil industries	70	69	–	–	30	31
Wood and paper goods	17	19	43	44	40	37
Building materials	77	79	–	–	23	21
Glass and china	–	–	–	–	100	100
Total retail trade	49	48	23	22	28	30
Services	41	49	18	13	41	38
Handicraft and free market goods	–	–	–	–	100	100
Total private consumption	45	45	21	20	34	35

At the producer stage there was an approximate balance between increasing administration (primarily in construction) and a declining proportion of official prices (in agriculture and engineering). At the consumer stage too, movements in both directions could be observed. What is noteworthy is that the flourishing liberalization of industrial producer prices overall was not reflected at the consumer stage.

Of course, the distribution of price types over time is not by itself sufficient to evaluate the price policy of the 1970s satisfactorily. There are a number of indications that the problems of the mixed price system manifested themselves in practice in an almost textbook fashion. There were disruptions in the functioning of both the 'market prices' and the officially regulated prices.

The difficulties with the free prices relate particularly to the fact that in Hungary functioning markets are the exception rather than the rule. An efficient market requires a minimum measure of competition, which in turn assumes a certain morphology. Partly as a relic of the period of strict centralization, but also as an economic consequence of the highly restricted domestic market and the farreaching central control of foreign trade, the number of suppliers is very limited. This natural monopoly situation at the beginning of the reform was above all characteristic of the industrial enterprise (J. Nagy, 1972). True, in 1968 the 'open market principle' was introduced, that is, the 'restricted profile' of the enterprise was abandoned. The possibility of entering new markets was thus legally established. But the economic pressure to safeguard this possibility could not be created artificially (Wilcsek, 1967). Thus very strict legislation on competition was needed to fill the gaps. This was considered necessary particularly because the achievement of the largest possible profit was linked to corresponding material advantage for management, so that the enterprise had a concrete interest in exploiting the scope for monopolistic pricing. In those cases where, despite a distinct concentration of power, free price setting was permitted, arrangements to check on abuses had to be made. In the first two years after the economic reform 'unjustified price increases' were the object of much publicity. Price increases which represented a response to increased demand were also denounced (J. Nagy, 1972, p. 236). The selective price controls were extended until the middle of the 1970s, applying primarily to consumer prices, although these were greatly influenced by producer prices. Further problems which appeared were that:

(1) The sanctions were either not effective at all or were too small in comparison with the 'damage inflicted on the economy';
(2) The price checks were carried out at too long intervals;
(3) The inspection apparatus was neither quantitatively nor qualitatively equipped to discharge its duties; this deficiency was brought clearly to light by the shift of supervision of the independent price setters onto the local Councils;

(4) The legal regulation of the state of affairs in enterprises (calculation formulae, surcharges) inevitably had to be drawn up in very general terms, so that it was very hard to produce proof of 'excessive prices' (Nyul, 1977, pp. 40ff.).

It was not only the inadequate degree of competition which disrupted the allocation function of prices but also the imperfections in the pricing of supplies, in other words in cost calculation. According to the original 1968 conception prices were to reflect the socially necessary expenditure, except when this principle was overridden by other preferences which required prices set on a different basis. In practice these preferences were reflected in the imposition of turnover taxes or the grant of subsidies to modify 'prime cost price' plus a profit margin (Csikos-Nagy, 1969, p. 155). In the interindustry price system the preference structure was bound to become evident everywhere since even the apparently freely calculated prices indirectly reflected the taxes and subsidies because of the techical interrelationships of production. This aspect was particularly important in the linking of the domestic price system to the world market: the prices of imported inputs were heavily manipulated by means of differential exchange rates and tariffs; for exports the degree of financial promotion varied with the commodity group and country of destination. The alterations in these 'financial bridges' and changes in the rates of and liability for indirect taxes in the first half of the 1970s caused considerable price movements which had only little connection with market changes in the strict sense. This problem affected all types of prices equally – both free and officially regulated prices.

The need to harmonize the domestic and world market price levels proved especially urgent where exported intermediate and finished goods were produced on the basis of imported raw materials. In the iron and steel industry, for example, it emerged that the foreign currency revenue obtained for the exported product could not even cover the foreign currency expenditure on the imported raw materials. Because of the 'financial bridges' (artificial cheapening of material imports through tax preferences) a transaction which was economically senseless for the country appeared advantageous: 'at the enterprise level the accounts showed a profitable export business' (Nyul, 1977, p. 15).

Between 1971 and 1974 the rise in the level of industrial producer prices for domestic sales amounted to 1.5% per year and was thus well below the rate of inflation abroad. Even the sharp revision in 1975 (when producer prices rose by 10.7%) was not sufficient to restore the link with the world market. But at least the domestic prices of the most important imported raw materials (energy, metals, chemicals, leather, wool, cotton) were raised by up to 150%. In this way around 20 billion forints were 'added' to the domestic price level through increased prices of imports and the state budget enjoyed a substantial relief. A second wave of import-determined price revisions of approximately the same size took place in 1976 (amounting to about 17 billion forints), with the effect concentrated this time on energy, timber and some other agricultural raw materials. As a result of this a balance was reached for the first time between import subsidies and import taxes (customs duties). From the allocation aspect this balance is not in itself important, but it is from the point of view of the state budget. An 8–12% revaluation of the forint against the convertible currencies and the transfer ruble offset the rise in the domestic price level in 1976 in relation to foreign trade. A number of consumer prices were also raised sharply in 1975–1976 by administrative decrees: energy prices were increased by about 25%, sugar by 50%, building materials by 22%, meat and meat products by 30%.

Despite the drastic scale of some of the increases, the raising of consumer prices in 1976 was not completely sufficient to reflect the full extent of the imported inflation in the consumer price level, although this had been more or less achieved with producer prices. Thus the second harmonization problem, that of the relationship between producer and consumer prices, was also not fully mastered as had been wished.

Even before the 1968 economic reform one of the political maxims was the need to create an integrated overall price system ('egyszintü arrendszer' – 'uniform price system') (Vajna, 1969, pp. 82f.). According to this principle price at the producer stage is determined from the socially necessary expenditure; in the course of interindustry processing it is raised by the creation of additional value and finally reaches the consumer including an allowance for the costs of distribution. (This vertical integration of the price system is, of course, found very widely in the Western market economies, and indeed applies to each individual price.) In Hungary at first the intention was to integrate only the overall price level, so that in particular cases deviations arising from considerations of social and health policy were to be accepted. In 1956 the consumer price level was 38% higher than the producer price level, in the first half of the 1960s it was still 14% higher and in 1968 4% – the 'gap' was entered in the state budget accounts as revenue from consumer taxes (Csikos-Nagy, 1969, p. 135). This declining disparity was eventually reversed in the middle of the 1970s: in 1976 the consumer price level was 2% below the producer price level, and if the prohibitive taxes on certain luxuries are excluded the gap came to 10%. This swing is contrary to the most recent conceptions of price policy. Since the middle of the 1970s the integrated price system has no longer been the watchword (Nyul, 1977, pp. 107ff.). The intention now is rather to return to conscious disparity as it existed in 1968 and earlier years: in future the producer price level is to be lower than the consumer price level. Underlying this is the aim of again financing a larger part of the state budget than at present through consumer taxes. In order to attain this goal there are two possibilities: further price rises at the consumer stage or relieving producer prices by reducing indirect taxes. There are already clear signs that both approaches are likely to be adopted simultaneously. The officially decreed consumer price increases in 1975–1976 were accompanied by a reduction in the capital charge imposed on producers. This charge was previously levied on the gross capital stock, but since 1975 the considerably smaller net capital stock has been the basis of assessment.

In conclusion it remains to be noted that the conceptions of price policy entertained in 1968 have been only partially fulfilled, possibly because of external circumstances:

(1) The liberalization of price setting was indeed successfully asserted as a conception, but in practice the proportion of 'free' prices remained frozen.
(2) The linking of the domestic price level to the world market was successfully achieved overall, although only after lengthy delay (Antal, 1976, p. 155).
(3) The vertical integration of the price system was abandoned as a conceptual task of price policy; this is to be regarded as a retrograde step.

Income policy

Under the 1968 reform conception the system for controlling incomes was allotted the most difficult task: it was supposed to provide for constant harmony between central and decentralized interests.

The original draft of the set of instruments to be used for income policy started from the following considerations:

(1) In order to ensure that the impulses emanating from the market through prices were in fact picked up, income policy had to generate – even if indirectly – pressure for reaction; in this way income policy was charged with a supplementary allocation function (Csikos-Nagy, 1967).
(2) Economic policy was to correct the new price system in order to guarantee a functional distribution of incomes which corresponded to the overall interests of the economy (Csikos-Nagy, 1966, p. 218).
(3) In order that all persons participating in economic life could be motivated in accordance with central objectives, income policy had to include the distribution of personal incomes in its task of harmonization without transgressing the limits of socially acceptable income differentiation (Berenyi, 1974, p. 30).
(4) Finally, the set of instruments used for income policy was to guarantee the financial provision necessary for the tasks of the state and the economy, regulating the institutional distribution of value created between state, enterprises and private households (Friss, 1969).

If we try to translate the demands placed on income policy in Hungary into the mode of thought of a market economy, the difficulty of the venture becomes especially clear. First, the principle of economic gain had to be introduced into an economic order with virtually no private ownership of the means of production in order to create a corresponding motivation. Second, in the absence of real land, labour and capital markets, a 'market-justified' functional distribution of income had to be simulated. These two functions of income policy disappear in a market economy, where the redistribution of income can be concentrated in the two remaining fields of activity (social policy and financial policy).

In view of its multiplicity of functions, it is not surprising that from the start the system of income control in Hungary was very complicated, and that in the course of the 1970s this system had to be reworked particularly frequently. The evidently unconcealed need for revisions to the income policy steering system gives cause to doubt whether it is in fact possible to find a consistent and efficient and at the same time permanent set of regulations at all. Despite all the detailed revisions, of course, one cornerstone of the 1968 conception remained untouched: the orientation of interest towards profit. The manual on medium-term income policy for the first half of the 1970s underlines the importance of profit:

> Successful implementation shows that the profit motive, which constitutes the fundamental factor in our income policy, has proved itself suitable for the purposeful harmonization of enterprise and national economic interests. (Ferge and Antal, 1970, p. 49)

Corresponding statements are to be found in the description of medium-term economic policy for the second half of the 1970s:

> Our steering system rests on the fact that enterprises are directly interested in raising their profits. Profit is the most comprehensive indicator of enterprise performance, because it reflects on the one hand the result of economical (or extravagant) practice on the cost side and, on the other hand, changes in the production structure in the right direction and improvements in the rate of sales. (Bagota and Garam, 1976, p. 198)

A profit-oriented system of this kind can only perform its tasks satisfactorily under three conditions. First, the profit motive must be predominant for enterprise managements and workforces, so that their behaviour is dictated by the link between personal income and enterprise profits. Second, the size of the incentives must be sufficient to exceed the threshold of perception. Third, and finally, the profits of the enterprise must be closely related to the degree of urgency of the production concerned – in other words, costs and revenues must mirror scarcities on the relevant factor and product markets as well as possible.

A survey of 130 leading managers, admittedly relating to an earlier time, showed that only 30% saw the maximization of the total profit, and a further 11% the maximization of profit per head, as the enterprise's goal. Growth of output, satisfaction of needs, utilization of capacity and job security, on the other hand, together accounted for 56%. Responsiveness to incentives can be deduced indirectly from the same survey: 28% of those questioned were reluctant to take risks because in their view the profit which could be expected was relatively too modest. Fear of losses caused 36% of those surveyed to be shy of risk taking (Komonyi, 1970, p. 49), not surprisingly, since the maximum personal liability of management in the case of loss amounted to three months' salary.

The regulations on profit sharing in 1968 left much to the decisionmaking powers of enterprises: not only the absolute but also the relative size of bonuses depended on the hierarchy within the enterprise. For top management bonuses up to 80% of annual salary, and for middle management up to 50%, could be paid out of profits; the remainder of the workforce was considerably worse off, with a maximum share of 15% of salary (Buda and Pongracz, 1968). All the same, in order to attain such rates the enterprise would have had to have a really fantastic profit performance. *Table 6.3* shows that in 1968–1970 additional income derived from profits in state industry was equivalent to only one month's basic income. In some

Table 6.3 *The trend of the profit-sharing fund (in percentages of wages and salaries)*

		State industry		Cooperative industry
	Lowest rate	Highest rate	Average rate	Average rate
1968	7.1	14.3	8.7	15.0
1969	4.6	11.6	6.7	15.0
1970	2.4	11.5	5.5	14.4
1971	7.7	18.3	10.1	14.2
1972	5.1	17.7	10.2	14.7
1973	3.9	16.1	10.6	14.8
1974	3.9	16.7	11.4	14.6
1975	4.1	16.6	11.5	14.7

enterprises the profit-sharing fund had indeed reached considerable orders of magnitude and evidently the profit-sharing provisions within enterprises adhered to the regulations – senior managers, who enjoyed high basic salaries in any case, received substantial bonuses. The trade unions, whose self-assurance has increased over the years since the reform, successfully intervened several times. As early as 1969–1970 the workforce was in practice rewarded at the expense of senior and middle management (Nemeslaki, 1973). In 1972 the trade unions secured the standardization of the maximum rate of profit sharing at 25% of annual income.

Since the beginning of 1976 the relevant regulations have again been changed. Profit sharing is now distinctly differentiated once more, although not so sharply as in 1968. Managerial personnel can receive a maximum of 30% of their annual income from profit sharing, plus a further 10–20% dependent on individual performance. This second component is intended to reward the successful introduction of rationalization measures in production and improvements in the product range even if the effects of the measures are not yet reflected in the enterprise's profits. Strictly speaking, this bonus calls into question the general validity of motivation according to profit. The maximum rate of profit sharing for the rest of the workforce is in practice around 15% of annual income (to be precise, the equivalent of 36–42 days' pay), as larger shares in profits are scarcely thinkable because of the tax regulations. The minimum share of the rest of the workforce amounts to 7% of annual income (Bagota and Garam, 1976, p. 201).

The changes in incomes policy which came into force with the fifth five-year plan extend far beyond the regulations on maximum rates of profit sharing – they affect broad sections of the original reform conception. Concerning the allocation function of income policy, an important change is that labour was made noticeably dearer in comparison with capital. For one thing, the transition to the net principle for the capital charge brought relatively greater relief for capital-intensive manufacturing processes, enterprises and branches. Capital assets financed from external sources became basically free of tax, and for some branches there were additional reliefs or even complete exemptions from the capital charge. These measures, which were discussed for many years (Kadar, 1972), led to an overall reduction in the capital tax burden by around one third. Second, the payroll tax was raised steeply: the original rate of 25% which was introduced in 1968 was put up to 35%. About two thirds of this tax goes to finance social security and the remainder is interpreted as payment for public investment in 'human capital' (Vajna, 1969, p. 69). The changes in the tax rates and arrangements made labour inputs over the whole economy dearer by about 13 billion forints – this is equivalent to some 3% of total value added. The necessity of such an artificial alteration in relative factor prices was becoming more and more urgent as the labour scarcity continued to increase during the 1970s – not least because of the failures of income policy, in the opinion of some critics (Nyul, 1977, p. 96). At present there are possibly around 200 000 more jobs in Hungary than members of the labour force, so that some 2% of all jobs are unfilled. The reasons for this shortage are certainly partly exogenous: the potential labour force is static and the scope for migration out of agriculture is already largely exhausted. Yet it is the unanimous opinion that industry is overstaffed and conceals a massive reserve of productivity the mobilization of which would eliminate problems of shortage. The fact that during the fourth five-year plan at least 90% of the growth of the economy was derived from increasing labour productivity does not contradict such views: despite all the growth in the first half of the 1970s the level of labour productivity is demonstrably too low. The reasons for the large reserve of productivity are numerous: excessive turnover, high absenteeism, unjustified downtime, disorganization, irregular production growth and slack labour discipline are the ones most frequently mentioned (Marton, 1977, pp. 14ff.). The increased mobility was quite in accordance with the reform conceptions: a number of administrative obstacles to mobility were removed ('authorized personnel'), so that a pent-up demand to change jobs was bound to be satisfied at a rush. In the meantime the turnover rate has settled down at 17% – though this is still considerably higher than in the 1960s. The least-skilled workers are the most prominent among those changing jobs, which on the other hand is not at all consistent with the idea of loosening up an ossified employment structure. This is all the more true, since the wave of movement between enterprises can be demonstrably attributed to the perverse effects of the income policy, as experts pointed out as early as 1968 (Revesz, 1968): wrongly defined 'incentives' in the 1968 conception made it lucrative for all participants to employ workers on below-average pay. In this way the profit–sharing fund could be increased and central wage controls evaded (Antal, 1968). By employing 35 low-skilled workers whose average pay was 25% below that of the original workforce a thousand-man enterprise could finance a 1% 'hidden' increase in pay in excess of what central regulations permitted (Bodnar, 1968):

> Enterprises increased their already underemployed internal labour capacity with industrial workers whom they could not utilize. (Marton, 1977, pp. 44ff.)

Certain quite obvious faults in the structure of the income policy steering system were gradually eliminated, primarily in the major revision of 1 January 1971 (Ferge and Antal, 1970, pp. 51f.). The central problem remained, however: the close link between enterprise profits and the opportunities for earnings. For beside the explicit profit sharing the possibilities of raising contractual incomes were also indirectly connected with enterprise results. There was little change in this until 1975, so that highly profitable enterprises attracted labour while those which made losses or earned little profit had to tolerate the loss of labour because they paid low wages. In principle this, too, would have been quite in the spirit of the reform conception, if economic policy had succeeded in keeping profits under control. In fact – for a variety of reasons – high profits also arose where this was contrary to central interests. Because of the legacy already described, on many individual markets profits also ran counter to the state of the market. The multiplicity of overlapping and partly contradictory levies and subsidies, which exerted substantial influence on the level of profits, further complicated the assessment of profits. Thus no-one could really judge any longer what the source of above-average profits ultimately was: market power, a fortunate combination of fiscal burdens or relief, or genuine scarcity. 'Excessive profits' were indeed taxed away by means of a specially created levy ('production tax'), yet the scope for increasing wages was largely unaffected.

The waves of movement between jobs made the clash between central, enterprise and personal interests plain. Metalworking enterprises had to accept considerable net losses of labour, although this was precisely the industry in which the state was assisting investment and wanted to carry out modernization of manufacturing capacity. Owing to the peculiarities of the income policy steering system, however, not all the costly new jobs could be filled. For the expansion of the stock of machinery had a negative effect on the level of the profit-sharing fund by cutting into enterprise profits; the changes in 1971 did bring some relief, but without eliminating the basic income discrimination against workforces employed in capital-intensive manufacturing. Small auxiliary and specialized enterprises, some organized as cooperatives, registered increased employment because they understood how to plug gaps in the market, even if their stock of machinery was obsolete. Thus it proved worthwhile for individual enterprises to adhere to combinations of factors of production which from a national point of view were disadvantageous (Ferge and Antal, 1970, pp. 48f.).

In the middle of the 1970s income policy thus found itself at the watershed between more tolerance and more administration. Theoretically, at least, there was the possibility of accepting the movement of labour towards small and medium specialized enterprises and waiting until the point of natural saturation was reached. At the same time measures could have been taken to improve the technology of the production capacity in these evidently very flexible economic units. The foundation of new auxiliary and ancillary enterprises would have offered the opportunity to create an enterprise structure corresponding to the domestic market and at the same time to weaken the monopoly power of the large enterprises. All the same, such a strategy clearly ran counter to the increased international division of labour which was the longer-term objective of the central plans, which can only think in terms of large enterprises. Furthermore, the deconcentration of the enterprise structure would have reduced the central bodies' possibility of supervision and potentially undermined their influence on the course of the economy. These must presumably have been the major reasons favouring the alternative of 'more administration'.

This alternative was broadly implemented in 1976. Enterprise wage policy was confined within narrow limits, while a 'minimum wage increase' was fixed for every enterprise, independent of its results. The previous spread of rates of wage increase, 0–15%, is now limited to 2–8%, but because of further regulations the actual range is likely to be only 4–6% (Bagota and Garam, 1976, p. 205). There are four different variants of the new wage policy in operation: relative wage level regulation, relative total wage regulation, central wage level regulation and central total wage regulation. In the last two cases (they apply to the various branches of the energy sector, large parts of the services sector and few branches of manufacturing industry) wage rises and total wages are completely independent of results. In the first two variants the enterprise results are still important for the growth of wages or of the total wage bill, but not nearly as much so as before; these variants apply to broad sections of manufacturing industry, state agriculture and certain services. The levelling of inter-sectoral and inter-enterprise wage and salary growth does not, of course, mean that differentials within enterprises would also be evened out. But it must be assumed that in practice the two go together. In order to upgrade the branches which were shunned because of their unattractive wage level and uncomfortable working conditions, revised wage rates finally came into force in 1976. Among general wage increases, the lower-paid groups are favoured and supplements are introduced for shift-work (Bagota and Garam, 1976, pp. 205f.).

As far as influencing contractual incomes is concerned, income policy remains at least as complicated as it was in 1968. Considerable simplification has been achieved, however, in the field of controls over the use of profits. This change, too, has been a gradual process, which was started at the beginning of the 1970s, when the shortcomings were already distinctly visible (Jancsi, 1972). In the original conception pre-tax profits were divided up according to specified formula – which depended on the total wage bill and the fixed capital employed – into various funds, of which the profit-sharing fund and the development fund, used to finance investments, were the most important. Transfers between funds were forbidden, so that profits were utilized in accordance with a central scheme. The two major funds were taxed separately, with the profit-sharing fund subject to a steeply progressive tax (top rate 50%), whereas the development fund bore a high but linear rate (60%). The changes from 1971 onwards did not affect the principle but changed the arrangements for obligatory distribution of profits. Revision of the distribution formula (the 'wage multiplier' was raised from 2 to 3) led to a noticeable increase in the gross profit-sharing fund. But at the same time the taxation was made more steeply progressive, with the initial exemption – originally 3% of the wage bill – abolished, the starting rate doubled to 40% and the top rate raised from 50% to 70% (Ferge and Antal, 1970, p. 57).

The regulations in force since 1976 have eliminated the obligatory division of profits. The rigid system of fund formation has given way to a somewhat more flexible utilization of profits. All the same, this freedom does not apply to the establishment and build-up of the obligatory reserve funds. Profits tax is initially set at a linear rate of 36%. Distributions to the workforce are in addition subject to further progressive taxation, while the part of profits used for self-financing of investments is exempt from tax beyond the basic 36%. The steepness of the progressive taxation on distributions to the workforce is shown by the following example: in order to be able to give the workforce a share in profits in excess of 40 days basic pay, 8 forints would have to be paid in tax for every 1 forint distributed. The alternative is to use 9 forints, tax-free, for investment. Distributions which do not exceed 15 days' basic pay are, however, relatively favourably treated. The tendency for levelling is thus clear, not only in relation to contractual incomes but even more so in relation to profit sharing. Evidently social policy objectives of equality have been implemented here too and the profit motive almost completely dropped in practice as the yardstick for income policy.

A tendency towards levelling can also be seen at the macro level in the medium-term trend of the distribution of income between the enterprise sector and the state budget. As a proportion of net value added, the tax burden in 1968 was 50.6%; in 1974 it was 63.5%. At the same time the rate of subsidies (overt subsidies only) rose from 16.7% in 1968 to 25.1% in 1974. The 1968 intention of cutting back indirect taxes and subsidies has not succeeded: turnover taxes increased by 120% in 1968–1974 and price subsidies by 135%, while net value added grew by only 63%. The importance of taxes on factor utilization – the wage bill tax and the capital charge – within total tax revenue declined considerably. It was precisely these two taxes which were intended to provide the incentives for a more economical approach to factors of production. The 1976 tax reform will initially increase the portion of net value added taken by the state even further; only in 'later years' is there to be some relief (Bagota and Garam, 1976, p. 195).

In conclusion we can say that the conception of income policy outlined in 1968 had to be revised at fundamental points, as it was unable to handle the multiplicity of tasks which it was expected to perform:

(1) The place of profit in the steering system has indeed remained basically high, but in practice the consequences resulting from this were not accepted;
(2) The linking of wages and additional personal incomes to enterprise profits was not in principle abandoned, but the scope for income differentiation was greatly restricted;
(3) Some fundamental weaknesses in the construction of the 1968 income policy steering system and the rigid fund-formation scheme have been eliminated, but the 1976 reformed conception features an increase in direct regulations;
(4) The measurable influence of the state in the circulation of income has risen perceptibly; contrary to the 1968 conceptions there has been an increase in the importance of redistribution by means of indirect taxes and subsidies.

Investment policy

It is no accident that the new investment policy introduced in 1968 has proved the most stable component of the economic reform. Its design has the advantage of being based on a strict conception, which has found an acceptable compromise between central and decentralized powers. Added to this was a tried and tested set of instruments which operated in a comprehensible manner and were never at all experimental. In one point investment policy enjoyed a natural advantage compared with price and income policy, which should not be underestimated: in Hungary at any rate it has virtually no unprotected political flank. In contrast to the multiplicity of functions of income policy, investment policy from the beginning had been allocated a consistent set of functions:

(1) Provision of an up-to-date combination of men and machinery in individual enterprises so as to keep abreast of technical progress;
(2) Shaping of a sectoral and regional economic structure which corresponds to the central conceptions;
(3) Development of the infrastructure, that is to say 'non-productive' specialized capacity (Sulyak, 1969).

The first of these functions applies predominantly to replacement and rationalization investment, the latter two to investment in expansion, even if a strict separation between them cannot really be made. At any rate, the 1968 reform conception started from the assumption that replacement and rationalization investment can be left to be decided autonomously by enterprises, since they rather than central bodies possess the detailed knowledge which this needs. Investment in the expansion of the 'productive sphere', which influences the structure of the economy, and infrastructure investment were on the other hand reserved for central decision. This clear division of responsibility as a basis for the whole of investment policy was to be retained even at later stages of the economic reform in the 1968 conception. In this way the centre was assured of free scope for active moulding of the structure of the economy without the risk of irksome clashes of authority. In the first reform year over 60% of total investment was decided centrally. Even then this proportion was regarded as far too high, and it was intended to decline gradually thereafter. No long-term limit was set for the reallocation of the central share of decisionmaking (Seidenstecher, 1972).

The investment decisions taken by the enterprises are subject to supervision by means of various instruments which work through the financing of the investment. For one thing this took the form of compulsory levies: 40% of depreciation allowances and 60% of the development fund, formed out of profit to finance investments, had to be surrendered to the state budget. Second, investment grants from the budget were offered for preferred projects, to top up enterprises' own development funds. Finally, the banking system granted additional external finance under a selective policy with strict profitability criteria. Differentiated interest rates and graduated terms (periods and repayment arrangements) offered additional opportunities for the transmission of preferences. Credit policy guidelines were to provide information annually from which enterprises could reckon their chances of obtaining a bank loan for investment purposes in good time. The idea of the selective credit policy was that the total volume of credit available should first be disaggregated among branches in accordance with structural plans, after which the most efficient investment projects would compete for the branch credit funds. The principle of competition was put into effect in practice by means of a 'rank number': this rank number, formed from the reciprocal of the profitability of investments and their repayment period, was designed to guarantee that, within the branch, loans would go where the degree of economic urgency of the investment was highest (Madarasi, 1967; Filipszki, 1967).

This mixture of direct and indirect investment policy was put through a severe test in the very first years of the economic reform. The release of enterprise initiative unleashed an investment boom, which clearly exceeded the planned figures: in 1969 investment rose by 30%, and again by 20% in 1970. This overheating of the investment climate was interpreted – presumably rightly – as an inevitable transitional phenomenon. All the same, it provided a good opportunity to test the new investment policy. It emerged that tension in the investment goods markets could be noticeably alleviated through counter-cyclical central investment decisionmaking. Thus severe restraint was exercised in centrally decided projects in 1970 (+6.5%), in order to offset the strongly expanding decentralized investment (+31%). Credit policy, on the other hand, was less efficient than at first expected in stopping the investment boom, even though it was taken to the limits of the possible with a tightening of the conditions to the point of a complete credit freeze. The reason this instrument could not work effectively was that economic policy clearly underestimated enterprises' own financial resources. Evidently in the years up to 1968 enterprises formed reserves which – with the additional help of the 1 January 1968 revaluation – were then openly shown as profits. In the years 1968–1969 gross profit on turnover reached 14%, a substantially higher figure than could be expected according to the model calculations before the reform. Enterprises therefore also had correspondingly higher development funds available, which were fully spent for the purpose of investment (Bagota and Garam, 1971, pp. 113ff.).

Despite this negative experience the investment policy conceived in 1970 for the fourth five-year plan showed only changes of nuance compared with the original reform ideas. Surprisingly, some changes were even made which increased enterprises' disposable financial resources. For example, the formation of an obligatory reserve out of the depreciation allowances left to the enterprise was abandoned from 1972 onwards. At the same time there was a reduction in the proportion of non-returnable investment grants, in place of which interest-bearing public loans on favourable terms were introduced. For projects which conformed especially closely to central plans there was the prospect that the state budget would take over the costs of credit if an enterprise had two projects promising approximately equal profitability, but one of which was closer to central conceptions. The testing of credit policy showed that in 1968–1969 its selective effect could not operate 'for lack of mass', since it had to be conducted in a very restrictive manner in order to keep the total volume of finance in the economy within limits. In addition, large portions of the total volume of credit, which was in any case small, had to be reserved to complete the financing of projects begun earlier (Berend and Dancs, 1970). The tightening of the credit terms, especially of the repayment periods, also had an unexpected effect on the structure of credit allocation. Enterprises of different branches were able to meet the steep demands for the granting of loans to varying degrees, so that the proportion of the branch credit allocation which was taken up varied widely. In this way substantial discrepancies came about between the centrally planned and the actual structure of new borrowing. An important factor here was that enterprises with a large development fund found it easier to get a favourable 'rank number'. Even if the profitability of their investment projects was not particularly high they could gain an advantage *vis-à-vis* enterprises which were short of capital by offering quick repayment. Following this discovery the authorities concluded that in future there would have to be different types of investment credit for more specific purposes:

(1) Bridging loans with a maximum period of two years, designed to overcome short-term bottlenecks in financing investment; they are granted outside the competition for the branch credit fund and depend only on repayment on time;
(2) Medium-term investment loans (for a maximum period of five years) are given strictly according to 'rank number';
(3) Long-term investment loans, for a maximum of twelve years, are offered in close accordance with state preferences, with 'rank number' only a secondary consideration (Antal, 1976, pp. 66ff.).

These minor revisions left the original reform conception largely untouched. The same applies to the changes in investment policy which came into force in 1976. (The temporary freeze on investment loans and grants for the first half of 1978 was connected only with the level of activity in the economy, not with investment policy.) The most important innovation relates to major investments affecting the structure of the economy, which are centrally decided. Here there has been a noticeable shift of responsibility since 1976, in that the enterprises concerned now have to answer for the construction, the financial burden and the profitable utilization of the new plants. In order to make this completely clear, the enterprises must pay back the investment grant to the state within ten years, irrespective of how long the installation of the plant has taken. If the enterprises achieve a low rate of profit, so that the returns from the investment are not sufficient to repay the capital advance, they must make up the shortfall from their own enterprise development fund. If the investment involves higher costs than planned, the enterprises must cover the excess from their own reserves. These regulations are designed to prevent enterprises submitting their projects as major investments for central decision merely in order to secure more favourable financing terms (Bagota and Garam, 1976, p. 208). The preference aspect of credit policy is once again to take second place to the profitability aspect.

Higher demands on the borrower in respect of rapid amortization of capital mean that mostly short- and medium-term loans are given. The preference system is confined almost exclusively to new capacity which will enable exports to be increased. State investment aid for projects decided by enterprises is only given in extremely exceptional cases as non-returnable grants. The 1976 profits tax reform favoured internal financing of investments. As we have described above, distributions to the workforce above a specified limit are subject to prohibitive taxation, so that a larger part of profits necessarily went into enterprise development funds.

If we try to sum up these measures, they mean more decentralization, rather than recentralization, of financing. The opposite conclusion must be drawn, however, if we consider the trend of decisionmaking powers. In 1970 the share of central investment decisions was 45.9% of the total volume of investment in the socialist sector, and it rose slightly to 47.3% in 1975. According to the fifth five-year plan, the proportion is to reach some 53.5% in 1980. This would still be below the 1968 level, yet over the medium term the tendency to comparative recentralization is clear, without, however, amounting to a fundamental change in the conception of investment policy. The increase in enterprise's share in investment financing on the one hand and the reduction in their share of the decisionmaking on the other, will bring their proportions of financing and decisionmaking closer in the second half of the 1970s: in 1970 enterprises had decided more than half of investment but financed only about 35% out of their own resources (Bagota and Garam, 1971, p. 57); according to Antal, the proportion of autonomous investment decisions is around 25% and the central authorities influence a further 25% through their participation in financing it.

The 1968 investment policy which, unlike the price and income policies, has remained almost unscathed has shown only limited effectiveness in relation to its objectives. 'During the fourth five-year plan, too, investment was the weakest point in the operation of the economy' (Bagota and Garam, 1976, p. 45). It was least successful in achieving an up-to-date combination of men and machinery. It must remain an open question how far a different investment policy would have produced better results under the given circumstances, the more so as the indirect influence exerted on enterprise investment decisions was designed to assist the price and income policies to fulfil their functions. To the extent that the evolution of the market-oriented price mechanism was stopped and the profit motive weakened, the meaningfulness of profitability calculations and the striving for profit were inevitably bound to suffer. But this removed the necessary reference basis for the indirect investment policy.

Whatever particular steering systems are to be held responsible, it must be noted that at best gradual improvement was registered in connection with the following aspects of investment:

(1) Too much time elapses between investment planning, the start of installation work and final commissioning, so that useful capacity, on the one hand, and capital tied up, on the other, are out of proportion;

(2) The structure of investment by purpose, that is, replacement, rationalization or expansion, is unbalanced. Although the level of utilization of existing capacity is unsatisfactory, too much additional plant is installed (Drecim, 1977, p. 22; Bagota and Garam, 1976, p. 45; *A Magyar . . .*, 1975, p. 34).

Table 6.4 shows that after the economic reform the level of uncompleted projects could not even be successfully stabilized. At the end of 1975 it

Table 6.4 *Completed and uncompleted investments in the socialist sector (in current prices, billion forints)*

	Total investment	*Completed investment*	*Change in uncompleted investment*
1968	56	57	− 1
1969	76	64	+12
1970	90	82	+ 8
1971	101	85	+16
1972	103	94	+ 9
1973	108	103	+ 5
1974	120	105	+15
1975	142	134	+ 8

reached the figure of 112 billion forints in the socialist sector; this was equivalent to 7% of the total capital stock of the economy. In the first half of the 1970s uncompleted investment led to an annual loss of production of around 60 billion forints. According to various estimates it takes about twice as long in Hungary to complete an investment as in Western economies, but also longer than in most other socialist countries. The delays are attributed to lack of capacity in the contracting enterprises, but also to shortages of building materials, difficulties with machinery deliveries, lack of materials and finally to mistakes in planning. The fact that almost identical conclusions concerning this problem can be read at the beginning of the fourth and fifth five-year plans as in the 1960s (Nemenyi, 1967, pp. 39ff; 1966, p. 69f.) is disquieting.

Delay in completing investment projects is in most cases an indication that the cost of the project has turned out to be higher than planned – and thus its profitability lower than the estimated level. For example, the machinery delivered to a Budapest paper factory from Poland exceeded the agreed dimensions, so that the enterprise buildings which had already been erected had to be pulled down and rebuilt (Papanek, 1977, p. 70). In such cases the enterprise has to review its financial position. If it does not succeed in obtaining the necessary bridging through bank credit, two possibilities remain: either other investment projects already started can be stopped or the project affected can be carried on gradually out of the enterprise's own financial resources. The continuing excess of investment expenditure over the national plan is probably still attributable more to deliberately over-drawn investment budgets than to genuine additional improvements. The changes in investment policy which came into force in 1976 aim to remedy this situation by making the enterprise liable even if the investment project has been decided centrally. The second problem area is the still too-expensive structure of investment. The share of buildings is regarded as far too high: it amounts to a good 30% of the total volume of investment, excluding housebuilding, and is thus, for example, about twice as high as in the Federal Republic of Germany. With machinery, too, the desire to expand currently plays the decisive role, as the share of replacement and rationalisation investment is only 15% – in the Federal Republic of Germany this proportion was 50% even in the boom years of 1970–1971. The fact that only 1–1.5% of the capital stock is scrapped annually is a further sign of an unbalanced investment structure (Bagota and Garam, 1976, p. 45); all the same, this figure is no different for the Federal Republic (1.4%). The predominance of expansionary investment clearly contradicts the aim of appropriate factor proportions, for new jobs are continually being created before the already available jobs have been filled. A balanced relationship between rationalization and expansion would have solved this problem: the correct investment structure can harmonize the release of and the demand for labour. The raising of the wage bill tax from 1976 may possibly lead to pressure in the direction of rationalization. At this point we should also note the introduction of the 10% tax on building, which is intended to exert a preference for investment in equipment rather than buildings.

There exist studies, in the form of spot checks, on how a more balanced investment structure could ensure better use of the productive capacity of the economy. If, for example, there were a concentrated effort at rationalization of intra-enterprise transport systems considerable labour reserves could be mobilized. Around 15% of all labour is used to move materials (in the GDR the figure is 5%), since the level of mechanisation of intra-enterprise transport is only 29% (40% in the GDR). Fitters spend up to 20% and turners up to 15% of their working time on such auxiliary jobs (Marton, 1977, p. 57). Labour is also wasted because obsolete machines which need frequent repair are kept in service, tying up undue amounts of labour. The consequence is that the older plant, which is in any case less productive, requires so much labour altogether that there is inevitably underutilization of modern plants; the overall level of capacity utilization is distinctly below the optimum. In industry on average only 1.4 shifts per day are worked, but from this time lost due to absenteeism and downtime must be deducted. According to one estimate, of the 10 to 11 billion hours of work theoretically possible in a year according to the labour legislation in fact only 7 to 7.5 billion are spent in productive work (Marton, 1977, pp. 50, 52); capacity, meanwhile, is evidently planned at the maximum possible value. Such states of affairs show just how closely price and income policy on the one hand and investment policy on the other are connected. For there is no basis for a more economical regrouping of enterprises' man–machine systems as long as the market rewards uneconomically produced, unnecessarily labour-intensive goods with correspondingly high prices and allows sizeable profits to be earned in such cases. The relatively poor utilization of the modern manufacturing capacity and the general excess of capacity have other causes, too – above all, the far from smooth functioning of the supply and distribution systems. Uneven flow of materials transmits short-run swings in production figures from one enterprise to others. The supply of spare parts, too, is still a hard problem to solve. Therefore, from the enterprise point of view there must often be reserve capacity to enable it to catch up again after interruptions in production. In some enterprises large fluctuations in production are almost built into annual plans: a temporary doubling of production from one quarter to the next is by no means a rarity (Marton, 1977, p. 65).

In comparison with these problems of investment – which are well known from the time before the reform – the size of the product, sector and regional allocations of specialized capital is not so important. Within relatively close tolerances investment policy can ensure the provision of the 'correct' capacity in the 'correct' branches and in the 'correct' regions – be it only by financing a complete new enterprise out of central resources. How efficiently the new capacity is ultimately used remains an open question. All the same, if misallocation within enterprises is aggravated by wrong product ranges and also by problems of sectoral and regional structure, it can only redound to the discredit of investment policy. As far as the product range of Hungarian industry is concerned, a study is frequently quoted, according to which only 20% of all products was up to the standard of the world market in terms of quality and modernity, about 30% came near to that standard and 50% was far below it (Papanek, 177, p. 32). Such simplified statements are open to the charge that they do not take account of the cost and price aspect. Traditional products of good quality are quite saleable on the world market at low prices; modern products can linger on the shelves despite being of good quality if their prices are excessive. In the quest for an up-to-date product structure little attention was paid to costs in the 1970s. Consequently, even marketable goods had to be subsidized on export markets. On the other hand, however, the modernization of the product range has been impeded by the fact that in many branches no adaptable capacity had been installed. In many export-oriented enterprises the result was underutilization due to lack of sales.

It is particularly hard to judge the efficiency of investment policy in moulding the sectoral structure. Of course, the planned and the actual structure can be compared in a purely mechanical way, as in *Table 6.5*. But

Table 6.5 *Planned and actual investment structure, 1971–1975 (%)*

	Plan data	Actual figures
Total socialist sector	100	100
Non-productive sectors	19.5	20.4
Productive sectors	80.5	79.6
Industry	42.2	38.9
Construction	3.1	2.7
Agriculture and forestry	13.7	14.9
Water supply	5.2	5.5
Transport and communications	12.6	12.5
Trade	3.7	4.1

the divergences between the two figures would only be a valuable measure if we could be certain that the planned structure was optimal. There may be good reasons why industry did not reach its planned share of total investment in 1971–1975 – some major centrally decided projects were held back in order to allow investment to be concentrated on completing outstanding projects. What is to be regarded as an unequivocal failure, on the other hand, is the construction industry's inability to achieve even its scant investment quota. The capacity of this branch of the economy – and of its principal supplier, the building materials industry – is permanently overloaded; some of the delays in completion of investments are attributable to this state of affairs.

Investment policy has been distinctly successful on the other hand in moulding the regional structure. By consistently locating new plants outside the industrial conglomeration in and around Budapest the proportion of the labour force employed in the overcrowded capital conurbation was reduced from 46% in 1970 to 41% in 1975 (Bagota and Garam, 1976, p. 46). The number of industrial jobs in the least developed regions in the east and south-west of the country increased by more than the average owing to a

Table 6.6 *Indicators of regional development (%)*

	Change in industrial employment	Change in investment per capita	Change in industrial investment
	1971–1975 / *1965–1970*	*1971–1975* / *1965–1970*	*1971–1975* / *1965–1970*
Selected less-developed districts (Szabolcs, Szatmar, Bacs-Kiskun, Hajdu-bihar, Tolna, Somogy)	+13	+79	+78
Selected developed districts (Veszprem, Komaram, Fejer, Heves, Borsod-Abauj-Zemplen)	+5	+62	+61
Budapest	−14	+78	+54
National average	+1	+72	+63

levelling investment policy, while Budapest lost one seventh of its industrial jobs (see *Table 6.6*).

To sum up, we can say of investment policy in the 1970s:

(1) The 1968 conception, which was based on a division of authority between central offices and enterprises and on indirect steering through fiscal and credit policy, has basically been maintained; the revision involved placing greater responsibility on enterprises for the execution and utilization of centrally decided projects.

(2) Investment policy was only moderately effective all the same, and in particular the problem of overinvestment and the associated low and uneven level of utilization of capital could not be solved with the set of instruments available.

(3) To ascribe this inefficiency entirely to the investment policy conception would certainly be unfair; the disruptions in the functioning of the investment sector are partly due to the price and income policies pursued.

6.3 Ten years of the new economic mechanism – an attempt at a balance sheet

The first decade after the introduction of the New Economic Mechanism has surely been a disappointment only to those whose expectations in the euphoria of reform were from the start too high. For no-one can argue convincingly that the new direction of economic policy at that time has collapsed. In fact, in view of the external economic and domestic political pressures it is remarkable how party and government in Hungary have held fast to the basic ideas of the reform. The fact that at the turn of the year 1977–1978 new advances in the development of the economic steering system in the direction of more decentralization were announced shows all the same that the representatives of the reform conception are under strong pressure to succeed – the chances of more comprehensive implementation of their alternative depend to a high degree on the results achieved.

Just as the sparkling economic results of 1977 brought a new impetus to the reform ideas, the rather moderate results in the first half of the 1970s stifled the consistent implementation of the reform conception. The interim balance sheet of the first decade of the reform shows, however, that the idea of distilling out only the advantages of the market and the plan conceptions of economic steering by harmonious coordination of the two is an illusion. This is true above all when the blend of central and decentralized steering elements varies in particular areas of economic policy. In practice it is evidently not possible to pursue a predominantly liberal price policy without at the same time accepting the temporary negative consequences for income and investment policy. But there are just as many problems in relying on the initiative of the individual enterprises if they are left with the possibility of solving all their problems by means of budget funds. The majority of Hungarian enterprises chose this comfortable alternative because the economic policy makers realized much too late that this was not consistent with the conception of the reform. For the representatives of the reform idea it may have been depressing that enterprises should have consciously misinterpreted the profit principle: the more difficult methods of cost reduction were rejected in favour of obtaining – to some extent even by false pretences – state grants or monopolistic price increases. All this cannot, of course, exculpate economic policy completely. It was afraid of the risk involved in penalizing uneconomic behaviour to a sufficient degree. Instead of liquidating unprofitable enterprises or sections of enterprises, production units which were no longer economically viable were supported. This tolerance towards enterprises with low levels of productivity and profitability is all the more incomprehensible as it was in no way the outcome of an emergency situation: in the mid-1970s at least, redundancies would have created no problems for the labour market.

On the other hand, anyone who has a feeling for political realities must have a good measure of understanding for these deviations from the reform conception which had pacifying social effect in the field of income policy. The trade unions' objections to a wage policy related tightly to profits were in many cases also justified on strictly economic grounds. As long as large wage increases are only possible due to a favourable combination of monopoly position and claim on subsidies, the movements of labour which they cause must appear very questionable from the allocation point of view.

In the long run the profit principle can only prove itself a useful aid to motivation and steering if the thicket of preferences and subsidies is cleared and sales are taxed at a uniform rate. Sooner or later the harmonization of taxes and elimination of subsidies must also be extended to the private consumption basket of goods, which hitherto, despite all the good resolutions of 1968, has been far from the case: the range of price subsidies in the major group of necessities stretches from 0% to 36%, the range of consumption taxes from 2% to 41% (Csikos-Nagy, 1976, p. 16).

The disruptions in the functioning of investment policy in turn could only be alleviated if uneconomic behaviour and violation of contracts were more heavily penalized. Important steps in this direction were taken in 1976, when the individual enterprise's liability for the construction and utilization of its new capacity was increased. But it remains to be seen whether the threatened sanctions will just fizzle out ineffectively in many cases: as long as an enterprise contributes to the fulfilment of quantitative export targets it can continue to rely on sure subsidies, which, in turn, make plant that is installed late and is underutilized 'profitable'. Here we again encounter the problem of coordinated use of instruments in an economic system, where economic policy must not only steer the macro-level aggregates but must also share substantial allocation functions with the market. The short-term considerations of current policy rarely coincide with the longer term requirements aimed at the optimization of factor utilization.

The compromises which are characteristic of both the original reform conception and present economic policy in Hungary will also continue to prevent optimal results being achieved from the particular policy functions in the future. As in the first decade of the reform, instruments which in themselves are effective will still have to be abandoned in order to conceal the imperfections in other spheres. This process impairs the medium- and long-term consistency of policy and burdens enterprises with frequent revisions of their mode of calculation. The political efficiency of the New Economic Mechanism is therefore bound to be continually called into question again.

To examine economic efficiency on the basis of the usual criteria – rates of growth of production and profitability, employment situation, price stability, balance of payments and budget equilibrium – involves the danger of an extremely mechaical approach. The decade before the economic reform in Hungary was distinguished by social and economic consolidation after the events of 1956. The beginnings of a more serious CMEA integration and the slow incorporation of Hungary into the division of labour on the almost uninterruptedly expanding Western markets created relatively calm conditions for domestic economic development. In the decade after the reform, on the other hand, the hardly predictable effects of the new concept had to be mastered. The powerful waves of the world market situation and the 1973 increases in energy and raw material prices held a considerable potential for disruption of an economy which in precisely this field is very import-dependent.

The superficiality of the apparently objective 'before and after comparison' is illustrated particularly clearly by the example of the trend in monetary values. The annual rate of inflation in 1958–1967 was not even 0.5%, in 1968–1977 on the other hand it was 2.5–3% – yet even the latter was really too low a figure to reflect fully the burden of the worsening in the terms of trade. In view of the circumstances, the annual average increase in national income in 1968–1977 of around 6% is to be rated more highly than the similar 6% growth rate in the pre-reform decade. The slowdown in the growth of industrial production to 5.5% (1958–1967: + 7%) presumably reflects the longer term trend in the degree of maturity of the economy – it is notable that since 1970 the increment in output has been provided almost completely from higher productivity; in 1958–1967, on the other hand, the labour force in industrial enterprises rose by around 2.5% annually (all data from the various issues of *Statisztikai Evkönyv* unless otherwise indicated). In neither period was there open underemployment. The fact that the rate of growth of productivity was raised despite a reduction in working time is indirect evidence that at least some concealed underemployment has been eliminated.

The foreign trade balance has undoubtedly deteriorated in the decade following the reform. The cumulative deficit in the trade balance for 1958–1967 was around 4–5 billion foreign trade forints. (Because of the change in valuation complete comparability is not possible.) Even when we consider that foreign trade turnover has grown greatly meanwhile, the current deficits are of an order of magnitude which is insupportable in the long run: around one-sixth of imports are being bought on credit. Hungary's foreign debt to the West is estimated at some 2 billion US dollars, of which half is in the form of credit taken from suppliers (*FAZ*, 20 January 1977).

Beside abstract aggregate economic statistics the most impressive achievement is the visible improvement in living conditions, of which the catch-phrase 'goulash communism' gives only a distorted reflection. The situation is more accurately described by noting that the level of equipment of households with consumer durables is in some cases close to saturation (radios, television sets, refrigerators and washing machines) and in the remainder is growing rapidly. Thus the number of private car registrations has already reached 100 000 per year and the stock is likely to pass the one million mark in 1980–1981 (*Blick durch die Wirtschaft*, 3 December 1977). What is noteworthy is that the selection of consumer goods is supplemented by articles from Western markets, so that a broad range of choice is offered, which in the general view is not to be found in the other CMEA countries. On the other hand, there has been scarcely any change in many cases of shortage: spare parts and accessories are still the weakest point of consumption – numerous letters to the press and exchange arrangements for wanted goods draw economic policy makers' attention to the problem daily. The provision of housing is unsatisfactory. True, the activation of private building led to a rise in the number of houses completed to 100 000 per year, double the level during the 1960s, but housing is still scarce: on average there are 1.5 persons per room (1970: 2.0; 1960: 2.4).

All in all, the balance sheet of the first decade after the introduction of the New Economic Mechanism is respectable, even if not so impressive that the other socialist countries would be compelled to follow the Hungarian example. A good part of the deficiencies in the functioning of the economy which have not been eliminated by the new policy may be ascribed to the compromises which are presumably immanent in the system in view of the ideological conditions of property ownership and the primacy of central planning.

6.4 Revision of strategy for the 1980s

On 1 November 1979 the official gazette of the Hungarian People's Republic, *Magyar Közlöny*, published 56 new regulations relating to economic policy, which came into force on 1 January 1980. Almost all important regulations previously in force were subject to revision. The overall effect of this renewed 'reform of the reform' is hard to assess. For just as with earlier reviews of the reform concept, simultaneous tendencies towards recentralization and decentralization are discernible. On the one hand, the autonomy of individual enterprises was *de facto* restricted, but on the other hand it was decided that price policy should move closer to a market basis.

The change of course in these two crucial areas of the 1968 economic reform must be seen against the background of the overall economic development during 1978. The most striking indicator of the difficulties with which Hungarian economic policy had to cope was certainly the doubling of the foreign trade deficit from 29 billion forints in 1977 to around 60 billion forints in 1978. The plan to close the trade gap in 1978 by a freeze on imports and a double-digit rise in exports more than failed ('Weltwirtschaft . . .'). In reality, exports stagnated while imports increased by well over 10%. The planned investment expenditure was exceeded by about 10% and consumption, too, rose somewhat faster than according to plan. In this way aggregate domestic expenditure exceeded the growth of domestic productivity more than ever. But it should have been the other way around, since Hungary, like the other small East European countries, should really have had to undergo a significant transfer of resources in the wake of the deterioration in its terms of trade. The failures of 1978 also included a further increase in the excessive level of stocks, which was interpreted as an indication that quantitative thinking had once again got the upper hand in enterprises; the effort to educate them to concentrate on profitability showed no visible success. The same may be said of the still-unsolved problems in connection with uncompleted investment, the level of which increased further, contrary to the intention of economic policy. The associated dispersion of investment funds obstructed the planned structural change in the economy, which was one of the principal goals of the five-year plan (Hoós, 1979).

To be sure, 1979 proved considerably more successful than 1978, especially in foreign trade. And the cutback in the volume of investment to the desired order of magnitude was at least nearly achieved too (Havasi, 1979). All the same, the criticism of the 'Mechanism' continued: the blame for the failures was attributable not so much to enterprises as to economic policy, which had evidently set the wrong signals – this was the formula adopted by the party leadership as the justification for deciding on a distinct change of strategy (Szikszay, 1979).

Changes in price policy

The principal idea underlying the changes in price policy, which are officially designated 'the 1980 price reform', remains basically unaltered: it is the creation of the greatest possible vertical integration of prices, which should function smoothly from the world market right through to the consumer stage. In some respects these conceptions, which have prevailed since 1968, are now being put into action substantially more radically than hitherto. The toughest stipulation relates to the raising of a series of industrial producer prices: this is only permitted on domestic sales to the extent that the enterprises concerned can prove equal price increases on Western markets. Csikos-Nagy, the long-serving president of the Materials and Prices Office, speaks of a 'transition from the prime cost price system to a competitive price system' and sees the latter as existing 'when the input price of natural resources is determined by the import price, and the final product price is determined by the export price in non-ruble terms' (Csikos-Nagy, 1979). The intention was that this principle should apply to 80% of industrial turnover from 1 January 1980.

The objective of the price reform is that, as far as possible, the enterprise should only be able to improve its profit situation if costs per unit of production are reduced or the product range is appropriately revised. In comparison with prime cost pricing, which is substantially more comfortable for enterprises, the 'competitive' prices require economical use of labour and material inputs. Since in view of the continuing concentration there is scarcely any competition on the domestic market, an attempt is being made to simulate it by means of the link between domestic prices and export prices on Western markets. With only 700 or so enterprises and about the same number of cooperatives in the whole of Hungarian industry it is, in fact, likely to be difficult to rely on the competitive mechanism in the domestic economy.

In practice, of course, the concept of 'competitive' prices encounters substantial difficulties. A number of Hungarian enterprises which it is hard to estimate would have to declare themselves bankrupt if they could only charge for domestic sales the prices they achieve on the Western market. One reason is because the market position of the Hungarian products in the West is too weak to allow them to sell at profitable prices at all. Another is because trade restrictions have to be overcome, which *a priori* limit the scope for export prices. This latter applies primarily to agriculture and the food industry. The transition to the 'competitive' price system will therefore only be able to occur gradually – either the full adaptation of prices will be left until subsequent years or supporting subsidies will be paid. In the longer run, problems could arise from the fact that the Hungarian price level will be inflated to the same degree as that in the West. All the same, the automatic import of inflation could be prevented by changes in the exchange rate. Until the deficit in the trade balance is eliminated, of course, no revaluation of the forint can be expected (Havasi, 1979).

As a whole, the reform of producer prices, in so far as it can be implemented, can be regarded as conceptual progress. However, it only makes sense if at the same time consumer prices are more flexibly linked to producer prices. This is the political dynamite of the 1980 price reform. The linking of consumer prices to the producer price level is indeed an organic part of the 1980 price reform, yet the transition times are considerably longer here than for producer prices. This scepticism appears unjustified if one takes a look at the price increases which have actually been put into effect. The price of bread, held stable for twenty-eight years as a political price, was raised on average by 50%. Until then substantial quantities were fed to livestock, thanks to the subsidized price. Meat and meat products prices increased by 26%, sugar by more than 20%, and there was also a steep rise in the price of dairy products. Nevertheless, this was not even sufficient to cut the absolute burden of food subsidies on the state budget. Only bread is now sold at a price which is correctly related to the producer price.

The same is true of energy prices. The price of electricity, untouched for fifteen years for political reasons, was raised by 50% – but it would have had to be 90% in order to cut out the subsidy altogether. The charges for district heating increased by 40%, yet they cover only one third of its costs. The private consumption of the Hungarian population is subsidized by a total amount of around 40 billion forints (Nyül, 1979), so that rapid dismantling of the disproportions would be bound to affect severely the standard of living of the population. The price increases, which added a full 5% to the cost of living, were therefore accompanied by income supplements. In this way the dissatisfaction of the population could be at least partly contained, and the long-overdue correction of the consumer price structure more quietly handled than in Poland.

Income policy

The income policy revisions which came into force on 1 January 1980 are at least in one respect consistent: the experimentation with incentive formulae continues, with no end in sight. The recurrent deficiencies in functioning, which are concealed in the details of the regulations, have once again been met by a multitude of special provisions. The system of material incentives has now become so complicated that, for that reason alone, the intended effects are bound to fail to materialize: with the exception of the chief accountant scarcely anybody is likely to be in a position to follow the entire complex of guidelines. To that extent these revisions are disappointing; further changes in the foreseeable future can hardly be avoided. Only a thoroughgoing simplification and standardization could offer a solution here.

Enterprise wage policy is conducted by branches along six different lines ('Decree . . .' (12), 1979). These are (a) performance-related regulation of the total wage bill, (b) central regulation of the total wage bill, (c) 'relations-determined' central regulation of the total wage bill, (d) perform-ance-related regulation of the wage level, (e) central regulation of the wage level and (f) 'relations-determined' central regulation of the wage level. The use of the different types of regulation in particular branches seems almost arbitrary. The confectionery industry appears in group (b), the sugar industry in group (a), and the bakery industry in group (e). In addition to these economically unsustainable differences the respective departmental ministers or supreme supervisory organs have the possibility of taking decisions in their branch which deviate from the general guidelines. The trend of pay in individual enterprises is thus primarily determined by their grouping and their supervising authority; there can therefore be only very limited feedback from market success to scope for pay increases.

There is most opportunity for this in versions (a) and (d) of wage policy, in which the total wage bill or the wage level are derived from the economic performance of the enterprise. The differentials which could in principle arise from this are, however, considerably restricted by the imposition of an extremely progressive compulsory levy on wage increases beyond a specified threshold. If, for example, the limit on the increase in total wage bill is exceeded by 2%, three times the excess amount must be paid to the state. In the case of the wage level transgression of the limit is even more heavily taxed ('Decree . . .', 1979). However, the 1.5% general tax on the wage bill was abolished. A further concession is that an increase in wages by 6–8%, which in view of the 5% rise in consumer prices seems by no means high, is taxed relatively less than in the past.

Enterprise profit may be intended to be the yardstick for wage differentiation, but in 1978 this incentive mechanism scarcely functioned. For enterprises which achieved no increase in profits at all raised the level of wages by 8.1%, while enterprises with profits growth of more than 20% were able to do little more – 9.3% in fact – for the average member of their workforce (Havasi, 1979). A special problem in this connection is 'unfair profit'.

According to a decision of the Council of Ministers unfair profit occurs when the enterprise's price policy infringes state guidelines, especially when its selling price is 'disproportionately high' ('Decision . . .', 1979). In assessing this, quality, modernity, foreign trade prices and the prices of comparable products should be used as yardsticks. 'High' prices are permissible when this is justified by the relationship of demand and supply – whatever that may mean. There is the threat of commercial law (compensation), disciplinary law and even criminal law consequences for enterprises whose domestic sales prices:

(1) Are unjustifiably higher than for exports to the West;
(2) Are raised when the costs of inputs increase but are not reduced when input prices decline;
(3) Are excessive because the goods have been made artificially scarce by the choice of sales outlets or by the exclusion of certain trade channels;
(4) Are the result of misuse of monopoly power;
(5) Are 'structurally' excessive because cheaper goods have been deleted from the product range and not replaced or deliberately made scarce;
(6) Remain unchanged while quality or fittings are reduced;
(7) Do not pass on the benefits of price subsidies from the budget.

Besides these there are still other situations, like exploitation of an emergency, which resemble the corresonding provisions of German law. All together, however, it is clear that in practice competition policy in Hungary is even more than before taking the form of price controls. This generates a kind of obligation for enterprises which have earned profits to justify them.

The link between individual material interest and the total profitability of the enterprise (profit as a percentage of capital employed plus total wage bill) is basically unchanged in that a prescribed part of profit can be allocated to the profit-sharing fund. The taxation of the profit-sharing fund is based on a well thought-out principle: the higher the total profitability, the larger the amount which is exempt from tax. Thus enterprises which have achieved a level of profitability of more than 16% can distribute an additional 4% on their wage bill in tax-free shares in profit. But there is no exemption from tax for enterprises showing a profitability of less than 2%. The importance of the tax exemption level can only be appreciated by looking at the rates of taxation: once the exemption level is exceeded the rate of tax starts immediately at 200%, with no transition. The peak rates are completely prohibitive. Even an enterprise which attained a total profit of 20% would have to pay a top rate of 800% (!) in profits tax if it distributed more than 14% of its annual wage bill to its profit-sharing fund ('Decree . . .' (17), 1979).

When we try to estimate the importance of the incentives, it rapidly becomes clear how marginal the workforce's interest in maximizing total profitability must be. Let us assume that an enterprise has achieved a profitability of 10%, has an annual wage bill of 100 million forints, and wishes to give its workforce a share in profits of 5% of the wage bill. In this profitability zone the tax exemption level is 2% of the wage bill; on the next 2%, 200% must be paid in profits tax and on the last 1%, 300% must be paid. This by no means excessive rate of profit-sharing of 5%, then, results in an average tax burden of 110% of the sum distributed, or a rate of tax of over 52%.

Viewed realistically, then, the potential differentiation of workforces' incomes in relation to profitability is hardly more than a few per cent. Compared with the financial possibilities opened up by taking a second job this is far too little. Hence it is not surprising that no worthwhile improvements in labour morale can be achieved by means of the material incentive. The desired impetus to labour productivity remains correspondingly limited.

Statistical studies of the level of profit sharing show that since the middle of the 1970s there has been a clear downward trend. In 1975 it amounted on average to 5.7% and by 1978 had dropped to 3.8% (Racz, 1979). At the same time differentiation in rates of wages growth increased somewhat. In view of the wage policy regulation already mentioned, the actual wage differentiation is likely to be more clearly dependent on central decisions than before. What deviations from the general trend of increase in wages should be allowed in individual cases is a topic of continual discussion. The present position is that the need for differentiation can be satisfied by variations of 40–50% of the average rate of increase (Racz, 1979). Thus if wages rise by an average of 6%, the permissible spread is from 3% to 9%.

In trying to sum up the changes in income policy a certain trend towards centralization can scarcely be mistaken. Beside the trimming of enterprises' financial autonomy the over-bureaucratization of economic policy plays an important part here. Voices are now again to be heard which see no further scope for progress in increasing economic 'levers' (Drecin, 1979). On the other hand, there are no alternatives to the present exceedingly complicated system of economic steering in sight. For neither a complete market economy solution nor a return to tight central planning are feasible under the given political circumstances. Hence the forecast for Hungarian economic policy in the 1980s can only be: further experimentation with the 'socialist market economy' – with more or less success according to the world economic situation.

References

A Magyar Szocialista Munkaspart XI Kongresszusa (1975). Budapest

Antal, E. (1976). *Das Wirtschaftslenkungssystem des ungarischen Sozialismus.* Münich

Antal, I. (1968). Vallalati erdekeltseg es letszamstruktura. *Közgazdasagi Szemle,* pp. 925ff.

Bagota, B. and Garam, J. (1971). *A nepgazdasag fejlesztesenek negyedik öteves terve.* Budapest

—— (1976). *A nepgazdasag fejlesztesenek ötödik öteves terve.* Budapest

Berend, I. and Dancs, I. (1970). A fejlesztes szabalyozasa. *Közgazdasagi szabalyozo rendszerünk tovabbfejlesztese.* Budapest

Berenyi, J. (1974). *Lohnsystem und Lohnstruktur in Österreich und in Ungarn.* Vienna and New York

Blick durch die Wirtschaft, 3 December 1977

Bodnar, L. (1968). Megegyszer a jövedelemszabalyozasrol. *Penzügyi szemle,* p.233

Buda, J. and Pongracz, L. (1968). *Szemelyi jövedelmek, anyagi erdekeltseg munkaerogazdalkodas.* Budapest

Csikos-Nagy, B. (1966). Die ungarische Preisreform. *Osteuropa Wirtschaft,* No. 3, p. 218

—— (1967). A gazdasagiranyitasi rendszer Küszöben. *Közgazdasagi Szemle,* pp. 1400ff.

—— (1968a). A magyar gazdasagiranyitasi reform elso tapasztalatai. *Közgazdasagi Szemle,* pp. 1269ff.

—— (1968b). Az uj magyar arrendszer. *Közgazdasagi Szemle,* pp. 1397ff.

—— (1969). The New Hungarian Price System. *Reform of the Economic Mechanism in Hungary.* (ed. by I. Friss) Budapest

—— (1976). Die Preispolitik zu Beginn der gegenwärtigen Fünfjahrplanperiode. *Marketing in Ungarn,* No. 3, p. 16

—— (1979). Die Betriebe müssen sich stärker nach den Weltmarktpreisen richten. *Handelsblatt,* 14 November 1979, pp. 29ff.

Decision 1028/1979 (XI.1.) of the Council of ministers, *Magyar Közlöny,* 1979/77, pp. 963ff.

Decree 12/1979 (XI.1.) of the Minister of Labour, *Magyar Közlöny,* 1979/77, pp. 965ff.

Decree 17/1979 (XI.1.) of the Minister of Finance, Magyar Közlöny, 1979/77, pp. 988ff.

Drecin, J. (1977). *A hatekonysag szerepe gazdasagi fejlödesünk jelen szakaszaban.* Budapest

—— (1979). Nehany gondolat a gazdasagi erdekeltsegröl es a szemlelet modosulasanak szüksegessegeröl. *Tarsadalmi szemle,* No. 5, pp. 13ff.

Ferge, S. and Antal, L. (1970). A vallalati jövedelemszabalyozas es tamogatas rendszere. *In Közgazdasagi szabalyozo rendszerünk tovabbfejlesztese.* Budapest

Filipszki, Z. (1967). A hitelpolitika iranyevei a reform kezdeteben. *Penzügyi szemle,* pp 892ff.

Frankfurter Allgemeine Zeitung, 20 January 1977

Friss, I. (1969). Principal Features of the New System of Planning, Economic Control and Management in Hungary. In Friss (ed.) *Economic Mechanism*

Haffner, F. (1972). Reformen der Preissysteme. In *Die Wirtschaftsordungen Osteuropas in Wandel,* Vol. II (ed. by H.-H. Höhmann, M. Kaser and K. C. Thalheim). Freiburg

Havasi, F. (1979). Az 1979 evi nepgazdasagi terv vegrehajtasanak eddigi tapasztalatai. *Tarsadalmi szemle,* No. 7–8, p. 4

Hoós, J. (1979). Soron levö gazdasagpolitikai feladatainkrol. *Tarsadalmi szemle,* No. 4, pp. 7ff.

Jancsi, G. (1972). A nyereseg es a jövedelemszabalyozas szerepe a vallalati döntesben. *Penzugyi szemle,* pp. 586ff.

Kadar, J. (1972). Report to Central Committee session of 14–15 November 1972

Komonyi, Z. (1970). Some Aspects of Enterprise Behaviour. In *Progress and Planning in Industry.* Budapest

Madarasi, A. (1967). A beruhazasok uj finansirozasi rendszererol. *Penzügyi szemle,* pp. 196ff.

Marton, J. (1977). *Hatekony munkaerogazdalkodas.* Budapest

Nagy, J. (1972). Das Monopolproblem in Ungarn. *Osteuropa Wirtschaft,* no. 4, pp. 221ff.

Nemenyi, I. (1966). *A nepgazdasag fejlesztesenek harmadik öteves terve.* Budapest

—— (1967). *Beruhazasi politikank.* Budapest

Nemeslaki, T. (1973). Ber-es kereseti aranyok. In *A szocialista gazdasag es a szakszervezetek.* Budapest

Nyul, E. (1977). *Arpolitikank az ötödik öteves terv idöszakaban.* Budapest

—— (1979). Gazdasagi fejlödesunk es az arrendszer. *Tarsadalmi szemle*, No. 6, p. 18

Papanek, G. (1977). *Az ipari termekszerkezet javitasanak idöszerü feladatai*, Budapest

Racz, A. (1979). Mvnka szerinti elosztas, ösztönzes. *Tarsadalmi szemle*, No. 9, p. 16.

Revesz, G. (1968). Jövedelemszabalyozasi rendszerünk varhato hatasainak elemezesehez. *Penzügyi Szemle*, pp. 132ff.

Seidenstecher, G. (1972). Die Wirtschaftsreform und die Planung und Finanzierung von Investitionen. In Höhmann, Kaser and Thalheim (eds) *Die Wirtschaftsordnungen Osteuropas im Wandel*

Statisztikai Evkönyv, various issues

Sulyak, B. (1969). Major Financial Regulators in the New System of Economic Control and Management. In Friss (ed.) *Economic Mechanism*

Szikszay, B. (1979). A szabalyozok 1979 evi modositasa. *Tarsadalmi szemle*, No. 2, p. 11

Vajna, T. (1969). *Die Reform der ungarischen Wirtschaftspolitik* (Dissertation). Cologne

Vallus, P. and Racz, L. (1970). Az arrendszer ertekelese es tovabbfejlesztesenek iranyai. In *Közgazdasagi szabalyozo rendszerünk tovabbfejlesztese*. Budapest

Weltwirtschaft zur Jahresmitte, Ungarn, Supplement to *NJA*, 29 Jg. Nr. BM 235

Wilcsek, J. (1967). A gadasagi verseny helye es szerepe az uj gazdasagi mechanizmusban. *Közgazdasagi Szemle*, pp. 817ff.

Economic development and planning in Bulgaria in the 1970s

George R. Feiwel

In the 1950s and 1960s, Bulgaria, together with Romania, was considered to be the fastest growing economy in Eastern Europe. In the 1960s the growth rates had begun to decelerate but they were still fairly respectable. However, during the first half of the 1970s Bulgaria was bested by Romania and Poland in growth rates of both national income and industrial output – a matter of considerable concern to the central planners. This was probably a major reason why the targets of Bulgaria's 1975–1980 five-year plan (FYP) were much higher than those of its CMEA partners. But performance fell disastrously behind plan.

In the 1970s Bulgaria continued to struggle with an attempt to infuse dynamism throughout the economy, but without much success due to the resistance to innovation built into the economy and the much more cautious, than in the other East European economies, shopping spree for new technology in the West. But it did succeed in substantially expanding and modernizing its machine building industry and becoming an important exporter of machinery, primarily to its CMEA trade partners.

Bulgaria was also an innovator in Eastern Europe in reorganization and 'industrialization' of agriculture. But the agricultural apparatus thus created proved to be overcentralized and unwieldy and contributed in the 1970s to a much slower growth of agriculture than in the 1950s and 1960s. Yet agricultural products remained a major source of earning foreign currency, especially hard currency. At the same time, the poor performance in agriculture adversely affected living standards. Improvement of living standards was long overdue. In the early 1970s the leadership made a valiant attempt at redressing the situation. But because of the overheating and consequent poor performance of the economy, after only a couple of years of relative improvement, the consumers' lot again fell by the wayside. In the latter part of the 1970s real incomes grew at much slower rates than in the late 1960s and the first half of the 1970s. By the mid-1970s the goals for improvement of living standards by 1980 and 1990 were lower than those enunciated in the early 1970s.

The attempts at reforming the Bulgarian economy were primarily initiated in response to deteriorating performance. The fruits of increased efficiency were going to be used to improve living standards and for further indus-trialization, but the various redesigns of the management system did not provide the necessary measures for increasing efficiency, nor did the high-investment growth policy pursued afford the release of tensions necessary for such measures to take root. The modifications in economic management introduced in the late 1970s somewhat relaxed the highly monopolized, cumbersome, and bureaucratic structure established in the early 1970s. But the devolution of decisionmaking was only to a larger number of monopolistic organizations (combines rather than associations) and not to the production units themselves. Moreover, the system remains centralized in its tight control over formation and disbursement of resources and open to further recentralization. In essence the traditional system has been preserved. For many cogent reasons the regime remains opposed to market-type reforms and democratization of the economic process.

7.1 Aspects of economic development at the threshold of the 1970s

A distinguishing feature of Bulgarian industrialization was the speed and character of the structural transformation, that is, the striking rapidity of industrial growth and the disproportionate rates of sectoral advance, with priority of heavy industry as a hallmark, as reflected in the shifting composition of the structure of production by sectors of origin over time[1].

Agricultural performance seems to have been much better in the 1950s in Bulgaria than in the other CMEA countries. However, in the 1960s Bulgarian agricultural growth was slower than in the 1950s and about the same as in the other countries. The prewar backwardness and inefficiency of Bulgarian agriculture contributed to the relatively good showing of the immediate postwar period. Moreover, investment allocation favoured this sector more in Bulgaria than in the other countries.

Throughout the postwar period Bulgaria exhibited extraordinarily high rates of capital formation, considerably above the very rapid rates of output expansion (see *Tables 7A.1, 7A.3* and *7A.4* in the appendix to this chapter, pp. 242–250). Most conspicuous is the upward trend in the share of accumulation and, *ipso facto*, the downward trend in that of consumption. A remarkable feature was the spectacular speeds and aftermaths of recurring investment drives, partly reflected in the notable fluctuations in the shares of accumulation (see *Table 7A.3*).

Generally, investment was allocated by according a strikingly discriminatory preference to growth-forcing, rather than to welfare-oriented, activities. This policy was periodically tempered. By and large there were rather limited modifications of the leading-links approach. The factors favouring perpetuation of the existing structure must have been strong, as illustrated in *Table 7A. 5*. Whatever other problems beset food processing and light industry, the key one seems to have been deficiency of capital and its antiquated and sometimes dilapidated state.

Two basic features of development in Eastern Europe were: fluctuating and declining rates of activity. The fluctuations were particularly pronounced in Bulgaria and especially in terms of investment, as illustrated in *Table 7A. 3*[2].

The intensive rural–urban migration reached exceptional proportions in Bulgaria between 1953 and 1963. Between 1948 and 1964 the number of farm workers declined by nearly 50%, with the slowdown thereafter partly achieved by 'administrative means' (*Economic Developments . . .*, 1970, p. 150). The exodus from agriculture benefited primarily industry and construction.

If the sectoral shift of employment is to be a rough yardstick for measuring industrialization, *Table 7A. 6* indicates the progress accomplished by Bulgaria. But such a yardstick is not particularly reliable, since it gives relatively greater weight to the undermechanized (and hence often less privileged) sectors and branches. During the early 1950s the increase of employment in Bulgaria was predominantly in the traditional industries (woodworking, textiles, and food processing), where considerable unused capacity existed. But investment allocations favoured heavy industry, making them much more reliable as a gauge of state priorities than increase of employment. By 1970 the more traditional industries (woodworking, food processing, glassware and china, textiles, garments, and leather and footwear) still accounted for 42.8% of the workforce in state-owned industry, as against 48.5% in producer-goods industries (electricity, fuels, metallurgy, machine building, chemicals, and building materials) (*Statistical Yearbook . . .* 1971, p. 93).

Despite their wide divergences, both official and recalculated data place Bulgaria and Romania at the top in terms of average growth rates of aggregate output per employee in 1952–1967. Both these countries seem to have done better in the 1960s than in the 1950s; Romania (with 4.8 and 7.6% respectively) outdid Bulgaria (with 5.7 and 7% respectively) – a notable source of disquietude in Bulgaria in the 1960s and 1970s (*Economic Survey . . .*, 1972, p. 6).

Foreign trade reflects the benefits, costs, and shifts in industrialization policy. The question is not so much the size as the composition and efficiency of external trade. Autarchy – a feature of past Soviet-type development – is in the process of erosion. There are demonstratively compelling empirical reasons for drawing on the theory of comparative advantage and exploiting the advantages of backwardness, which are obviously limited by political considerations.

It appears that during the 1960s the fastest rate of growth of foreign trade was registered in Bulgaria, with exports growing considerably faster than imports. By 1972 the CMEA countries could be ranked as follows, in descending order of foreign trade growth rates: Bulgaria, Romania, Poland, Hungary, the USSR, the GDR, and Czechoslovakia (Feiwel, 1977, p. 327). In comparing average annual rates of growth of industrial output and exports one should note that both in 1950–1960 and 1960–1964 Bulgarian exports (16.6 and 15.9% respectively) grew faster than industrial output (14.8 and 11% respectively) (*Handel zagraniczny . . .*, 1969, p. 62).

7.2 Performance in the 1970s

Despite all the well-known shortcomings of comparing plan and performance (retailoring of plans to fit performance and other manipulations) some interesting observations can be deduced from *Table 7.1.*

At first glance, looking at the overall plan fulfilment performance, at least three general observations stand out: (1) The plans for national income and agricultural performance are usually or often underfulfilled and the others are overfulfilled. In this connection, observing performance during FYPs, the overfulfilment is most noticeable in industrial output (with the exception of 1966–1970) and by a much lesser margin in retail trade (except in 1961–1965) or in real personal incomes (except in 1961–1965). (2) Frequently performance alternates from a good to a bad FYP, for example the relatively satisfactory performance in 1949–1953 (at least in terms of industrial output) was followed by a more disappointing one in 1953–1957 when, however, the indicators which suffered in the previous quinquennium (agriculture) seem to have recovered ground. Similarly, the almost exemplary performance in 1958–1962, when even the recalcitrant index of agricultural production seems to have been overfulfilled, was followed by a disastrous performance in 1961–1965 which, for the first time, set the leadership thinking about economic reforms. In 1966–1970 the FYP was again somewhat better fulfilled, but in 1971–1975 performance proved disappointing, and, as we shall see later, the seesaw effect was reversed – performance in 1976–1980 proved to be more disappointing still. (3) Since the early 1960s, in the index most likely to be overfulfilled (industrial output) the rate of overfulfillment has been diminishing rapidly, and the index of industrial growth, though still substantial, has been on the wane.

The publication date of the 1971–1975 FYP almost coincided with the report on the execution of the first year's plan. The poor results achieved in 1971 might have prompted some scaling down of FYP targets before the plan was finally approved (Iliev, 1971, p. 23). The Sixth FYP followed a period of overexpanded investment activity, overheating, and manifest growth barriers. The targets postulated for the Sixth FYP were slightly below those for the preceding period.

Table 7.1 indicates that in 1971–1975 the target for national income was slightly underfulfilled, industrial and agricultural output were as planned, but the plans for real income and retail trade were considerably overfulfilled. But, as contrasted with the preceding FYPs, the average annual growth rates

Table 7.1 Bulgarian five-year plans (P) and their fulfillment (R) in selected indexes, 1949–1975

| FYPs | Average annual growth rates | | | | | | | | | |
| | National income | | Industrial output | | Agricultural output | | Retail trade | | Real incomes | |
	P	R	P	R	P	R	P	R	P	R
1949–1953[a]	n.a.	8.4	17.1	20.8	9.5	−0.8	10.2	10.3	n.a.	8.4
1953–1957	8.5	7.7	9.9	13.1	10.7	4.9	11.2	14.9	7.0	7.1
1958–1962[b]	8.5	11.6	9.9	16.3	6.2	6.6	7.0	13.5	5.4	8.3
1961–1965	9.8	6.7	11.2	11.7	7.5	3.2	7.5	7.3	5.9	4.6
1966–1970	8.5	8.8	11.2	11.0	5.5	3.7	7.0	8.6	5.4	6.1
1971–1975	8.0	7.9	9.1	9.1	3.2	3.2	6.7	8.0	4.6	5.8
1952–1975[c]	8.6	8.3	10.3	11.8	6.5	4.1	7.9	10.2	5.6	6.2

(a) Reported as fulfilled during 1949–1952;
(b) Reported as fulfilled during 1958–1962;
(c) Average for a 24-year period.

Source: P. Shapkarev, *Planovo Stopanstvo*, No. 9, 1976, pp. 11–24.

of national income and agricultural output were very low and that of industrial output the lowest of all FYPs. On the whole, the central planners were haunted by the deteriorating position of Bulgaria in terms of growth rates of national income and industrial output *vis-à-vis* the other CMEA countries (Feiwel, 1977, pp. 332–4). Bulgaria shifted from its pre-eminent position in the 1950s and 1960s to third place behind Romania and Poland (see *Table 7.A.2*).

The largest beneficiaries of the investment effort in 1971–1975 were to be fuels and power, machine building, and the chemical industry (continuing along the lines of the fifth FYP), followed (after a wide gap) by building materials, food processing, and ferrous metallurgy (*Rabotnichesko Delo*, 17 December 1971, p. 2). Throughout the period the largest rates of increase of output were to be in petroleum (100%), machine building (more than 100%), chemicals (more than 100%), ferrous metallurgy (95%), building materials (77%), and electric power (59%) (Dulbokov, 1972, p. 9). But by 1975 the fuels industry had grown by 50% compared with 1970, machine building by 99%, chemicals by 73%, ferrous metallurgy by 68%, building materials by 55% and electric power by 30% (*Statistical Yearbook of Member Countries*, 1977, pp. 68–9) – a sizable underfulfilment in almost all priority branches. Also by 1975 the share of machinery in total exports was planned to reach 43% whereas it was reported to be only 40.7% (Ivanov, 1972, pp. 2–6; *Statistical Yearbook of Member Countries...*, 1977, p. 343).

Despite its relatively more modest targets the 1971–1975 FYP proved to be very taut. From the very beginning enormous difficulties were encountered in construction. This was a legacy of the previous FYP, which had left an extended construction front, but was also due to the sixth FYP's high rate of investments. Since 1972 every year emergency measures were being taken to complete the most important projects in construction and to give precedence to key projects. The main stress was on concentration of investment resources on fewer projects. But by 1975 unfinished construction was higher than total investment, whereas the 1971–1975 FYP had called for it to be 55–60% of total investment (Iliev, 1974, p. 2; *Rabotnichesko Delo*, 17 December 1971, p. 1).

The average annual increase of real wages in 1971–1975 was to be 4%. During the first two years real wages grew very slowly (3% in 1971 and 2% in 1972). By 1973 the rate of growth was still below the low average planned. In 1973 nominal wages increased by 3.8%, but on 1 June 1973 consumer prices were modified. In 1975 average nominal wages rose by 3%, and per capita real incomes by 5%. (*Statistical Pocketbook . . .*, 1970, p. 140; Szabo, 1974, p. 1184; *Rabotnichesko Delo*, 1 February 1975, p. 2). During the 1971–1975 FYP the average annual growth rate of real per capita income was 5.8% as against 4.6% planned – only slightly below the rate of increase reported in the 1966–1970 FYP.

As a result of the poor showing throughout the period there was a proliferation of accusations of mismanagement and slack discipline, together with mounting exhortation for mobilizing planning and campaigns to put the house in order. Such campaigns are a built-in feature of the Bulgarian way of life, but they are usually on the increase in a deteriorating economic situation, and their intensity is a good indication of the acuteness of shortfalls.

In many respects the targets set for 1976–1980 were similar to those set for 1971–1975, with the notable exceptions of higher rates for investment and lower for real wages[3]. In this respect the Bulgarian goals differed from those of the other CMEA countries which scaled down their targets for the second half of the 1970s. The most obvious explanation was the need and desire to catch up with the more developed neighbours and the persistent disregard for the overheating in the preceding period, which was apt to raise all sorts of growth barriers and ceilings. In the investment area the 46% growth rate was above the planned 33% (and reported 40%) increase in 1971–1975, which probably partly reflected the inflationary rise in prices of investment goods.

By the end of 1978 performance again showed how taut and overoptimistic the seventh FYP was. The targets for the next two years (1979–1980) were scaled down considerably, as shown in *Table 7.2*. By the end of 1979, Western estimates indicated that even assuming fulfilment of the lowered 1979–1980 targets, the planned growth targets for 1980 (over 1975) would be fulfilled as follows: national income (planned 45%) 38%, industrial output

Table 7.2 *Bulgarian plan targets and reported fulfilment of 1976–1980 FYP, selected indexes and annual percentage growth rates*

Indexes	Plan fulfilment reports			Planned targets		
	1976	1977	1978[a]	1979	1980	1976–1980[b]
National income	6.7	6.3	6.0	6.7[c]	7.0[c]	8.4
Industrial output	8.0	6.8	7.0	7.8	8.6	9.0
Agricultural output	3.1	−6.3	5.0	7.0	4.8	5.0
Real per capita income	4.4	2.0	3.1[d]	3.2	3.6	4.0
Retail domestic trade	7.3	3.2	4.6	4.1	4.7	7.0

(a) Estimates;
(b) Annual average;
(c) This is according to the law on the plan published on 2 December, 1978. The speech by the Chairman of the State Planning Commission, Kiril Zarev, included the following slightly higher targets: 1979, 7.0% and 1980, 7.2%.
(d) Average annual earned income.

Sources: Rabotnichesko Delo, 7 April and 30 October, 1976; K. Zarev, *Rabotnichesko Delo*, 21 December, 1977; *Rabotnichesko Delo*, 9 February, 1978; Zarev *Rabotnichesko Delo*, 30 November, 1978; *Rabotnichesko Delo*, 2 December, 1978; and *Rabotnichesko Delo*, 31 January, 1979.

(55%) 45%, machine building (100%) 79%, chemicals (80%) 62%, investment (46%) 21%, agricultural output (20%) 14%, and foreign trade (60%)
64% (*Quarterly Economic Review* . . ., 1979, p. 14).

Some of the causes for poor performances in 1976–1978 were attributed to
climatic conditions and the economic downturn and inflation in the West.
Some of the internal causes stressed were delays in implementing technical
progress, delays in commissioning new capacities, underutilization of
existing capacities and ineffective use of working time (Zarev, 1978). The
most severe shortcomings were the delays in completing construction and
failure to achieve rated capacity in the new or rebuilt plants. Machinery and
equipment was underutilized. New machines remained uninstalled. The
shift index was low. Work stoppages were frequent. Absenteeism increased
as did all sorts of violations of discipline (Rudnichar, 1978; Mishev, 1979).

As could be expected, the major trouble spot was once more the
investment programme. Again the seventh FYP was left a legacy of a wide
construction front which was further expanded in its earlier years. To recall,
by the end of 1975 the volume of unfinished construction was higher than
total investments. To narrow down the construction front was a prime goal,
and unfinished construction was planned at 65% of total investments by
1980, which was revised to 78% in the 1979–1980 plan. But the actual
proportion was 98.9% in 1977 and 95.6% in 1978 (*Rabotnichesko Delo*, 31
August 1976; Zarev, 1978). Twenty construction projects of national
priority (controlled by the Council of Ministers (CM)) were singled out in
the 1976–1980 FYP. After two years' work all was not well. Even these top
priority projects suffered from delays in design and documentation, in
supply of machinery and equipment, and shortages of building materials and
skilled construction workers (Ekov, 1977; Vladimirov, 1977; *Stroitel*, 28
September 1977; Krustev *et al.*, 1977).

Another serious problem area was the underutilization and ineffective use
of capacity. By 1975 nearly 70% of all fixed assets in industry were no more
than 10 years old (installed since 1965) (Tsoneva, 1977). Imported Western
machinery was being underutilized or remained uninstalled for long periods.
There were failures in adapting foreign technology purchased under licence
(Tuzharov, 1977). In 1976–1977 machinery in industry was utilized by
50–60%, construction 45–50%, and agriculture 40–60%. Some of the
reasons for this drastic underutilization were interruptions in the flow of
supplies, poor planning of production and poor labour organization (Koev,
1978).

In 1976–1980 the growth industries continued to be machine building and
chemicals. But during the first years performance again fell short of plan.
Machine building grew at 13.8% in 1977 (21% planned) and 11.4% in 1978
(13.7% planned). The respective figures for the chemical industry were
12.3% (15.9% planned) and 10.0% (11.1% planned) (*Rabotnichesko Delo*,
29 March 1978 and 31 January 1979). The shift to a lower gear in the last two

years did not evince a corresponding relenting of priority for group A. Thus the volume of output of machine building, chemicals, metallurgy, and power was to increase from 49.9% of total industrial output in 1978 to 52.3% in 1980. The specific growth rates of various industries in 1979 and 1980 respectively were planned at 11.6% and 12.1% for machine building and electronics, 9.1% and 14.3% for chemicals and rubber, 4.0% and 5.1% for light industry, and 5.8% and 7.1% for the food industry (Zarev, 1978).

By the mid-1970s Bulgaria (like other East European countries) was beginning to feel the energy crisis and has been labouring under its rapidly growing stringencies (evinced in shortages and high prices of imported fuels, power breakdowns, etc.) (Radeva, 1978; Todoriev, 1978; Elenska and Konstantinova, 1978). By mid-1979 severe cuts in the use of fuels and power were decreed (*Durzhaven vestnik*, 25 May 1979; *Rabotnichesko Delo*, 22 May 1979). Petrol prices were raised by almost 100% (on top of the 38–52% increases in 1977)[4], which resulted almost immediately in much-reduced traffic, as a good number of the 620 000 private car owners could no longer afford to pay for petrol and simply stopped driving (*Rabotnichesko Delo*, 14 June 1979).

7.3 Technical progress and foreign trade

Diffusion of foreign-generated innovations appears to be at present the most important agent of technical change and a key factor in productivity growth. A fundamental problem is the rate at which new techniques are adopted and incorporated into production and spread throughout the system. There seems to be a major difference between the technical change in high priority activities – which benefit not only from discriminatory allocation of the best resources but also from removal of some of the obstacles to new technology – and the rest of the economy.

The first rumblings of reform echoed the calls for technical progress, which have been growing to crescendo proportions, in contrast to other reform desiderata which slowly waned. Attention was paid to planning and decisionmaking, with increasingly delineated competence and delegation of decisionmaking to the medium levels of management and the research and development organizations. Reorganizations followed each other with little success (Feiwel, 1977, pp. 192–6).

The central planners' forcing of machine building is a major determinant of structural change, of direct and indirect production, and of qualitative performance of the system. It is also a tension-producing factor. In 1971–1975 a structural break was to take place. In fact, as illustrated in *Table 7A.5*, by 1977 machine building (27.7%) had usurped first place from food processing (22.5%) as Bulgaria's leading industry. The ambition was to establish Bulgaria as an important machinery exporter in the world market.

The Soviet economy's requirements were a determinant of the Bulgarian production profile (Dakov, 1972, p. 9; Ivanov, 1972). The clue to the pushing of exports of machinery so hastily lies, *inter alia*, in competition and rivalry with other CMEA members in terms of this important 'index of industrialization', which in 1970 found Bulgaria (29%) not only behind the GDR (51.7%) and Czechoslovakia (50.4%), but also behind Poland (38.5%) and Hungary (32.6%). By 1976 Bulgaria (42%) had taken third place behind the GDR (51.2%) and Czechoslovakia (50.0%), but ahead of Poland (41.4%), Hungary (33.7%), Romania (26%), and the USSR (19.4%) (*Statistical Yearbook of Member Countries...*, 1977, pp. 343–345). A further illustration of the structural break that occurred in Bulgaria during the 1960s and 1970s is provided by *Table 7A.10*. Whereas throughout the period the negative trade balances in producer goods were paid for by positive balances of consumer goods, in the 1970s the negative balances of machinery have been gradually decreasing, until by 1975–1977 they were turned into rather considerable positive balances. On the other hand, the negative balances of raw materials and semifabricates have been growing apace.

The Bulgarian economy is heavily dependent on foreign trade, being poorly and lopsidedly endowed with raw materials. Throughout the 1970s close economic integration with the USSR has been the goal – with particularly detrimental effect on the attempts to infuse the Bulgarian economy with technical progress borrowed from trading partners and with negative repercussions on Bulgaria's economic performance due to the sluggishness of the Soviet economy. We can only allude to the impact of Soviet technology and technocratic style in Bulgaria (Petrov, 1974; Sokolov, 1974; Kolev, 1973). Apparently by 1977 Bulgarian enterprises built with Soviet aid produced 70% of electric power, 100% of iron, copper, zinc, artificial phosphate fertilizers, soda ash and caustic soda, almost 100% of the steel, rolled products and lead, almost 80% of battery operated fork lift trucks and electric hoists, 80% of pulp and 60% of artificial nitrogen fertilizers (Kaprielova, 1977). Most scientists and technicians have specialized in Soviet institutions.

As *Table 7A.9* indicates, more than three quarters of Bulgarian foreign trade remains with socialist countries, whereas that of its CMEA trading partners was gradually shifting to the West, at least until the late 1970s. Throughout the 1960s and 1970s Bulgaria registered very high foreign trade growth rates, far surpassing those of national income, industrial output, and investment (see *Table 7A.1*). Officials acknowledge that the benefits of trade are lower and costs higher than usually claimed. In many cases import and export costs tend to be understated; export returns do not cover cumulative import outlays; investments are ineffectively allocated on the basis of overstated investment efficiency claims. More reliable foreign trade and investment efficiency criteria are sorely needed (Ivanov, 1973).

The impact of foreign trade on reform is blunted by several factors. By securing a relatively stable outlet for about four-fifths of exports Bulgaria can postpone the internal changes required to modernize and upgrade output, which can be limited only to the strength of the increasing demands of CMEA partners. Also, if a substantial share of imports originates from the CMEA countries, the beneficial competition effect is weakened.

However, the share of trade with the West has a much greater impact than the mere statistics suggest or than the continuous official stress on trade with the USSR indicates. The record seems to show that, granted the powerful constraints, by and large the Bulgarians have displayed a fair amount of flexibility in trade with the West. It was in 1974 and 1975 that trade with the West grew most rapidly. According to Polish estimates, by 1980 Bulgaria's trade with the West was expected to amount to $2460 million – i.e., a threefold increase since 1975 ($820 million). Bulgaria remains primarily an exporter of agricultural products to the West, and these constitute about 12–20% of its shipments to Italy and France and 35–40% to West Germany and the UK. Metals and metal products contribute about 10% of exports to West Germany (Bulgaria's most important Western trade partner), fabrics about 20% and machinery less than 20%. About 30–50% of imports from the West consist of capital goods, 10–30% chemicals, and 10–15% metal goods (Zamek, 1979).

Apparently, Bulgaria is substantially liberalizing its terms for joint ventures with Western enterprises. From 1 January 1979, according to Atanas Ginev, Deputy Minister of Foreign Trade, Bulgaria would no longer insist on a majority holding in foreign investments. It would even allow 100% foreign management. However, the joint venture company would have no right to the land on which the plants would be built. Until now Bulgaria has participated in joint venture companies with the West in third countries. Bulgaria now apparently wants to go into partnership with well-established high-technology Western firms. This project would make Bulgaria's joint-venture policy among the most liberal in the CMEA countries (*Financial Times*, 8 September 1979; *Handelsblatt*, 18 May 1979).

Understandably, the central planners must have mixed feelings about major expansion of trade with the West, even irrespective of political constraints. Such trade makes plan fulfilment more difficult. The demanding buyer is a problem and the complaints and pressures he generates might not be disposed of so easily as those from CMEA partners. Adaptation to such trade disturbs the structure of output, disrupts the way of doing things, and necessitates more radical reforms.

7.4 Agriculture

In the 1970s Bulgaria was pioneering large scale 'industrialization' of agriculture. The agricultural — industrial complexes (AIC) were originally set up in the early 1970s on the basis of horizontal integration of neighbour-ing state and cooperative farms and their servicing centres. The widespread integration with industry and procurement and distribution centres was undertaken on the heels of the horizontal integration. Large unified branch managements were set up, e.g., cattle, poultry, grain, fruit, etc. One of the dire consequences of this gigantomania was the high concentration of decisionmaking managerial personnel and specialists at the branch levels, while the production centres were bereft of on-the-spot guidance and technical expertise. Overcentralization of management was admitted to have caused a setback in effective operational management (Vasilev, 1978; *Rabotnichesko Delo*, 14 April 1978; Tsanov, 1978).

The inefficiency and sluggishness of the agricultural apparatus contributed to inappropriate use of inputs and production costs rising faster than output. A comparison between Bulgaria and the developed European countries for the period 1971–1977 indicated that Bulgarian crop yields of wheat and corn per unit of arable land were behind those of France, West Germany, Denmark, Belgium, and the Netherlands (*Zamedelso zname*, 12 August 1976; Ganev, 1976; Gatev, 1978).

The Bulgarian Communist Party (BCP) Central Committee (CC) Plenum of 2–3 March 1979 dealt with the introduction of a new management system in agriculture. Briefly, a National Agro-Industrial Union (NAIU) would manage the Agro-Industrial Complexes, previously under the aegis of the Ministry of Agriculture and the Food Industry. The Ministry was criticized for ineptitude, overcentralization and overbureaucratization, which ham-pered the development of agriculture and stifled initiative. The management of the NAIU was to be elected by rank and file members and not centrally appointed (*Kooperativno Selo*, 30 and 31 March 1979).

The AICs were to be reorganized generally on a two-level basis to reduce the bureaucratic process and bring management closer to production. The AICs would be reduced in size and some of the central employees transferred directly to production (Tsanov, *Kooperativno Selo*, 1978; *Dur-zhaven vestnik*, No. 7 (23 January), 1979). The number of binding indicators would be reduced and output of needed agricultural products would be influenced by contracts between producers and procurement agencies and by bonus prices paid over and above the fixed prices. All agricultural units would become self-supporting and taxation would be related to the size of land rather than income in an attempt to induce larger yields. Agriculture would no longer benefit from state subsidies. The unit's wage funds and individual wages would depend on its financial results (*Rabotnichesko Delo*, 6 and 7 March 1979). However, the implementation of the AIC reform was slow. According to the Chairman of the Central Council of the NAIU, many AICs lagged behind in the recomputation of norms. There were also serious manipulations of indicators and infractions in payment of wages (Tsanov, 1979).

In Bulgaria, private plots amounted to 12.7% of arable land in 1975 and provided 25% of total agricultural output (32.9% of livestock, 42.4% of milk, 48.3% of eggs, between 27% and 63% of various fruits and 14.8% of vegetables), accounting for 25.9% of the incomes of agricultural workers (Kazandzhiev, 1977; 1979). Recently the policy towards private plots was again relaxed and their cultivation encouraged in an attempt to increase agricultural output (*Pogled*, 3 October 1977; *Durzhaven vestnik*, 28 February 1978).

7.5 Living standards and conditions

Even in Bulgaria, whose population is relatively conformist and inarticulate, due partly to the stronger police-state tactics, there have been rumblings of discontent with the low living standards. The expression of discontent was not confined to the usual dissatisfaction, absenteeism, slack performance on the job, refusal to buy, etc.; it also assumed politically explosive forms. The response of the leadership to the demands for improving living standards has vacillated considerably in recent times. For example, the pre-Congress (April, 1971) slogan of 'concern for man' was dropped in favour of 'increased labour productivity'. But shortly thereafter and at the December 1972 Plenum (hereafter in this section referred to as the Plenum) Zhivkov stressed that economic plans should 'satisfy the growing material and spiritual needs of the people (Zhivkov, 1972). Early in 1976 the BCP CC issued a set of Theses on the Standard of Living (hereafter in this section referred to as the Theses) which seemed to have toned down some of the goals proclaimed by the Plenum (*Rabotnichesko Delo*, 12 February 1976) as illustrated in *Table 7.3*.

The vicissitudes in living-standards policy roughly parallel the fluctuations in growth performance. In general, when an overambitious and unrealistic FYP is set its early years are characterized by a high rate of investment, imbalances and neglect of the consumer. These are often mitigated by a shift in policy halfway through the FYP reducing the rate of investment and giving greater weight to consumption. This is again reversed by a resumption of the investment momentum. The length of the periods and intensity of shifts depend, *inter alia*, on the abruptness of the increase of the investment rate and the existing state of the construction front.

In recent years there has been a marked improvement in living standards in Bulgaria, particularly if measured by 'extensive'-type indicators. From 1952 to 1970 per capita consumption rose by 225%, by 80% from 1960 to 1970, by 36% from 1965 to 1970, and by 50% from 1970 to 1977. Thus it rose by 387% from 1952 to 1977 (by 170% from 1960 to 1977) (*Statisticheski Godishnik . . .*, 1978, p. 75). Even if official claims are exaggerated, the Bulgarians are indeed better off than they were some years ago, and they are

Table 7.3 *Reported and projected consumption of selected goods in Bulgaria, 1970, 1975, and 1980*

Products	Units per capita	'Scientific norm'	Reported for 1970	1972 Plenum for 1975	Reported for 1975	1972 Plenum for 1980	1976 Theses for 1980
Meat	kg	80	41.4	55.0	57.0	75	70
Fish	kg	12	5.5	8.0	6.2	10	8
Milk	litres	260	152.0	196.0	174.0	250	220
Eggs	number	265	122.0	159.0	145.0	250	200
Flour	kg	135	170.0	182.0	157.0	150	150
Vegetable oil	kg	13	12.5	13.9	13.8	14	14
Sugar	kg	32	32.9	37.0	34.0	36	36
Vegetables	kg	180	89.0	136.0	94.0	160	150
Fruit	kg	200	148.0	179.0	118.0	200	190
Cotton fabric	metres	36	22.2	24.7	26.5	33	30
Wool fabric	metres	7	3.8	4.7	4.9	6	6
Shoes	pairs	4	1.7	2.1	2.1	3	2.2
Radios	number*	130	100.8	104.0	106.9	100	130
TV sets	number*	105	42.0	53.0	60.3	80	80
Washing machines	number*	70	50.0	50.0	50.0	60	65
Refrigerators	number*	100	29.0	59.0	61.0	90	90
Cars	number*	40	6.0	13.5	16.0	30	26

* per 100 families

Sources: T. Zhivkov, *Rabotnichesko Delo*, 14 December, 1972; *Rabotnichesko Delo*, 12 February, 1976.

better off than the populations of some other CMEA countries (*Economic Developments* . . ., 1970, pp. 41–64).

Western recomputations of per capita personal consumption (in West German marks) ranked CMEA countries as follows in 1970: GDR (3954), Czechoslovakia (3017), Hungary (2678), Bulgaria (2479), USSR (2030), Poland (1924), and Romania (1732) (*Handelsblatt*, 4 February 1971). According to other Western estimates of the dynamics of personal consumption, taking 1965 as 100, some of the East European countries could be ranked as follows in ascending order by 1978: Czechoslovakia 130.3, Bulgaria and Hungary 146.5, GDR 146.8, and Poland 157.5 (Alton, 1979, p. 16).

The consumption index would also have to be adjusted for the loss of welfare due to poor quality of goods, restricted choice and general shopping frustrations. The system displays some advantages in restricting the modern Western 'bamboozling' of the consumer through spurious and unnecessary product differentiation and 'brainwashing' through advertising. But it has been unable to elicit the required flexibility and responsiveness of the producer to demand.

Improvement of consumer goods supply depends not only on restructuring allocation of investments in favour of the consumer goods sector and increasing the output of that sector but also on restructuring foreign trade in favour of larger imports of consumer goods and raw materials for the production of such goods, and especially on reforming the system of functioning so as to improve the quality, variety and attractiveness of the available consumer goods. The Plenum offered the first official denial of the absolute priority of producer over consumer goods production. In fact, in some years, in order to readjust the production of consumer goods, output of these goods can grow at a faster rate than that of producer goods 'as long as this does not become a permanent trend'. In more immediate terms this meant a review of the possibilities of increasing output of consumer goods. But throughout most of the 1970s output of group A outpaced that of group B (*Statisticheski Godishnik* . . ., (1978, p. 172).

Concurrently the Plenum announced something of a revision of policy as regards import of consumer goods. Previously, imports of consumer goods were notoriously limited. By 1973 imports of consumer goods would constitute 10% of total imports, and would increase to 15% by 1975 and to 20–25% in 1976–1980. According to the Theses this share was to be about 20% in 1976–1980 and to rise to 25–30% by 1990 (Zhivkov, 1972; *Rabotnichesko Delo*, 12 February 1976). This share is difficult to verify in practice. However, the share of all consumer goods (agricultural and industrial) in total imports was reported as 12.2% in 1973, 14.0% in 1974, falling to 12.5% in 1975, 12.9% in 1976, and 13.2% in 1977. The respective figures for the shares of industrial consumer goods in total imports were: 9, 9.6, 8.9, 8.6 and 10% (*Statisticheski Godishnik*, 1976, p. 348; 1978, p. 353).

The Plenum strongly castigated all the shortcomings in consumer goods availability and production, but it was less forceful in proposing methods for overcoming them. Conditions were not created to compel the seller to react and adapt output to consumer demand and to interest him in introducing really new and better products at terms advantageous to the consumer. It appears that the post-Plenum supply of consumer goods and services did not improve noticeably. The well-known complaints of poor quality, unavailability, lack of supplies and consequent idleness of consumer goods plants abounded (Dimov, 1975; Georgieva, 1977).

The intensified postwar urbanization gave rise to serious shortages of housing in cities, with concurrent underutilization of housing facilities in rural areas. Aside from its qualitative and spatial shortcomings, even quantitatively housing construction in the CMEA countries falls considerably behind that in the West. Within the CMEA in the 1960s and early 1970s Bulgaria was trailing behind most other countries (except for the GDR) in this important index of consumer welfare (Feiwel, 1977, p. 325). Some of the problems in housing construction are: (1) insufficient allocation of resources to housing construction at the planning stage, with further inroads during plan execution; (2) drabness in design and poor quality of execution; and (3) commissioning of semi-finished dwellings (Martinov, 1978; Vulchanov, 1978; *Tekhnichesko Delo*, 20 August 1977). The sixth FYP called for 250 000 housing units to be built and only 237 000 were reported finished by the end of 1975 (*Rabotnichesko Delo*, 1 January 1976).

In the postwar period the public consumption fund grew considerably (i.e., by 589% from 1952 to 1968, and by 416% from 1960 to 1977) (*Statisticheski Godishnik* . ., 1978, p. 87). The sheer quantitative expansion and the scope of the undertaking is remarkable, even if we discount the frequent inclusion of military and other 'secret' state expenditures in this fund. However, the distribution of the public consumption fund suffers from many misallocations. By 1977 the largest share (66%) was claimed by social security payments, allowances, and health and sports, followed by education (22%), others (8%) and culture and arts (4%) (*Statisticheski Godishnik* . . ., 1978, p. 87). Concurrently there are appalling shortages of nurseries and daycare centres. Public health facilities and health care remain unsatisfactory. There are serious shortages of hospitals and sanitoriums, with considerable delays in their construction. The existing facilities are not equipped with modern conveniences and are understaffed (Gocheva, 1973, p. 8; Genchev, 1974; Zhivkov, 1972).

The postwar period was marked by a tendency for relative levelling of wages (Feiwel, 1977, pp. 223, 321–2). This tendency is perpetuated by periodic wholesale revisions of wages, which tend to stress increases in minimum wages, rather than in those above the minimum level. As illustrated in *Table 7A. 7*, in the 1970s Bulgaria's growth in real wages was the lowest among its East European neighbours, and that of labour productivity among the highest. With the exception of 1976, the annual growth rates of real per capita income were well below the 4% average in 1977 and 1978 and were also planned below that rate for 1979–1980, as indicated in *Table 7.2*.

In the last quarter of 1979 considerable increases of staple food prices were announced coupled with wage, family allowances, scholarship and pension rises. New higher retail prices for most staple foods (see *Table 7.4*) went into effect on 12 November 1979. Prices of clothing, furniture, household

Table 7.4 *Price increases of foodstuffs in Bulgaria, 12 November 1979*

Goods	Unit of measure	Old price (leva)	New price (leva)	Percentage increases
Bread (standard loaf)	kg	0.15	0.26	73.3
Bread (Dobrudza loaf)	kg	0.26	0.36	38.5
Bread (fine, white)	kg	0.34	0.48	41.2
Milk	litre	0.30	0.36	20.0
Yoghurt	kg	n.a.	0.46	n.a.
White sheep cheese	kg	2.50	3.60	44.0
Kashkaval cheese	kg	3.60	4.00	11.1
Butter	kg	4.00	5.40	35.0
Poultry	kg	n.a.	2.40	n.a.
Beef and pork	kg	2.40	3.40	41.7
Veal	kg	2.80	5.40	92.9
Sugar	kg	0.70	1.00	42.9
Rice	kg	0.72	1.00	38.9
Beans	kg	0.44	0.80	81.9
Vegetable oil	litre	1.20	1.50	25.0

Sources: Statisticheski Godishnik na Narodna Republika Bulgaria 1978 (Sofia, 1978), p. 340; *Bulgarian News Agency*, 12 November 1979.

appliances and medicines were unchanged. Prices of building materials rose by 40% and of alcoholic beverages by an average of 45%. Prices in canteens and retaurants would be raised accordingly. Post, telephone and telegraph were to increase prices by 1 January 1980 and theatre and cinema tickets by 1 December 1979. Dressmaking and carpentry would also become more expensive. Home heating fuels would cost more, e.g. home heating oil doubled in price (from 0.12 leva per litre to 0.24 leva). In the spring of 1979 limits for electricity use were set, with above-limit rates costing about 45% more. In November electricity rates went up above those listed in the spring for above-limit consumption.

Concurrently wages and salaries were increased retroactively to 1 November 1979: wage scales for blue-collar workers by about 30% and for white-collar workers by about 25%. The minimuim monthly wage was raised from 80 to 100 leva. However, these increases were not equally distributed. Particularly large increases were granted to young specialists.

Among blue-collar workers preference seems to have been given to the more skilled and experienced workers.

On the whole, it would seem that the new price-wage manoeuvre was motivated by the need to increase the prices of the subsidized foodstuffs, but it is not known by how much the subsidies were reduced. At the same time, it appears to be an attempt at restructuring personal real incomes in favour of the higher income groups. Food price increases always hit hardest the lower income groups (or large families with one or at the most two breadwinners) where expenses on food represent the largest share of the family budget. In this case, as shown in *Table 7.4*, it appears that (with the exception of veal) some of the staple foods consumed in larger quantities by the poorer families (such as standard bread and beans) have had the highest price increases. Also the wage rises seem to have favoured the more skilled workers and technicians, who were already better off, at the expense of those on minimum wages. Family allowance increases blatantly discriminated against larger families (with a 200% increase for one child, 100% for two children and only 55% for three children).

In closing this section on living standards we should be remiss if we did not mention the moral climate. The Plenum hinted at indifference of the broad masses, at alienation and general lack of participation (Zhivkov, 1972). Aside from alienation and lack of democracy, the system suffers from an erosion of morality at all levels that can be partly attributed to the high-pressure economy and unrealistic planning. The most obvious man-ifestation is the widespread practice of falsification of plan fulfilment reports (Panev, 1977). All levels, from the very top to the very bottom of the economic hierarchy, use well-known techniques to camouflage poor per-formance (Tsekov, 1977; Markov, 1977). In the 1970s increasing concern over economic crimes and 'several large encroachments on socialist property' have been revealed. Workers and managers in different enterprises and organizations were involved. In discussing this state of affairs, the press listed as the main causes slack control, general apathy, lack of criticism and condonement of unprincipled behaviour (Vachkov, 1973; Fidanov, 1975; Kolev, 1979; Balkamski and Naydenov, 1979)[5]. However, the real causes are much deeper. They stem from the very low living standards during the initial rush for industrialization and are perpetuated by disrespect for social property, a cynical attitude towards theft and manipulations, and the bureaucratic system of management[6].

7.6 The system of planning and management

The central planners usually refer to increased efficiency derived from economic reform as an additional source of economic growth or as a possible source for redressing some flagrant disproportions. However, they do not readily perceive the essence of the inverse relationship between growth policy and reform – that is, that reform implementation requires an appropriate degree of slack in the economy. Reform encounters insurmountable obstacles in an economy overheated by overcommitment of resources to investment[7].

Since the early 1960s, particularly between 1963 and 1966, the usually prosaic Bulgarian economic literature was enlivened by various reform proposals[8]. The discussion flourished after official recognition of past abuses and calls for reform were sounded. Most of the proposals were along the lines officially propounded and were in a similar 'quasi-profit-oriented' family. Concurrently a series of experiments was initiated along the lines that were later given official sanction in the 'Draft Theses of the Politbureau of the Bulgarian Communist Party on the New System of Planning and Management of the National Economy' (hereinafter referred to as the blueprint). The system outlined in the blueprint was perhaps closest to that tried at that time in Czechoslovakia, particularly as regards the three-tier price construct (also a feature of the Hungarian reform) and the concept of gross income, borrowed and adapted from Yugoslavia. The blueprint attempted to restrict the scope of direct administrative orders and to enlarge that of economic calculation. More specifically, it aimed at curtailing the number of binding plan indicators, enhancing the role of profit, tying wages in with performance more closely, and extending horizontal relations. The blueprint also affirmed 'planning from below' – in essence the aggregation of plans prepared by lower units on the basis of a restricted number of state directives and limits. The *à tâtonnement* process of reform implementation was fraught with a number of snags, resulting in numerous amendments.

Within four years of the initial experiments the general direction of Bulgarian reform was reversed at the July 1968 Plenum of the BCP CC – the real clue to what the Bulgarian reform had become (Zhivkov, 1968). The reform's three most 'progressive' features – i.e., planning from below, the lifting of controls over the wage fund and the three-tier price system – were abandoned. Considerable stress was laid on catching up with world technical standards and on more effective administration. The list of directive indicators was expanded, but the blueprint's skeleton of the financial system was preserved, although its meaning was largely lost. All this foreshadowed the technocratic approach to management evinced in the 1971 modifications of the traditional system.

At the end of 1970 the number of associations was reduced from 120 to 64 by means of combination, presumably to provide for intensified concentration, improved synchronization of investments, and tighter links between research and development and production (*Dürzhaven vestnik*, 19 January 1971). The Bulgarian experience featured the transformation of the association from an intermediary link in the chain of command into a fully integrated 'economic management' organ. The association became the basic unit which not only grouped enterprises of a given branch or subbranch but also encompassed the entire production process of given products. It also became the basic unit of *khozraschet* with enterprises functioning on a form of internal *khozraschet*[9].

The potential advantages and drawbacks of associations notwithstanding, in practice much was attenuated by the fact that these units were staffed by old-time bureaucrats used to getting orders from above and distributing them peremptorily and often arbitrarily among their wards. There was a lack of economic intelligence and managerial ability at that level. The associations' work-style was bureaucratic and sluggish, and they showed little initiative in solving the problems of their wards (Iliev, 1971, p. 15).

The strengthening of associations created a considerable vacuum in the functioning of the ministries – at least on paper. It is not entirely clear to what extent the ministries tended to interfere in practice in the operative functions of their associations. In the early 1970s one might have presumed that this could be a first step toward the withering away of ministries, at least as we know them from the traditional system. In 1969 there were four industrial ministries. However, by mid-1973 the ministries showed a tendency to multiply with the establishment of three new industrial ministries – an indication that the enlarged and more powerful associations were not doing as well as was expected.

By 1976 yet another in the series of administrative reorganizations, that had been 'particularly painful' in the past (Fidanov, 1975), was in the offing. The role of associations was considerably underplayed and combines got some attention (Todorov, 1975; *Durzhaven vestnik*, No. 100 (30 December), No. 101 (31 December) 1975). The establishment of such combines on an industrywide basis took place in 1975 in the chemical industry, where 11 autonomous combines were set up under the direct aegis of the ministry. In this scheme the associations were bypassed entirely. The new combines were formed around a basic plant, with an eye to localization (Pankov, 1975).

Since the reorganization in the chemical industry there has been a rush to set up combines, which have replaced a good number of the unwieldy associations. At the April 1978 Party Conference Zhivkov praised the combine as the organization of the future bypassing the intermediary level (association) (Zhivkov, 1978). Unfortunately horizontal and local integration is more prevalent than vertical concentration. If pushed to the logical conclusion of integration along the lines of vertical concerns, this might offer a more viable model of organization for devising a more realistic mechanism of functioning within the existing constraints of an economy without slack.

A direct post-Conference result was the new set of regulations governing the prerogatives and responsibilities of the combines (*Durzhaven Vestnik*, No. 51 (June 30) 1978; *Rabotnichesko Delo*, 26 June 1978; *Ikonomicheski Zhivot*, No. 27 (5 July) 1978). The much-vaunted expansion of the combines' independence was, however, limited and open to all sorts of constrictions by the ministries and control agencies:

(1) The number of binding directives was reduced to eight: output in value added (net production), specific physical production targets of selected goods and their quality grade indicators, foreign currency earned on exports and to be spent on imports, costs of materials per 100 leva of marketable output, employment limits, average gross wage, profit per 100 leva of fixed assets, and the coefficient of shifts. The content of the indicators could be modified to fit the specific nature of the particular combine, but their number could not be expanded. But, as past experience with the reduction of binding directives showed, almost every one of these directives lends itself to multiplication. Again stress was placed on stability of directives.

(2) Financial independence was given prominence, but it remained restricted by central determination of special purpose funds – how to replenish them and on what to spend them. Only 5% of planned profit was to be left with the combine, which would receive 50% of the 'above plan' profit declared in the counterplan. The budget constraint was lessened by amplifying the special purpose funds and allowing the combines to spend them with less interference. The Bulgarian National Bank's influence over the combines' activities was enhanced through its credit policy and control functions.

(3) The combines were granted much greater freedom to enter into contracts with domestic and foreign buyers, thus allowing them greater flexibility in responding to demand.

(4) The director's prerogatives and responsibilities were the mainstay of the new regulations. He could be held personally responsible for losses caused by his decisions. The Committee for State and People's Control and the party cells were enjoined to become more active in ferreting out misconduct and all sorts of aberrations.

The counterplan campaign began in 1972. It was created as a device to overcome what the central planners considered to be slack in the early years of the sixth FYP. The point of the exercise is for units to undertake and fulfil obligations in addition to their regular plan. This could also be termed as a 'plan of plan overfulfilment'. It is supposed to reveal additional reserve capacity and augment tautness. But the material, technical and financial coordination of the counterplans must take place without additional investment, foreign exchange or materials and manpower (*Rabotnichesko Delo*, 15 January 1972; Filipov, 1973).

Despite the many references to the counterplan as democratization and increased participation of workers in the planning process (Zh. Zhivkov, 1973, p. 4; Dakov, 1972, p. 17) it is nothing but another attempt at 'mobilizing' planning. Obviously, the plan supplements do not really originate from below. Whatever the political advantages, the results are often disruptive and abortive, with predictable upsets in coordination, balances and internal consistency. Overfulfilment is not always desirable and non-uniform plan fulfilment in various activities might be conducive to waste. Predictably, the original plan is understated by the extent of the counterplan (*Rabotnichesko Delo*, 15 January 1972). The experience with counterplans was chaotic. Many shortcomings resulted from lack of specification, concretization and dovetailing of counterplans with remaining plan indicators. The central planners blamed the executants for focusing their attention mainly on fulfilling the volume indicators at the expense of the qualitative ones and attempting to secure initially the lowest possible control figures (*Ikonomicheski Zhivot*, 3 October 1973, p. 1). Apparently, in formulating quality indicators, the units tend to ignore changes in product mix. This is reported to create real difficulties in the coordination of physical indicators and makes for unrealistic counterplans of cost reduction, profits and gross income.

In late 1977 a 'new planning technology' was pompously announced and given particular prominence at the 1978 Party Conference, where Zhivkov stressed in particular the FYP as law at all levels and the counterplan as the basis for planning. However, there seems to be nothing essentially 'new' in the widely publicized methodology – perhaps the novelty might lie in the determination with which the leadership intends to implement it (Zhivkov, 1978; *Rabotnichesko Delo*, 26 April, 29 April 1978, 14 October 1977; Zarev, 1977; *Ikonomicheski Zhivot*, 19 October 1977; *Trud*, 28 October 1977).

Concurrently a new wage system to apply in industry, construction, and agriculture was announced (*Durzhaven Vestnik*, No. 19 (8 March) 1977; *Zamedelso zname*, 11 March 1977; *Narodna Mladezh*, 11 March 1977). Blue-collar workers were to be classified into seven wage groups ranging from the monthly minimum wage of 80 leva to 224 leva. Five salary groups were instituted for white-collar workers: three for managers and specialists starting at 110, 125, and 140 leva per month, depending on educational levels, and two for office and other personnel, starting at 80 and 90 leva each. The top salary for general directors of combines was to be 500 leva.

Within each group employees would be entitled to a range of pay from the minimum up to a certain given maximum. Numerous criteria were to be used for determining a person's particular pay within his scale, including in most cases fulfilment and overfulfilment of the quantitive and qualitative plan. Premiums for overfulfilment of norms would no longer be paid; the flexible gross pay would reflect performance. This was to be evaluated annually by appraisal commissions which, obviously, are open to all sorts of arbitrariness and favouritism.

All strata of employees were to be held responsible for losses incurred due to personal negligence or error. The managers of enterprises which did not meet their contractual deliveries to others or produce their quota of spare parts would have their salaries blocked until such deficiencies were made up.

In combines (or associations) the wage fund would be determined on the basis of the planned labour force and the average gross wage amended by an indicator of increase of labour productivity resulting from the counterplan (*Durzhaven Vestnik*, No. 62 (8 August) 1978; Krustev, 1978). Savings of the wage fund from a reduction of the labour force would increase the average gross wage and be used as premiums for the personnel directly responsible for such savings. Labour productivity gains derived from savings of raw materials would have the major influence on the average gross wage. The latter would be reduced by 1% for each percentage point underfulfilment of the labour productivity plan.

Individual salaries of managers would be reduced by a given share of the losses incurred by subordinate units or by losses due to deterioration of quality and breakage of contractual obligations. These individual salaries were to be determined either in relation to the unit's performance or on the basis of an assessment of the individual's personal contribution. The unit's internal regulations would determine into which category an employee falls. The ratings of these employees would be determined by their immediate superiors, and for the director and his deputies (including the chief accountant) by the superior unit.

The implementation of the 1977 wage regulations was very protracted partly due to the complications and arbitrariness involved in determining the workers' and employeees' contributions[10]. The new wage system was cautiously introduced in the last quarter of 1978 into only 12 medium-size industrial enterprises in heavy and light industry. Zhivkov implied that the delays would persist not only due to the new system's complexity, but also that each combine which embarked on this system would have to make sure of the availability of funds to pay for increased productivity (*Rabotnichesko Delo*, 26 April 1978).

Simultaneously an attempt was made at labour reorganization on the basis of self-supporting brigades to provide for peer control since each person's pay would depend on the performance of the entire brigade (Zhivkov, 1978; *Rabotnichesko Delo*, 17 April 1978). Thus far, construction had the most experience with the brigade system (in direct imitation of the Soviet experience). But the unsatisfactory performance thus far was attributed mainly to erratic supply and faulty scheduling of projects. The malaise lies in the system of planning construction work and the supply system, hence at the roots of the growth strategy and plan construction[11]. Organization of work by brigades in industry was lagging due to difficulties in introducing internal *khozraschet* (*Rabotnichesko Delo*, 16 April 1979).

In enumerating the most recent changes in Bulgarian planning one should point to the continuous reshuffle of top administrators (ministers, party secretaries, etc.) in a search for 'culprits' for the economic malaise. By mid-1976 strong criticism was also voiced against overstaffing at the top management echelons (Markov, 1976). That the individual dismissals were to be numerous was indicated by the issue of a special decree on how these dismissals were to be conducted (*Durzhaven Vestnik*, No. 66 (17 August) 1976). Possibly they affected a good number of hitherto privileged party members and gave rise to much infighting. The overall campaign to reduce administrative personnel was still in full swing in 1978. The administrative and managerial personnel, who comprised 13% of the workforce in 1975, were supposed to have been cut down to 9% in 1978. By April 1979 this reduction was apparently achieved and about 150 000 white-collar workers had been released (Todorov, 1978; Zhivkov, 1979).

The stress on computerization of the economy and on automated management systems (AMS) began in the early 1970s. Having abandoned market-type reforms the leadership still had to grapple with the exigencies that made them turn to these reforms in the first place. Computerization seemed to be favoured because it permits a high degree of centralization and control. At one time it appeared as if the USSR were using Bulgaria as a willing guineapig to test the feasibility and advisability of a nationwide AMS. But in the latter part of the 1970s wholesale computerization of the economy seems to have faded away as a goal.

7.7 Impetus for and resistance to change

One of the similarities of East European reforms has been their advocacy of a shift from extensive to intensive growth and from quantitative to qualitative indicators for evaluating performance. But the crucial questions are whether the system has actually adapted itself to such an evaluation in practice and whether under conditions of a sellers' market it can do so. Some of the reasons for the extremely poor Bulgarian qualitative performance are as follows.

(1) The high-pressure economy stresses maximization of output volume, pushes qualitative improvement of production to the background and gives rise to inefficiencies and bottlenecks that pervade the system.

(2) Postulation of targets tells us something about the planners' intentions, the acceptable rate aimed at and the recognition of limitations. But the executant knows that not all targets are equally important, and he will discriminate among them if they conflict or if their execution is endangered.

(3) The system instils a short time horizon into the executant: his primary task is to fulfil the annual (or even quarterly or monthly) targets.

(4) The rhetoric and exhortations toward greater efficiency notwithstanding, the various levels of management are still, in fact, judged in terms of physical plan fulfilment; incentive systems might be tied into qualitative indicators, but they are largely counteracted by the severe penalties for not fulfilling the physical plan.

(5) Other reasons include the poor technical and organizational level of production, the proverbial inefficiency of organization, bottlenecks in

supply, labour laxity, etc. As a rule, although the quantitative plan indicators are usually fulfilled, the qualitative ones are not (Feiwel, 1977, pp. 177–81).

Palpable incentives are required in any system to elicit better performance or compliance. The traditional system and even the more radical reforms tend to stress material incentives. In Bulgaria, more than in other CMEA countries, non-material incentives have received shifting emphasis, though material incentives have been used considerably. The high-investment and highly politicized Bulgarian economy has relied much on campaigns, moral suasion, and exhortations of all sorts to fulfil 'mobilizing' plans, together with political advancement and all kinds of orders and decorations.

One of the answers to the often-posed question 'how to make workers work' is to reward them according to their relative productivity, granted that in many cases this is difficult to quantify. Rewards related to productivity call for wider income differentials, and they conflict with egalitarian distribution. But established patterns of income distribution are difficult to change. This seems to be one of the fundamental obstacles to a reform linking rewards to performance A resolute implementation would mean that earnings would fluctuate, and employees are apprehensive of downward earnings flexibility. Moreover, if the higher pay cannot buy high-quality, desired goods, the worker might prefer leisure.

In Bulgaria prices remain more or less arbitarily set: they tend to be inconsistent with other instruments of plan execution. Domestic prices are only tenuously related to world market prices[12], and within the system, producers' prices are insulated from consumers' prices[13]. Naturally the planners want production to be elastic to some prices and inelastic to others, and this is a source of many inconsistencies. Executants will make whatever decisions they can on the basis of existing prices (and will try to influence new prices to their own advantage). One of the most expedient measures for reducing the distorting impact of prices is to restrict the periphery's sphere of decisionmaking.

Periodic price revisions – quite distinct from reform of principles and methodology of pricing – eliminate some distortions and shortcomings and tighten up the system. But here again, elimination of some accumulated inconsistencies tends to create new ones. The problem is to make price setting more consistent with plan construction and with the other instruments of plan execution (such as performance criteria and incentives) and also to allow for more flexibility to reflect changing environment and desiderata.

Reforms have to cope with moderating the sources of inefficiency. But the crux of the matter is dynamic efficiency, which requires a reform capable of instilling the spirit of innovation and risk-taking at all levels of economic activity. So far the Bulgarian 'reforms' have not only failed to introduce the necessary stimuli for generating technical progress from below but have not succeeded in eliminating the built-in obstacles to implementation of technical progress imposed from above.

The major problem remains one of diffusion of technical progress and spillover from growth-promoting and defence activities to the rest of the system. The system-made obstacles to technical progress derive primarily from the disruptive effect of its introduction on current activity, which is at the forefront of attention. The underlying factor is again the high-pressure economy which, despite the leadership's rhetoric regarding technical progress and the extension of the planning horizon, stresses quantity at the cost of quality, and current plan fulfilment at the cost of long-term benefits, and results in instability even in the short run, so that executants have to provide larger reserves for current plan fulfilment which otherwise could have been used for technical progress measures.

In the final analysis the system of functioning should be consistent and dovetailed with the development strategy. There is an obvious interaction between the plan and the *modus operandi*. Choice of an appropriate growth rate, structure and techniques of production, as well as a more effective planning system, would jointly produce better results than could be achieved by attacking the economic riddle on one front only.

The organizational structure of Bulgaria now features a high degree of monopolization. Whatever the economic reasons, benefits of scale, propensity for gigantomania and equating high concentration with progress, there are strong political reasons for such organization. It facilitates central control, shortens and reduces the number of channels of communication and coordination and provides an opportunity for restricted 'decentralization'. Such an arrangement avoids some of the excesses of overcentralization but also precludes devolution of decisionmaking to the actual production units. Thus, the system cannot be expected to benefit from the initiative and ingenuity of economic actors at the time and place of action. But it seems that the planners have traded off the potential gain in efficiency for maintenance of control, which is necessary in a high-pressure economy.

The strongest opposition to reform is not on grounds of economic merit but on those of the gains which the different interest groups expect to derive from it and the losses they fear. It might seem paradoxical that in view of the recognized needs, consistent reforms are not introduced. But economic solutions are increasingly political questions. By their very nature market-type reforms shift the focus towards interaction between contracting parties and checks from below – and divert it from the vertical command system. It is a democratization process that not only weakens the rulers' monopoly over economic decisionmaking but threatens to spread into other domains. A real movement toward political democratization would essentially expropriate the ruling clique, which, though it is not the legal owner of the means of production, possesses all the prerogatives and privileges of a collective owner. Even those among the leadership who favour reform are reluctant to commit themselves to such a course, for it is usually costly, entails some unpopular measures and does not pay off quickly.

The Bulgarian system relies heavily on the political apparatus, and a growing bureaucracy plays an important role. The aparatchiks are compensated by relatively very high earnings (which grow apace, even when salaries and wages in production units are stagnant or fall) and a broad and growing network of privileges that include special stores where they can acquire at special prices high-quality goods and luxuries unavailable elsewhere, their own hospitals and resorts, private villas, expensive gifts, proliferation of jobs at full pay for one individual, special luxury holidays abroad, etc.

An expanding industrialized economy has to rely increasingly on the technocracy to keep the wheels turning. There is understandable friction between the old-time privileged apparatchik and the increasing aspirations of the technocrat for a share in power, prestige, position and income.

In the final analysis meaningful reform cannot be implemented by individuals who fear its consequences and resent it. Neither can it be introduced by those who have been inculcated with the bureaucratic way, for sooner or later their well-ingrained habits will predominate and overrule the attempted reform. The vertical hierarchic chain of command is staunchly defended by the bureaucracy. Such a system is incompatible with market-type reforms and perpetuates the salient features of the traditional system. In particular, despite pronouncements about differentiation between guiding and directive indicators, the executants depend on the source from which these instructions emanate and thus superiors can *de facto* turn guiding into directive indicators, and reduction of the number of binding indicators is not a measure of decentralization. On the whole, it is difficult to judge to what extent the bureaucracy has deliberately exerted its energies on thwarting reform. At any rate, one should remember that the Zhivkov regime is cast in the traditional conservative mould, with strong allegiance to the USSR. Although it has shown some pragmatism and flexibility, it lacks imagination and daring and is particularly skillful in the centralistic and autocratic ways.

The present timid and tired leadership can hardly be counted on to generate and institute the requisite changes in policy and working arrangements. As such, the present system not only lacks the capacity to generate economic progress but suffers from its inability to adapt and adjust to change and to modify radically the growth strategy and the institutions to reflect the profound shifts in domestic and external conditions and the aspirations of the economic actors. At present it is difficult to be optimistic and to identify a social force sufficiently powerful to act soon as a strong catalyst of economic and social progress.

7.8 Statistical appendix

Table 7A.1 *Major economic indicators of Bulgaria: selected years,
1965–1976 (1960 = 100)*

Indicators	1965	1970	1971	1972	1973	1974	1975	1976
National income produced	138	210	225	242	262	281	306	326
Gross industrial output	174	293	319	348	380	411	450	480
Producer goods (group A)	193	339	379	421	458	498	548	593
Consumer goods (group B)	157	251	266	283	309	332	362	379
Investments	146	263	268	294	315	339	398	400
In industry	192	349	345	356	384	389	467	475
In agriculture[a]	97	140	146	161	166	193	197	200
Gross agricultural output	117	139	141	149	151	149	160	167
Crops	112	133	133	144	144	134	144	152
Livestock	127	149	159	161	166	178	191	195
Retail trade[b]	139	211	225	239	261	284	306	329
Foreign trade[c]	195	319	357	398	452	562	694	755
Labour force in socialized economy	124	155	161	169	184	193	207	219
In industry	124	150	154	157	162	166	169	171
In construction	140	189	194	196	196	196	197	195

(a) Including forestry and in 1975–1976 excluding costs of forest planting;
(b) Including public catering;
(c) At current prices.

Sources: Statisticheskii Ezhegodnik Stran-chlenov Soveta Ekonomicheskoi Vzaimopomoshchi
1975 (Moscow, 1975), pp. 21; Statistical Yearbook of Member Countries of the
Council for Mutual Economic Assistance 1977 (Moscow, 1977), p. 21.

Table 7A.2 Average annual growth rates of national income (Y) and gross industrial output (O) in CMEA countries, 1951–1977

Periods		Bulgaria	Czechoslovakia	GDR	Hungary	Poland	Romania	USSR
1951–1967	Y	9.6	6.0	7.7	5.7	7.1	9.8	8.8
	O	13.6	8.6	9.1	9.2	11.0	13.2	10.5
1961–1972	Y	7.6	4.5	4.5	5.5	6.6	8.9	6.7
	O	10.9	6.1	6.1	6.8	8.5	12.6	8.3
1951–1955	Y	12.2	8.1	13.2	5.7	8.6	14.2	11.3
	O	13.7	10.9	13.8	13.2	16.2	15.1	13.2
1956–1960	Y	9.6	7.0	7.4	6.0	6.6	6.6	9.2
	O	15.9	10.5	9.2	7.6	9.9	10.9	10.4
1961–1965	Y	6.6	1.9	3.4	4.1	6.2	9.2	6.5
	O	11.7	5.2	6.0	7.5	8.5	13.8	8.6
1966–1970	Y	8.7	6.9	5.2	6.8	6.0	7.6	7.8
	O	10.9	6.7	6.5	6.2	8.3	11.9	8.5
1971–1975	Y	7.8	5.5	5.4	6.3	9.8	11.3	5.7
	O	9.1	6.7	6.5	6.4	10.5	12.9	7.4
1976–1978	Y	6.0	4.2	4.2	5.1	5.0	8.9	5.1
	O	6.6	5.4	5.7	5.7	7.0	10.8	5.4

Sources: *Rozwoj gospodarczy krajow RWPG 1950–1968* (Warsaw, 1969), pp. 44 and 47; *Rocznik statystyki miedzynarodowej 1973* (Warsaw, 1973), pp. 97 and 118; *Rocznik statystyczny 1974* (Warsaw, 1975), pp. 563 and 572; *Rocznik statystyczny 1978* (Warsaw, 1978), pp. 466 and 474; *Rocznik statystyczny 1979*, pp. 485 and 493.

Table 7A.3 *Annual growth rates (rounded) of national income, gross industrial output, gross agricultural output, and investment in Bulgaria, 1951–1977*

Years	National income	Gross industrial output	Gross agricultural output	Investment
1951	41	19	40	27
1952	−1	16	−16	22
1953	21	15	22	9
1954	0	11	−12	6
1955	5	8	9	5
1956	1	15	−7	2
1957	13	16	17	−3
1958	7	15	−1	22
1959	22	20	18	63
1960	7	12	3	18
1961	3	11	−3	4
1962	6	10	4	7
1963	7	10	2	15
1964	10	10	12	10
1965	7	15	2	8
1966	11	12	15	22
1967	9	13	3	25
1968	6	12	−9	9
1969	10	9	4	1
1970	7	10	4	11
1971	7	9	2	2
1972	8	9	6	10
1973	8	9	1	7
1974	8	8	−3	8
1975	9	10	8	17
1976	7	7	4	1
1977	6	7	−5	n.a.

Sources: *Rozwoj gospodarczy krajow RWPG 1950–1968*, pp. 14–41; *Rocznik statystyki miedzynarodowej 1973*, pp. 96, 117, 195; *Rocznik statystyczny 1971*, p. 661; *Rocznik statystyczny 1972*, p. 628; *Rocznik statystyczny 1975*, pp. 563, 570, 572 and 596; *Statisticheskii Ezhegodnik Stran-Chlenov Soveta Ekonomicheskoi Vzaimopomoshchi 1976*, p. 141; *Statistical Yearbook of CMEA 1977*, pp. 59 and 139; *Rocznik statystyczny 1978*, p. 474; *Statisticheski Godishnik na Narodna Republika Bulgaria 1978* (Sofia, 1978), pp. 122 and 229.

Table 7A.4 *Growth of national income, accumulation and consumption in Bulgaria, selected years 1939–1977 (1952 = 100)*

Years	National income	Per capita national income	Consumption	Accumulation
1939	72	83	n.a.	n.a.
1948	73	74	n.a.	n.a.
1955	127	124	128	107
1956	128	123	142	76
1957	145	138	149	120
1958	155	146	164	126
1959	189	176	183	252
1960	202	187	195	237
1961	208	190	211	194
1962	221	201	221	241
1963	237	214	233	317
1964	261	233	251	374
1965	279	248	269	353
1966	310	273	286	495
1967	339	296	313	533
1968	360	312	341	539
1969	396	341	360	594
1970	424	363	380	590
1971	454	386	408	522
1972	488	414	433	632
1973	528	445	462	733
1974	568	476	495	910
1975	618	515	533	1081
1976	658	546	565	956
1977	699	577	588	1041

Sources: Statisticheski Godishnik 1968, pp. 100 and 102; Statistical Yearbook of the People's Republic of Bulgaria 1971 (Sofia, 1971), pp. 56 and 58; Statisticheski Godishnik 1977, p. 122; Statischeski Godishnik 1978, pp. 122 and 124.

246

Table 7A.5 Structure of Bulgarian industry (1) and growth (2) of the various branches (1960 = 100), selected years 1960–1977

Branches	1960		1965		1970		1975		1977	
	1	2	1	2	1	2	1	2	1	2
Total industry	100.0	100	100.0	174	100.0	293	100.0	450	100.0	513
Electric power	2.0	100	2.3	200	2.5	373	2.2	483	2.3	570
Fuels	2.8	100	3.8	238	4.6	484	3.8	727	3.5	776
Ferrous metallurgy	1.1	100	2.2	333	3.1	778	3.5	13x	3.7	16x
Machine building	12.4	100	16.5	232	20.2	478	24.8	948	27.7	12x
Chemicals	3.7	100	4.8	219	7.5	580	7.6	10x	7.8	12x
Building materials	3.1	100	3.8	215	3.7	350	3.9	542	4.0	631
Timber and woodworking	6.3	100	4.8	134	3.7	170	3.5	224	3.3	241
Paper	0.9	100	0.9	174	1.0	355	1.4	625	1.3	662
Glassware and china	0.6	100	0.8	243	0.9	448	0.9	672	0.9	777
Textiles	13.5	100	10.1	131	9.1	198	7.8	281	7.5	310
Clothing	5.5	100	4.4	142	4.9	263	3.6	373	3.3	386
Leather and footwear	2.3	100	1.8	139	1.9	243	1.7	334	1.6	347
Printing	0.6	100	0.4	126	0.5	223	0.4	270	0.5	375
Food	33.5	100	31.8	165	25.4	222	23.5	294	22.5	321

Source: Statisticheski Godishnik 1978, p. 170.

Table 7A.6 *Structure of employment in Bulgaria by sectors in selected years, 1948–1977*

Years	Industry	Construction	Agriculture	Transport	'Non-productive sector	Distribution and procurement	Administration
1948	7.9	2.0	81.9	1.2	4.3	2.2	1.5
1956	12.9	3.3	70.1	2.5	7.2	3.0	1.4
1960	21.9	5.2	54.7	3.5	9.2	4.0	1.4
1965	26.3	7.0	44.9	4.4	10.8	5.2	1.2
1970	30.4	8.4	35.2	5.2	13.1	6.1	1.5
1973	32.2	8.3	31.0	5.2	14.5	7.1	1.5
1975	33.5	8.0	27.6	5.6	15.7	7.8	1.5
1977	34.2	8.3	25.3	5.9	16.3	8.1	1.5

Sources: Statistical Yearbook of Bulgaria 1969, p. 38; *Statisticheski Godishnik 1978*, p. 100.

Table 7A.7 *Growth of real wages (1) and labour productivity (2) in some CMEA countries, selected years 1960–1976 (1970 = 100)*

Years		Bulgaria	Czechoslavakia	Hungary	Poland	Romania	USSR
1960	1	70	79	77	84	68	74
	2	52	65	66	61	49	60
1965	1	77	84	84	91	84	80
	2	72	77	84	78	70	76
1971	1	102	104	102	106	102	103
	2	106	106	107	105	105	106
1972	1	105	109	105	112	104	106
	2	109	113	114	111	110	112
1973	1	111	112	108	122	107	110
	2	121	119	120	122	119	119
1974	1	113	115	114	130	112	114
	2	128	126	129	132	127	126
1975	1	116	118	118	141	120	119
	2	139	134	135	144	136	134
1976	1	117	121	118	147	127	123
	2	148	141	142	158	148	138

Sources: Statisticheskii Ezhegodnik Stran-chlenov Soveta Ekonomicheskoi Vzaimopomoshchi 1975, pp. 48 and 131; Statistical Yearbook of CMEA 1977, pp. 48 and 131.

Table 7A.8 *Estimated personal consumption of goods in Bulgaria, selected years, 1960–1967 (1968 = 100)*

Years	Foods	Beverages	Clothing and shoes	Furniture and household durables	Cultural durables	Transport durables
1960	78.4	53.9	62.2	50.6	17.8	41.2
1965	93.3	75.4	81.5	71.0	41.0	71.4
1970	102.7	95.7	107.0	139.7	90.5	96.3
1971	105.1	102.3	109.5	137.6	74.7	155.9
1972	107.3	106.4	112.4	147.1	68.3	167.0
1973	109.5	117.0	119.3	165.4	64.2	196.0
1974	111.9	118.2	125.1	162.4	52.6	221.5
1975	117.4	119.4	130.2	185.9	57.0	232.6
1976	121.6	130.7	134.0	199.3	73.7	252.9
1977	120.5	129.2	125.9	211.8	67.3	288.6

Source: T. P. Alton et al., Personal Consumption in Eastern Europe, Selected Years, 1960–1978, OP-57 (New York, 1979), pp. 29–32.

Table 7A.9 *Distribution of imports (1) and exports (2) of CMEA countries by geographical areas, selected years 1950–1976*

Countries	Regions	1950 1	1950 2	1960 1	1960 2	1970 1	1970 2	1974 1	1974 2	1976 1	1976 2
Bulgaria	Socialist	85.8	91.8	83.9	84.0	76.2	79.3	70.1	76.0	77.2	80.2
	Developed capitalist	13.1	7.3	13.7	12.5	19.1	14.2	22.5	11.7	18.3	10.5
	Developing	1.1	0.9	2.4	3.5	4.7	6.5	7.4	12.3	4.5	9.3
Czechoslovakia	Socialist	56.6	54.8	71.3	72.3	69.4	70.6	65.0	67.4	69.9	74.2
	Developed capitalist	34.9	34.7	18.9	16.7	24.5	20.4	27.7	24.0	24.9	18.2
	Developing	8.6	10.5	9.8	11.0	6.1	9.0	7.3	8.6	5.2	7.6
GDR	Socialist	75.9	68.2	73.8	75.7	69.4	73.9	60.2	68.4	63.6	71.6
	Developed capitalist	24.0	31.1	22.0	20.2	26.7	21.9	34.2	27.4	31.6	24.0
	Developing	0.1	0.7	4.2	4.1	3.9	4.2	5.6	4.2	4.8	4.4
Hungary	Socialist	56.6	66.0	70.9	71.5	65.0	65.6	57.6	67.1	54.6	60.5
	Developed capitalist	37.3	27.4	24.7	21.9	28.8	28.0	34.6	26.1	36.0	30.8
	Developing	6.1	6.6	4.4	6.6	6.2	6.4	7.8	6.8	9.4	8.7
Poland	Socialist	61.1	56.9	63.5	62.6	68.6	63.9	44.4	55.7	46.9	59.7
	Developed capitalist	35.7	39.7	29.7	29.9	25.8	28.4	50.8	36.3	48.9	32.0
	Developing	3.2	3.4	6.8	7.5	5.6	7.7	4.8	8.0	4.2	8.3
Romania	Socialist	78.1	89.2	73.1	73.0	53.9	58.1	39.2	43.3	45.4	45.7
	Developed capitalist	16.5	5.5	23.4	21.3	39.5	31.9	48.6	42.1	36.7	34.9
	Developing	5.4	5.3	3.5	5.7	6.6	10.0	12.2	14.6	17.9	19.4
USSR	Socialist	78.0	83.6	70.7	75.7	65.1	65.4	54.7	53.5	52.5	58.7
	Developed capitalist	15.6	14.6	19.8	18.2	24.0	18.7	32.6	30.2	37.7	28.0
	Developing	6.4	1.8	9.5	6.1	10.9	15.9	12.7	16.3	9.8	13.3

Sources: Kraje RWPG 1950–1973 (Warsaw, 1974), pp. 105–106; *Kraje RWPG 1960–1975* (Warsaw, 1976), pp. 117–118; *Kraje RWPG 1977* (Warsaw, 1977), pp. 132–133.

Table 7A.10 Foreign trade balances of product groups in Bulgaria, selected years 1960–1977 (millions of foreign currency leva)

Products	1960	1965	1970	1971	1972	1973	1974	1975	1976	1977
Producer goods (group A)	− 311.9	− 444.4	− 651.2	− 821.0	− 810.0	− 875.8	− 1296.0	− 1918.5	− 1569.3	− 1435.8
Machinery	− 204.5	− 202.0	− 59.8	− 133.9	− 76.4	+ 71.8	− 58.4	− 75.9	+ 163.0	+ 464.0
Raw materials and semifabricates	− 107.4	− 242.4	− 591.4	− 687.1	− 733.6	− 947.6	− 1237.6	− 1842.6	− 1732.3	− 1899.8
of agricultural origin	+ 73.8	+ 98.4	+ 0.2	+ 17.2	+ 49.4	− 44.3	− 252.3	− 181.2	− 82.5	− 46.1
of mineral origin	+ 181.2	− 340.8	− 591.6	− 669.9	− 783.0	− 903.3	− 985.3	− 1661.4	− 1649.8	− 1853.7
Consumer goods (group B)	+ 240.4	+ 442.2	+ 853.4	+ 894.4	+ 874.8	+ 904.8	+ 821.0	+ 1224.3	+ 1333.1	+ 1396.1
Crops	+ 210.6	+ 389.4	+ 690.1	+ 750.7	+ 734.6	+ 782.8	+ 780.8	+ 978.2	+ 1092.7	+ 1136.3
Livestock products	+ 62.3	+ 99.8	+ 172.7	+ 206.0	+ 197.5	+ 183.4	+ 162.6	+ 282.8	+ 292.8	+ 324.5
Industrial consumer goods	− 32.5	− 47.0	− 9.4	− 62.3	− 57.3	− 61.4	− 122.4	− 36.7	− 52.4	− 64.7
Total	− 71.5	− 2.2	+ 202.2	+ 73.4	+ 64.8	+ 29.0	− 475.0	− 694.2	− 236.2	− 39.7

Sources: Statisticheski Godishnik 1976, p. 348; Statisticheski Godishnik 1978, p. 353.

Notes

1. The growth strategy in post-war Bulgaria and the development of the economy in the 1950s and 1960s were analysed in Feiwel (1977, chs 1 and 2).
2. For an evaluation of economic fluctuations in CMEA countries see Feiwel (1977, pp. 38–49) and the references therein.
3. Some of the targets set for 1980 (increase over 1975) were: national income 45%; investment 46%; industrial output 55%; (machine building 100%, chemicals 80%, light industry 43%, food industry 40%, electric power 50%); agricultural output 20%; foreign trade 60%; retail trade 40%; services 65%; real per capita incomes 20%; public consumption 35% labour productivity (national income per employee) 45%; labour productivity in industry 50%. About 420 000 housing units were to be built. The distribution of national income between consumption and accumulation was to be 74:26 (*Rabotnichesko Delo*, 30 October 1976; *Durzhaven Vestnik*, No. 88 (5 November) 1976.
4. 96-octane increased from 0.5 to 1.00 leva per litre, 93-octane from 0.44 to 0.80 leva and 83-octane from 0.36 to 0.70 leva.
5. Along with the broadening of international contacts, foreign currency violations have also become an important aspect of economic crimes (Boev and Balkanski, 1979; Kayrov, 1979; Kharalampieva *et al.*, 1979; Lazarov, 1977).
6. For a masterly analysis of economic crimes in a 'socialist system' see Kalecki

(1964, pp. 83–90); cf. Feiwel (1977, pp. 227–230).
7. For an explanation of this relationship see Feiwel (1977, pp. 234–235 and 253–254).
8. For an analysis of the early stages of Bulgarian economic reforms see Feiwel (1977, pp. 91–100).
9. For an exposition of the financial and bonus system in the mid-1970s see Feiwel (1977, pp. 143–162).
10. For criticism of the complexity of this new system see *Rabotnichesko Delo*, 22 February 1978.
11. For some of the problems of the construction brigades see Minev (1979).
12. For example, when the 1971 wholesale prices were introduced they were already obsolete. Their continued use in the 1970s deepened their obsolescence. This became particularly acute in the prices of fuels, energy and raw matrials. The domestic prices of oil were only a fraction of what Bulgaria had to pay for it. Oil refining became astronomically profitable. Its high earnings were siphoned off to make up the difference between the import and domestic prices of oil. But this branch benefited from high bonuses linked to profitability. Moreover, the artificially depressed prices of all raw materials had a distorting effect on domestic economic calculation and encouraged waste. New wholesale prices were apparently to be introduced in 1980 (Ilev, 1978, p. 14).
13. For the Bulgarian experience with price formation see Feiwel (1977, ch. 5).

References

Alton, T. P. *et al.* (1979). *Personal Consumption in Eastern Europe, Selected Years, 1960 –1978*, OP-57. New York

Balkanski, B. and Naydenov, V. (1979). *Anteni*, 7 February

Boev, P. and Balkanski, B. (1979). *Anteni*, 31 January

Dakov, M. (1972). *Planovo Stopanstvo*, No. 9

Dimov, K. (1975). *Partien Zhivot*, No. 6, pp. 26–8

Dulbokov, S. (1972). *Planovo Stopanstvo*, No. 1

Durzhaven Vestnik, 19 January 1971, pp. 1–3; No. 100 (30 December) 1975; No. 101 1975; No. 66 (17 August) 1976; No. 88 (5 November) 1976; No. 19 (8 March) 1977; 28 February 1978; No. 51 (30 June) 1978; No. 62 (8 August) 1978; No. 7 (23 January) 1979; No. 41 (25 May) 1979

Economic Developments in Countries of Eastern Europe (1970). US Congress, Joint Economic Committee. Washington, D.C.

Economic Survey of Europe in 1971 (1972). Part 1, United Nations, New York

Ekov, I. (1977). *Trud*, 19 October

Elenska, V. and Konstantinova, Z. (1978). *Pogled*, 23 January

Feiwel, G. R. (1977). *Growth and Reforms in Centrally Planned Economies*, New York

Fidanov, D. (1975). *Anteni*, 21 February

Filipov, G. (1973). *Ikonomicheski Zhivot*, 3 October

Financial Times, 8 September 1979

Ganev, A. (1976). *Ikonomicheski Zhivot*, 14 April

Gatev, G. I. (1978). *Novo Vreme*, No. 3

Genchev, T. (1974). *Narodna Mladezh*, 25 July, p. 2

Georgieva, E. (1977). *Anteni*, 24 August

Gocheva, R. (1973). *Ikonomicheska Misul*, No. 2

Handelsblatt, 4 February 1971; 18 May 1979

Handel zagraniczny a wzrost krajow RWPG (1969). Warsaw

Ikonomicheski Zhivot, 3 October 1973; 19 October 1977; 5 July 1978

Ilev, B. (1978). *Planovo Stopanstvo*, No. 3

Iliev, I. (1971). *Naruchnik na Agitatora*, No. 24; *Rabotnichesko Delo*, 30 October 1974

Ivanov, I. (1972). *Vunshna Turgoviya*, No. 10, pp. 2–6; No. 6, 1973, pp. 2–10

Kalecki, M. (1964). *Z zagadnien gospodarczo-spolecznych Polski Ludowej*, Warsaw

Kaprielova, Y. (1977). *Vunshna Turgoviya*, No. 11

Kayrov, G. (1979). *Anteni*, 31 January

Kazandzhiev, M. (1979). *Otechestven Front*, 8 October; 27 March 1979

Kharalampieva, N. *et al.* (1979). *Pogled*, 12 February

Koev, D. (1968). *Ikonomicheska misul*, No. 7, pp. 3–13

Kolev, K. (1973). *Novo Vreme*, No. 12, pp. 23–4

Kolev, S. (1979). *Rabotnichesko Delo*, 4 June

Kooperativno Selo, 30 and 31 March 1979

Krustev, T. (1978). *Planovo Stopanstvo*, No. 8, pp. 73–8

Krustev, V. *et al.* (1977). *Rabotnichesko Delo*, 1 September

Lazarov, A. (1977). *Trud*, 19 October

Marinov, G. (1978). *Stroitel*, 22 February

Markov, M. (1976). *Rabotnichesko Delo*, 3 August

Markov, R. (1977). *Statistika*, No. 6, pp. 62–9

Minev, M. (1979). *Tekhnichesko Delo*, 1 June

Mishev, M. (1979). *Trud*, 12 January

Narodna Mladezh, 11 March 1977

Panev, B. (1977). *Trud*, 23 March

Pankov, G. (1975). *Ikonomicheski Zhivot*, 13 August

Petrov, M. (1974). *Rabotnichesko Delo*, 10 January

Pogled, 3 October 1977

Quarterly Economic Review of Romania, Bulgaria, Albania, 4th quarter, 1979, The Economist Intelligence Unit

Rabotnichesko Delo, 17 December 1971; 15 January 1972; 1 February 1975; 31 January 1976; 12 February 1976; 31 August 1976; 30 October 1976; 14 October 1977; 22 February 1978; 22 March 1978; 14 April 1978; 17 April 1978; 26 April 1978; 29 April 1978; 26 June 1978; 31 January 1979; 6 March 1979; 7 March 1979; 16 April 1979; 22 May 1979; 14 June 1979

Radeva, M. (1978). *Tekhnichesko Delo*, 28 January

Rudnichar, 16 November 1978

Sokolov, A. (1974). *Narodna Armiya*, 17 January

Statistical Pocketbook 1970. Sofia

Statistical Yearbook of Member Countries of the Council of Mutual Economic Assistance 1977. Moscow

Statistical Yearbook of the People's Republic of Bulgaria 1971. Sofia

Statisticheski Godishnik na Narodna Republika Bulgaria, 1978. Sofia

Stroitel, 28 September 1977

Szabo, A. (1974). *Közgazdasagi szemle*, No. 10

Tekhnichesko Delo, 20 August 1977

Todoriev, N. (1978). *Energetika*, No. 1, pp. 3–6

Todorov, S. (1975). *Rabotnichesko Delo*, 5 December; 22 March 1978

Trud, 28 October 1977

Tsanov, V. (1978). *Rabotnichesko Delo*, 5 May; *Kooperativno Selo*, 21 December 1978; *Rabotnichesko Delo*, 22 June 1979

Tsekov, G. (1977). *Anteni*, 24 August

Tsoneva, I. (1977). *Planovo Stopanstvo*, No. 2, pp. 72–6

Tuzharov, D. (1977). *Novo Vreme*, No. 8, pp. 35–44

Vachkov, I. (1973). *Rabotnichesko Delo*, 29 June

Vasilev, D. (1978). *Rabotnichesko Delo*, 27 February

Vladimirov, V. (1977). *Trud*, 19 October

Vulchanov, V. (1978). *Stroitel*, 1 May

Zamedelso Zname, 12 August 1976; 11 March 1977

Zamek, U. (1979). *Rynki zagraniczne*, No. 22 (19 February)

Zarev, K. (1977). *Rabotnichesko Delo*, 18 October; 30 November 1978

Zhivkov, T. (1968). *Rabotnichesko Delo*, 25 July; 14 December 1972; 12 February 1976; 26 April 1978; 28 April 1979

Zhivkov, Zh. (1973). *Ikonomicheska Misul*, No. 1

Economic reform in Romania in the 1970s

Michael Kaser and Iancu Spigler

8.1 Publications on the Romanian system

Romania has not received the same attention as the more developed economies of the CMEA countries in the matter of its management system. Five English-language works which have appeared since the present writers contributed to an earlier collective volume sponsored by the Bundesinstitut may particularly be mentioned (Kaser, 1975)[1]. Of these the only one to focus in detail upon the Romanian economic mechanism is that by Granick, who selected it as one of four in Eastern Europe (Granick, 1975)[2]. His analysis, much of it based upon interviews, chiefly with industrial managers, provides invaluable insight into the microeconomic control system. A World Bank study has been devoted to Romania (which joined it and the International Monetary Fund in 1974), and discusses planning as well as performance and prospects (Tsantis and Pepper, 1979). Montias has drawn upon his long specialization on the Romanian economy (Montias, 1967) in comparing three forms of contemporary economic system (Montias, 1976). Although Wiles no more than mentions the specific case of Romania, his investigation of the common and divergent features of economic institutions raises many issues of the planning mechanism and enterprise objectives in a 'Soviet-type economy' (Wiles, 1977). The Joint Economic Committee of the United States Congress (JEC) has brought together studies on all the East European economies. That which appeared in 1977 included a paper which devoted attention to foreign-trade organization (Brada and Jackson, 1977) and another with brief reference to the general economic mechanism (Jackson, 1977). A new JEC compendium was in preparation as this study was being completed[3] and NATO devoted its annual colloquium on the East European economies to economic reform[4]. Finally, a forthcoming University of Wales symposium on East European economic reform will contain a study on Romania[5].

It is significant that the only two detailed studies are based on interviews and documentation gathered during visits to Romania – Professor Granick in 1970–1971 and the World Bank mission in 1975 and 1976. This is largely because of the paucity of material on economic organization published in Romania. The two journals which drew on academic and research institutes as well as officials, *Probleme economice* and *Finanţe şi credit*, ceased publication in 1974 and the successor of the first-named, a weekly, *Revista economică*, offers little more than the simple presentation of government decisions with superficial elaboration, general industrial surveys and brief annotations on detailed economic issues. At about the same time the theoretical and policy-studies organ of the communist party, *Lupta de clasă*, was also replaced by the more popular-styled *Era Socialistă*, and the flow of official statistics began significantly to diminish[6]. The natural calamities which struck the country in that period – disastrous floods in 1975 and an earthquake in 1977 – may have rendered the authorities more reticent about performance, while the increasing personal control of affairs by the President since the creation of the office has disinclined officials and scholars to publish on current topics due to the requirement for clearance at the highest level.

There has, of course, been a great deal of published elaboration of the changes decided upon in March 1978 which have been drawn upon for this study. Two books edited by Professor Ioan Totu, the Director of the Central Institute of Economic Research (*Institutul central de cercetări economice*), have also been used, but they were completed before the implementation of the new practices. They contain chapters surveying planning methods in 1972–1976 (Părăluță, 1977) and covering the 1978 decision (Russu, 1978).

Two important institutional studies bearing on the economic mechanism should also be mentioned – on the budget by the late Kurt Wessely of the Österreichisches Ost- und Südosteuropa Institut, Vienna (Wessely, 1978) and on the constitution of 1965 as amended up to March 1975 by Janina Zakrzewska of Warsaw university (Zakrzewska, 1978).

8.2 The period between reforms, 1972–1978

The first economic reform in Romania, announced in 1967 and operative during the four years 1969–1972, was brief[7], and little more than the intermediate organizational form, the *centrală*, was retained during the ensuing period of recentralization. Some indication of the hesitation with which the Romanian Communist Party approached the issue of economic reform was the delay in its introduction; there had been neither a careful sifting of proposals for a once-and-for-all change as in Hungary, nor a marked change in the political structure, as in Czechoslovakia. The first hint that some reform was in the air came in July 1966, when every other CMEA member in Europe had taken definitive measures of reform; the relevant resolution of the party Central Committee was in October 1967; experimental change was launched in April 1969; and the new institutions (*centrale*) were created in October 1969. Another contrast was that whereas the rest of the CMEA countries made planning 'slacker' by decentralization, the aim of the Romanian changes was to 'tauten' relationships. In December 1969 the Party Leader, later President, Ceauşescu put among the reasons for the measures then just introduced: 'Still more negative in fact is the failure at all levels – enterprises, ministries and the Planning Committee – to draft a plan utilizing all the available resources' (*Scînteia*, 14 December 1969). Granick, visiting enterprises and ministries in 1970, saw that 'the original plan targets are not set at a particularly demanding level' (Granick, 1975, p. 98) and he concluded in another study that Romania remained a more centralized economy even than the GDR or the USSR (Granick, JEC, 1974, p. 234). Finally, the Romanian authorities never termed the changes a 'reform' but spoke of 'improving the management and planning of the national economy' (*perfectionarea conducerii şi planificarii economiei naţionale*).

Around 1972 there was a halt to further change along the lines sketched in 1967, and the industrial ministries regained much of the authority they had had to surrender. Writing of 1972–1977 Jackson considered (in our view erroneously) 'that what has been most interesting about Romanian economic organization, especially by comparison with other CMEA members, is not change, but a relative lack of change' (Jackson, 1977, p. 890). He interpreted that period as one of deliberate alteration of 'organizational mood' rather than of formal variation in decisionmaking procedure and finds 'the best term for describing the phenomenon [is] the word "mobilization", defined by Montias as "the form of pressure on individuals and their families, usually channelled through local party cadres, to make them contribute as much as they can to the pursuit of the regime's goals"' (Jackson, 1977, p. 890)[8]. Our interpretation is that the period between the formal 'reforms' was used to establish a more pervasive structure of macroeconomic control by the Communist party and to evolve a microeconomic criterion of 'own effort'.

The first of these developments was the insertion of 'consultative' councils at the national level within the pyramidal economic structure. Bodies of workplace consultation had been part of the original reform, being created in April 1968; they were accorded much greater weight by being given a national forum in July 1977 in the Congress of Councils of the Working People in Industry, Construction and Transport. 'Workers' control teams', established in December 1956, were convened in a first national conference in February 1977. Elected members of provincial councils, as reconstituted in February 1968, became *ex officio* the Legislative Chamber of People's councils in July 1976. The common feature of the three groupings was to evoke a voice of those elected at workplace or residence which, while by their large numbers susceptible to Party manipulation, are a safety valve for genuine grievances among the labour force or citizenry at large.

The second development was the introduction of a distinction between external impact on enterprise performance and the enterprise's 'own efforts' in the calculation of workplace and enterprise bonuses: targets underfulfilled by the fault of outide circumstances (such as the non-delivery of materials or blueprints) are not automatically disqualified from consideration for reward (Tagle).

The trends at both levels had been fully established by 22–23 March 1978, when a resolution of the Party Central Committee on 'the Improvement of Economic and Financial Management and Planning' heralded a new economic reform (*Revista economică* No. 13, 1978). In the following text this document is referred to as the 'Resolution'.

The enhancement of party control

The formal interlocking of party and governmental hierarchies in a manner never adopted in any other country with a ruling Communist (or Workers') Party had been initiated in 1967: the party national conference of December 1967 required integration of executive posts at key points in the party and government. This was largely effected by the establishment of common bodies in the central administration and by the appointment of a single individual to posts at the head of each local administration. The First Secretary of the Party Committee for a county (*judet*) became, for example, *ex officio* the chairman of the local government authority, the secretary of a town committee became the mayor. The process culminated in the establishment in 1974 of the office of President, which was forthwith filled by the party leader, Nicolae Ceauşescu. The party and, increasingly, the law came to assume major roles in the mobilization of the individual Romanian for macroeconomic objectives.

Jackson points out that membership of the Romanian Communist Party grew by 20% between 1969 and 1974. At some 2.5 million, its ratio to population was the highest of any CMEA member (Jackson, 1977, p. 891). The high rate of recruitment sought to permeate management and labour alike with those commissioned to interpret and implement the party's objectives, a function also served by the merger of party and government administrations. The local administrations themselves were brought together in 1976 into a Legislative Chamber of People's Councils. This is the assembly of all members of county (*judeţena*) councils and of the Bucharest city council (which has county status), and its function was defined as to 'analyse major problems of economic and social development in the provinces, cities and localities and to debate and vote on draft legislation on development in administrative territorial unions before presentation to the National Assembly (*Scînteia*, 15 April 1976)[9].

At the other end of governmental authority, the President is chairman both of the Central Committee of the Party and of the Council of State,

which, under the 1965 Constitution, exercises the power of the National
Assembly between its sessions (Spigler, 1973, p. 29). The Council came to
be endowed not only with executive but also with legislative functions. In
October 1971 it delegated much of its routine intersessional making of
decrees and regulations to a Legislative Council, subordinate to it, but
independent of the executive (then the Council of Ministers) and the
judiciary[10]. In March 1974 it assumed many duties of the Council of
Ministers, putting a formal stamp on the pre-eminence of the President over
the Prime Minister. The Central Committee and the Council constituted
from 1974 the 'higher Party and State authorities' (*conducerea superiora de
partid şi de stat*), supervising the 'central administration' (*organele centrale*),
of more than twenty ministers and ten other officers of state (the Procura-
tor-General and the chairmen of State Committees). Two thirds of the
ministerial portfolios or committees are concerned with branches of the
economy. Seats on the Council of Minsters, unlike the practice in any other
CMEA state, are also given to the chairman of the National Union of
Collective Farmers and of the Central Council of the General Confederation
of Trade Unions and to the First Secretary of the Communist Union of
Youth. The responsibilities of members of the Council of Ministers thus
extend to every field of political, economic and social activity in the country;
those members can execute the directions of the Council of State far beyond
the confines of the ministries of which such Councils are elsewhere
composed.

A significant change in the agencies of economic decisionmaking had
taken place in early 1973, the chairmen of the two bodies then created having
seats on the Council of Ministers. The former Economic Council – since
1968 a joint subordinate of the Party Central Committee and of the Council
of Ministers – was demoted into the Central Council for Workers' Control
of Economic and Social Activities. A new body was established, the
Supreme Council on Problems of Social and Economic Development,
whose high coordinating role was indicated by chairmanship by the party
leader with the Prime Minister as his deputy.

The March 1978 resolution made the control of the party and of its leader
still more specific. Its preamble to the second part of the resolution stated
that economic planning is based on the fundamental objectives set by
congresses and conferences of the party and on the 'orientations and
indications' of its General Secretary. The Supreme Economic Council,
under his chairmanship, and not the government under the Prime Minister,
is named as the principal agency for executing the resolution; the Council of
Ministers is accorded a more subordinate role.

It is of interest to compare the organization chart produced by the World
Bank (*Figure 8.1*) with that in the article by the Prime Minister, Manea
Mănescu (*Figure 8.2*), particularly with respect to the decisive role of the
party in the latter. Academician Mănescu was Prime Minister between 1974

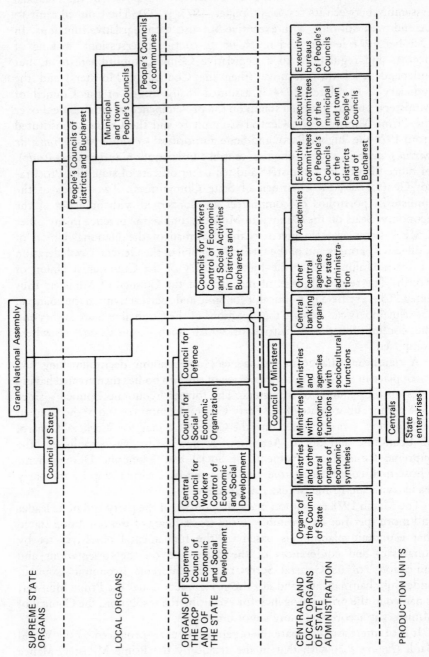

Figure 8.1 *The structure of the government*

SUPREME STATE ORGANS

LOCAL ORGANS

ORGANS OF THE RCP AND OF THE STATE

CENTRAL AND LOCAL ORGANS OF STATE ADMINISTRATION

PRODUCTION UNITS

Grand National Assembly

Council of State

People's Councils of districts and Bucharest

Municipal and town People's Councils

People's Councils of communes

Councils for Workers Control of Economic and Social Activities in Districts and Bucharest

Supreme Council of Economic and Social Development

Central Council for Workers Control of Economic and Social Development

Council for Social-Economic Organization

Council for Defence

Organs of the Council of State

Ministries and other central organs of economic synthesis

Ministries with economic functions

Council of Ministers

Ministries and agencies with sociocultural functions

Central banking organs

Other central agencies for state administration

Academies

Executive committees of People's Councils of the districts and of Bucharest

Executive committees of the municipal and town People's Councils

Executive bureaus of People's Councils

Centrals

State enterprises

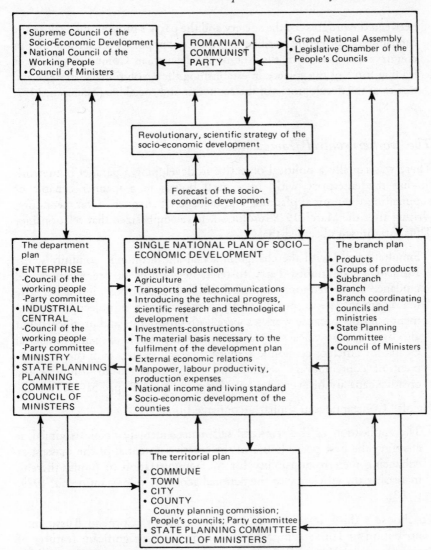

Figure 8.2 *The relationship between party and state agencies in planning*

and 1979 and may be seen as an architect of the scheme, but his replacement by Ilie Verdet could suggest an eventual divergence of view with the President. In the article from which the figure is drawn, he wrote:

The experience gained in building socialism proved that the creation of the new social system is the result of a vast political and organizational work, of the guidance of all the fields of social life by the Romanian Communist Party. . . . Social management has a primordial political character. . . . The management of the whole activity of planned socio-economic development by the Romanian Communist Party, the interdependence between the progress of the society and the party's programme, evince the fundamental principle verified by the contemporary evolution of our country: the growth of the role of the Romanian Communist Party as leading force of the society in establishing the revolutionary strategy and tactics of the development of the economic and social life (Mănescu, 1979, p. 228).

The 'workers control' framework

There was equally a political objective in developing a parallel framework linking the enterprise with the central bodies in a manner capable of supplanting the normal planning and managerial channels. Commentators, writing after the March 1978 resolution, have emphasized that relationship. Thus Grigorescu observed that:

> Simultaneously with the change in social and economic conditions, the Romanian Communist Party fostered new forms of organization and guidance in the economy and methods to bring workers into enterprise management. The deepening of democracy became an objective requirement not only because workers were both proprietors and producers, but also because it was necessary as rationally as possible to manage material means for efficient economic activity, keeping in step with the development of contemporary science and technology and to stimulate the creative capacity of every worker (Grigorescu, 1979, pp. 51–2).

Nicolae Constantinescu similarly confirmed that:

> The application of the workers' self-management principle is aimed at ensuring the best possible use of the creative potential of the masses, at enhancing their responsibility for the administration of funds, thereby increasing the efficiency of the national economy (Constantinescu, 1979, p. 60).

To choose a third among many such observations, Corneliu Russu, in a contribution to Totu's symposium, took one of the significant features of the resolution of March 1978 as 'raising the role of the mass of the working people in the organization, management and development of production' (Russu, 1978, p. 200).

The model for the new structure was the creation of a Legislative Chamber of Local Councils which federated those entities into a national body separate from the normal constitutional chain of administration. The systems of relevance to the enterprise were of enterprise councils, which constituted a Congress of Councils of the Working People and of workers' control teams which were convened into a national conference. The first followed the enterprise principle, the second the territorial principle. The developments made still clearer the Party's policy of appearing to provide outlets for the expression of rank-and-file opinion, while keeping such expression under its own control; in terms of economic management they bypassed the formal hierarchy and could be used to exert pressure on managements and their supervisory bodies in directions and for purposes formulated by the Party.

The economic reform of 1967 had envisaged a replacement of 'one-man management' on the Soviet model by collective management under a board of management (*comitete de direcţie*)[11]. The board was not merely advisory but a management body, empowered to approve or reject the decisions of the enterprise director, who, in turn, had to implement the policies ratified by the board. Overt opposition by enterprise directors kept *de facto* interference by boards at bay until the protagonists were strong enough to reduce their formal powers on their redesignation in October 1971. The new title, 'committee of the working people' (*comitetul oamenilor muncii*), had implications of 'workers' control', which was later to be more actively promoted, but between 1971 and 1977 they served as a constraint on the director to limit any excessive display of authority. They lacked independent managerial powers, since all key decisions after 1972 were returned to the supervisory agencies above the enterprise. The 1971 reorganization did, however, endow the committees with a subsidiary body, a 'collective economic management' of three to seven members, which maintained a closer watch on the director's performance. Each central office, to which authority had been devolved in 1969, was given a corresponding 'council of the working people' (*consiliul oamenilor muncii*), which had correspondingly been converted in 1971 from a 'council of administration'[12].

A parallel set of participatory agencies had been long established on a territorial basis (as distinct from the enterprise basis of the committees of the working people), namely the 'public control teams' set up in 1956 (*Buletinul oficial*, 22 December 1956). They did little other than act as channels for complaint about inadequate consumer supplies, but in 1972 they were put under the aegis of the Socialist Unity Front (the coalition in the Grand National Assembly under the leadership of the Communist Party) and their remit was widened to every form of state and cooperative agency supplying consumer goods and services and the entire range of social consumption and to assistance in the protection of the environment (Law No. 6, 1972). In the following year the Economic Council, a joint body of the Central Committee of the Party and Council of Ministers, was retitled the Central Council of Worker Control of Economic and Social Activities. This was the first appearance of the term 'worker control' and it was accorded still wider currency in 1977. In April 1976 it was announced that representatives of the public control teams should be appointed for a national conference later that year (*Scînteia*, 16 April 1976): in the event the meeting was not held until February 1977 (*Scînteia*, 18 February 1977). The 40 000 control teams then in being (on which 170 000 workers, peasants, technicians, students, pensioners and housewives were stated to be serving) elected their representatives at county conferences, which took place in January 1977: the scale of the promotion can be judged by the report that over 15 000 persons participated in the county conferences and that one in five of them made a speech *Scînteia*, 23 and 30 January 1977). Predictably, President Ceauşescu spoke at the national conference, and proposed a change of title to the more evocative 'workers' control'. The teams would work closely with the Central Council of Worker Control, but were not formally federated, for that national role was reserved for the enterprise-based committees of the working people. It may be that when the World Bank missions came to Romania at about this time their function had not been clearly defined; that the Bank's interlocutors preferred not to dwell on them; or that the missions disregarded them. Although both the councils in the counties and the Central Council are shown in its organization chart of the 'Structure of the Government' (*Figure 8.1*), not a word is accorded them in an otherwise exhaustive survey of planning procedures. A corresponding Romanian chart is reproduced in *Figure 8.2*, stressing the importance of the party. It can certainly now be seen that they were being groomed for a more prominent role, as two exhortations of 1976 indicated. The first was the distinction made by the Central Council itself between 'Party democracy' through the channels provided and the 'anarchism' which could prevail without them (*Scînteia*, 2 July 1976); this echoed a speech by President Ceauşescu which had called for the participation of every worker and employee in the work of management (*Scînteia*, 3 July 1974). A research study in 1976 (possibly commissioned to prepare the way for change) found that the committees of the working people had not actively encouraged genuine participation: the election of staff representatives was formal, the turnover of representatives was low and representatives spoke at meetings far more rarely than management. The main shortcomings were of the adequacy of information: the enquiry showed that representatives had little access to management documentation, that their electorate were very seldom asked what topics should be discussed and that they were poorly briefed on the legal competence of management (Zara, 1976). The follow-up came soon: in May 1976 the Executive Committee of the Party Central Committee resolved that these bodies, at enterprise and central office level, be federated into a Congress of Councils of the Working People in Industry, Construction and Transport (*Congresul consilillor camenilor muncii dîn industrie, construcţi şi transporturi*), which would be governed by a National Council between quinquennial sessions of the Congress (*Scînteia*, 12 May 1976). The inaugural Congress met in July 1977 and proved to be little more than an adjunct to the Party in tautening the plan. The Congress resolution called, for example, for the raising of the industrial output target for 1980 by 120 to 130 billion lei. Not only was that in itself a substantial increment, but it was well above the 100 billion lei supplementary target which had been written into the draft resolution circulated at the opening of the Congress. The creation of the National Council to serve as an executive body between Congress sessions was made a further opportunity to enhance the place of President Ceauşescu, for it was he who was elected the first Chairman of the National Council (*Scînteia*, 15 July 1977).

Other enterprise-level agencies, 1970–1977

Two sets of organizations established on 1 June 1976 drew in the cooperative Sector. The Central Council for the Coordination of Consumer Cooperatives, Handicraft Cooperatives and Agricultural Production Cooperatives was created to coordinate the operations of the entire cooperative sector, though each cooperative remained legally independent and the property of its members. The Council for the Coordination of Consumer Good Production for the Entire Economy was set up with general oversight of all consumer-good production whether in the three types of cooperatives or by state enterprises. It was stated that it would not interpose itself as a supervisory agency in the public-sector hierarchy, but rather participate in plan formulation at the ministerial and territorial levels.

Two measures on inter-enterprise relations may be noted. One enhances quality control of physical goods, the other the quality and technical parameters of construction[13]; the latter, the first of its kind as comprehensive building legislation in Romania, was made necessary by the shortcomings tragically exposed by the earthquake. The former may be seen as a supplement to the quality discipline imposed by inter-enterprise contracts, which from a 1976 enquiry, left much to be desired: thus, although contracts for 1977 should all have been signed by 30 September 1976, by 12 November only 85% had actually been concluded ('How are . . .', 1976).

Since 1970 enterprises may make use of 'organization offices' (*cabinete de organizare*), which provide consulting services on organization and methods on a fee-for-service basis. In one county (Braşov) in 1975 29% of overfulfilled profits in local industry were reported as attributable to the counsel of the office (Stefanescu, 1976).

The variety of forms of control over management came at a time when the authority of the enterprise director was more restricted than in the 1969–1972 period of reform. The key elements in that constraint were firstly a very great widening of the scope of centrally allocated products. As from the 1974 annual plan 720 products were so allocated, against 180 previously (*Probleme economice*, No. 11, 1973, p. 23). The uses of those products were regulated by energy input norms in that plan for 250 products and in the 1975 Plan for all centrally allocated products (*Revista economică*, No. 12, 1975, p. 9). The second element was the withdrawal of enterprise authority on capital formation in 1973 (*Scînteia*, 29 November 1974). By 1975 President Ceauşescu was able to say that 'in future, not a single investment including local industry, can be made without central approval' (*Scînteia*, 24 July 1976; Jackson, 1977, p. 891).

Within the enterprise the role of foreman was raised. Regulations of 1977 required new foremen to be graduates of a special technical school or with a minimum of eight years experience as skilled workers; the foreman became formally responsible for the work of his team and for its supplies and conditions, that responsibility being recognized by higher wages[14].

8.3 The 'new economic mechanism' and its implementation, 1978–1980

Constantinescu identifies four objectives of the reforms introduced by the 1978 resolution. First, 'the affirmation and improvement of workers' self-management as a basic principle of economic management alongside the principle of democratic centralism'; second, the enhancement of enterprise responsibility by economic and financial self-administration; third, 'the improvement of the economic incentives system so as to ensure a better interrelation between the system of interests and the plan', i.e. through profit-sharing; and finally, 'the improvement of the system of planning and of the system of economic indicators' (Constantinescu, 1979, p. 58). In most commentaries two principles are particularly stressed: one is microeconomic, that of self-management (*principiul autogestiunii*), the other is macroeconomic, the principle of a unitary national plan (*principiul planului naţional unic*) (Russu, 1978, pp. 206–7). But the contradiction between them is left unexamined, for an expansion of inter-enterprise negotiation and enterprise freedom to manoeuvre in the light of changing demand and supply conditions must be constrained by the tighter control of a unitary plan.

That the prime criterion is conformity rather than flexibility was made plain by President Ceauşescu speaking in June 1980, a year and a half after the mechanism had been introduced: 'It must be understood that the new economic mechanism assumes proceeding under disipline, order and respect for regulations' (*Scînteia*, 14 June 1980). The role of the central bodies may well be enhanced under the 1978 resolution because it requires the extension of special (i.e. centrally directed) programmes, of which 150 had been elaborated under the previous planning practice, for the 1976–1980 Plan[15]. Similarly, the number of centrally operated material balances was to be increased:

The number of material balances adopted for a five-year plan, and those thereof which the Council of Ministers and ministries are authorized to approve, shall be increased, and at the same time control over material balances drawn up by ministries and central offices shall be strengthened[16].

Finally, the resolution emphasizes, 'at all organizational levels firm action must be taken for strengthening plan discipline'[17].

In the light of such assertions, we find it difficult to accept the conclusion of the ECE Secretariat that 'the reform aims to increase the decisionmaking power of enterprises' (*Economic Survey* . . ., 1978, p. 130), but it does make the decisions open to the enterprise qualitatively more effective. As the ECE Secretariat rightly goes on to say

> The principle of economic accountability is being enhanced, and enterprises will be expected to make greater use of their own funds in implementing expansion plans. Profits are to serve as a main yardstick of performance, and will provide the resources to build up the various 'funds' which will be left at the disposal of the enterprises (*Economic Survey* . . ., 1978, p. 130).

The key to the new financial and plan-implementation relationships between the enterprise and its supervisors is the value of 'net output'. The Resolution requires it to

> be introduced as the basic indicator in industry, state agriculture, construction and transport. The value of net output constitutes the newly created value of productive activity and is composed of the following main items: the transfer, in the form of a tax on net output, of a part of newly generated revenue to society's fund for development; directly paid wages and other remuneration to workers; costs of research and expenditure on the introduction of new technology; overhead costs net of material costs; the tax on the remuneration fund; social insurance premia; and net profit. The calculation of net output is effected by deducting material costs from gross output[18].

Leaving the 'tax on net output' for discussion later in this section, it is important to note that 'net output' itself is only one among a multiplicity of other plan indicators which comprise many of those previously imposed on the enterprise. 'To ensure the firm orientation of economic activity towards satisfying the real, concrete needs of the economy, the use of physical indicators shall be extended in the elaboration of the plan and in monitoring its execution'[19]. The targets in physical terms are production, investment, exports, imports, deliveries to the home market and technical progress. The multiplicity of plan targets for the enterprise – with all its problems of ambiguity and tradeoffs – was criticized at the time of the first economic reform (Simon, 1969, p. 90), and there is no reason to believe it to have lost that inherent power of dysfunction. The central bodies seek to diminish such deviation by frequent verification of plan indicators against targets and it is significant that this process of monitoring has been widening. Thus until 1975 reports on 800 product plan-fulfillments of the top ('ARP') category had to be submitted by enterprises quarterly and annually. From 1976 the number of products was raised to 1200 and from 1978 the frequency of reporting was increased by requiring monthly reports (Munteanu, 1978, p. 13).

Within the constraints imposed by the use of obligatory plan indicators (either of the enterprise or of its suppliers), the self-finance criterion is intended to enhance enterprise efficiency. Although provision is still made for centrally financed investment (the only East European country which has wholly liquidated this being Hungary), profits are intended to furnish the five internal funds – for economic development (i.e. fixed capital investment), supplemented by depreciation charges; for working capital; for research, technological development and the introduction of technical progress; for housing and social investment; for social actions; and 'for working people's participation in profits'[20]. Enterprises can borrow from the banks on a repayment and interest-bearing basis. The Law on the Formation, Planning and Utilization of Profits, enacted in November 1978, specifies these funds and sets the profits tax at 10%[21].

Coherence within a central financial plan is assured by the maintenance of price and wage controls (discussed further below) and by a requirement for ratification of planned outlay and income by the supervisory body. On output and output price controls, the Law of November 1978 states in Article 6 that 'the earnings and expenses incurred during the period of the plan are determined in keeping with the prices and tariffs in force'. The ratification provision was set out in the Resolution as follows:

> The budget of revenue and expenditure of the enterprise shall be integrated into the system of budgets of revenue and expenditure drawn up at central office and ministry level, in conformity with the unitary national plan, the state budget, the credit plan and the centralized financial plan of the state, in order to ensure the financial equilibrium of the national economy[22].

Finally, the 'tax on net output' serves as an instrument for assuring conformity to plan. It is differentiated first by product (according to the profit margin authorized in the wholesale price) and secondly in relation to the achievement of the plan target. The latter provision is, however, in the classic Soviet tradition of rewarding plan overfulfilment, i.e., the tax is smaller for above-plan net output and not on the symmetry advocated by Liberman for the USSR in 1962, i.e. divergence from the plan target either way should be penalized. The argument deployed for the practice adopted is that a reward for effecting a higher-than-plan net output (an indicator freed from the abuses of overfulfilment of gross output by buying outside materials) is necessary when 'hidden reserves' have to be extracted from enterprises. It remains a source of abuse that enterprise managers will seek to minimize planned net output in order to mitigate their tax burden.

The administration's determination to enforce discipline within a self-financing scheme may be seen from two of the President's pronouncements in May and June 1980. In a speech to the National Council of the Working People in June he warned enterprises working inefficiently that they could be closed in 1981 and that 'it must be understood that the new economic mechanism assumes procedure under discipline, order and respect for regulations' (*Scînteia*, 14 June 1980). In a declaration the previous month, he had criticized those

who have taken for granted that the issues of the economic mechanism consist only in the sharing out of profits. Some seem to think that they have the right to spend as much as they like without being accountable to anyone. . . . This is not the new economic mechanism!

He consequently called for more supervision of self-management decisions:

There are also signs of serious deficiencies in the organization of labour and production in the implementation of the new economic mechanism. It is difficult enough in fact, to affirm that the principles of the new mechanism are properly understood or that effective action has been taken to implement them. . . . No competent organization nor proper qualified control . . . has been secured. We must state that many inspections are lacking in scope, avoiding problems and trying to justify a series of shortcomings, and transgressions of laws and decisions (*Scînteia*, 1 June 1980).

Wages and profit-sharing

The President doubtless had in mind both managers administering the allocation of profits and workers seeking their share, for both are novel in this form in Romania. The tax on the wage fund, however, just antecedes the new economic mechanism, for it had been introduced in 1977 to replace the earnings tax levied on the earner. Romania thereby joined Albania (1967) and Poland (1976) in abolishing direct taxes on public-sector earnings. The payroll tax was set at a range of 14.5% to 17.5% (Dumitrescu, 1977).

Conceptually there is no need for a socialist state which itself determines wage rates to levy taxes on wages, and the abolition of the wage tax paradoxically reflected increasing control over wages in the 'Law on Labour Remuneration' of November 1974 (*Buletimul oficial*, No. 133–4, 1974).

It had always been government policy in Romania to discriminate between industrial branches as to the basic wage level. The 1974 law confirmed this by fixing basic wage levels for 52 separate industrial branches, sub-branches and other economic activities into which the economy is divided. The basic wage rate in a given branch is determined by criteria which include the importance of the branch, the quality and quantity of work and the level of qualification of staff. Within a branch, wage differentials are determined according to a single basic wage and three wage ranks, on the one hand, and eight separate wage scales for each of these four, on the other. Wages are paid either as piecework or as timework, the trend being – as the law made clear – to make as wide use as possible of piecework and to fix quantitative and qualitative criteria for those working on timerates. Wages account for about 90% of average gross planned earnings of manual workers and about 90–95% of salaries of technical, administrative and maintenance staff. The balance is made up by long-service awards amounting to 3, 5, 7 and 10% of the monthly wage for continuous seniority of 5–10, 10–15, 15–20 and over 20 years respectively, and some extra incentive payments for outstanding performance. Extra money rewards in the form of annual bonuses (*gratificatii*) introduced in 1970 were maintained in the new law.

The law contains a special section on financial penalties for failure to reach plan targets and for other types of poor performance. Deductions from wages and salaries, amounting to 1% of the monthly wage of workers, 4% of salaries of management and 2% of other staff salaries, are applied for failure to fulfil the plan and other indicators.

The regulations governing the establishment of wage and salary levels, pay differentials, annual bonus payments and economic penalties, as well as the rules and procedures of wage planning make Romania's incentive system the most comprehensively regulated and tightly controlled in the whole of Eastern Europe.

The three wage ranks were reformulated by a decree of the Council of State in July 1977. All jobs and workplaces were differentiated according to circumstances, complexity, requirement for and importance of, the work done. As a rule, workplaces and jobs performed in more difficult conditions are permanently classed in groups I or II, but such classification may also be temporarily decided for other jobs and may be annually reviewed according to changes in work circumstances. Work of category I is, for instance, that of underground miners, workers employed on oil rigs, civil aviation flight personnel, and workers producing and handling ammunition and explosives. The appointment of employees in groups I and II is made according to the maximum number of such jobs stipulated in and approved by the annual plan; for permanent posts the number of jobs in groups I and II is established according to the number of employees required to produce the amount of output planned. Ministries, central offices and other organizations were required to take measures by the end of 1978 to eliminate causes of special working conditions which would require extra wages than those laid down in the three ranks (*Scînteia*, 17 July 1977). The pressure on individuals to 'discharge their basic social obligation to work' was made explicit in a law of November 1976, which was passed in tandem with one providing that labour should be recruited only in the county in which the employing body is located (although the worker may be recruited for another location run by the same body) (*Scînteia*, 6 November 1976).

The narrowing of differentials which these policies are promoting may be seen from *Table 8.1*. But egalitarianism, coupled with poor supplies of

Table 8.1 *Earnings differentials in Romania*

	Average net wage	Minimum net wage
1950	22.81	10.89
1960	11.62	6.52
1970	6.87	4.26
1975	5.53	3.86
1980 (Plan)	5.53	2.92

Source: M. Bota, *Revista economică*, No. 27, 1977.

foodstuffs in shops, went too far for coal miners in the Jiu Valley (which supplies about 70% of Romanian coal output). Western press reports spoke of a strike of 35 000 miners and the holding as hostages of a Central Committee Secretary, Ilie Verdeţ (later Prime Minister) and the two Ministers concerned (*The Times*, October 1977; *Time* (New York), 24 October 1977; *Radio Free Europe Research* (Munich) 26 October 1977). After a personal plea by President Ceauşescu in which it is reported that he said that unless he could maintain discipline 'we will be trampled on by others', a 5% pay rise and a daily free meal before starting work was accorded miners (*Bulletin oficial*, No. 100, 19 September 1977), a disputed pensions scheme was replaced and the central office for the coal field disbanded (*Bulletin oficial*, No. 94, 29 August 1977). The President followed up these concessions by a personal 'working visit' in November (*Revista economică*, No. 45, 1977, p. 1) but although the concessions were maintained, the ringleaders were soon victimized by transfer to work in other parts of the country.

The profit-making provisions of the 1978 Resolution may be seen as a further and generalized concession, certainly as a politically motivated measure to reduce the antagonism of 'Them' and 'Us' in industrial relations.

In the new system there are three profit shares which benefit personnel. The 'Fund for the participation of the Working People in Profits' (*Fondul de participare a oamenilor muncii la beneficii*) is composed principally of 3% of planned profits on average: the actual rate for ministries, central offices and counties (for locally run enterprises) is to be varied within that overall mean. To it is added in each enterprise a share not exceeding one quarter of the excess of profits over planned if that excess is earned by a reduction of costs as planned; a share not exceeding 14% of the excess profit over plan if it has accrued by overfulfilment of plan for physical output; a share of 8% of the excess profit over plan if obtained by other means; and a share not exceeding 10% of the excess profits if they derive from overfulfilment of the export plan. For enterprises producing export goods and services 2% of above-plan earnings may be retained in foreign exchange 'for collective trips abroad' by the staff. While this retention provision was carried over from the Resolution of March into the Law promulgated in May, another, allowing the enterprise to spend 25% of above-plan foreign earnings on imports, was dropped in the interval. They would have to have been spent on products which would 'assist the development of exports, improve product quality or contribute to the introduction of new technology or to the modernization of productive equipment'.

The Fund for Housing Construction and other Social Investment (*Fondul pentru construcţia de locuinte şi alte investiţii cu caracter social*) is the investment fund for facilities benefiting personnel and is carried over from previous practice.

Price control

Since, as we have shown, quantities of inputs and of outputs remain controlled in physical terms, the retention of central price fixing at both wholesale and retail level removes all flexibility for the enterprise under market-type signals. 'Enterprises and central offices are bound to execute all contracts and orders which accord with the demands of the national economy' ran the Resolution, meaning for 'demands' the decisions of the central bodies. The establishment in 1973 of a Higher Court for Financial Control (*Curtea Superioară de Control Financial*), on the lines of the French Cour de Comptes or the Federal German Bundesrechnungshof but applicable to the entire state sector, and a law on financial control in March 1974 added to the enforcement of directive financial planning and price controls. The attachment of much capital formation and some staff remuneration to profits requires a more rational ordering of the prices of inputs and outputs from which profits derive.

The World Bank report has concisely described the Romanian pricing system, and it is enough here to recall that the 1971 Law on Prices and Tariffs amended the practice operative since 1955 of fixing wholesale prices as the average cost of production within an industry for the product plus a profit mark-up on that cost. The 1971 Law added into the wholesale price taxes on capital assets (which served as a charge on capital, previously absent) and on land (which stood for some sort of a rent charge) and a 'regularization tax' (Tsantis and Pepper, 1979, pp. 56–9)[23]. The latter is rather more clearly defined by Spigler as the margin required to align actual wholesale prices with 'accounting prices' (*preţuri de calcul*). The accounting price is current branch average cost plus a 10% profit mark–up which, as a result of changes in production costs since the establishment of an official price list, may diverge significantly from the enterprise wholesale price (*preţuri cu ridicată ale intreprinderii*). Only when the accounting price was significantly below the wholesale price (or the export price converted into domestic currency) was the tax levied (Spigler, 1973, pp. 120–127).

The immobility of prices over long periods was a cause for the introduction of the regularization tax: industrial price lists were revised – the Romanian term is reassessment (*reasezarea*) – in 1955, 1963 and 1974–1976, the latter applying the factor charges authorized in the Law of 1971[24]. By a revision of that Law in 1977, the land tax was considered a charge on profits and not as an expenditure (i.e. it was excluded from 'net product') and the regularization tax was abolished (since the reassessment completed at the end of 1976 removed its immediate *raison d'être*). In the extractive industries intra-industry 'settlement prices' allow for variations in differential rent: the principle is the standard Soviet procedure, but those applicable after the last reassessment are reported as inadequate (Săvoiu, 1977, pp. 10–11).

After the reassessment the President made plain his opposition to any devolution of price fixing:

> The price problem is a fundamental issue of our society. . . . How much profit margin is added to one product or another, at what price it sells – that is no longer a problem concerning an enterprise, but it is a matter of the state's general policy which we cannot leave to the initiative of the Councils of the Working People (*Scînteia*, 15 July 1977).

Retail price control – applied also to 'free market' sales by farmers – has been strictly applied to keep consumer goods prices nominally constant, but frequent reports of shortages indicate how far they are from market-clearing levels. The 1971 Law on Prices and Tariffs laid down that retail prices could only be increased with the express permission of the Council of State; from 1974 the approval of the President was enough (*Buletinul oficial*, No. 83, 19 January 1974). After the law revising wholesale prices procedure was promulgated on 1 January 1977 it was officially stated that no retail-price change was foreseen (*Scînteia*, 3 July 1976); in fact, the cost of living index for urban households in 1979 was 6.1% above that of 1975[25].

The price of foreign currency

It was the intention under the March 1978 Resolution to replace on 1 January 1979 the coefficients which relate the foreign-trade price to the price received by exporters or paid by importers by a normal exchange rate, but it was soon decided to defer the change until 1 January 1981.

Before 1973 the disorderly margin between foreign prices converted at the official exchange rate[26] and the domestic prices which importers paid or exporters received was absorbed by the foreign-trade corporation (and thence taxed off) as the *Preisausgleich*. From that year a 'discounted rate' (*rata de decontare*) was applied which converted one US dollar as 20 domestic lei (foreign-trade statistics remained converted at the official rate, i.e. were in *valuta lei*) (*Comerţul* . . ., 1974, p. viii); at the time this appeared to devalue the lei further than was justified: Wessely estimates 15 lei to the dollar for the period (Wessely, 1978, p. 136, fn. 2), but the World Bank report declares, doubtless on the basis of interviews, that 'it approximated the weighted average of all actual exchange rates for export and import transactions over the previous three years; it therefore represented the average rather than the marginal cost of foreign exchange' (Tsantis and Pepper, 1979, p. 63).

The enterprise selling an export or buying an import did not necessarily receive the equivalent of the foreign-trade price at the 'discounted' rate (or 'trading' rate in the World Bank usage): indeed, since the wholesale-price reassessment, exports actually have been compensated within a range of 5 to 50 domestic lei per dollar. The rate of 20 was probably an undervaluation but the devaluation of the dollar also contributed to a revaluation to 18 lei in March 1978 and to setting of the 'commercial' rate for 1 January 1981 at 15 lei to the dollar. No change was envisaged at the time in the 'non-commercial' rate which is applied to remittances, tourism and other personal transactions: when the official rate was at 4.9 lei valuta to the dollar, the non-commercial rate was 14.38 domestic lei to the dollar; on revaluation to 4.47 in March 1978, it became 12, at which relationship it was reported that it will remain from January 1981.

As the World Bank explains the practice, the 'trading' rate determines whether a good should be traded and how foreign exchange gains should be divided between the foreign trade corporation (whence it is taxed away) and the domestic enterprise concerned (Tsantis and Pepper, 1979, pp. 64–66).

The second component of the foreign exchange reform to be implemented in January 1981 is to devalue the transferable ruble, the 'collective' currency of the International Bank for Economic Cooperation (whose membership is identical with that of the CMEA), so that it is at par with the dollar. At the time this announcement was made in July 1980 the Soviet valuta ruble (to which the transferable ruble is itself at par) was quoted at $0.6435, so that for a cross-rate of $1.00 to apply, the ruble in terms of lei would have to be notionally devalued to 64.35% of its official value. Such an act can take place (as it has in Hungary) without danger of arbitrage because no free transactions are permitted in either Soviet or transferable rubles. The Hungarian procedure just mentioned has succeeded in devaluing the transferable ruble with respect to the forint to a cross-rate of $0.91. The 'unification' of directional exchange rates at one transferable ruble to one dollar will terminate the system of 'relations difference' (*diferiţ pe relaţie*) introduced experimentally in 1970 and definitively from January 1971.

Foreign trade organization

The first economic reform decentralized some authority in foreign trade: in January 1970 most foreign trade corporations were transferred from the competence of the Ministry of Foreign Trade to the appropriate central office and a further devolution took place in 1971 (Kaser, 1975, p. 182; Matejka, 1975, pp. 450–458). These measures were, however, nullified by the retrocession of those corporations in May 1974.

By the end of that year only four foreign trade corporations remained subordinate to a central office (Ceauşescu, 1973, p. 632; Brada and Jackson, 1977, p. 1270). Other measures of recentralization included the establishment of a single agency to deal with licences and transactions for each product group, under a decree of 22 March 1974 (*Buletinul oficial*, No. 43, 1974). Furthermore, the distinction between 'centralized' and 'departmental' imports was abolished, by the suppression of the latter: as a result from 1 January 1974, all imports were subject to centrally issued licences.

The Ministry of Foreign Trade, to the title of which 'and of International Cooperation' was added the same year, was virtually in sole command of all foreign economic relations, a fact to which President Ceauşescu drew attention in a speech to foreign trade staff in May 1975. 'I believe that from this point of view the Ministry cannot complain that it does not know what it has to do, that it does not have clear attributions, or that legislation does not give it enough powers to fulfil its responsibilities' (Brada and Jackson, 1977, p. 1270).

Brada and Jackson consider that the decentralization of Romanian foreign trade under the reform of 1969–1973 was 'a properly conceived organizational response to the needs of Romania's international strategy of increased trade with the West and of expanded exports of manufactured goods'. They conclude that it had to be abandoned 'due to internal shortcomings, including the inability to provide skilled personnel to operate the new organizations and because of the hostile external environment which greeted the new organizations' (Brada and Jackson, 1977, p. 1276).

Agricultural organization

Even less attention than to industry and trade seems to have been paid by Western economists to the cooperative sector of agriculture[27]. Jackson observes that

as far as is known, Romanian agriculture was not touched by economic reforms. Here it is significant that Romania has never dismantled the machine-tractor stations as other CMEA countries did. Creation of various types of intercooperative associations in the 1970s appears to be a form of centralization. By far the most important change in Romanian agriculture has been the thorough overhaul of peasant incentives (Jackson, 1977, p. 892).

The present study reaches the same conclusion, although – as the writer suggested in an earlier paper (Kaser, 1975, pp. 186–8) – the reorganizations of 1966–1968 could be considered a 'reform'. Indeed, in retrospect, the creation of the Union of Cooperative Farms in 1966 can be seen as the first measure in the federations of enterprises which, as described above, were established for industry, construction, transport and local services a decade later. The Union was paralleled at the county and district level by 'agricultural councils' which, since 1962 (and the first such in Eastern Europe), had brought formally together cooperative-farm and local-authority representatives, and had been brought into conformity with the Party–state mergers in 1970[28].

Both state farms and machine-tractor stations were redesignated: the former became 'state agricultural enterprises' (*întreprinderi agricole de stat – IAS*), and the latter were until 1971 'agricultural–mechanization enterprises' (*întreprinderi de mecanizarea agriculturii – IMA*). The number of IAS was reduced by merger: by the end of 1971 there were only 215, against 721 at the end of 1965 (and 370 existing at the end of 1970). This conformed to the policy of concentration pursued in the cooperative farm sector (*cooperative agricole de producţie – CAP*), the maximum number of which was attained just after collectivization – 6424 at the end of 1961; the number was down to 4601 at the end of 1971.

During 1971 the contrary process began for the *IMA*, their stock and staff being divided so as to provide a one-for-one service to every inter-cooperative council. Their title reverted to 'station', replacing the word 'enterprise' (*staţiun pentru mecanizarea agriculturii – SMA*)[29]. Their number leapt from 293 at the end of 1970 to 772 at the end of 1971, while the operations each undertook for cooperative farms declined from 126 000 hectares of conventional ploughing units to 52 000.

The intercooperative councils, to which the *SMA* were attached, were created at the same time, but were more than federal assemblies of local *CAP*: that function was adequately provided for by the Union. Each council is composed of representatives of the constituent *CAP*, of the appropriate *SMA*, and of the Bank for Agriculture and the Food Industry (which in 1971 was authorized to grant long-term credits to *CAP*) (Spigler, 1973, pp. 158 –60) as well as of local government officials responsible for farming.

The Party Programme elaborated by the Party Congress in 1974 called for a 'strengthening' of intercooperative councils, but the Party Political Executive Committee delayed specific action until its meeting of 27–28 December 1976. The consequences were evident in new constitutions adopted by the councils in the first half of 1977, after compliance with the formalities of discussions in general assemblies of constituent *CAP* and in their country Unions (*Scînteia*, 1 March 1977; Telescu, 1977). The councils were joined by representatives of the councils on coordination of consumers', handicrafts and agricultural cooperatives, and were to be chaired by the director of the *SMA*. The old predominance of the machine-tractor station was evoked by this provision, and by the politico-economic leadership (i.e. with local Party representation) to be ensured by an executive bureau, to take decisions between general assemblies of the council. An even smaller group within the bureau has day-to-day powers vested in it, the director of the *SMA* and three officials of the council, the agronomist, the animal specialist and the economist. Since the council is responsible for drawing up the production plan for the cooperative agriculture of the area, the constituent *CAP* – though nominally autonomous – can only fulfil the targets given to them. The council also supervises the fulfilment of *CAP* delivery contracts and, as the recipient of production and financial plan targets proposed by the supervisory agencies, became in effect the intermediary between the state plan and the farm.

As yet no scheme has been mooted for integrating state farms (*IAS*) with the councils but their parallel existence can only suggest some eventual merger. The councils have already been urged to establish industrial-type activities, either for agricultural needs or in the processing of farm produce, and a Romanian economist has observed that today 'the agricultural enterprise tends to acquire all the more the organizational and structural interests of the industrial enterprise' (Topor, 1971, p. 125). President Ceauşescu is on record as urging *CAP* to apply 'the superior method of organization of production' of the *IAS* (*Scînteia*, 20 March 1973). In the 1970s a considerable amount of cooperation was fostered between *CAP* and *IAS* in livestock breeding and water resources (Miculescu, 1971, p. 6).

Just as in industry, construction and transport, the degree of participation by the individual *CAP* member in the assemblies of which they are constituents tends to be formal. An opinion survey of two *CAP* showed that in one 42% of members considered that the management of the *CAP* took no account of proposals by members and 31% thought they could not inscribe topics for discussion at the general assembly; in the other, however, the respective proportions were 7% and 9%; in both farms around one-third of members had never attended a general assembly (Otopeleanu, 1971, pp. 196–207).

The practice of making monthly advances to *CAP* members in place of the annual dividend in cash or kind was instituted in 1970 and was in force in all cooperatives by the end of 1973; a minimum wage of 300 lei per month was guaranteed, provided that a man had contributed 20 days' work and a woman 15 days. The codification and amendment of the legislation on remuneration in *CAP*, enacted at the end of 1976[30] (*Buletinul oficial*, 31 December 1976), raised the monthly guarantee to 1500 lei in the livestock sector and 1200 lei in horticulture provided that 25 days were actually worked. For those working on crop cultivation the minimum was 40 lei per day. The total advances should amount to 90% of the eventual year's dividend in the livestock sector and 80% in the cultivation sector, but it was explicitly laid down in the final law (though not in the draft)[31] that 'members of a *CAP* cannot be paid unless they have performed useful work which contributes to implementing production in such a unit'[32]. The high degree of farm concentration justified a calculation of dividends on the basis of work by the team, which is, under the 1976 Law, paid on the basis of its production results, irrespective of the record in the cooperative as a whole.

The 1976 Law was the culmination of a substantial improvement of the remuneration of a cooperative farm member with respect to the industrial worker. Thus when the minimum on a *CAP* for livestock work was 400 lei a month (1971), the minimum wage for a state employee was 800 lei; but when it reached 1500 in 1976, the minimum for the state employee (as set in July 1975) was 1200 (Jackson, 1977, p. 936).

The final change to date is also of 1976, a lightening of the tax burden on the cooperative farmer[33]. The previous fiscal concept had been a tax base of notional income from household plots and the few private farms left in mountainous areas: assessments had to be made annually and were based on land use, marketings and livestock numbers. The new tax system is a flat rate per hectare. The same principle is appplied to the *CAP*: a flat rate is paid per hectare, varying with the 'zone of fertility' in which the farm is located (arable land in the worst districts pay 30 lei per hectare, but in the most productive districts 55 lei). In order to encourage the ploughing back of profits, the *CAP* is in addition liable to a tax varying with the remuneration paid to its members: if up to 3000 lei is distributed annually per member the tax is only 3% of the aggregate paid-out dividend, but at over 12 000 lei, the rate is 9%.

The corresponding change in the non-farm sector was the abolition of the individual tax paid by employees in the following year and to which reference has been made above.

Notes

1. As the acknowledgement indicated, Mr Spigler was a collaborator. For a detailed description of the first economic reform, 1967–1971, see Spigler (1973).
2. Some key conclusions, notably on 'plan slackness', were previously presented in Granick (*Soviet Studies*, 1974).
3. Under the provisional title *East European Economic Assessment*, it includes a paper by M. R. Jackson on Romania and a comparison of Czechoslovakia and Romania by A. E. King and D. E. Schlagenhauf.
4. Papers by A. Smith and by Elizabeth Clayton will be published in the colloquium report in 1981.
5. Paper by A. Smith.
6. Thus the last commodity-by-country trade statistics published were *Comertul* . . . (1974).
7. Granick (1975, pp. 37–42) puts the end of the reform in 1973, Jackson (1977, p. 891) says 'decentralization lasted from 1969 through 1972 or 1973'; the present writer's 'Foreword' to Spigler (1973, p. xiv) suggested July 1971 as the first shadow of the end of the reform period. See also Kaser (1975, pp. 172–174 and 182–183) and Spigler (1973, pp. 4–9).
8. The citation is from Montias (1976, p. 117).

9. The local councils themselves were endowed with new statutes (*Scînteia*, 3 July 1976).

10. Sessions are brief and only twice or three times a year; the practical authority of the Council of State is correspondingly great.

11. On their history 1968 to 1971 see Spigler (1973, pp. 81–86).

12. For the history 1969 to 1971 see Spigler (1973, pp. 62–65).

13. Both were enacted at the July 1977 session of the Grand National Assembly (*Scînteia*, 2 July 1977).

14. Draft law in *Scînteia* (7 May 1977), report on final text in *Scînteia* (2 July 1977). The final version substituted eight years experience for a minimum of five and was less precise about the wage differential to be accorded foremen.

15. Part 2, point 1, para (c) of the Resolution (*Revista economică*, No. 13, 1978, p. 3).

16. Part 2, point 4, para A of the Resolution (*Revista economică*, No. 13, 1978, p. 4).

17. Part 1, point 1 of the Resolution (*Revista economică*, No. 13, 1978, p. 2).

18. Part 1 (*Revista economică*, No. 13, 1978, p. 2).

19. Part 1, point 2 (*Revista economică*, No. 13, 1978, p. 2).

20. Resolution, Part 3, point 1 (*Revista economică*, No. 13, 1978, p. 4).

21. *Economic Survey* . . . (1978, p. 130) interprets this provision (Article 2 of the law) as a ceiling (10% of profits) on the reimbursement from profits of state subsidies, but our interpretation follows Constantinescu (1979, p. 61).

22. Part 3, point 1 (*Revista economică*, No. 13, 1978, p. 4).

23. The report only mentions the institution of price controls in 1950, not the price formation system of 1955.

24. The World Bank report discusses the reassessment of 1974–1976 (Tsantis and Pepper, 1979, pp. 59–62).

25. Derived from a comparison of the increase between those dates of money wages (32.2%) and of real wages (24.5%), cited in *Revista economică* (No. 7, 1980).

26. In valuta lei to the US dollar: 6 until December 1971, then 5.53 until February 1973; then 4.97 until March 1978 and 4.47 subsequently.

27. Spigler (1973) and Granick (1975) limit themselves to industry (although the former considers procurement from agriculture and credits to cooperative farms). The present writer has benefited from seeing an unpublished paper on 'The organization of Romanian agriculture' (1973) by Dr Paul Wiedemann for a collaborative research project under the direction of Everett Jacobs, Professor Alec Nove and Professor Karl-Eugen Wädekin ('A Comparative Study of the Organization and Efficiency of Socialist Agriculture'). The paper for the NATO colloquium by Clayton (see note 4) describes farm enlargement as the only 'economic reform' in Romanian Agricultural organization in the 1970s.

28. Thus a senior official of the *judet* party committee would become chairman of the *judet* branch of the union; the national chairman of the union was a secretary of the party central committee.

29. The pre-1967 machine-tractor station had been *SMT*.

30. The procedure had been experimentally applied during 1976 pursuant to a Grand National Assembly resolution of 21 December 1975.

31. The draft was published in *Scînteia* (11 December 1976); see Miculescu (Minister of Agriculture and the Food Industry) (*Scînteia*, 30 December 1976).

32. Article 4 of the law as enacted.

33. The draft, which appeared in *Scînteia* (31 March 1976) was approved basically unchanged by the party central committee on 3 November (*Scînteia*, 11 November 1976).

References

Brada, J. C. and Jackson, M. R. (1977). Strategy and Structure in the Organization of Foreign Trade Activities, 1967–1975. In *East European Economies Post-Helsinki*, Joint Economic Committee, US Congress, Washington, D.C., pp. 260–276

Buletinul oficial, 22 December 1956 (Decree No. 665); No. 43, 1974; No. 83 (19 January 1974); No. 133, 1974; No. 134, 1974; 31 December 1976; No. 94 (29 August 1977); No. 100 (19 September 1977)

Ceaușescu, N. (1973). *România pe drumul desavirisirii socialiste*, Vol. 8. Bucharest

Comertul exterior al RSR 1974 (1974). Bucharest

Constantinescu, N. N. (1979). Remarks on the Measures Designed to Perfect the Economic-financial Mechanism. *Revue roumaine des sciences sociales; Serie des sciences economiques*, Vol. 23, No. 1 (January–June)

Dumitrescu, F. (Minister of Finance) (1977). *Scînteia*, 1 July

Economic Survey of Europe in 1978, Part I, The European Economy in 1978

Granick, D. (1974). Variations in Management of the Industrial Enterprise in Socialist Eastern Europe. In *Reorientation and Commercial Relations of the Economies of Eastern Europe*, Joint Economic Committee, US Congress, Washington, D.C.

—— (1974). The Orthodox Model of the Socialist Enterprise in the Light of Romanian Experience. *Soviet Studies*, Vol. XXVI, No. 2 (April), pp. 205–223

—— (1975). *Enterprise Guidance in Eastern Europe: A Comparison of Four Socialist Economies*. Princeton, N.J.

Grigorescu, C. (1970). The Deepening of Workers' Democracy in the Conditions of the Economic and Social Development of Romania. *Revue roumaine des sciences sociales: Série des sciences economiques*, Vol. 23, No. 1 (January–June)

How are We Preparing for 1977 Production? (1976). *Revista economică*, No. 19

Jackson, M. R. (1977). Industrialization, Trade and Mobilization in Romania's Drive for Economic Independence. In *East European Economies Post-Helsinki*, pp. 886–940

Kaser, M. C. (1975). Romania. In *The New Economic Systems of Eastern Europe*, pp. 171–197 (ed. by H.-H. Höhmann, M. C. Kaser and K. C. Thalheim). London

Law No. 6, 1972

Mânescu, M. (1979). The Romanian Communist Party: the Vital Centre of the Unitary Management of the Socio-economic Development of the Country. *Revue roumaine des sciences sociales: Série des sciences economiques*, Vol. 23, No. 2 (July–December)

Matejka, H. (1975). Foreign Trade Systems. In Höhmann, Kaser and Thalheim (eds) *New Economic Systems*

Miculescu, A. (1971). *Probleme agricole*, No. 1

—— (1976). *Scînteia*, 30 December

Montias, J. M. (1967). *Economic Development in Communist Rumania*. Cambridge, Massachusetts

—— (1976a) *The Structure of Economic Systems*. Yale, New Jersey

—— (1976b). Types of Communist Economic Change. In *Change in Communist Systems* (ed. by C. Johnson). Stanford, California

—— (1977). Romania's Foreign Trade; An Overview. In *East European Economies Post-Helsinki*

Munteanu, C. (1978). Statistics. *Revista economică*, No. 12

Otopeleanu, V. (1971). The Functioning of Management in Cooperative Agriculture. In *Conducerea proceselor economica din agricultură*, (ed. by D. Dumitriu *et al.*). Bucharest

Paraluta, M. (1977). The Development and Improvement of the Organization and Management on the Basis of the National Economic Plan. In *Progresul economic in România 1877–1977* (ed. by I. V. Totu) pp. 596–610. Bucharest

Probleme economice, No. 11, 1973

Radio Free Europe Research, Munich, 26 October 1977

Revista economică, No. 12, 1975; No. 45, 1977; No. 13, 1978; No. 7, 1980

Russu, C. (1978). Industrial Organization and Management on a Scientific Basis. In *Politica Partidului Comunist Român de Industrializare socialistă a tării* (ed. by I. V. Totu). Bucharest

Săvoiu, N. (1977). The Functions of Settlement Prices. *Revista economică*, No. 4

Scînteia, 14 December 1969; 20 March 1972; 3 July 1974; 29 November 1974; 31 March 1976; 15 April 1976; 16 April 1976; 12 May 1976; 2 July 1976; 3 July 1976; 24 July 1976; 6 November 1976; 11 November 1976; 11 December 1976; 23 January 1977; 30 January 1977; 18 February 1977; 1 March 1977; 2 May 1977; 2 July 1977; 15 July 1977; 17 July 1977; 1 June 1980; 14 June 1980

Simon, I. (1969). Economic Reality and Statistical Indicators. *Revista de Statistică*, No. 2

Spigler, I. (1973). *Economic Reform in Romanian Industry*. London

Stefanescu, L. (1976). *Revista economică*, No. 7, pp. 14–15

Tagle, F. *Labour Policy in Romania*. Unpublished

Telescu, M. (1977). *Era socialistă*, No. 4

The Times, 6 October 1977

Time (New York), 24 October 1977

Topor, B. (1971). The Organizational Structure of the Enterprise. In Dumitriu *et al.* (eds), *Conducerea proceselor*

Tsantis, A. C. and Pepper, R. (1979). *Romania*. The World Bank, Washington, D.C.

Wessely, K. (1978). Le budget d'état de la Roumanie. *Revue d études comparatives Est-Ouest*, Vol. 9, No. 1 (March), pp. 135 –163

Wiles, P. J. D. (1977). *Economic Institutions Compared*. London

Zakrzewska, J. (1978). Les Révisions de la Constitution de la Republique socialiste de Roumanie. *Revue d'études comparatives Est-Ouest*, Vol. 9, No. 2 (June), pp. 151– 169

Zara, I. (1976). *Revista economică*, Nos 40 and 41

CHAPTER 9

Objectives and methods of economic policies in Yugoslavia, 1970–1980

Fred Singleton

9.1. Introduction

The first independent South Slav state of modern times – the Kingdom of Serbs, Croats and Slovenes – was proclaimed by the Serbian Regent, Alexander Karadjordjević, on 1 December 1918. It included elements which had never previously been united under a single political authority or a single unit of economic activity. During the previous 500 years some areas had been under Turkish rule and some under the control of the Habsburgs. Two small independent principalities emerged within the Turkish occupied area of the Balkans – Serbia, which had achieved *de facto* independence for part of its territory by 1830, and Montenegro, which was never fully mastered by the Turks.

When these disparate elements were brought together in 1918 the new political entity which was created did not possess any semblance of economic cohesion. Areas which had previously been linked to the 59 million strong Habsburg Monarchy were now forced to look to a domestic market of only 12 million. Once on the least developed fringe of a major European power, they became the industrial centres of a poor Balkan state with a predominantly peasant population[1].

The new rulers attempted to integrate the separate economic units into an autarchic, centralized economy, protected by tariff walls and other forms of state support from foreign competition. Politically, the new state was dominated by the Serbian ruling classes, and economic policy tended to favour Serbia against the interests of the more developed regions of Croatia and Slovenia. Because of the weakness of domestic capital resources, foreign investment was sought, but this tended to be attracted to the extractive industries of the underdeveloped south – especially non-ferrous metal mining – rather than to the manufacturing industries of the more developed north.

In many ways, royal Yugoslavia's economy displayed many of the characteristics of underdevelopment which are apparent today in countries of the Third World. A nationalist-minded bourgeoisie wielded political power in order to protect its infant manufacturing industries; foreign capital controlled much of the primary raw material production[2], and in the countryside there was a vast untapped reservoir of cheap labour living on inefficient peasant holdings in conditions little above subsistence level. A specifically Yugoslav characteristic, however, was the wide difference in cultural traditions and historical experience which reinforced the differences in economic levels which existed between the peoples of the different parts of the country.

When Yugoslavia was drawn into the Second World War in 1941 the country was split asunder, and separate political and economic entities were again established. The war brought crippling human and material losses. It also prepared the seedbed for a political revolution, which brought into power a new Communist-led government and which laid upon itself the formidable task of rebuilding the shattered and fragmented economy on the basis of state-socialist principles.

Whatever the political objectives, however, there were certain basic facts which no regime could ignore, and which placed objective limitations on the range of options open to the new rulers. In addition to the historical problems of inherited cultural differences, regional economic inequalities and rural overpopulation there were also the limits placed by economic geography on the possibilities of rapid industrialization, which was the new regime's central economic goal.

Resource base

(a) Power supplies

Yugoslavia is deficient in fossil fuels and in the immediate post-war period its hydroelectric power potential had scarcely begun to be realized. The majority of rivers suitable for hydroelectric development flow through remote mountainous regions, where problems of accessibility create serious technical troubles and involve heavy capital expenditure. Power shortages have been a major limiting factor in the exploitation of the mineral resources of the south and the expansion of industry in the north.

(b) Mineral resources

Yugoslavia has some reserves of mainly low-grade iron ore, but a richer endowment of non-ferrous ores, especially lead, zinc, copper, bauxite and mercury. Most of these ores, however, are to be found in the less accessible mountainous regions of the south, a fact which presents obstacles to their exploitation.

(c) Agricultural potential

Geographically, Yugoslavia has the possibility of achieving self-sufficiency in basic foodstuffs, but has not yet done so. Until the Second World War more than 75% of the people lived from agriculture, and it was not until 1960 that the proportion fell to 50%. Despite this, Yugoslavia has been a net importer of food for most of the postwar period. The size of the food deficit fluctuates wildly from year to year, depending mainly on the vagaries of the climate, but also affected by the trade policies of importing countries and other factors.

(d) Transport problems
The topography of the country adds greatly to transport costs, and by placing obstacles to movement between different regions reinforces the centrifugal tendencies which arise from the historical and cultural diversity already mentioned. Transport problems add greatly to the costs of manufacture, and restrict the possibilities for the exploitation of the mineral wealth of the interior.

(e) Human obstacles to economic development
In addition to these geographical constraints, the revolutionary leaders of Yugoslavia were faced with massive human problems. Most of the population was steeped in the traditions of the Balkan peasantry. They lacked experience of industrial life, they were untrained in modern skills and 40% were illiterate. Poverty, ignorance, individualism, suspicion of urban politicians, local loyalties – all these were elements in the background of the rural population, which the revolutionaries had to overcome if they were to create a modern industrial society.

9.2 The economic objectives of the Yugoslav revolution

Post-revolutionary economic development had two principal objectives – rapid industrialization, leading to a higher material standard of living for the Yugoslav people, and a lessening of income differentials both between social groups and between regions. The methods employed to achieve these broad objectives have changed from time to time.

Centrally directed command economy
The first five-year plan (1947–1952) was modelled on those of the USSR, and used administrative methods, backed by the coercive power of the state, whose directives came from the Communist Party. Most industrial property was taken into state ownership. Emphasis was laid on the building of heavy industry, power supplies and communications. Investment in agriculture was given a low priority, but nevertheless efficiency and output were expected to rise. The consumer-goods industries were also neglected.

The rupture of political and economic relations with the Soviet Union and its East European allies following Yugoslavia's expulsion from the Cominform in 1948 dealt a mortal blow to the five-year plan, and ultimately to the whole concept of the centralized command economy too. This was not immediately apparent, as a drive for collectivization began during the following year, and by 1950 17% of farm land was included in collectives. The collectivization drive was abandoned in 1953, and within a short time most land reverted to the private sector.

'Parametric planning'

After a period of adjustment to the economic and political consequences of the break with the Cominform, a new strategy was developed during the mid-1950s. This was based on decentralization of economic decisionmaking, workers' self-management and a separation between political and economic power. The Second Five-Year Perspective Plan (1957–1961) has been described by Bičanić as introducing 'a system of *parametric* planning. Parameters of action, called economic instruments, were set, and it was left to those planning the enterprises to find their own optimum' ((Bičanić, 1973, p. 52). The average rate of growth of the national income during the period of this plan was 12.6% per annum, compared with a target figure of 10.9%; the share of the social product derived from industry rose from 39% to 45%. Despite these successes, the new system generated problems of its own. The rapid industrial growth rate was achieved within a framework of protectionism. Within this closed, autarchic system problems began to accumulate – e.g. inflation, low productivity of labour, disguised unemployment and a growing foreign trade deficit. The rate of growth began to decline, unemployment rose and many of the problems which existed during the period of the 1957–1961 Plan became so acute during the next planning period (1961–1965) that the Plan was abandoned after the recession of 1961–1962.

The economic reform of 1965

A way out of these dilemmas was sought in the economic reform of 1965, which broke with the autarchic principle and opened the Yugoslav market to foreign competition 'so that its growth should be measured and evaluated and its success verified by world standards, i.e. on the world market at competitive prices' (Bičanić, 1973, p. 165). Yugoslavia's entry into the 'international division of labour', as these changes were described, went hand in hand with the development of 'market socialism'. An element of competition was introduced, state controls were relaxed and the yardstick of success on the market was given a high priority. Since 1965 the concept of 'market socialism' has been presented by Yugoslav economists and politicians as a *via media* between the Scylla of Stalinism and the Charybdis of capitalism. In fact, 'market socialism' as practised in Yugoslavia after 1965 did not solve any of the basic structural weaknesses of the economy, although it did offer some palliatives. For example, the encouragement of workers to find employment in Western Europe, and the opening up of the tourist industry helped to ease both the balance of payments and the unemployment problems. The 1967 law which permitted foreign capital to participate in joint enterprises with Yugoslav firms brought some new investment, and, what is perhaps more important, brought new technology. The scale of the investment was small, however, in relation to Yugoslavia's needs (Horvat, 1976, p. 205). Equally important, the more liberal approach to foreign trade encouraged some Western firms to enter into licensing and marketing agreements with Yugoslav enterprises.

The results of the 1965 reform were in many ways disappointing. If followed to its logical conclusion, 'market socialism' should have led to the closure of uneconomic enterprises and a restructuring of the economy. But, as Marijan Hanžeković wrote in 1973, 'Inefficient enterprises and those with no future have not closed down. Enterprises which have a future for development but are in temporary difficulties have not received assistance. Growth-inducing enterprises . . . have not been given adequate credit to allow them to develop to the full.[3]. Those who introduced the system did not have the courage of their convictions. It was politically impossible to allow the discipline of the market to force the closure of firms. Those who got into debt were rescued by intervention from the banks or the government. Government intervention by administrative and fiscal measures interfered with market relations. Long before inflation rates of over 10% became common in Western Europe, Yugoslavia led the field with rates which rose steadily between 1967 and 1971 from 7% to 15%. At the end of 1974 it was running at an annual rate of 26%, and it reached over 30% in May 1975. Inflation was fuelled by unproductive government expenditure financed by the printing of money, and by workers councils which paid themselves higher wages, which they recovered by increasing the prices of their products.

9.3 The Yugoslav economy in the 1970s

When the 1971–1975 five-year plan was introduced the Yugoslav economy was suffering from an accumulation of chronic weaknesses which 'market socialism' had done little or nothing to remedy. There was also a serious political crisis involving the fundamental relationship of the republics to the federation. The 1971 Constitutional Amendments represented an attempt to come to terms with nationalism by conceding as much political and cultural autonomy to the republics and provinces as was consistent with the maintenance of the federation. It also envisaged inter-republican economic cooperation which would preserve the unity of the Yugoslav market and assist the less developed areas to overcome their economic backwardness.

The concessions to the republics, rather than diminishing the nationalist pressure, appeared to encourage it, especially in Croatia. There were some specifically economic grievances. Two of the slogans shouted by the Zagreb students who demonstrated in the streets in November 1971 were 'Abolish the retention quotas' and 'End the plunder of Croatia'. The retention quotas were introduced in 1967. Enterprises were allowed to retain a proportion of their foreign currency earnings from exports, tourism, etc. – the amount varied from 4% to 20%. The retained currency could be used at will by the enterprise. The rest had to be sold for dinars to one of a number of appointed banks, the most important of which were in Belgrade. The banks then allocated foreign currency to potential importers, and as demand always exceeded supply the banks had considerable influence in deciding priorities. The banks were under greater influence from the federal government, and thus the retention quotas system was seen by many Croats as a device to recentralize in Belgrade powers which had formerly been decentralized.

After the 'Croatian crisis' of 1971 some concessions were made. Retention quotas were increased to 20% for most enterprises and to between 40% and 50% for tourism. In 1973 foreign currency regulations were again relaxed, meeting most of the Croatian demands.

The other Croatian demand ('End the plunder of Croatia') refers to the deeply held conviction of many Croats that the resources taken from more developed areas to assist the industrial development of the less developed republics were frequently squandered, and that if Croatia were allowed to utilize to the full her own resources, the more rapid development of the Croatian economy would in the long run benefit the whole federation. The less developed areas, in their turn, feel that they are exploited by the more developed northern republics, which receive cheap raw materials, food and unskilled labour from the poorer south. It is an almost impossible task to measure accurately the balance of advantages and disadvantages between the republics as a result of their being involved in a common Yugoslav market. As Bakarić is reported to have remarked, 'Who *does* receive something in Yugoslavia if we are all plundered?' (Lendvai, 1969, p. 143).

The five-year plan 1971–1975

The 1971–1975 Social Development Plan was worked out in conformity with the new principle of planning which evolved during the 1960s when 'decentralization' and 'market socialism' were two key concepts in the minds of Yugoslavia's rulers[4]. Under these principles the federal planning laws laid down

> General lines of development of economic and social activities; general policy regarding the standards of living, employment and cadres; basic relations in the distribution of the social product and national income; the

policy of economic relations with other countries; the policy of accelerated development of underdeveloped republics and regions; the strengthening of the defensive ability and security of the country (Stajner, 1971,
p. 27).

Within these general guidelines, detailed planning is devolved to republican
and local government organs and to the organizations of associated labour in
the self-managed enterprises. A complex system of joint consultation
between the various bodies involved – including banks, federal and local
financial institutions, trade unions, organizations of workers and managers,
socio-political bodies – takes place both during the period when the Federal
plan is being discussed and after its enactment by the Federal Assembly,
when the circumstances of its implementation are worked out at local level.
The Federal Executive Council (*Savezni Izvršni Savet*) submits a report
annually to the Assembly, and the progress of the five-year plan is
monitored.

The process of discussion took much longer than expected in 1969–1971,
when the successor to the 1966–1970 plan was being prepared. As a result,
the draft of a new medium-term plan which should have come into
operation in 1970 was not passed by the Assembly until November 1971,
and did not come into effect until 1972. The main cause of the delay was the
fierce inter-republican struggle which was being fought on the economic as
well as on the cultural front.

The year 1971 saw the introduction of a series of major constitutional
amendments, and at the end of that year the eruption of Croat anger which
was largely inspired by a sense of economic grievance. The plan was thus
launched against a stormy background of internal dissension. Before it had
run its course, the disruption of world trade consequent upon the action of
the OPEC countries in raising the price of oil had seriously affected the
Yugoslav economy.

Despite these difficulties, the Yugoslav economy weathered the storm,
although not without considerable battering. For a summary of the targets
and achievements of the 1971–1975 plan, see *Table 9.1.*

The social plan of Yugoslavia for 1976–1980

This plan was adopted in July 1976. It looked forward to an annual growth
of the social product of 6.9%, compared with the 1971–1975 target of 8%
and the actual achievement of 6.3%. Agriculture was expected to grow at a
rate of 4.3% per annum, compared with the 3.0% attained under the
previous plan, and industry by 8% compared with the actual growth of
8.1% during 1971–1975.

The planners correctly identified the main problems facing the Yugoslav
economy in the second half of the 1970s. Priority was given to the reform of

Table 9.1 *Targets of 1976–1980 plan (percentage increases in volume) and targets and achievements of 1971–1975 plan*

	Target	1971–1975 Outcome	1976–1980 Target
Private consumption	7.0	5.3	6.0
Gross fixed investment	7.0	7.1	8.0
economic sectors	9.5	6.2	8.5
non-economic sectors	9.5	8.4	7.5
housing	–	8.5	8.0
Total domestic demand	–	5.7	6.5
Exports of goods and services	13.0*	7.3	8.0
Imports of goods and services	11.0*	5.8	4.5
Social product	8.0	6.3	7.0
Industrial output	9.5	8.1	8.0
Agricultural output	3.0	4.1	4.0
Social sector employment	2.5	4.1	3.5
Productivity	6.0	2.4	4.0

* In value terms
Source: OECD Economic Survey, May 1977, p. 26.

the structure of industry, the narrowing of regional inequalities, improvement in labour productivity, the reduction of inflation and of unemployment and the improvement of the chronic balance of payments deficit. Unfortunately, the close involvement of Yugoslavia in the world economy means that the Yugoslav economy cannot be isolated from world trends over which the Yugoslavs have no control, and the instruments devised to achieve these objectives have proved inadequate for the solution of the problems which had to be faced. Apart from the problems arising from the world economic crisis, there are also peculiarly Yugoslav problems, some of which are inherent in the situation of a developing country attempting a programme of rapid industrialization, and others which arise from the unique methods of controlling the economy by the instruments of self-management.

Since the passing of the 1974 Constitution and the 1976 Law on Associated Labour, great emphasis has been placed on 'self-management agreements' (*samoupravni sporazumi*) and 'social compacts' (*društveni dogovori*) as means of implementing economic policies. These methods imply an acceptance by decisionmaking bodies such as 'Basic organizations of associated labour' (*osnovni organizacije*) and enterprises, of a degree of civic responsibility and economic sophistication which few countries would expect of their workers. In Yugoslavia's decentralized, self-managed system there are three main instruments of social control which attempt to bring cohesion to the functioning of the economy. They are the market, the machinery of self-management and the so-called 'socio-political organizations', of which the most powerful is the League of Communists.

The role of the federal government in the management of the economy has been considerably weakened during the last ten years, although it still has an important part to play, especially in foreign economic relations and in regional economic policy. It also retains powers in the field of price and credit control. For example, in August 1979 the government ordered a temporary price freeze, pending the introduction of new criteria for fixing prices (*RAD* . . ., 21 August 1979, p. 2). This was accompanied by a squeeze on consumer credit. The role of self-managing institutions in determining economic policy has been strengthened by the 1974 and 1976 legislation in furtherance of the policy of devolving power to the workers. In theory, organizations of associated labour are free to make agreements covering such matters as income and price levels, trading practices and more general questions of economic policy. Once concluded, these agreements are enforceable at law. In practice, however, the self-management system does not work in a vacuum, and elaborate consultations occur with local, republican and federal government agencies, banks, trade unions and the League of Communists. The machinery is cumbersome and is often ignored when conditions require swift decisions to be taken. The coordinating functions of the League of Communists are important in trying to ensure that decisions are taken within the framework of agreed policy objectives, and the state – which theoretically ought to be 'withering away' – is often forced to intervene directly in order to prevent a crisis. The state also influences the banks in determining interest rates, credit policy and money supply.

The 1976–1980 plan envisaged a growth of 8% per annum in gross fixed investment. By 1979 it appeared that the high level of investment was a major factor in fuelling inflation and in accentuating the unfavourable trade balance. The level of investments in housing and industrial construction soared well above the planned targets. Much of it was financed through bank credits, and by a 30% increase in the money supply (*RAD* . . ., 10 May 1979, p. 2). Figures issued by the Federal Institute of Statistics showed a steady increase in investments year by year (see *Table 9.2*).

Table 9.2 *Investment indices (preceding year = 100)*

1976	1977	1978
108.2	109.4	110

Source: Saopštenje No. 333, 1978, Federal Institute of Statistics.

An analysis of the sectoral pattern of investments shows that the largest increases during the period 1976–1978 were in investments in social welfare, education, housing and other non-economic activities. The main sources of finance were the banks (46.5% in 1978), although there was a steady increase in investments by 'self-management communities of interest'[5]. Financing of economic activities is mainly channelled through the 'organizations of associated labour', either by direct financing from an enterprise's own resources or through bank loans.

Table 9.3 shows that housing construction funded through the banks was the fastest growing sector of investment. Much of the housing financed by bank loans is for private ownership.

Table 9.3 *Sources of finance for fixed investments (percentage share in total)*

	1976	1977	1978
Organizations of associated labour (economic sector)	34.8	36.5	34.4
Self-management communities of interest (social)	2.4	3.0	3.5
Banks	38.1	42.3	46.5
of which, investment in housing construction	9.1	8.7	10.47
Federal, Republican and local government	24.7	17.2	15.6

Source: Statistički Bilten, No. 12, 1978.

Of total investment in the social sector (i.e. excluding private house building and private farming and business activities) the share of housing was also large and rising during the late 1970s. In 1977 16.7% of all investment was for housing. This had risen to 17.2% in 1978. Between the same years the percentage of investments in industry and mining fell from 39.7% to 38.5%.

Inflation

Throughout the 1960s Yugoslavia's rate of inflation was the highest in Europe, reaching double figures by the end of the decade. During the first few years of the 1970s the rate rose even more steeply, climbing from 12.5% in 1970 to 30% in 1975. Until then, all the efforts of the various 'stabilization programmes' had been of no avail. For example, in October 1970 the Ribičič administration declared a six-month price freeze, at a time when inflation was running at 12.5%. By March 1971 the rise in prices had accelerated to 15%. This was attributed at the time to the deliberate evasion of the price regulations by worker-run enterprises. One device was to reclassify goods under different names, and enter them on the market as new goods, not subject to price control (Singleton, 1976, p. 303, n. 7). With the increased income from sales, workers' councils were able to vote themselves higher personal incomes, thus increasing the inflationary pressures. Other causes of inflation were uncontrolled government expenditure, the issuing of an ever-increasing volume of currency, the sanctioning of investment programmes which were not backed by adequate resources and the tendency for enterprises to run up large deficits. The general malaise can be summed up by the phrase 'lack of social discipline' – an attitude of irresponsibility which seemed to afflict all levels of Yugoslav society. These domestic causes were massively reinforced by world pressures, especially the rise in oil prices after 1973.

Anti-inflation measures

In 1975, with the rate of inflation at 30%[6], the government became seriously alarmed. The old recipes of administrative intervention to impose temporary wage and price freezes, coupled with a deflationary monetary policy, seemed to have been ineffective. A new policy emerged in 1972, based on the Social Price Control Act (1972) and greatly extended by two Laws of 1975 – one on the Establishment and Determination of Incomes in Basic Organizations of Associated Labour, and the other on Payments to Beneficiaries of Social Property. The 1975 legislation compelled enterprises to behave with greater responsibility over the repayment of debts, to reduce unnecessary expenditures and to rationalize investments. The initial impact of these measures was favourable in reducing the rate of inflation during 1976, although it did result in some bankruptcies and a rise in unemployment. However, in 1977 the rate of inflation began to rise again, partly as a result of enterprises raising prices to prevent losses which previously would have been incurred and then recouped from the public purse when the enterprise was threatened with insolvency (*Table 9.4*).

Table 9.4 *Rise in retail prices (%)*

1971	1972	1973	1974	1975	1976	1977	1978	(first 5 1979 months)
1970	1971	1972	1973	1974	1975	1976	1977	1978
14	16	19	26	26	9	13	13	16

Source: Indeks-Savezni Zavod za Statistiku (appropriate monthly isues 1971–1979).

By the end of 1979 the rate was still rising, and exceeded 20%. Certain administrative measures taken by the Federal Government appeared to have been effective in reducing the rate of price rises. For example, in May 1976 the federal government substantially reduced the turnover tax on some

consumer durables, building materials, leather goods and beverages, resulting in price reductions on those items of between 2% and 10.5% (*RAD . . .*,
26 May 1976). The main instruments of price control, however, are under
the Social Price Control Act (1972) which relies heavily on 'social compacts'
(*društveni dogovori*) and 'self-management agreements' (*sampoupravni sporazumi*). It would appear that these methods worked for a time in 1976 but
they presuppose a high level of social discipline, the momentum of which is
maintained by the various informal pressures which can be exerted through
such bodies as the League of Communists and the Socialist Alliance.

In the spring of 1977 there were signs that inflationary pressures were
again becoming a serious problem. In February the Central Committee of
the League of Communists of Yugoslavia devoted a whole session to the
deteriorating economic situation. Dr Šefer, a Federal Vice-President with
special responsibilities for economic affairs, was reported as attacking 'the
lack of discipline in individual economic enterprises . . . and a lack of
respect for the social compacts on prices, investments, etc.' (*Borba*, 25
February 1977).

The Federation also has a general responsibility over certain prices:

> The Federation will continue to regulate the system of price controls to
> ensure direct social control of prices and products and services of concern
> to the country as a whole. According to need, federal agencies will spell
> out measures for direct social control over producers' prices of industrial
> products . . . . In addition, cement, rail transport, postal rates, and basic
> agricultural products are subject to Federal price control, whilst republics,
> provinces and communes have some control over other products and
> services (e.g. building materials, rents, some food products) (Govedarica,
> 1972, p. 27).

The rapid rise in the rate of inflation which occurred in 1979 clearly
indicated that the instruments available to the government were inadequate.
The first reaction was to appeal for a reduction in investments. Croatia
responded immediately, by announcing a 40% cut in the current investment
programme, and some other republics followed suit. In July price increases
on bread (10%), petrol (35%) and some consumer goods were decreed
(*Tanjug*, 9 July 1979). This was followed in August by a two-month price
freeze and credit restrictions to dampen down the demand for consumer
goods. The easy credit facilities and low rates of interest on bank borrowing
had stimulated a consumer boom, which in turn led to an increased demand
for imports, and to inflationary price rises. In future, buyers would be
required to make a down-payment of 50% on all goods, except on solid fuel
stoves, where the down-payment remained at 10% in the hope of encouraging householders to change from oil or gas-burning appliances to those
which did not require imported fuels.

In September, petroleum prices were again allowed to rise, as a further measure in the battle to reduce Yugoslavia's dependence on increasingly expensive imported oil. In the short run, however, this would be expected to increase inflation.

The general rise in world prices and the steady decline in the value of the dinar also led to price increases over which the government could have no control. Yugoslavia had no means of defending itself against imported inflation if, at the same time, it planned to develop its industries on the basis of imported materials.

Foreign trade

During the 1960s Yugoslavia's foreign trade became linked very closely to that of Western Europe, and especially to the EEC countries, West Germany and Italy alone taking almost 22% of Yugoslavia's exports and supplying 31% of imports in 1961 (*Table 9.5* and *Figure 9.1*). Proportions

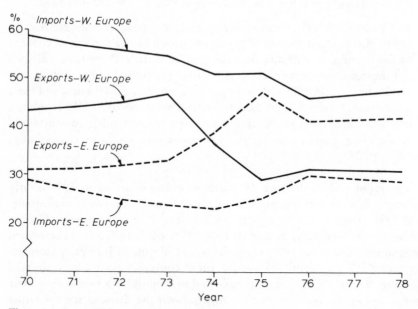

Figure 9.1 *Eastern and Western Europe's share of Yugoslav trade*

similar to these were maintained throughout the 1960s. In 1973 trade with these two countries accounted for over 25% of Yugoslavia's exports and 31% of imports. After 1973, however, there was a marked change in the geographical pattern of Yugoslavia's foreign trade as a result of the world

Table 9.5 *Yugoslavia's foreign trade (percentage distribution by area)*

	1961 Export	1961 Import	1970 Export	1970 Import	1973 Export	1973 Import	1974 Export	1974 Import	1975 Export	1975 Import	1976 Export	1976 Import	1978 Export	1978 Import
Western Europe	45.3	48.6	42.1	59.8	46.5	54.3	36.4	51.4	28.3	50.5	31.3	46.4	31.0	47.2
Eastern Europe	31.0	20.1	31.8	28.1	32.3	24.4	38.6	22.7	46.8	24.2	41.2	30.2	41.9	28.7
North America	6.4	20.2	5.9	6.1	8.6	5.0	8.7	5.3	6.9	6.2	7.2	6.3	7.0	6.0
Non-aligned	10.9	6.8	11.2	10.1	11.6	13.6	15.0	18.0	17.0	16.4	16.2	14.8	18.2	13.3

Source: Statistički Godišnjak, appropriate years.

economic crisis of the early 1970s (*Figure 9.2*). As the share of Yugoslavia's exports taken by Western Europe, and especially by EEC members, declined, a higher proportion was taken by the CMEA countries. In 1973 exports to Western Europe accounted for 46.5% of Yugoslavia's total exports, of which EEC members took 35.8%. By 1978 Western Europe's share had dropped to 31%, and the EEC's share was down to 23%. Ironically, the decline began in 1973, the same year in which Yugoslavia negotiated a five-year trade agreement with the Community, based on the Generalized System of Preference (GSP), introduced by the EEC in 1971. It

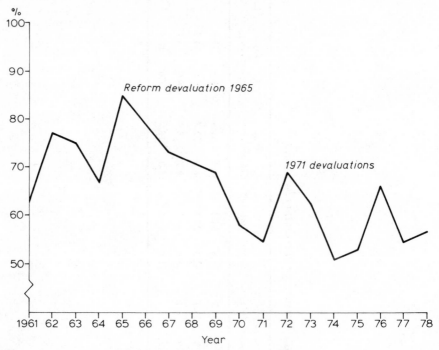

Figure 9.2 *Yugoslav trade balance: exports as a percentage of imports*

allows 'industrial products to enter the EEC duty free up to certain ceilings or quotas, with additional targets (*butoirs*) fixed for each beneficiary country' (*European Trends*, No. 6, August 1979, p. 27). Once the ceiling has been reached certain customs duties are introduced. The Yugoslavs, of all users of the system, have most frequently broken through the ceiling and have had to face discriminatory duties. Restrictions on the importation of agricultural produce have borne particularly harshly on Yugoslavia. In 1973 agricultural produce accounted for 29% of Yugoslavia's exports to the EEC: 10% were of beef and veal to Italy alone. In July 1974 severe restrictions were imposed on this trade. Difficulties have also been encountered with the entry of Yugoslav wines, slivovic and fruits. The proportion of agricultural produce fell to 17% in 1978.

The Yugoslavs complain that they are unable to reduce their enormous trade deficit with the EEC because of the artificial restraints on their exports imposed by the Community. Negotiations to replace the 1973 agreement began in 1977, but encountered serious difficulties. The first negotiating mandate had to be replaced by new guidelines at the end of 1978, but a year later agreement had not been reached. The 1973 agreement should have expired in September 1979, but its life has been prolonged until a replacement can be found. Meanwhile, certain other forms of Yugoslav–EEC cooperation have been able to make progress. The EEC members have a strong interest in improving communications through Yugoslavia, as it lies across the main routeways between Western Europe and the Eastern Mediterranean. The European Investment Bank has therefore approved a $600 million loan to assist in the construction of a motorway through Yugoslavia to replace the present inadequate *autoput* (E5) which runs from Ljubljana to the Greek border. The World Bank has also made a credit of $40 million available for part of this scheme (*RAD* . . ., 4 April 1977).

As the EEC countries restricted their imports from Yugoslavia, the Yugoslavs turned eastward to find markets for their products. The share of exports to CMEA countries increased from 32.3% in 1973 to 41.9% in 1978. Unfortunately a similar shift in the source of imports could not be made, as the goods which Yugoslavia needs to sustain its industrialization programme are not available from the Eastern bloc. Western Europe provided almost half of Yugoslavia's imports in 1978, of which 38.2% originated in the EEC. The CMEA countries could only supply 28.7%. Similar problems arise in dealing with the Third World. They have been able to take a larger share of Yugoslavia's exports, the proportion rising from 11.6% in 1973 to 18.2% in 1978, but the proportion of imports from these countries has remained at about the same level – 13.6% in 1973 and 13.3% in 1978.

The implications for the balance of payments are, of course, extremely serious. There was a total foreign trade deficit of $4300 million in 1978, of which $2500 million was with the EEC. It seems likely that the 1979 figures will be even worse. Preliminary estimates suggest a deficiency of $6000 million.

The structure of foreign trade

The structure of foreign trade has undergone a steady change since the economic reforms of 1965. In general, the share of industry has increased whilst those of agriculture and forestry have declined, a fact which reflects the changing structure of the economy as Yugoslavia moves into the status of a medium-rank industrial power (*Table 9.6*).

Table 9.6 *Sectoral composition of exports and imports*

	1965		1975		1978	
	Exports	*Imports*	*Exports*	*Imports*	*Exports*	*Imports*
Total	100	100	100	100	100	100
Industry	81.2	83.9	91.1	94.8	94.0	91.0
Agriculture	17.3	15.9	7.6	4.5	6.0	9.0
Forestry	1.5	0.2	1.3	0.7		

Source: Statistički Godišnjak, 1966 and 1976; Statistical Pocket Book, 1979.

There has also been a change within the industrial sector. The share of both exports and imports of raw materials and unworked products has declined, whilst exchanges of goods in the higher stages of processing has increased (*Table 9.7*). As most imports of goods in this category come from EEC countries, USA and Austria, the effect of this tendency has been to increase the visible trade deficit with the hard currency areas of the West, while trade with CMEA countries and the developing world has generally shown a balance in Yugoslavia's favour.

Table 9.7 *Sources of machinery imports*

	1970	1974
Machinery (excluding electrical goods)		
EEC and USA	62%	62%
Eastern Europe	9.4%	9.8%
Electrical machines and apparatus		
Western Europe	66%	72.5%
Eastern Europe	6.8%	6%
Domestic electrical equipment		
Western Europe	64%	80%
Eastern Europe	5.6%	6.5%

Source: Statistički Godišnjak, 1975.

For most of the post-war period Yugoslavia has carried a large deficit in visible trade:

	Percentage of cost of imports covered by export earnings				
1950–1954	*1955–1959*	*1960–1964*	*1965–1969*	*1970–1974*	*1975–1979*
59.5	63.9	70.2	74.9	59.5	55.5

Until the mid-1960s the deficit was mainly met by borrowing and by foreign aid in various forms, but during the last decade invisibles have become increasingly important.

Table 9.8 *Balance of payments (billions of US dollars)*

	1971	1972	1973	1974	1975	1976	1977	1978
Exports	1.81	2.24	2.85	3.81	4.07	4.87	5.25	5.67
Imports	3.25	3.23	4.51	7.54	7.70	7.36	9.63	9.98
Trade balance	−1.44	−0.99	−1.66	−3.73	−3.63	−2.48	−4.38	−4.31
Services and transfers (net)	−1.11	1.28	1.82	2.27	2.31	2.28	2.49	3.3
of which								
Tourist income	0.36	0.46	0.53	0.64	0.70	0.72	0.74	0.93
Emigrants' and workers' remittances	0.65	0.79	1.17	1.43	1.45	1.40	1.44	1.74
Transport	0.22	0.23	0.27	0.39	0.43	0.42	0.56	0.58
Current balance	−0.35	+0.42	+0.48	−1.18	−1.0	+0.16	−1.58	−1.02

Source: Economic Survey, Yugoslavia, OECD 1979, Table M.

Invisible earnings

The main sources of invisible earnings are remittances from Yugoslav workers temporarily employed abroad, earnings from the tourist industry and from transport services. In 1972, 1973 and 1976 these earnings more than covered the visible trade deficit, bringing the current balance of payments into surplus (*Table 9.8*). It seemed possible that the objective of external convertibility of the dinar was within sight, but the effects of the world economic crisis caused yet another postponement of this aim of the 1965 reforms (Horvat, 1977, p. 204).

The reason for the small surplus in 1976 was primarily an improvement in the visible trade balance. Exports rose in value by 20% and imports fell by 4%. There was, however, for the first time in recent years, a drop in invisible earnings. This tendency is a reflection of the world economic crisis. Many Yugoslav workers in Western Europe have been forced to return home, and the German recession triggered off by the oil crisis of 1973 has reduced the amount of surplus cash which those who remain have available for sending home. In addition, there was a fall in the number of foreign tourists entering Yugoslavia, from a peak of over 6 million in 1973. There was a slow recovery in numbers during the next few years, and by 1978 the 1973 figures had been surpassed (*Table 9.9*).

Table 9.9 *Foreign tourists entering Yugoslavia (millions)*

	1970	1971	1972	1973	1974	1975	1976	1977	1978
Number of tourists	4.75	5.25	5.1	6.15	5.5	5.85	5.6	5.6	6.4
Overnight stays	22.5	25.85	25.8	32.0	29.75	31.6	29.3	29.0	34.9

Source: Statisticki Kalendar Jugoslavije, 1977.

Foreign capital in the Yugoslav economy

There are two main sources for the flow of foreign capital into the Yugoslav economy; first, loans from the International Bank for Reconstruction and Development (World Bank), of which Yugoslavia was a founder member and, second, from Western banking consortia, both private and governmental, and from investments made under partnership agreements which permit foreigners to invest up to 49% of the capital in a Yugoslav enterprise. Between 1949 and 1975 World Bank loans at rates of interest varying from 3.0% to 7.5%, repayable over periods of from 3 to 30 years, have contributed $1205 million to the Yugoslav economy. Most of this money has been for infrastructure projects, flood control and hydroelectric schemes, and for the modernization of industry (see *Table 9.10*).

It is likely that the involvement of the World Bank will increase, as both partners seem to be satisfied with the relations which have developed between them during the three decades of their cooperation.

Table 9.10 *World Bank loans*

	($ million)		
1949–1969	381.1	Varying rates from 3% (1949) to 6.5% (1969)	Mainly for communications, hydroelectric power and river control
1970	98.0	7%	Industrial and communications modernization, roads
1971	110.0	7.25%	Roads, hydroelectricity (Bosnia), tourism (Dalmatia)
1972	75.0	7.25%	Electricity generation
1973	104.9	7.5%	Agro-industrial projects in Macedonia. Gas pipeline. Metal industry (Vojvodina)
1974	226.5	n.a.	Industrial modernization in less developed areas. Port of Bar (Montenegro)
1975	170.0	n.a.	Agriculture, roads. Hydroelectricity (Bosnia)

Source: Nedelja Informativne Novine, 25 August 1975.

Note: A comparison of *Tables 9.10* and *9.11* suggests that private investment is more interested in manufacturing industry in the developed areas, whilst World Bank credits go to infrastructure projects in the less developed areas.

By the end of 1976 the World Bank had loaned $1500 million to Yugoslavia. In February 1977 a further two loans, of $56 million each, were approved, the first to support a programme of modernization of agriculture in Serbia and Kosovo and the second for highway construction in several republics. In June 1977 a further loan of $75 million was granted from a nationwide agricultural programme, in which special consideration was to be given to the less developed republics. During 1979, World Bank and European Investment Bank Loans of $40 million and $600 million respectively were given for highway construction.

It was perhaps appropriate that in October 1979 the Yugoslavs should have been the hosts for the annual meetings of the IMF and the World Bank in Belgrade. The Yugoslavs took the opportunity to plead with some of their creditors for a renegotiation of up to $600 million of the country's foreign debts. Although a detailed breakdown of the figures is not available for

1979, at the time it was stated that Yugoslavia's total indebtedness to Western Banks was between $11 000 000 and $13 000 000 million and debt servicing of these loans was estimated to be $1800 million in 1979 rising to $2900 million in 1981. Approximately 22% of all foreign currency earnings are needed to cover the servicing of these debts. In Belgrade in 1979 the bankers negotiated a rescheduling of Yugoslavia's debts to ease the burden of repayments (Antic, 1979, p. 2) as it was obvious that unless this was done the development of the Yugoslav economy would suffer a serious setback.

In addition to World Bank Loans, Yugoslavia has received aid from consortia of Western Banks, from foreign governments and from organizations such as the EEC and the CMEA. Aid from Soviet and East European sources has been much less than that from the West, and has often been hedged round with restrictions imposed for both economic and political reasons which have limited its usefulness to the Yugoslav economy.

Joint enterprise investments

In 1967 a law was passed which permitted foreign nationals to hold up to 49% of the capital in a joint enterprise with a Yugoslav firm (*Službeni List*, No. 31, 19 July 1967). At first there were stringent conditions concerning such matters as the export by foreigners of profits from joint enterprises, the proportion of profits which had to be reinvested in Yugoslavia, and the rate of taxation on profits. In August 1971 these restrictions were eased, in the hope of attracting more funds, but the total sum invested in this way has been disappointingly low. The main purpose from the Yugoslav point of view was to assist in the improvement in technological standards and business efficiency through collaboration with advanced Western firms (Sukijasović, 1970, p. 11). It was also hoped to persuade foreign firms to invest in the less developed republics, in order to raise the level of industrialization in these areas. The first objective has been realized only to a limited extent. The total investment in 1968–1972 from this source was only 4% of the total inflow of medium- and long-term capital (Horvat, 1976, p. 205). A glance at *Table 9.11* will show clearly that this second aim has not been realized, as most of the investment has gone to the motor car and other consumer goods industries in the developed north.

Table 9.11 *Private foreign investment in Yugoslavia under joint venture agreements, 1968–1972*

(1) Investment in developed areas	$84 166 970
Of which, Fiat Crvena Zastava automobile works, Kragujevac	$30 million
(2) Investment in less developed areas	$9 338 582
Of which, A.B. Svenska Kullagerfabriken and Volkswagen in UNIS, Sarajevo	$5.5 million

Source: International Investment Corporation for Yugoslavia, London

Regional economic policies

At its birth in 1918 Yugoslavia inherited problems of regional economic inequalities, and little was achieved during the period of the Yugoslav kingdom in reducing the gaps between the rich and poor areas. The Communists declared one of their primary objectives to be the reduction of these inequalities. Despite all their efforts the Yugoslavs have seen the gap between the rich and poor areas, measured in income per capita, grow steadily during the last three decades. Everyone's standard of living has improved, but on the whole that of the rich has improved at a faster rate than that of the poor. In 1947 the gap between Slovenia (the richest) and Kosovo (the poorest) was 1:3.3. At the end of the First Five Year Plan, in 1952, it was 1:3.8. In 1974 it had grown to 1:6.1. During this period Serbia Proper, which includes Belgrade, has remained at about the national average, and Croatia's relative position has changed little since 1957 (*Table 9.12*).

Table 9.12 *Index figures of national income per capita, 1965–1977 (Yugoslavia = 100)*

	1965	*1970*	*1974*	*1977**
Slovenia	174.5	186.9	192.8	200.1
Croatia	121.7	122.7	121.3	124.8
Vojvodina	122.0	115.2	124.9	117.6
Serbia Proper	99.1	100.1	100.0	98.5
Montenegro	70.6	69.7	68.5	71.1
Bosnia-Hercegovina	69.3	64.0	61.9	65.1
Macedonia	69.2	69.3	70.4	68.1
Kosovo	37.0	33.8	31.3	30.4
Ratio Kosovo/Slovenia	1:4.7	1:5.5	1:6.1	1:6.5

* The 1977 figures are based on social product per capita (*Statistical Pocket Book 1979*, p. 48). The 1965–1974 figures are of national income per capita (*Statistički Godišnjak*, 1976).

As Yugoslav economists and policy makers tend to take the per capita income figures as the effective determinant of whether a region is underdeveloped (Colanović, 1967), the fact that the less developed regions have a higher birth rate than do the more developed regions accentuates the size of the gap[7].

During the first five-year plan (1947–1951) allocations were made through the federal republic for investment in basic industries in Montenegro, Bosnia-Hercegovina and Macedonia, with the intention of accelerating the economic growth of these areas at a rate above the national average. This policy was continued after the relaxation of the rigid system of centralized planning, but during the 1950s the instruments of allocation became more flexible. For example, the areas designated as underdeveloped were more precisely defined; a distinction was made between credits and grants; investment funds, separated from the federal and republican budgets, were required to consider the 'rentability' of investments in addition to the social and political factors which were predominant during the earlier period. In the 1961–1965 plan provision was made for a General Investment Fund, which would allocate investment resources to the less developed regions through republican and provincial government agencies. The 1963 Constitution defined Bosnia-Hercegovina, Montenegro, Macedonia and Kosovo as 'insufficiently developed areas'. The fund was allocated 1.85% of the social product of all republics. In the 1971–1975 plan an additional 0.09% was specifically allocated to Kosovo. Special treatment for Kosovo was continued in the 1976–1980 plan.

Under these various enactments, a considerable investment has been made in the less developed areas. There are also funds available from republican and federal sources for assistance to less developed areas within republics which are considered to be in the more developed category – for example, some of the regions of Croatia along the Bosnian border.

Investment in underdeveloped areas is often less productive than investment in the more developed regions. There are several reasons why this should be so. The less developed areas lack infrastructure, they lack trained personnel both in production and administration, and their industrial development tends to be based on the basic operations of raw material extraction and primary processing, where the terms of trade are unfavourable. The more developed areas, with their longer traditions of manufacturing and their greater experience in marketing, concentrate on the more lucrative operations, gaining some advantage by virtue of the fact that they are within the same economic unit as their raw material suppliers from the less developed south. To give one small example, much of the wine sold on West European markets by Slovene wine merchants is, in fact, of Macedonian origin. The Macedonians have excellent wines, but they lack the business skills and experience to enable them to market them profitably on the international market. The Slovenes can buy Macedonian wine in bulk cheaply and sell it at an enhanced profit through their well-established trade outlets. The market mechanism tends to favour the more developed areas, when the poor raw material producers and the richer manufacturers happen to be within the same economic unit.

There is no doubt that the Yugoslav federal authorities, for overriding political reasons, genuinely desire to reduce the economic inequalities which exist between the regions. They have tried several methods – direction of resources administratively through the budget (1947–1951); loans and grants centrally administered but having regard to the 'rentability' of the investment (mid-1950s); the establishment of a national fund distributed according to market criteria (mid-1960s); and variations on all these themes. None of these methods has had a noticeable effect on the narrowing of the gap between the richest and the poorest regions. As long as these disparities exist, they will provide fuel for nationalist propaganda.

Agriculture

All communist regimes in Eastern Europe have had difficulties with the agricultural population and Yugoslavia has been no exception. In the immediate post-war period there was a land reform which distributed land from larger estates to smallholders and landless peasants. Between 1949 and 1952 there was a programme of collectivization, intended to achieve the 'socialist transformation of the village'. This was abandoned after about 25% of the arable area had been collectivized, and most of the land was taken back into the private sector. During the next 20 years the attitude of the authorities to the private farmer shifted from one of suspicion and even of hostility to an acceptance of the persistence of a private sector, and an attempt to cooperate with it in raising food production.

The number of private holdings has remained fairly constant at about 2.6 million, but the population dependent upon agriculture has fallen from 10.6 million (64%) in 1948 to 7.8 million (36%) in 1971. 82% of arable land is privately farmed, the remainder being farmed by worker-management agricultural enterprises, mainly in the lowlands of Vojvodina, Pelagonia and Kosovo. Various forms of cooperation between public and private sectors are encouraged.

In 1973 a 'Green Plan' (1973–1985) for agriculture was launched, after the signing of three agreements in Belgrade between representatives of the republics and autonomous provinces and the federal government. The first envisages an average annual growth of agricultural output of 2.8% overall, and 6% within the public sector between 1973 and 1985. The other two are concerned with providing the means to promote this increase. The measures include assistance to private farmers in purchasing machinery, fertilizers and seed, and in financial and taxation measures designed to secure a stable market for farm produce. In the seven years since the Green Plan was launched the rate of mechanization of the private sector, measured by the number of tractors per farm, has increased, whilst in the public sector it has remained constant. In 1978 there were 316 000 tractors on private holdings and only 26 000 in the public sector (*Statistički Godišnjak*, 1979, Table 102.17). On the other hand, agricultural yields from the private sector have remained much below those in the public sector (*Table 9.13*).

Because of the small percentage area devoted to the public sector, the private peasant, despite his lower level of efficiency, still provides most of Yugoslavia's food output. In 1970 this accounted for 60% of wheat, 70% of meat and 95% of vegetable production.

Table 9.13 *Index of agricultural output 1970–1976*
(1955 = 100)

	Total	Private	Public
1970	154	129	550
1971	164	133	671
1972	159	129	654
1973	171	138	690
1974	181	146	786
1975	177	142	735
1976	189	151	834
1977	198	157	889
1978	185	144	882

Source: Statistički Godišnjak, 1979, Table 102.17.

The proportions did not change significantly during the first few years of the Green Plan, but since 1975 the public sector has been supplying an increasing share of the nation's food. This is partly because many ageing private peasants have been persuaded to sell or lease their holdings to agricultural organizations, and because increased investment in agriculture has begun to produce higher yields in the public sector. The average wheat yields, for example in the period 1965–1969 were 35.7 quintals per hectare in the public sector and 25 quintals per hectare in the private sector. In the period 1975–1979 the figures were respectively 45.5 quintals per hectare and 32 quintals per hectare. In 1978 the private sector provided approximately 50% of wheat and meat (*Statistički Godišnjak*, 1979, 102.17, 102.18). The major fluctuations in output can be attributed more to the weather than to any act of man.

Banking and monetary policy

Banking policy, like every other aspect of the Yugoslav economy during the last 30 years, has been subject to frequent changes. There have been at least nine important reorganizations of the banking system. Under the centrally planned economy, the banks were instruments of the state planners and all banking functions were concentrated in two institutions – the National Bank and the Social Investment Bank. The distinction between short-term and long-term investments which is reflected in the different functions of these two institutions is based on Marx's distinction between fixed and circulating capital. Despite many institutional changes, this distinction is still maintained in present-day Yugoslav banking practice. After 1948 communal banks and regional banks were formed. The former acted as bankers to the local enterprises, as well as being general banks to serve the local community, and enterprises were obliged to conduct most of their transactions through them. The regional banks were mainly concerned with loans to agricultural cooperatives and socialist farms.

As the economy was decentralized during the 1950s the banking system was, paradoxically, recentralized, possibly as a deliberate counterbalancing act and as a means of enforcing financial discipline, as well as freeing the banks from local pressures (Ugrčić, 1968, pp. 167–8). Thus in 1952 the communal banks disappeared, and all banking functions were taken over by the National Bank, with its 460 branches. The Bank had supervisory powers over enterprise accounts, and was able to influence economic decisions in the interests of federal government policy. After 1959 these social accounting functions were separated from the bank and put under the control of the autonomous Social Accounting Service.

In 1954 decentralized local banks re-emerged, and by 1959 more than half the branches of the National Bank had been replaced by communal banks (Waller, 1973, p. 78). During the late 1950s three specialized federal banks were created – the Yugoslav Bank for Foreign Trade (1955), the Yugoslav Investment Bank (1956) and the Agricultural Bank (1958).

In addition to the financing of investment through the special business banks, various government investment funds were established, the most important of which was the General Investment Fund.

In the reforms of 1961 banks were given a greater degree of autonomy, and the Communal Banks were given the major role in financing the economy. In 1963 Social Investment Funds were transferred to the banks, and the following year the General Investment Fund was abolished.

The 1965 reforms freed the banks from much of the political control under which they had operated during the previous 20 years, and enabled them to make investment decisions primarily on economic criteria, where market considerations normally took precedence over political pressures. Under the Banking Law of 1965 the management of banks was placed under the authority of an Assembly, on which were represented all the enterprises which were designated as Founders by virtue of the size of the credit funds which they had contributed to the bank.

The workers in the bank enjoy the rights of self-management in so far as the determination of their own incomes is concerned, and also had, until 1971, a 10% share of the vote in the Assembly (Waller, 1973, p. 128). Reforms of the banking system in 1971–1972 increased the influence of the Founders in the control of the banks and diminished the roles of the socio-political communities and the bank employees. The effect of these changes was to give greater priority to purely economic considerations and to give enterprises greater control over investments. By 1971 51% of all investment in fixed assets was made through the banks, and a further 27% directly by enterprises. Only 15% came from federal or republican government sources. Most of this was expenditure of the Fund for Underdeveloped Republics.

The increased control over investment by banks and enterprises led to certain difficulties because of the tendency of enterprises to undertake investments irresponsibly, and for banks to be too liberal in their credit policies. Eventually the federal authorities stepped in, proposing in 1974 that the banks should reach agreements amongst themselves regulating the supply of credit. At the beginning of 1975, when no such agreements had been reached, the Federal Executive Council (i.e. the government) issued a Policy Resolution threatening the banks that 'unless an agreement is reached in the first part of the year the FEC will provisionally prescribe a structure of credit growth, binding on all commercial banks . . . . The National Bank will again provide, besides agricultural rediscount credits, more or less automatic coverage for exports and imports' (OECD, 1975, p. 35).

It had also been intended that the role of the central bank should diminish, but, as so often happens in Yugoslavia, the intention to decentralize was frustrated by the need to meet an emergency by 'temporary' intervention from the centre.

The federal pressure did produce inter-bank agreements, but they were not considered to be stringent enough. In 1976 the government increased bank reserve requirements (*Quarterly* . . ., 1976, p. 9) and introduced a new system of settling accounts between enterprises, which ended the bad old practice of settling accounts in kind, rather than in cash. 'It is now required that all transactions should be made in cash, letters of credit, bills of exchange or any other bank paper readily convertible into money' (*Economic Survey* . . ., 1976, p. 103). Settlement must be made within 15 days of receiving goods or services. This measure was designed to bring a note of realism into the management of the enterprises and to curb the tendency to illiquidity which has been a curse of the Yugoslav economy since the 1965 reforms. It also caused a large increase in the money supply, which grew by 51.7% during 1976, compared with a target of 18%. It has often been argued by monetary theorists that a principal cause of many of Yugoslavia's inflationary troubles has been the uncontrolled growth of money supply, but in this case it could be argued that the temporary increase in money supply brought about by this measure will be offset by the reduction in credits which accompanied it.

In June 1977 it was again apparent that the government was putting pressure on the banks, this time to secure a reduction in interest rates. Dr Šefer reported to the Federal Assembly on 29 June 1977: 'If the appropriate reduction in interest rates is not settled by an accord reached by business banks, the FEC will adopt the appropriate regulations on this matter within the scope of its powers' (*Tanjug*, 30 June 1977).

The federal government influences investment and credit policy to some extent through the budget. Deficit budgeting has been a common feature of the 1970s and there has been a tendency to have recourse to borrowing from the National Bank to cover budget deficits. In 1976, however, another method was used, namely a 3.8 billion dinar bond issue. Bond issues have been used on occasions to finance projects such as the Belgrade–Bar railway and experiments have been made with 'enterprise bonds'. There are some theoretical difficulties for communists in the issuing of interest-bearing bonds, and there has been some controversy over them.

In fact, bond issues are usually issued by republican authorities for particular schemes which have a 'national' aspect to them – e.g. a road from Zagreb to the Dalmation coast which attracted Croatian money, and the already mentioned Belgrade–Bar railway, which was the fulfillment of a century-old Serbian dream of a link with the sea.

There are similar theoretical difficulties regarding the creation of a money market. Yugoslavia has a free market in the exchange of goods and services and a free labour market. There is, however, no free money market. Some of the difficulties which the banking system has encountered and some of the problems which enterprises have encountered regarding investments arise from the strain between the 'socialist' and the 'market' elements in a system of market socialism.

Personal incomes

During the period of administrative socialism workers employed in publicly owned industries were paid on fixed income scales determined by the state. After the introduction of self-management, the workers councils of the enterprises had an increasing degree of control over the distribution of personal incomes, although they have never been completely free from external constraints, both formal and informal.

The 1976 Law on Associated Labour[9] enshrines the principle that 'Workers shall freely dispose of the net income of basic organizations[10] under conditions of responsibility to one another and to society as a whole and under other conditions as determined by the present Law' (Art. 52).

There was a period during the late 1960s when the right of workers to determine their own incomes led to great differences in earnings both between republics and between workers within the same industry. There are two alternative principles between which Yugoslav income policy has oscillated. The egalitarian principle seeks to lower differentials. The policy of the liberal reformers is to permit differentials based on skill and on the success of an enterprise on the market. The reformers frequently speak of the right of workers to be rewarded according to the results of their work, and of their right freely to dispose of the fruits of their labour. The enunciation of these principles does not, however, solve the problem of income differentials, or of how to measure the results of work. If the measure of success is that of the market, then inequalities will inevitably arise. These may be based on accidental factors, which are not related to the efforts or skills of the workers, or may result from the exploitation of a monopoly position by a particular enterprise or group of enterprises. This was particularly true of banks and foreign trade enterprises.

There is some evidence that the inflation of the late 1960s and early 1970s was partly caused by enterprises paying their members incomes which were not justified by the commercial performance of the firm. According to Branko Horvat

> Prices are determined predominantly by changes in wages, and so most of the time inflation is a cost-push inflation . . . . Wage increases in privileged work organizations initiate wage increases throughout the economy, and whenever prices cannot bear a cost increase, they are revised upward (Horvat, 1977, p. 226).

Although considerable pressure has been exerted since 1972 to prevent the workers' councils from acting irresponsibly over income distribution, it is clear from recent speeches of ministers concerned with economic policy that the problem is by no means solved.

In a speech to the Federal Conference of the Socialist Alliance on 23 June 1977, the Premier, Veselin Djuranović, spoke of the need to ensure that

> the use of income is firmly brought into harmony with the demands for strengthening the economy's reproductive capacity, for the distribution of income according to the results of work and for the elimination of spending of unearned income or spending in excess of available income (*Tanjug*, 29 June 1977).

In a report to the Federal Assembly on 29 June, Dr Berislav Šefer, the Vice-President responsible for economic affairs, urged all organizations of associated labour not to violate the income of policy which had been agreed between the governmental and socio-political organizations. For example, 'organizations with current losses during the year should not raise personal incomes while they are planning on a loss'. He also hinted that if 'social action . . . based on carrying out income policy in accordance with . . . the Law on Associated Labour' is ineffective, the Republican and Provincial governments 'should ensure this implementation of income policy and personal incomes by means of appropriate regulations'. It is clear from these statements that the state retains the right to regulate incomes by administrative regulation if workers in self-managed enterprises pay themselves too much.

During the 1970s efforts have been made, with some degree of success, to regulate incomes by means of voluntary agreements. These 'self-management agreements' (*samoupravni sporazum*) are the method by which the income levels within a particular industry can be made more comparable. They are fostered and encouraged by the Federal and Republican governments and by a whole range of 'socio-political' organizations such as the League of Communists and the trade unions.

Price policy

During the period of administrative planning, prices of manufactured goods were first set on the basis of actual costs, and therefore varied from producer to producer. During the first five-year plan (1947–1952) uniform prices were fixed for most commodities by taking average costs and adding average rate of profit; losses were subsidized through the budget and excess profits were passed into the budget. Only small amounts of consumer goods were allowed onto the free market.

Agricultural prices were fixed by the government, and there was a system of compulsory deliveries (*obavezn otkup*) which forced peasants to sell to the state at arbitrarily low prices. Compulsory deliveries were abandoned in 1952 at the same time as the pressure for collectivization was relaxed. After a further period of experimentation, in which the federal government was the prime agent in determining prices, the Federal Price Office was established in 1955. Since 1958 enterprises intending to raise prices must register the new prices with the Price Office, which has a 30-day period to examine the reasons for the proposed rise, and the ultimate power of veto during that period.

Enterprises have in the past shown considerable ingenuity in evading these restrictions, a common device being the introduction of ostensibly new products, which are in effect old lines which have been slightly modified. In addition to the power of veto by the Price Office, the Federal Government has power to set fixed prices for electricity, transport and certain commodities – for example, sugar, salt and cigarettes. It can also set maximum prices for some basic raw materials – e.g. coal, petroleum, steel – and can order a general price freeze for a limited period of time. Republics exercise control over trade margins of wholesalers, and local authorities have similar powers over retailers. In addition, agricultural prices are influenced by the policy of the Federal Food Reserve Board which purchases food products at guaranteed prices[11].

The economic reform of 1965 involved, in theory, a fundamental change in price policy. The principle for determining price levels was that the basis should be the world price as set by the international market (in practice the levels of Yugoslavia's chief trading partners in Western Europe).

In the first stage of the reform most prices rose, but a temporary freeze was declared at the new, higher levels. The ultimate objective was to use competition on the international market as the spur to goad Yugoslav industry into greater efficiency. Free convertibility of the dinar, the removal of artificial barriers to trade, and the withdrawal of the state from intereference in the workings of the economy were to be achieved within as short a time as possible. Meanwhile, some short-term administrative measures were seen as being inevitable in the transition period. The dinar was devalued by 66%, multiple exchange rates were abolished, customs duties were reduced to approximately half their previous value, and quota restrictions on imports were removed. All these measures had important effects, especially on producer prices. Retail prices were affected by the introduction of a sales tax.

In fact, the Yugoslav market economy never fully emerged, and during the fifteen years since the reform, policy regarding prices has never been free from administrative intervention.

In the early post-reform era, administrative intervention was usually intended to raise Yugoslav prices closer to the international level. In the late 1960s and during the 1970s administrative intervention has been intended to curb inflation, and to cushion Yugoslavia from the effects of the world inflation to which the country's economy was so vulnerable. The apparant success in bringing down inflation to single figures in 1976 was followed by a resumption of the upward trend in wages and prices during the subsequent two years. In 1979 government intervention again became necessary, when inflation had climbed to 20% and a new stabilization programme was initiated.

Employment

Throughout the three decades of socialist Yugoslavia employment in the public sector has risen steadily, with only occasional setbacks (*Table 9.14*). So, also, since the early 1960s, has the number of unemployed, or, as Yugoslav statistics list them, 'persons seeking work'. These two facts – rising employment, especially in industry, and an increasing number of people seeking work – are a reflection of the massive shift of population from self-sufficient private agriculture to urban and industrial occupations. In the 1960s some of the pressure was relieved by the flow of *Gastarbeiter* to Western Europe. Since 1973 this flow has been reduced, although the number temporarily abroad is still approximately one million. Nevertheless, there has been a substantial rise in unemployment, which must in part be due to the decline in opportunities for work abroad.

Between 1973 and the end of 1978 300 000 Yugoslav workers returned home, but about 80 000 left to find work abroad. Most of those returning came from Western Europe, but the number of Yugoslavs abroad did not fall as dramatically as these figures suggest. This is because as the number of workers employed in Western Europe fell as a result of stricter immigration controls and the slowing down of the Western economies, the number of dependents increased. It has been estimated that between 1977 and 1979 the number of dependents rose by 100 000, so that in September 1979 there were still 1 185 000 Yugoslavs living in Western Europe. These comprised 695 000 employed workers and 490 000 dependents, of whom 250 000 were children of school age (Antić, 1979). This reflects a more generous policy towards dependents in the receiving countries, and possibly also an increasing tendency amongst the Yugoslavs to regard their stay abroad as a

Table 9.14 *Employment in the public sector (in millions)*

1965	1966	1967	1968	1969	1970	1971	1972	1973	1974	1975	1976	1977	1978	1979	1980 (1st quarter)
3.68	3.64	3.60	3.66	3.81	3.95	4.1	4.31	4.38	4.6	4.66	4.9	5.1	5.3	5.5	5.6

Unemployed (annual averages) (thousands)

1965	1966	1967	1968	1969	1970	1971	1972	1973	1974	1975	1976	1977	1978	1979	1980 (1st quarter)
237	257.6	269.1	311	330.6	319.6	291.3	315.3	381.6	448.6	537	635	700	738	762	797

Sources: Statistički Godišnjak, 1975. Quarterly review of Yugoslavia, 2nd quarter 1977, EIV, Appendix 1. Statistički Kalendar 1979. Indeks No. 8, 1980.

long-term proposition. The improvement in social security benefits for Yugoslavs promised by the EEC/Yugoslavia agreement of February 1980 may encourage more to stay (*Yugoslavia: a New Cooperation* . . ., 1980).

9.4. Prospects for the future

The Yugoslav economy has become so closely involved with the economies of Western Europe that its future development can only be assessed in the context of the economic crisis which was initiated by the rise in oil prices in the early 1970s. The underlying causes of the malaise go deeper than the oil crisis, but this was the occasion which exposed the sickness.

The impact on Yugoslavia was not at first as serious as might have been expected, and at the outset of the 1976–1980 Plan there was great optimism. Despite a high rate of growth in output, inflation was brought dramatically down from 26% in 1975 to 9% in 1976, and the balance of payments was almost in balance. Export earnings rose by 20% and imports fell by 5%. However, the performance during the next few years suggested that 1976 was an exceptional year. It seems that the mechanisms of self-management within an economy based on the concept of market socialism cannot induce a sense of discipline sufficient to control inflation. State intervention, which is contrary to the principles of self-management, has to be invoked from time to time to administer a short, sharp shock, as happened in 1976. The temporary improvement gained by this intervention soon evaporated, and ministers are again lecturing the workers about the need for restraint. During the late 1970s the Yugoslavs indulged in an investment boom which had to be brought under control by government intervention. Inflation resumed its upward path, the balance of payments deficit grew to an estimated $6000 million in 1979, unemployment rose to 16% of the social sector labour force, and there was little sign that measures to reduce regional inequalities were producing the expected results[12].

Once again, Yugoslavia had to look to foreign loans to give some relief to the overstrained economy

The immediate future will be difficult. The 1976–1980 plan was based on the assumption that the world economy would begin to emerge from its recession and that the volume of world trade would increase. This does not seem likely to happen. Some of Yugoslavia's troubles are directly related to the restrictionist policies of her EEC trading partners, and to the inability of Western Europe to absorb any more Yugoslav migrant workers.

Further difficulties may be experienced if the Yugoslavs, as intended, rely increasingly on voluntary agreements as a means of ensuring wage and price controls and curbing excessive investments. If past practice is a guide, 'temporary' intervention by the state will have to be used to achieve these objectives.

Nevertheless, although the fundamental changes envisaged in the 1976 –1980 plan are still only prospects for the future, some progress has been made in modernizing and restructuring both industry and agriculture, and growth in output has been high, but much remains to be done if the chronic weakness of the economy is to be corrected.

Notes

1. For an account of the economics of the infant Yugoslav state see Bičanić (1973), ch. 1, 'The Economics of the Creation of Yugoslavia'. In 1919 77% of the economically active population were engaged in agriculture.
2. Dimitrijević (1968) gives the following figures for the percentage of foreign capital in pre-war Yugoslav industry: cement – 97%, chemicals – 67%, food industries – 51%. The Bor copper mines were French-owned and the Trepča lead/zinc/silver mines were British-owned.
3. In Bičanić (1973, p. 231).
4. These principles were enunciated in a document entitled 'Teze o osnavama sistema društvenog planiranja' (Theses on the fundamentals of social planning) adopted by the Federal Assembly in 1966 and incorporated into a 'Basic Law' (*Osnovni zakon*) in 1970 (*Službeni List SFRJ*, No. 28, 1970).
5. These are bodies which bring together the users and providers of social services. They raise the funds from local enterprises, communes and banks.
6. A rate of 32% was reached during the first quarter of 1975. In a speech at Ljubljana on 5 September 1975 Tito declared that: 'The most important thing today is to liquidate the inflation in Yugoslavia, now running at the very high rate of 30% . . . . As everyone knows, we are much linked to the West . . . and the raw materials we import from the West have become more expensive. We have been particularly affected by oil.'

7. *Live births per 1000 population*

	1954	1974
Kosovo	46.4	36.1
Bosnia-Hercegovina	39.7	19.4
Macedonia	38.1	22.1
Croatia	22.4	14.7
Slovenia	20.9	17.3

Sicherl (1969) also makes the point that the use of per capita income as the criterion for determining underdevelopment accentuates the gap.
8. The figures for 1962 were: banks – 3%, enterprises – 30%, government agencies – 59% (*Statistički Bilten . . .*, No. 8, 1972, p. 69).
9. All quotations are from the authorized English translation of 'Zakon o udruženom radu' (*The Associated . . .*, 1977).
10. 'A basic organization of associated labour (*osnovna organizacija udruženog rada*) is the fundamental unit of the self-management system. It is the smallest unit which can be treated intelligibly as a separate entity from within the workforce of an enterprise, and in which the results of joint labour can be expressed in terms of value on the market or within the work organization concerned' (*The Associated . . .*, 1977).
11. For a summary of the position regarding price controls see Horvat (1977, p. 177).
12. The fostering of import substitution, which it was hoped would reduce imports, produced no significant results.

References

Antić, Z. (1979). Yugoslavia's Economic Difficulties. Radio Free Europe, *RAD Background Report*, No. 222 (15 October)
—— (1979). Many Yugoslav Workers still in the West. Radio Free Europe, *RAD Background Report*, No. 228 (18 October)

Bičanić, R. (1973). *Economic Policy in Socialist Yugoslavia*, Cambridge
Borba, 25 February 1977
Čolanović, B. (1967). Yugoslavia's Industrialization and the Development of the Underdeveloped Regions. UNIDO, ID/Conf. 1/927

Dimitrijević, S. (1968). *Strani kapital u privrede bivše Jugoslavije*. Belgrade

Economic Survey of Europe in 1976. Economic Commission for Europe. Geneva

European Trends, No. 6, August 1979, EIU Special Report 2, Yugoslavia and the EEC

Covedarica, S. (1972). Price System and Policy. *Yugoslav Survey*, Vol. XIII, No. 3 (August)

Horvat, B. (1977). *The Yugoslav Economic System*. IASP, New York

Lendvai, ?. (1969). *Eagles in Cobwebs*. London

OECD Economic Survey, Yugoslavia, April 1975

Quarterly Economic Review of Yugoslavia, EIU, 4th quarter 1976

RAD Background Report, Radio Free Europe Research, No. 122 (26 May) 1976; No. 73 (4 April) 1977; No. 104 (10 May) 1979; No. 185 (21 August) 1979

Sicherl, P. (1969). Analiza nekih elementa za ocenu stepena razvijenosti republika i pokrajina. *Ekonomska analiza*, Nos. 1–2

Singleton, F. (1976). *Twentieth Century Yugoslavia*. London

Službeni List SFRJ, No. 31 (19 July) 1967; No. 28 1970

Štajner, R. (1971). The System of Planning. *Yugoslav Survey*, Vol. XII, No. 1 (February)

Statistički Bilten SDK, No. 8, 1972, Belgrade

Statistički Godišnjak, 1979, Belgrade

Sukijasovic, L. M. (1970). *Yugoslav Foreign Investment Legislation at Work; Experiences so far*. Belgrade

Tanjug, reported in BBC Monitoring Service, EE/5548/CI/3 (29 June 1977); EE/5550/CI/5 (30 June 1977); (9 July 1979)

The Associated Labour Act (1977). Belgrade

Ugrčić, M. (1968). *Novčani Sistem Jugoslavije*. Belgrade

Waller, J. (1973). *The Yugoslav Banking System*. Unpublished MA thesis. Bradford University

Yugoslavia: a New Cooperation Agreement with the Community, European Communities Commission, ISEC/B12/80, 25 March 1980

The economic system of Albania in the 1970s: developments and problems

Michael Kaser and Adi Schnytzer

10.1 Conservative radicalism

Interrupting the revolutionary struggle, stopping the revolution halfway, is fatal to the destiny of socialism. (Report, 1968)

Ramiz Alia, a Secretary of the Central Committee of the Party of Labour of Albania (PLA), in presenting the report of the Politbureau to his Central Committee in 1968, employed a phrase which may be given a meaning other than that which he intended. It could be seen as reflecting the conservatism of the PLA in holding to the legacy of a dead foreign leader whom his Soviety countrymen have demoted. In 1960–1961 the PLA remained faithful to Stalin's codes when the communist parties of the USSR and of the rest of Eastern Europe were exposing his errors. From the early 1970s until the open break of July 1978 the PLA engaged in fierce debate with the Chinese Communist Party about the latter's perception of the international class struggle. Following the death of Mao Tse-Tung and the eventual emergence of policies under Hua Kuo-feng on research and the import of technology, scope for divergence clearly emerged over the Albanian watchword of 'self-reliance'. The long tenure of the General Secretary of the PLA, Enver Hoxha, appointed in March 1943 at the First Territorial Conference (*Konference e Vendit*) of the then newly founded Communist Party of Albania was, until his recent death, paralleled among governing communist parties only by Tito, whose general secretaryship of the Yugoslav Communist Party dated from October 1940. Their titles, and those of their parties, subsequently changed, but their tenure of the political leadership had been uninterrupted. Such continuity is by itself no evidence of a party's conservatism, but it does not suggest that new measures were brought in by new men[1].

There was, of course, no contradiction between maintenance of a Stalinist position and good relations with a Maoist state, for the rupture between the Chinese and Soviet Communist Parties left Peking, and with it Tirana, denouncing the revisions of Stalin's ideas and policies in Moscow. In terms of levels of development there was something in common between Stalin's USSR of 1930, Mao's China of 1949 and Hoxha's Albania of 1960 which argued for directive planning in which the goals were few and clear. When each embraced simple directive planning, national incomes per head were by no means equal – Albania ranked above China and below the USSR – but the magnitudes of their development task were comparable. The attainment of a substantial productive capacity to satisfy a wider range of requirements – among them a more sophisticated composition of consumer demand – called, on this line of thought, for the economic and political reassessments of a Khrushchev or a Teng Hsiao-P'ing. Hoxha, on the other hand, stresses, with some – though not full – justification, the continuity of his policies:

> Today, from thirty years' distance, we can see in all its magnificence and clarity the correct course adopted by the Party from the beginning . . . the correctness of the economic policy it worked out and implemented and the vitality of the principle of self-reliance. (Hoxha, 1974, p. 7)

Methods to which an attachment is long demonstrated may be no less revolutionary for being persistent and 'conservative radicalism' is not a misnomer when applied to Albania. One of the present authors has argued

> that the PLA leadership has maintained three major goals throughout its period in power and that the economic system today is the direct product of attempts to meet these goals subject to various constraints. These aims are to remain in power, to achieve the fastest possible rates of growth, particularly in industry, and to ensure that the PLA has the strongest possible direct influence on all economic outcomes. A major constraint on the first goal has been the PLA's determination to enter into external economic relations only when it has been convinced that its power to make its own decisions on economic matters would be unimpaired. (Kaser and Schnytzer, 1977, p. 584)

Both writers have described the turning point in economic organization that occurred in 1966 (Kaser and Schnytzer, 1977; Kaser, 1972 and 1975), but an understanding of that change in the context of Albanian continuity is essential to the analysis of 1970–1980 to which this volume is devoted.

10.2 Genesis of the present system

The Decision No. 15 of the Council of Ministers, dated 17–21 February 1966, 'On the Fundamental Principles of the Methodology of Planning' has never appeared in print, but was paraphrased in the journal of the Planning Commission by a staff member, A. Baçka, who stated that the Decision covered 'the general criteria and special instructions concerning the drafting of the plans for each activity, special plan indicators, the classification of indicators and preliminary plans at all levels, the path of planning and its relevant schedules (Baçka, 1966)[2]. The Decision was stated to be prefaced with four general points concerning the functioning of the Albanian economy. The first was that 'party spirit' (*partishmëria*) must apply in planning. Thus, it was argued, unless the party line was maintained throughout, the fundamental economic laws of socialism were in danger of violation[3], but with due account of domestic and international political circumstances. The second point reiterated Stalin's argument that the law of proportional development requires that the economy be planned. More specifically, it noted that the rapid development of the economy and its sectors was only possible if the interdependencies between the different sectors were fully understood: the implication was that a more thorough study of the economic system was required. The third point argued that workers must participate in planning since they were those who actually carried out the plans and could perceive 'hidden reserves'. Without the incorporation of these reserves into plans, no plan could be 'real, mobilizing and revolutionary'. Finally, the economic blockade against Albania by the Soviet Union required that 'in drafting plans it is necessary to start with the conditions of our country and to rely mainly on our own forces'.

In the first place the new methodology of annual planning ostensibly set the start squarely in the enterprise (or district council for small-scale activity). In June enterprises and in July Executive Committees of *rreth*, People's Councils, were instructed to submit a preliminary draft to the Ministry or relevant central body, which would coordinate them for their sphere of competence and send to the State Planning Commission in August a unified proposal. During September the State plan was to be drawn up and approved by the Council of Ministers who would ratify that plan, checking it against the Five-year Plan particularly for trade dependency and evolution of imports and construction project outlays. The second main feature of the Decision was to pare the number of targets ('indicators') in the State plan down to those considered essential for determining the principal trends of activity. The ratification of the Council of Ministers was required for only 77 industrial targets instead of 550, for 42 on agriculture instead of 320 and for 100 in investment and construction instead of 500. The third aspect was a corollary to the second in that the reduction in plan targets was effected by devolving authority to Ministries and the Executive Committees of district councils, and enterprises still had to elaborate plans, as detailed as before, dealing with particular issues.

The final change made by the Decision altered the basis of assessing enterprise performance, demoting the targets of global value of output in favour of those considered relevant to both quantity and quality. The incentives to achieve target performances were to rely more on moral imperatives than on material reward.

By 1966 several other socialist economies had already tried reform of the economic mechanism involving a decentralization of decisionmaking power within the policy, planning and administration hierarchy, and all – except

China – had decided that the solution lay in the direction of more freedom for enterprises in decisionmaking. Indeed, even in China that fraction of the Communist Party then in command of economic policy – later to be labelled by Mao Tse-tung as the 'capitalist roaders' – had come to the same conclusion. Outside Albania only the so-called 'socialist roaders' of the Chinese Communist Party maintained that the key lay in increased party activity at the local level.

The Decision made clear that Albanian economic ideology remained strictly Stalinist: it rejected any enlargement of the functions of the law of value and emphasized class struggle when the Soviet Union was enunciating the principle of the 'all-peoples' state'. Stalin had restricted 'commodity –money relations' to exchanges between the state sector and other entities (cooperatives, private persons or foreigners) and problems of information flow doubtless made difficult the compilation of rational scarcity prices.

The policy of politicizing the process of elaborating and fulfilling plans by propaganda and mass-mobilization, while fully consistent with Stalinism, was, on the other hand, adopted from China: an economic reform of the style being used in the USSR and elsewhere in Eastern Europe would have increased income differentials between managers and workers. An egalitarian line was manifest in a simultaneous pronouncement on the proposed social osmosis, that is, in a statement of the PLA Central Committee of February 1966 that many managers were volunteering to work in production. Shortly afterwards, on 4 March 1966, the Central Committee promulgated an 'Open Letter' (*Letër e hapur e komitetit gendror të PPSh*) which siezed upon the devolution of economic management to slim the civil service, cut higher salaries and integrate administrative with manual work.

The official *History of the PLA* recounts that 'within a record time the reorganisation was effected of the state and party organization in the centre and in the districts on a sounder revolutionary basis. The administrations of state enterprises and agricultural cooperatives were also reorganized and simplified. The number of ministries was reduced, unnecessary offices and branches were amalgamated. . . . The staff of the central state administration was reduced by half. About 15 000 senior staff went over to production, especially in the countryside; many, including leading officials of the Party and the state, were sent from the centre to the base. The simplification of the administrative organization was accompanied by a sharp reduction of correspondence, thus replacing red tape with living work with the people. Reductions and simplifications were made also in the system of accounting and planning. Numerous tasks in the fields of planning and fixing prices, concentrated in the Council of Ministers, were passed over to the ministries and the executive committee of the district councils, always in line with the principle of democratic centralism' (*History . . .*, 1971, pp. 568–569). Simultaneously with the expansion of productive manpower by the 15 000 transferred civil servants, a campaign began to involve all state employees in manual labour. According to the *History of the PLA* it was called 'a major movement to link mental work with physical work, with production. People engaged in mental work voluntarily went "en masse" to help the peasantry in agricultural tasks. In line with the decision of the Central Committee to reorganize on a sounder basis the direct participation in production of those engaged in mental work, all the employees of the administration, men and women engaged in scientific and cultural work, started to work in production, particularly in the countryside, one month every year; in addition, tens of thousands of young people from high and middle schools participated in voluntary mass actions of construction and production' (*History* . . ., 1971, pp. 568–569). There had been a precedent for involving all members of society in physical work, for in November 1958 the Central Committee of the PLA had required all state employees and members of the government, including Central Committee members, to spend a month each year in industry, agriculture, construction or communal works (*PPSh* . . ., 1972, p. 228). The 'Open Letter' of 1966 was thus a reflection of continuity in Albanian policy, and there has been since the Second World War – then on the Yugoslav model of 'youth brigades' – extensive unpaid projects, particularly by young people. But it was also expected that participation in physical labour would combat 'bureaucracy and petty-bourgeois tendencies' and improve relations between workers and state functionaries. The 'Open Letter' went beyond those practices to embrace the Chinese priority of 'redness' above 'expertness'.

Official encouragement of popular participation found further expression in September 1966 in the enactment of a new Labour Code, from which the key articles may be cited in full (*Përmbledhëse* . . ., 1971, pp. 89–100):

Article 3
In directing the economy of our country, our socialist state relies on the conscious participation of the workers and employees, and it supports the development of initiative and creative thinking in the working masses.

Article 6
The workers and employees have the right to organize in trade unions. The trade unions of Albania are social organizations of the masses. They unite the workers and employees on a voluntary basis, and operate as a school of Communist education under the leadership of the Party of Labour of Albania in accordance with its statutes.

Article 7
Organized into trade unions and conscious of the working class mission to build socialism, the workers and employees participate in directing the economy, in drafting and realising the state plans for economic development, in solving the problems of work and production, and in cultural activities and the increased well-being of the people.

The workers, employees and their trade union organizations fight to strengthen discipline in the state and at work, to continuously increase production, and to preserve and maintain state property. They control the administrative activity of enterprises, institutions, and organizations with the result that these groups function better, the people's government becomes stronger, and bureaucratic excesses may be avoided.

Article 9
The state organs take the position of the trade unions in the interpretation of the laws that regulate more important problems directly connected with work such as working conditions, wages, and social insurance for workers and employees.

Article 36
For work carried out outside normal work times, workers shall, in every case, be compensated only to the extent of 25 per cent above normal pay as fixed by the table of categories.

Article 48
The highest state organs and state inspection officers of the Health and Safety Division execute the provisions of this Code and its ordinance, resolutions and instructions dealing with problems of working conditions, working hours, vacation time, and safety and health measures. The rights and duties of the State Health and Safety Division are determined by decision of the Council of Ministers.

All reference from the previous Labour Code to penal sanctions against workers was eliminated and a determinedly revolutionary tone was struck, with the trade unions – permitted a consultative role by Article 9 or an educational function by Article 7 – removed from effective economic decisionmaking by Article 48. Article 36 is significant in discouraging overtime work as a means of increasing income in favour of voluntary overtime. The press frequently reports on workers who have finished their jobs for the day helping in public construction.

It was to the workers *en masse* rather than to their representatives that authority was purportedly passed, and in a speech of February 1967 Enver Hoxha bluntly told new directors or other senior or techical staff to stand before the workers' collective to give 'a frank account of himself so that the masses may pass judgement on him', and be warned that if he errs 'we will throw you overboard: bear well in mind that there is no one who can help you; the Party is ours, the regime is ours, it is we who are in power, it is the dictatorship of the proletariat which reigns. . . . The labouring mases should by all means and without hesitation strike down the director of this type or any other functionary of this kind, whoever and of whatever rank he may be in the Party or the government' (Hoxha, 1969, pp. 33–34 and 50–51).

The mechanism of 'workers' control' was soon formalized into commissions appointed at mass meetings, but these in turn allegedly succumbed to 'the efforts of some bureaucratic administrators to divert the workers' commissions into a bureaucratic framework under some sort of "Rules and Regulations". There was a tendency of some administrators to "institutionalize" and to keep the workers' control under "control"' (*Zëri i popullit*, 22 February 1968). The Party changed tack after a speech by Hoxha on 19 April 1968 entitled 'Working Class Control': workers' control commissions had 'become bureaucratic elements, eliminated grass-roots control and replaced the trade union committees, while administrative staff have entered them as heads of the commissions' (Hoxha, 1969, pp. 392 –393). Workers' control committees were henceforth elected on an *ad hoc* basis as particular problems arose and their membership was restricted to workers engaged directly in production. This microeconomic situation persisted until the late 1970s. Their current status is considered below.

Between 1966 and 1970 three other changes of significance for planning under the subsequent quinquennium were introduced. One was a ruthless pruning of the statistical service. The Party took the view that some four-fifths of enterprise statistical reporting was redundant. Not only were such 'excesses' proscribed and the duplication of returns forbidden (that is, a return could only be made to a single department), but it was even made illegal for an administration to demand more data than determined by the Directorate of Statistics (Jakubinim, 1967). The second was an attempt to reintroduce contractual relationships between enterprises (Ballco, 1968). The third was the transfer of bank control over investment outlays to the executive agencies, i.e. Ministries and district councils (*Bashkimi*, 25 July 1968), which was to have serious effects in the diffusion of capital spending.

10.3 The adaptations of 1970

The text of the governmental action which followed the recommendations of the Central Committee of the PLA in June 1970 went unpublished, like that of 1966. In brief, its import, as it emerged from scattered sources, was to undertake further devolution to local authorities and to foster more worker participation at the plan-drafting stage – each in the same direction as in 1966 – but also (in the words of the Central Committee Secretary Hysni Kapo in his report of June 1970) to 'eliminate routine and put management decisions on to a scientific basis' (Kapo, 1970)[4]. The latter might be interpreted as an acceptance of some 'expertness' in a spectrum previously oriented towards 'redness'. In the Chinese Communist Party a similar admixture of 'right' and 'left' factions was simultaneously being pursued in a policy of reconstructing the Party and the economy in the wake of the excesses of the Cultural Revolution. Chiang Ching, Mao's wife and the later leader of the 'Wang–

Chang–Chiang–Yao anti-Party clique' was noticeably much less prominent in her appearances and in the Chinese press.

The principal consequence of the decision further to develop planning powers was to double the number of state industrial enterprises under the management authority of district councils. There had been 40% of enterprises so run the previous year (accounting for 30% of gross output) – against a mere 20% in 1960 – but by the following year (1971), the number was 80% (Banja, Fullani and Papajorgji, 1973, p. 326). Because the biggest enterprises remained under the control of Ministries, the share of district-subordinated production less than doubled, but the proportion after the devolution was not officially revealed. The number of plan targets for industrial planning was further reduced, apparently from the 77 until 1970 to 36 (in 1973) (Hoxha, 1969, pp. 392–393), but without official details being given. The declared aim of the further devolution was to give workers more opportunity for voicing their observations, since they were more likely to influence local councils than Ministries in the capital city, and it was accompanied by a revision of annual plan scheduling which gave a more explicit role to *ad hoc* worker commissions. The initial elaboration of a plan draft for each enterprise was synchronized for Ministries and district councils to July of the year prior to the annual plan concerned (Xhuvani, Gurica, Sejko and Bollano, 1973, pp. 229–245).

Not only were 'planning commissions' of workers to be established at the enterprise, mainly composed of workers, but corresponding groups were to be set up at the brigade or workshop level. Each commission reviews the implications of the Five-Year Plan for its area of work, the record of the six months January–June and the prospects for the ensuing year and a half. The 'planning commission' draws up a set of proposals and it was a sign of a new institutionalization that the trade union and the local Party primary organization were drawn into the next phase of consultation. A 'project-plan' emerges from such discussion, ratified by a mass meeting in the enterprise and sent to the district council or Ministry for coordination and submission to the State Planning Commission. The national bodies finalize the draft and pass the eventual targets and plans down the same channels until they are presented to another mass meeting in each enterprise (Xhuvani *et al.*, 1973, pp. 229–245)[5].

The tension surrounding the decisionmaking of the enterprise director under the further formalization of 'workers' control' must have been increased by the measures of 1970. Moreover, those newly subordinated to district authorities must have had their normal channels of working relationships interrupted, both official and informal. This would have extended not only to issues of plan formulation and implementation but also to the negotiation of finance (under the 1968 transfer of authority from banks to superordinate bodies) and of supply and delivery contracts (under the same year's reiteration of these negotiations). The impact of 'workers' control' on his sphere of competence was marked by a shift of usage from *udhëheqje unike*, a literal translation of the Russian *edinonachalie*, one-man management, to *drejtim unik*, 'single guidance', a phrase modified by some such statement as 'under the leadership of the enterprise party organization'.

The operation of the rearranged practices during the 1971–1976 plan has been interpreted in the Press as enhancing the 'initiative' of enterprises in elaborating plans (*Zëri i popullit*, 1 April 1976). There is no documentary evidence that more decisionmaking power was, in fact, vested in the enterprise over 1970–1976[6], but the proximity of enterprises to district council offices, as against Ministries in Tirana, could have allowed informally some increased initiative to the director. Since the First Secretary of the district Party committee has an interest in the fulfilment of plans by local enterprises, there was patently more room for slack planning and the inclusion in the plan of what the enterprise management preferred. This consideration applies as much to enterprises located in Tirana and from 1966–1970 subordinated to its council.

One piece of evidence that planning was less taut in 1970–1976 was the complaint that the State Planning Commission's set of material balances were being drawn up incorrectly and not for all sectors of the economy (Bardhosi, 1976). To tauten plans in execution, the familiar practice of socialist emulation campaigns continued to be promoted. In the 1970–1976 period they ranged from competitions between brigades within an enterprise to between enterprises within a district. Typical prizes included some material rewards (such as a free package holiday) but invariably a 'moral' symbol, a red pennant.

The possible *de facto* decentralization of economic decisionmaking power from the hierarchy to the enterprises was hinted at by both Hoxha and Shehu at the Seventh PLA Congress, when they failed to single out excessive centralization or bureaucratization as problems for the Albanian planning system. These surprising omissions suggested that the PLA leadership might be contemplating a change to the system rules established by the 1970 reorganization. The first concrete change was reported in May 1977 in an article by the then newly appointed Chairman of the State Planning Commission, Petro Dode (*Rruga e partisë*, May 1977, pp. 5–19). He considered the crucial issues at Albania's level of development to be excessive stocks, low production efficiency and material and labour wastage. His solution lay in three directions. He first asserted that successful plan implementation could only be assured by a combination of workers' control, bank control and the work of the control agencies in the hierarchy. The former should, however, be set up with clearly defined tasks and 'experts' should be authorized to join the groups. Second, he argued for more financial discipline, condemning the tendency for enterprises to consider the financial plan as a mere supplement to the production plan: efficient planning demanded that both plans be seen as an organic unity.

Finally, Dode criticized central planning. Thus plans which are drawn up simply by adding a mark-up to the previous year's output figures inflated enterprise demands for inputs. The central planners must be fully informed, and this was clearly not the case when primary economic units had often reported 'global figures', upon which the ministries perform further 'roundings'. The only way, he argued, for society's needs to be fully met is for a realistic plan to be drawn up. But those 'needs' must be 'strictly in physical value quantity, assortment, variety and quality', and, further, not aggregated by price. In September 1977, Dode (*Probleme ekonomike*, July–September 1977, pp. 3–21) provided evidence of the recentralization when he noted decrees of the Council of Ministers designed to give ministries greater control over supply at the expense of local executive committees. Further, he accused his predecessor, Abdyl Këllezi – whose demise is discussed later in this chapter – of devolving decisions which were 'properly ministerial'.

The recent modifications to the planning system apparently culminated with the establishment of a new planning methodology in mid-1978. Although the methodology has not been made public, Dode later provided a summary of its contents (*Probleme ekonomike*, July–September 1978, pp. 9–34). It was based, in part, on the fact that Albania was no longer receiving aid from China and would need henceforth to develop on the basis of total self-reliance. This, it was hoped, would be facilitated by three changes in system rules. The first is pressure to bring enterprises up to the level of the 'best'. Prior to plan discussions with workers, the district executive committees must collaborate with enterprise planning bureaux to determine which were the best enterprises in each district; the planning departments of the ministries and the Central Planning Commission would determine the 'best' in each branch; and finally the evidence on 'leading experience' thus collected must be 'presented to the workers', so that they may discuss how – not whether – such experience might be incorporated into their own enterprise plan. Second, in the absence of foreign aid, the provision of new technology must be financed out of increases in labour productivity. Starting with the 1979 plan, all enterprises were to receive a special plan for research and technology while enterprises in those sectors providing capital goods would have a cooperation plan appended to their production plan. The aim of this latter measure was presumably to ensure the efficient production of high-priority goods. Third, the new methodology required strict economy in the use of materials and a tautening of work norms. Thus, whereas previously enterprises had submitted draft plans to the centre in aggregate form, henceforth, cost-reduction planning was to be carried out on the basis of cost per unit. However, the savings plan for input economies is not the only highly disaggregated document prepared by enterprises: according to the new methodology, all indicators will be sent to the central planners expressed in physical and financial units for all products.

The excursion into programming

In the early part of the five-year plan period – about 1970–1973 – prominence was given to the application of mathematical techniques to economic decisionmaking. At the macroeconomic level, the compilation of an input-output table was mooted (*Probleme ekonomike*, No. 1, 1973, pp. 55–76), but a change of policy seems to have intervened before its completion. At the microeconomic level a number of papers and at least one book (Kedi and Luci, 1970) advocated uses for testing the feasibility of the plan in terms of the targets given (on the model shown in the book which assumed that all the necessary inputs would be delivered on time and that the operations are linear). If the production plan is not feasible, the director can indicate this to the planners and seek appropriate adjustments.

The literature as published is cautious on the concept of duality. When linear programming is explained from a purely mathematical angle the existence of a dual problem for every primal is acknowledged, but economic interpretations of programmes invariably exclude mention of duality in favour of a statement of some such form as that economic problems can only be solved within the framework of the PLA interpretation of laws of political economy, and that the introduction of shadow costs, or other concepts of marginal economics, should be confined to capitalism or its revisionist form in the rest of Eastern Europe.

10.4 Incentives

Statistical data on the distribution of income in Albania are very scarce, but analysis is possible of the PLA's concept of the ideal income distribution and of the policy measures which have been taken to move society towards that ideal. For this purpose three income groups may be distinguished; workers, peasants and employees. An employee may be defined as any income earner who is neither a worker nor a peasant. Thus, managers, experts and members of the policy, planning and administrative hierarchy are all employees. In conceptual terms, workers and peasants are identified with physical work, while employees perform mental work. Workers and peasants are distinguished in the latest textbook of political economy in terms of their impact on the dictatorship of the proletariat: 'The social essence of the dictatorship of the proletariat is the alliance between the working class and the toiling peasantry, under the leadership of the working class (*Ekonomiâ . . .*, 1975, p. 16).

The only hint in Stalin's *Economic Problems of Socialism in the USSR* relating to the distribution of income in a socialist economy is his discussion of the distinctions between town and country, and mental and physical labour. Stalin argues that, under socialism, the 'antithesis' between these categories, which existed under capitalism, has been modified and has become a 'distortion'. In other words, although workers differ from managers they are no longer 'enemies, but comrades and friends'. Stalin expects the gap between mental and physical work to narrow as socialist emulation campaigns increase the educational level of the workers and thus make their work more 'mental' in content. For Stalin, the major difference between town (industry) and country (agriculture) lay in the fact that agricultural collectives are group-owned while industrial output is generated by state-owned enterprises. He provided no guidelines as to the way in which group may become state ownership, although direct nationalization was ruled out.

The PLA approach to the differentiation of mental and physical work agrees with Stalin on its ultimate disappearance, in that under full communism all members of society will engage in both physical and mental work, but diverges from his in stating that under socialism every employee must take part in physical production work for some period of each year. These measures have been discussed above, but of relevance for the distribution of income is the egalitarianism paramount in 1970–1980.

Until the mid-1960s pay scales were established on a basis similar to that employed elsewhere in Eastern Europe, the lack of suitably qualified experts in Albania giving rise to income differentials designed to induce people to gain higher qualifications. Remuneration was also higher for tasks which were judged to be physically difficult, so that not only were employees paid more highly than workers but there was also a significant spread in income between different branches. Thus in 1960 the average transport worker – the most highly paid sector – received 71% more pay than the average worker in the food industry – the lowest paid sector (Lika, 1964, p. 150). No figure relating the income of workers to that of employees has been published, although it seems reasonable to assume that the ratio was probably greater than 4:1.

The first sign that the PLA leadership was concerned that the ratio of employee income to worker income was too high came in the PLA Central Committee's 'Open Letter' of March 1966 to which reference has been made (p. 318). It argued that, although Party policy had always attempted to ensure that the increase in income of any particular individual was in line with increases in the earnings of the rest of the population, there were still anomalies in various categories of the pay scale. In particular, it is pointed out that the lack of experts had necessitated the provision of additional material incentives 'in this or that case'. In an attempt to eliminate the anomalies, and to ensure that everybody's standard of living was in accordance with the economic conditions of the time, it was announced that high salaries would be reduced (though the amount was unspecified).

The PLA's moves towards equalization of incomes initiated by the 'Open Letter' have been repeated twice since 1966. On 29 April 1967 a joint statement of the PLA Central Committee and the Council of Ministers announced that all wages over 1200 leks a month would be reduced, while the real income of workers would rise as a result of the abolition of all forms of income tax (*Information Bulletin . . .*, No. 3, 1967, pp. 10–12). Although the average wage of a worker in 1967 has not been published it is unlikely to have been much less than 550 leks – the value in 1975[7]. The statement also announced that, in response to the call for 'frugality and the spirit of sacrifice' made by the October 1965 Appeal, 'the workers of our country have widely aligned themselves with the revolutionary initiatives of the editors of the newspaper *Bashkimi* and have, of their own free will, expressed their willingness to renounce many supplementary and other incomes received over and above their basic salaries. Of major importance has been the initiative of the workers of some work centres in the Durrës district to turn over to the State all their state loan obligations, an initiative which has been supported by many other workers' (*Information Bulletin . . .*, No. 3, 1967, pp. 10–12).

On the other hand, the statement warned that placing moral incentives on a higher footing than material incentives did not imply 'petty-bourgeois tendencies of equalization and standardization' and indicated that good work would continue to receive good pay. It should be noted that, in Albania, payments above the basic wage were not insignificant. Thus, in 1961 supplementary payments in one Shkodër enterprise accounted for 34% of the wage fund, while in the 'Stalin' textile combine – one of the largest enterprises in the country – the relevant figure was 22% (Lika, 1964, p. 159). It has been stated that as a consequence of the 1967 measures the ratio of an enterprise director's salary to that of a typist was reduced to 2.5:1 (Sejko *et al.*, 1975, p. 279). The ratio was the same between the average wages of workers and the highest salaries of employees.

The second sudden change in the distribution of income between workers and employees took place on 1 April 1976 when the Council of Ministers and the PLA Central Committee issued a joint Decision. The lower limit on higher salaries was reduced from 1200 leks to 900 leks and all salaries above this level were to be cut by between 4 and 25% – presumably on a sliding scale. Lower and middle wages would not be affected, 'save in certain cases to preserve the necessary proportions'.

In addition to the pay cuts, it was announced that writers would no longer receive payments for their publications, that there would be a reduction in the bonuses paid for scientific titles and degrees and that the wages of state farm workers would be increased. Finally, it was decided that henceforth all specialists would be paid according to their area of specialization rather than the district or enterprise in which they worked.

The Decision reduced the ratio between the nominal wage of an average worker and the highest salaries of employees to 2:1, almost certainly the lowest in Eastern Europe. It seems reasonable to suggest that the distribution of income between employees and workers has always been relatively equal: a ratio of about 4:1 for the pre-1966 period was quite a narrow spread. The PLA has moreover diminished income differentials between town and country by regularly increasing grain procurement prices, reducing the retail price of industrial goods for agricultural use and altering the pattern of budgetary expenditure on services in favour of the agricultural sector. This is partially reflected in the 20.5% increase in per capita real income of the peasantry in the 1971–1975 period as against the 8.7% of workers and employees.

Prior to 1966, a policy of encouraging 'expertise' and a general neglect of the countryside led to the generation of distribution of income favourable to employees. On the other hand, it is unlikely that the real income of any one of the three groups actually fell. However, since 1966 there has been a considerable change in the shifts in real income. First, there can be little doubt that the real income of employees has fallen over the period 1966–1976. Second, although there are no figures for the 1966–1970 period, it seems clear that the real income of peasants has grown more rapidly than that of workers and employees combined and probably at a faster rate than the real income of workers. Thus, in terms of Stalin's prescriptions, there is no doubt that the distinctions between, on the one hand, town and country and, on the other, physical and mental work are being reduced.

So far as workers are concerned, the period since 1970 has seen some relaxation of the priority of moral over material incentives. On 27 December 1969 the Ninth Plenum of the Central Committee of the PLA issued a decision 'On the Work of the Organizations of the Party and of the Masses, of the Economic and State Organs to Further Increase Productivity and Enforce Proletarian Discipline at Work' (*Information Bulletin* . . ., No. 1, 1970, pp. 4–18). It complained that 'the non-fulfilment of the average work productivity in certain branches and [the slowdown of] the rate of production in general', could be partly attributed to the inadequacy of 'explaining the orientations and directives of the Party regarding the socialist organization of work, in acquainting the broad masses of workers with the objective economic laws governing them as well as with the consequences resulting from their correct or incorrect application'. The criticism implies both that the incentives offered to workers had been insufficient – or of the wrong kind – to induce them to tauten plans and that the superintending agencies which determine whether an enterprise has met the requirements for the receipt of bonuses from the Enterprise Fund, may have disregarded the 1967 regulations according equal weight to the fulfilment of production, cost-reduction and profit plans in the distribution of bonuses (*Përmbledhëse* . . ., 1971, pp. 426–427). The emphasis on plan fulfilment of any sort would nevertheless have induced workers to seek, in the same way as enterprise directors had previously done, the 'easiest' plan and to overfulfil it by a sufficiently small margin to prevent the imposition, from above, of a hard plan in the next period. Indeed, it is difficult to envisage any material incentive scheme which would have encouraged workers to put pressure on management if that pressure was going to lead to a reduction in leisure time without a compensating increase in wages. But the moral incentives implied by the ideological campaigns also failed, making reasonable the conclusion that, during the 1966–1970 five-year plan, capital productivity fell partly as a result of worker dissatisfaction with the PLA's continued efforts to entrench disinterested idealism on the shop floor.

In the light of the above arguments, the slight upswing in capital productivity during the subsequent five-year plan – particularly in the period 1971–1973 – might be thought to be partly attributable to some change in motivation policy implied by the new rules of 1970. But one sign of labour dissatisfaction with the trade-off persisted beyond 1970 and the only change in the regulations which was likely to contribute positively to productivity growth was the establishment of a special fund to be used in the implementation of workers' innovatory suggestions (*Information Bulletin . . .*, No. 3, 1970, p. 36). Of greater significance in this plan period was the reimposition of bank control over investments (Hoxha, 1976, p. 70) and the diminution of scope for enterprise choice among targets implicit in the reduction in the number of plan indicators.

On balance, it is difficult to determine whether PLA policy regarding the motivation of workers has had a positive or negative impact on the industrialization drive. Whereas the insistence upon continually increasing the workers' standard of living has probably contributed to popular support for the regime and its goals, it appears that PLA efforts to inculcate the population with its political doctrines may have had an unanticipated effect on labour productivity. Political socialization is, of course, a long-term process, but it is questionable how long it could survive a real decline in the workers' standard of living.

As Chinese aid has been suspended in the five-year plan 1976–1980 both consumption and accumulation will have been affected. To cite one Western press report among many, 'the loss of Chinese aid has already seriously affected the country's economy. Most consumer goods, including basic foodstuffs, are reported to be in short supply and major industrial projects have been abandoned' (Lederer, 1977). The formal announcement that the Chinese had decided to cease all aid, credits and technical assistance to Albania appeared in *Zëri i popullit* on 13 July 1978. It is not surprising that most subsequent discussion of the matter in the Albanian press has suggested that the Chinese presence had been detrimental to the Albanian economy[8].

One of the authors has derived from scattered Albanian and partner documentation that Chinese assistance, converted to US dollars at 1970 prices, was $227 million in the 1966–1970 plan period and $330 million in 1971–1975 (Kaser, 1977, p. 1335), but that in 1975 Albania received only half as much imports from China as it did in 1974 while selling about one-third more to China than the previous year (Kaser, 1977, p. 1340). The estimates are hazardous, because Albania has published no systematic trade returns since those for 1964 and China maintains complete secrecy. But if a further risky computation can be cited, Chinese aid in 1970 (still in 1970 prices in dollars) added 8% to Albanian gross territorial product to yield a gross domestic product of $693 million (Kaser and Schnytzer, 1977, p. 567). In that year gross fixed investment (at 1970 domestic prices in leks and hence not strictly comparable with price ratios ruling in foreign trade) was 25% of GDP and household consumption 54% (Kaser and Schnytzer, 1977, p. 580). If those proportions continued to rule in 1977, the loss of up to 8% of GDP cannot but have been serious.

10.5 Agricultural organization

Agriculture on official Albanian statistics was producing more than one third of net material product in 1970; the authors' estimate is 27% of gross territorial product (i.e. before inclusion of aid to make up to GDP), with 33% from industry and handicrafts, 8% from construction and 26% from 'productive' and 14% from 'non-productive' services (Kaser and Schnytzer, 1977, p. 581). The supply of produce from the land is hence still of considerable importance to the Albanian standard of living and stands behind the fluctuations of Chinese aid[9]. It is also highly relevant that, following an arduous and costly opening of new arable areas (above all in the uplands), self-sufficiency in grain was first achieved in 1976 and has been maintained in every year since that time.

The organization of farming is hence of crucial importance and the plan period 1971–1975 witnessed a new form of agricultural unit, the 'higher-type agricultural cooperative', first established in 1971 (Gazeta zyrzare, No. 8, 1971), and occupying 23% of arable land by 1976 (Hoxha, 1976, p. 55).

A textbook published in 1971 emphasized that while state farms operate under the authority of the director (as adapted to workers control), the cooperative farm is based on 'internal cooperativist democracy' (Kallapodhi, Dumani and Kote, 1971, pp. 520–523). An ordinary cooperative – and all farmland outside state ownership had been collectivized by 1966 – distributes its 'divisible' profits as a 'labour-day' dividend either in cash or kind. Members of cooperatives have the right to a private plot, the size of which has been reduced since collectivization was completed[10]. Monthly advances on the eventual annual dividend were introduced in 1971, aligning the Albanian collective with similar farms elsewhere in Eastern Europe.

But the 'higher-type agricultural cooperative' has the state as a partner and, when all cooperatives have become of this type, it will surely absorb both cooperative property and the private plot. At present, members of higher-type cooperatives retain their plots, and the condition for approved transition from ordinary to higher-type status is 'economic strength'. No higher-type cooperatives have as yet been absorbed into state farms, but, in launching the scheme in 1971, Enver Hoxha declared that 'life, the revolutionary practice of our socialist construction, will show us later the other stages through which this process will have to pass. It will indicate the measures that should be taken gradually to eliminate those differences which exist today between these two forms of socialist property' (Hoxha, 1971, p. 84). The new type of farm has a state shareholding to the extent of government investment finance (which replaces the repayable bank credit, as provided for ordinary cooperative farms) and has the exclusive use of a state-owned machine-tractor station (whereas ordinary cooperatives take their turn with neighbouring farms in MTS services). Finally, members of the higher-type cooperative are paid wages – on a piece-rate 'normed' basis – as to 90% of the planned wage bill; the residual 10% is settled at the end of the year only if the farm's plan has been fulfilled (Dodbiba, 1974)[11].

10.6 Sharp disputes on economic policy, 1974–1976

The three years 1974–1976 were marked by the sharpest divisions on economic policy since those surrounding the break with the USSR and the intimate alignment with China in 1960–1961. As then, the only sign in the official press that fundamental issues of policy had been in dispute were the dismissal, arrest, trial and (in some cases) capital punishment of those PLA and government leaders who had opposed the policies of Hoxha, Shehu and Kapo. The losers in the clash over the Sino–Soviet dispute included Liri Belishova, a Politbureau member, and Koço Tashko, a Central Committee member, for a pro-Soviet stance, whose trial was in May 1961, and Teme Sejko, Rear-Admiral, and Tahir Demi, an Albanian delegate to the CMEA, for participation in a 'Greek–Yugoslav–United States' plot, tried the same month (Pano, 1968, pp. 137–148; Griffith, 1963; Ash, 1975; Logoreci, 1976; Marmallaku, 1975).

The losers in the field of economic policy in 1974–1976 were the holders of the three principal economic ministries, Abdyl Këllezi, Chairman of the State Planning Commission, Koço Theodhosi, Minister of Industry and Mining, and Kiço Ngjela, Minister of Trade. So clean a sweep of the economic leadership – all were stated to have been dismissed in October 1975 – implied a fundamental divergence of view within the Central Committee of the PLA; the subsequent dismissal of the Minister of Agriculture, Piro Dodbiba (and, simultaneously the Minister of Education), the sole remaining economic portfolio, early the following year may not have been associated with that dispute. Its background was the scaling-down of Chinese aid in and the general underfulfilment of the 1971–1975 five-year plan, in contrast to the overfulfilment of the 1966–1970 plan.

Although more ambitious in its targets than the previous plan, the 1966–1970 plan called for an increase of only between 50% and 54% in global industrial production, representing an average annual rate of growth of around 8.7% (Shehu, 1971, p. 9). It was anticipated that industrial producers' goods (group A) production would increase at an average annual rate of 10.8% as against a rate of 6.2% for industrial consumers' goods (group B). In the event, the plan targets were significantly exceeded, global industrial production in 1970 being 83% greater than the value recorded for 1965, while group A production rose at an average rate of 15.8% and that of group B by an average 9.5% per annum (Shehu, 1971, pp. 17–18). As a result, the share of producers' goods in global industrial production rose from 26% in 1965 to 38.4% in 1970, the largest increase registered in any five years of Albanian history. The plan had not been fulfilled without tensions. The introduction of workers' control and the relegation of managerial staff must have posed problems, and labour productivity targets were not met. Hoxha provided no data, but observed at the PLA's Sixth Congress that 'as a consequence of the slow rate of increase of the productivity of labour, the increase of industrial production was due almost entirely to increasing the number of workers above the planned limit. This caused a disproportion between the increase of production and the wages fund' (Hoxha, 1971, p. 91). In fact, contrary to Hoxha's assertion, it was the increase in the labour force necessary to man the new industrial projects completed during the plan period which led to a slow increase in labour productivity. While the capital–labour ratio rose by 32 337 leks per man over 1966–1970, global industrial product per man increased by only 16 192 leks over the same period. Paradoxically, this marked decrease in capacity utilization was probably caused by the same factor which led to the high rates of growth of industrial output: whereas the Albanian balance of payments deficit on current account had been 670 million leks over the 1961–1965 period, the increase to 1139 million leks over the next five years provided Albanian industry with an increase in productive capacity for which the labour force was too small and insufficiently skilled to exploit fully.

As has already been stated, the volume of Chinese development assistance was greater in the 1971–1975 plan, which formulated higher targets than had the 1966–1970 plan, but more modest than had actually been achieved.

The Sixth Congress of the PLA approved a target of around 11.6 billion leks for the value of global industrial production in 1975, an increase of 61–66% over 1970; the increase in group A production was to be 78–83% while consumer goods production would rise by 40–44% (Shehu, 1971, pp. 52–62). Statistics published in 1974 suggest that progress was on lines which would allow these goals to be met. At 9608 million leks, global industrial production in 1973 (*30 vjet . . .*, 1974, p. 55) was slightly higher than the 9533 million leks which would have been achieved had the average annual rate of 10.3%, foreshadowed in the plan, been maintained over the 1971–1973 period. Further, the increase in output was in approximate accordance with the planned split between group A and group B production, the former having increased by 40% over 1970 and the latter by 29% (*30 vjet* . . ., pp. 55–56).

However, from the beginning of 1974 it was clear that the Albanian authorities felt that the industrial output targets of the fifth five-year plan were beyond their grasp. The 1974 annual plan called for an increase of 8% in global industrial production (*Probleme ekonomike*, No. 1, 1974, p. 8), while the rate achieved was 7.3% (*Probleme ekonomike*, No. 1, 1975, p. 4). The 1975 plan was even more pessimistic, calling for an increase of only 4.4% over the 1974 total (*Probleme ekonomike*, No. 1, 1975, p. 112). In the event, even this modest target was not reached, global industrial output increasing by only 4% over the year (*Probleme ekonomike*, No. 1, 1976, p. 5).

Thus, for the five-year plan period as a whole, global industrial production had risen by 50% according to Mehmet Shehu's report to the Seventh Congress of the PLA (*Rruga e partisë*, No. 12, 1976, p. 11), while the annual data suggested an increase of 51%. Given the degree of rounding off involved in the preparation of the data for publication this discrepacy is not significant. The changing structure of production does, however, represent an important problem, for whereas the production of industrial consumer goods rose by 45% and thus exceeded the plan target of a 40–44% increase, the value of group A production was only 57% greater than it had been in 1970 (against 78–83% planned). Thus over the last two years of the plan period, 1974 and 1975, the rate of growth of group B production exceeded that of group A, rates for the period having been 12.4% and 12.1% respectively.

A distinct change in the nature of Albania's industrial development at some stage in 1973 or 1974 is also indicated by the increase in labour productivity and the capital–labour ratio registered by Albanian industry during the fifth five-year plan. Between 1970 and 1973 the capital–labour ratio rose by 17.4% against an increase of 18.1% in labour productivity. In other words, industrial capital productivity had risen for the first time. Although the increase was less than 1%, the fact that the decrease experienced during the 1966–1970 plan was halted suggests that some of the labour misallocation problems besetting the earlier period had been solved. Further, the increase in experts and skilled workers forthcoming over time could only contribute positively to production efficiency.

In the 1974–1975 period, capital productivity again fell, industrial labour productivity rising by only 2.4% as against a 6.5% increase in the capital–labour ratio. Finally, it should be noted that, whereas the share of heavy industrial output in the total rose between 1970 and 1973, its share may have fallen between 1973 and 1975. This is suggested by the increase in the share of food and consumer manufactures, from 48.4% in 1973 to 49.3% in 1975 (*Rruga e partisë*, No. 12, 1976, p. 15); the share had been 51.4% in 1970 (*30 vjet . . .*, 1974, p. 65).

The absence of any official Albanian analysis of the change in industrial development experienced halfway through the fifth five-year plan – its existence is not even acknowledged – renders an explanation difficult. However, on the basis of the available evidence some tentative conclusions are possible. In the first place, one of the present writers has deduced that there may have been a reduction in Chinese aid in 1975 (Kaser, 1977, p. 1329). If this were the case, the downward revision in the five-year plan implied by the low 1974 target for global industrial production may be explained by the PLA's possible anticipation of the reduction in aid. Shehu's statement at the Seventh congress of the PLA that the failure of the industrial plan was in part due to a failure to complete the construction of important projects on time is consistent with this line of argument (Shehu, 1976, p. 15).

To explain the leadership disputes, the economic outcomes of the 1974–1975 period must be seen in terms of the PLA development strategy. On the basis of the PLA's reaction to the reduction in Soviet aid in 1961 it might have been predicted that resources would have been reallocated away from other sectors so that heavy industry would have a greater opportunity to fulfil its plans, the lack of foreign capital notwithstanding. On the other hand, the success of the light and food industries, coupled with the relatively modest increase in the industrial labour force between 1973 and 1975, suggests that a decisive change in industrial development policy took place at some time in 1973. Some evidence of this change is provided by statistics on Albania's trade with the developed capitalist economies over the relevant period (*Table 10.1*).

The doubling of turnover in the second quarter of 1974 and the return to 1973 levels in the first quarter of 1976 (even below in volume terms) suggests

Table 10.1 *Albanian trade with developed capitalist partners (millions of dollars)*

		Imports (fob)	Exports (cif)			Imports (fob)	Exports (cif)
1973	I	7	6	1965	I	26	15
	II	12	6		II	30	18
	III	15	7		III	15	19
	IV	10	12		IV	15	20
1974	I	12	9	1976	I	9	10
	II	26	15		II	11	14
	III	22	19		III	10	8

Source: M.C. Kaser, 'Trade and Aid in the Albanian Economy', in Joint Economic Committee, US Congress, *East European Economies post-Helsinki*. Washington DC, 1977, p. 1329.

a modification of Albania's trade policy. Further, although the planned increases in exports in 1973 and 1974 were only 5.4% and 11% respectively, the value of exports actually rose by 15% in 1973 and by 17% in 1974 (*Probleme ekonomike*, No. 1, 1973, p. 137; No. 1, 1974, pp. 6 and 8; No. 1, 1975, p. 6). Thus if there was a reduction in the level of capital imports from China in the 1974–1975 period, the PLA clearly responded with an export drive to the developed capitalist economies designed, possibly, to pay for capital imports. On the domestic front, it was evidently decided that other sectors should not be permitted to suffer losses from reallocations to heavy industry.

That the policy shift was only temporary was made clear when the three ministers already listed were dismissed at some time towards the end of 1975 – that is, when Albania's trade turnover with the West was beginning to drop. A possible reason for these dismissals emerges if it is assumed that there were sharp differences in the PLA leadership over the nature of the response to an aid reduction in 1973. It is likely, given the consistent attempts to maintain Stalinist development policies since the very early days of the PLA's rule, that some members of the leadership would have argued for a continuation of the current policy even in the face of anticipated difficulties. In the event, this faction was overruled and, although an 8% planned increase in global industrial production in 1974 represented a setback to the five-year plan, the deficit might still have been recovered if the switch in foreign trade yielded the desired capital imports to make the recovery possible.

The continued success of light industry in 1974 and the sharp increase in exports suggests that the low target for industrial production in 1975 was due either to an inability to obtain the desired capital imports from the West or to a further reduction in Chinese aid, which had not been anticipated in 1973. As has already been mentioned in section 10.6, the latter explanation is more plausible, it being calculated that China provided Albania with $75 million credit in 1974 while Albania ran a surplus of $25 million with China in 1975. Whatever the reason, the fifth five-year plan could no longer be met, the policy of temporary 'moderation' had failed and its advocates suffered the political consequences.

The accusations levelled at the dismissed ministers at the PLA's Seventh Congress in 1976 are not inconsistent with the above hypothesis. Thus Shehu accused the former Chairman of the State Planning Commission, the former Minister of Industry and Mining 'and others in the economic sector' of sabotaging the oil industry (Shehu, 1976, p. 15), while Hoxha, in his report, blamed those purged for the failure to complete certain construction projects as well as shortfalls in the (five-year) plans of the oil, chromium, copper, coal, bread grain and industrial crop sectors. Referring to the oil industry, Hoxha charged the two ministers with using 'refined methods to disorient exploration' and mismanage the industry, with preventing the exploitation of new sources of oil and gas, and with using 'barbaric' methods for the exploitation of existing wells (Hoxha, 1976, p. 39).

As has already been noted, the break with China was not explained in any official statement until mid-1977, and even then no explicit reference was made to prospects of Chinese aid. The significance and gradual growth of that aid as a ratio to gross investment is shown in *Table 10.2*.

Table 10.2 *Ratio of foreign aid to gross investment*

Plan period	1951–1955	1956–1960	1961–1965	1966–1970	1971–1975
	0.23	0.17	0.11	0.12	0.15

Source: A. Schnytzer, Economic Planning and Industrial Development in the People's Republic of Albania. Unpublished doctoral thesis, Oxford University, 1977, Appendix C.

A 1977 article (*Zëri i popullit*, 7 July 1977) criticized various of the theories underlying China's foreign policy, although China was not mentioned by name. In particular, it was argued that the United States and the Soviet Union were equally dangerous superpowers and that the Third World could not be considered as a shield to their power. Shortly afterwards the Chinese press attacked what it called 'splitism' in Albania. From the viewpoint of economic aid there was a significant report broadcast by Radio Tirana on 26 July, which contended that the Albanian government had asked the Soviet government for credits to assist in the construction of the metallurgy complex at Elbasan in 1960 and that they had been refused. The likely validity of this contention is supported by the fact that Romania's request to the USSR for a steel plant at Galaţi was also turned down at the same time (Kaser, 1967, p. 106). Moreover, the Czech government had earlier said that it could supply all of Albania's steel requirements if it received Albanian iron–nickel ores (*Zëri i popullit*, 30 April 1977). The report went on to add that the Albanians were thus forced to build the complex relying on their own resources and that this had been successfully achieved up to now. That the project could not have been undertaken without Chinese aid was not mentioned: in fact, the Chinese were not thanked for aid at all, nor, as already mentioned, in the November speeches of that year by Shehu and Kapo. Albania may be forced to embark on a policy of real 'self-reliance', with all that this implies for the already low level of current consumption in the country.

If the PLA leadership decides that Albania should maintain a balance of foreign trade it is possible that a large part of that trade will be with the developed capitalist economies of Western Europe. The agreement signed between the Albanian and Greek governments to open a Tirana–Athens air link may have been a first step in this direction. However, should Albania's pattern of trade alter in this direction and – given that China is no longer considered to be a socialist state by the PLA – any future Albanian requirement for foreign credit would pose constitutional problems for the PLA owing to the barring of such loans by the constitution.

It has already been argued that the dismissal of the three economic ministers Këllezi, Theodhosi and Ngjela in the autumn of 1975 may have been related to a dispute over the policy implications of a reduction in Chinese aid. It should be noted, however, that these were not the only important purges to take place in Albania during the period of the fifth five-year plan, and in a broader context the 1975 dismissals may be viewed as part of a continuing struggle by Hoxha to maintain the ideological purity of the Albanian Revolution. In this section the power struggle within the PLA leadership is linked with the gradual deterioration of the relations between Albania and China via the perceived requirements of ideological purity. To the extent that Albanian Stalinism is an all-pervasive doctrine, the implications of these political issues for economic policy have been considerable.

On the domestic front the first sector to feel the weight of a new ideological campaign was that of culture. In his report to the Fourth Plenum of the Central Committee of the PLA on 26 June 1973 Hoxha noted that the problems faced in the recent past by the Party in connection with 'the struggle against the influences of alien bourgeois and revisionist ideology . . . in particular under the present conditions of the hostile imperialist and revisionist encirclement of our country' (Hoxha, 1974, p. 309) had become acute. The most damaging element of alien ideology was 'liberalism'. This had been particularly marked in the arts: 'The various contradictions and the battle the Party and people wage against negative phenomena, obstacles and difficulties have been portrayed not from the position of the Party but from the opposing position. Thus in a number of cases the essence of the struggle against bureaucratism is wrongly presented as stifled by bureaucracy, and the working masses as entirely powerless to fight the bureaucrats. . . . In the name of the "new", the present is denied and the struggle between the old and the new is presented as an inevitable struggle between generations. Another consequence of alien influence is a departure from great social problems, and excessive treatment of insignificant intimate themes, the theme of the loneliness of man, the transformation of people into snails, figtrees and other absurdities, phenomena which are connected with the existence of existentialist philosophy' (Hoxha, 1974, p. 323).

Nor was music free from alien liberalism. Thus Hoxha noted that in Albanian light music, 'especially in rhythmic music, where the clear melodic line has been deformed, and the way opened to unrestrained beat . . . all our public opinion indignantly rejected that vulgar music, those worthless songs and the snobbish stage presentation at [a recent] festival' (Hoxha, 1974, p. 324).

The PLA attempted to solve these problems by dismissing those in the leadership who were allegedly to blame. Thus the president of the Writers' and Artists' Union, Dhimiter Shuteriqi, the Chairman of the People's Assembly and PLA Propaganda Secretary Fadil Paçrami and Todi Lubonja, the Director of the Albanian broadcasting service were all dismissed and expelled from the party.

Although no officials in the economic sector appear to have been purged at this time, Hoxha made it clear that 'a kind of liberalism of a more or less voluntary and subjective character' (Hoxha, 1974, p. 368) could be observed in the administration of the economy. He argued that state organs paid insufficient attention to the requirements of economic 'laws', in particular those concerning labour productivity.

> As a consequence, in a number of enterprises, districts and ministries there appeared signs of inflating plans for manpower, considering it a normal thing to maintain and request extra workers above the plans. Hence another negative phenomenon appeared: while the wage fund was exceeded, the production plan in certain enterprises was not fulfilled, or not fulfilled properly, thus causing inequality between the increase in purchasing power and the fund of goods required to cover it. The failure to pay sufficient attention to the requirements of economic laws accounts for the weakening of the self-supporting economic enterprises, for inefficient control over the use of the basic funds and means of circulation, and inadequate concern taken to calculate in detail the economic profitability of every product, and of every expenditure and investment, following the idea 'let us first produce, then the other things will fall into place'. The underestimation of the economic levers accounts for the temporary lifting and the weakening of control over the wage fund, and over-investment. (Hoxha, 1974, pp. 368–9)

Hoxha also stressed the need for rigid economy in the use of raw materials and criticized Theodhosi directly:

> Who gave the Ministry of Industry and Mining the right in 1972 to use, without the approval of the government, more crude oil for its enterprises than planned for, at a time when many enterprises of other departments were not supplied with their planned quotas? These activities and practices are not only a flagrant violation of the discipline of the plan and of the requirements of economic laws, but they also indicate a liberal interpretation of the internal and external political and economic situation under which we live and strive to build socialism. (Hoxha, 1974, p. 372)

The warning had been issued but apparently went unheeded, for when it was announced at the PLA Seventh Congress in November 1976 that Theodhosi had been dismissed, Shehu accused the former minister and others, as already noted above, of sabotaging the oil industry.

By 1974 the purges had spread to the armed forces. In October of that year Beqir Balluku, who had been Minister of Defence since 1953, was expelled from the government and the PLA Politbureau and, apparently, tried for unspecified crimes and executed. Thus, the years of the 1971–1975 Five-Year Plan had seen a significant change in the composition of the PLA leadership and a continued determination on the part of Hoxha to maintain the implementation of the Stalinist development strategy in all sectors.

Albanian foreign policy since 1970 has also reflected Hoxha's concern for doctrinal purity, particularly in the sphere of Sino–Albanian relations. Addressing the Sixth Party Congress in November 1971 Hoxha argued that a fierce struggle should be waged against both imperialist superpowers, the Soviet Union and the United States. Further, with a possible sideways glance at the Chinese, he noted with apparent concern that not all 'Marxist–Leninists' were being sufficiently resolute against the 'common enemy'. There seems little doubt that the emphasis placed on the problem of imperialism was related to Albanian concern over a possible Chinese rapproachement with the United States. Hoxha expressed his view unambiguously: 'Since American imperialism and revisionist imperialism are represented by the two imperialist super-powers and since they both support a counterrevolutionary strategy it is impossible for the people's struggle against them not to be channelled into a single current. It is not possible to use one imperialism in order to oppose the other' (Hoxha, 1971, pp. 20–29). In 1972 differences of opinion between China and Albania on such issues as the consolidation of the European Common Market, the Malta crisis, West Germany's *Ostpolitik* and Chancellor Brandt's re-election became evident. Whereas the Chinese government appeared to have embarked on a course of *Realpolitik*, and for the PLA ideological considerations remained paramount. Indeed, by the end of that year Hoxha felt able to suggest that Albania was leading the world revolution:

The party teaches the people to be vigilant in the face of any danger whatever which may come from abroad, be it danger of armed aggression or danger of loss of freedom and independence that may come through economic enslavement to the imperialist metropoles, with US imperialism at the head, and social-imperialist metropoles with Soviet revisionism at the head. In order to cope with the two dangers, the Albanian people and their party must be armed and must make no concessions at all. We stand for peaceful coexistence, on the known principles of the great Lenin, allowing nobody and at no time whatsoever to violate our legitimate rights. Someone may say smiling: 'But, would the imperialist powers be afraid enough of socialist Albania to act against her' We respond to him saying that the Albanian people are not afraid of them. Imperialism and social imperialism are afraid of the people's revolution and Marx's ideas, which inspire and lead them onward. Socialist Albania is at the head of this proletarian revolution and she is not alone. Her friends and faithful comrades are the peoples of the world; it is the world proletariat which is oppressed and pressured by imperialism and social imperialism in the most barbarous way (*Zeri i popullit*, 29 November 1972).

From the viewpoint of the economy the dangers inherent in a rift with China have already been indicated. The really interesting question – which, due to insufficient evidence, cannot as yet be fully answered – is whether Albania's ideological intransigence has been caused by dissatisfaction with China as an aid donor or whether the reverse is true, namely, that a reduction in aid from China has resulted from genuine ideological commitment on the part of the PLA leadership. It is possible to make a case for both hypotheses. Thus while the aid provided by China appears to have been fully in accordance with a policy stressing the rapid development of heavy industry, the geographic problems involved in commodity transport between China and Albania have probably led to difficulties in meeting project deadlines.

Shehu's statement at the Seventh Congress of the PLA that the failure of the 1971–1975 industrial plan was in part due to a failure to complete the construction of important projects on time (*Rruga e partisë*, No. 12, 1976, p. 15) is consistent with this line of argument. It is also clear that there were differences of opinion over the importance of granting aid to Albania within the Chinese leadership[12]. Given the frequent changes in influence within the Chinese government between the 'moderates' and the so-called 'Gang of Four', it would hardly be surprising if China had proved to be a rather unstable aid donor.

On the other hand, the PLA leadership by its actions over the past thirty years has indicated that it is quite willing to take economic risks where matters of ideology are concerned. The best example of this type of behaviour is, of course, the 1961 Albano–Soviet split. In any event, it is most likely that Chinese instability as an aid donor and Hoxha's political principles both contributed to the break of July 1978.

Notes

1. 'Measures, and not men, is the common cant of affected moderation' (*Letters of Junius, 1769–1772*).
2. An editorial in *Ekonomia popullore* (No. 1, 1966) had written that 'the new duties . . . demand a radical improvement in the management of the national economy as a whole and its planning in particular'.
3. The term 'fundamental economic laws of socialism' is, of course, Stalin's.
4. The Ninth Plenum in late 1969 had foreshadowed this turn towards a 'scientific content' for planning (*Information Bulletin . . .*, No. 1, 1970).
5. The full table of indicators is reproduced in translation in Kaser and Schnytzer (1977).
6. See the list of targets referred to in note 5.
7. This is based on Schnytzer's discussions in Albania in July 1975.
8. For an analysis of the claims on both sides as to the extent of the aid provided and the allegations about its withdrawal see Kaser (1979; *Comecom Reports*, Vol. 1, Nos 1, 2).
9. Aid from non-socialist countries need not be considered in the light of the prohibition in the 1976 Constitution of credits from 'bourgeois and revisionist capitalist monopolies and states'.

10. On each occasion some offsetting compensation has been offered – increases in procurement prices (which now require substantial subsidies), cuts in the prices of goods commonly bought by farmers and, lately, payments of pensions for invalidity and old age. *Albania Today* (No. 1, 1976, p. 20) wrote of 'hundreds of millions' of leks as farm subsidies in 1970–1975.

11. Dodbiba was then Minister of Agriculture; he was dismissed in 1976.

12. Hoxha released the evidence on his side in his 'Political Diaries' (Hoxha, 1979).

References

Albania Today, No. 1, 1976

Ash, W. (1975). *Pickaxe and Rifle*. London

Backa, A. (1966). The Simplification and Improvement of Plan Methodology. *Ekonomia populore*, No. 2, pp. 14–27

Ballco, I. P. (1968). For a Thorough Knowledge and Creative Application of Planning Methods. *Ekonomia populore*, No. 4, pp., 3–13

Banja, H., Fullani, J. and Papajorgji, H. (1973). *Probleme të organizimit e të drejtimit te ekonomisë populore në RPSh*. Tirana

Bardhosi, B. (1976). Strengthening the Scientific Character of Planning – an Important Basis for the Correct Execution of the Party's Economic Policy. *Rruga e partisë*, No. 8, pp. 36–47

Bashkimi, 25 July 1968

Dodbiba, P. (1974). *Albania Today*, No. 5, pp. 24–29

Ekonomia politike e socializmit, Vol. 1, 1975. Tirana

Ekonomia popullore, No. 1. 1966, pp. 3–12

Gazeta zyrzare, No. 8, 1971

Griffith, W. E. (1963). *Albania and the Sino-Soviet Rift*. Cambridge, Massachusetts

History of the Party of Labour of Albania (1971). Tirana

Hoxha, E, (1969a). *Raporte e fjalime 1967–8*. Tirana

—— (1969b). *Speeches, 1967–8*. Tirana

—— (1971a). *Raport në Kongresin VI të PPSh*. Tirana

—— (1971b). *Report to the Sixth Congress of the PLA*. Tirana

—— (1974a). *Our Policy is an Open Policy, the Policy of Proletarian Principles*. Tirana

—— (1974b). *Speeches 1971–3*. Tirana

—— (1976). *Report to the Seventh Congress of the PLA*. Tirana

—— (1979). *Thoughts on China*, 2 vols. Tirana

Information Bulletin of the Central Committee of the Party of Labour of Albania, No. 3, 1967, No. 1, 1970, No. 3, 1970

Jakubini, I. (1967). For a Better Understanding of the Simplification of Statistics. *Ekonomia populore*, No. 3, pp. 16–33

Kallapodhi, A., Dumani, N. and Kote, K. (1971). *Bazat e ekonomisë dhe organizimit dë bujqesisë socialiste*. Tirana

Kapo, H. (1970). Report to the Tenth Plenum of the PLA Central Committee, *Information Bulletin . . .*, No. 3

Kaser, M. C. (1967). *Comecon: Integration Problems of the Planned Economies*. 2nd ed. London

—— (1972). Albania. In *Die Wirtschftsordnungen Osteuropas im Wandel* (ed. by H.-H. Höhmann, M. C. Kaser and K. C. Thalheim). Freiburg-im-Breisgau

—— (1975). *The New Economic Systems of Eastern Europe*, London

—— (1977). Trade and Aid in the Albanian Economy. In *East European Economies Post-Helsinki: A Compendium of Papers Submitted to the Joint Economic Committee, Congress of the United States, August 25, 1977*, Washington, D.C.

—— (1979). Notes on Chinese Aid to Albania. In *Documents on Communist Affairs*, Vol. 2 (ed. by B. Szajkowski). London

—— Albania. *Comecon Reports*, Vol. 1, No. 1, pp. 45–53; Vol. 1, No. 2, pp. 60–3

Kaser, M. C.and Schnytzer, A. (1977). Albania – A Uniquely Socialist Economy. In *East European Economies*

Kedi, V. and Luci, E. (1970). *Programmimi linear në problemat ekonomike*. Tirana

Lederer, L. (1977). Crisis grips Albania. *Sunday Times*, 6 November 1977

Letters of Junius, 1769–1772

Lika, Z. (1964). *Dusa çështje mbi përmirësimin e metejshëm të planifikimit dhe të shpërblimit sipas punës*. Tirana

Logoreci, A. (1976). *The Albanians*. London

Marmallaku, R. (1975). *Albania and the Albanians*. London

Pano, N. C. (1968). *The People's Republic of Albania*. Baltimore, Maryland

Përmbledhëse e përgjithshme e legjislacionit në fuqi të RPSh (1971). Tirana

PPSh Dokumenta kryesore (1972). Vol. III, Tirana

Probleme ekonomike, No. 1, 1973, pp. 55 –76; No. 1, 1974; No. 1, 1975; No. 1, 1976; July–September, 1977, pp. 3–21; July–September 1978, pp. 9–34

Report to the Central Committee of the PLA, 27 September 1968. *Information Bulletin . . .*, No. 4, 1968

Rruga e partisë, No. 12, 1976: May 1977, pp. 5–19

Sejko, E., Papajorgji, H., Fullani, J., Murati, O. and Mara, G. (1975). *Bazat e organizi-mit socialist të punës dhe drejtimit*, Vol. II. Tirana

Shehu, M. (1971). *Report on the Fifth Five-Year Plan*. Tirana

—— (1976). *Report on the Sixth Five-Year Plan*. Tirana

Xhuvani, P., Gurica, I., Sejko, E. and Bollano, P. (1972). *Organizimi, planifikimi i veprimtarisë ekonomiko-produese të ndërmarrjeve industriale*. Tirana

31 vjet Shqipëri socialiste (1974). Tirana

Zëri i populit, 22 February 1968; 29 November 1972; 1 April 1976; 30 April 1977; 7 July 1977

Index

Agriculture,
  Albania, organization, 330–331
  Bulgaria, 225–227
    effects of investment allocation, 216
    exports to West, 225
    failure of modernization, 215
    industrialization process, 225–226
    plans underfulfilled, 218
    private plots, 226–227
    reform proposals, 226
    urban migration of workers, 217
  Czechoslovakia,
    good results since 1965, 153
    hierarchical organization, 156, 157
    reasons for growth, 175
  Poland,
    ambiguous policy on private land, 100
    failure to reach planned targets
      (1976–1980), 130
    improvements in early 1970s, 93
    need to encourage private farming, 127
    1976–1980 plan, 127–128
    productivity, 100
    wage differentials, 96–97
  Romania,
    organization, 273–276
    tax burden reduced on cooperative
      farmers, 276
  USSR,
    performance, 20
    policy objectives, 20–22
    policy on private plots, 22
    reasons for inefficiency, 22
  Yugoslavia,
    collectives revert to private sector, 283,
      303
    exports to EEC restrained, 294–295
    food deficits, 281–282
    Green Plan (1973–1985), 303
    modernization, 313
    output, private and public compared,
      303–304
    price setting, 309
  Albania, 315–342
    attempts to maintain ideological purity,
      337–338

Albania (*cont.*)
  conservative radicalism, 315–316
  loss of Chinese aid, 329–330, 334,340
  plan targets and results (1966–1970), 332
  political attacks in cultural spheres,
    337–338
  purges during 1971–1975, 331, 337–338
    in armed forces, 338–339
  'self-reliance' policies, 336
  Stalinist philosophy, 315, 318, 337
  see also country subheadings under
    principal subjects
Armaments policy, threats from economic
  reforms, 11
  see also Military expenditure
Associations of enterprises,2–3
  advantages, 77–78
  Bulgaria,
    as economic management instrument,
      233–234
    numbers reduced by combination, 233
    wage structure, 236–237
  Czechoslovakia,
    stable long-term plans proposed, 166
    structure, 156
  German Democratic Republic (GDR),
    application of profits, 62
    data preparation for annual plans, 59
    functions, 55, 56
    increased formation desirable, 77–80
    rise in numbers of combines, 78–79
  Poland,
    creates pilot 'large economic
      organizations', 113–114
    organizing own foreign trade, 112
    restructuring in 1960s, 109–110
  USSR, 35–36

Baikal–Amur railway project, 23
Balance of payments,
  Czechoslovak, in trade with developing
    countries, 176
  Yugoslav, 295, 297
    effect on invisible earnings, 298

Banking sector,
functions in German Democratic Republic,
67–68
Yugoslav policy, 304–307
Building *see* Construction industry
Bulgaria, 215–252
failure of five-year plan (1975–1980), 215
living standards, 227–232
plan for 1976–1980, 221–222
reasons for poor results, 222
see also country subheadings under
principal subjects
Bureaucracy,
in Bulgaria, privileges attached to, 241
in German Democratic Republic, causing
failure of new system, 69
losses feared from economic reforms, 13

Centralized economic planning,
characteristics, 2
Czechoslovakia, 165
fundamental defects, 25–36
German Democratic Republic,
in conflict with reform theories, 45–46
return to, 49
inefficiencies of territorial bodies, 36
over-complexity, 32–33
policy outgrown, 1
rationalization, 2–3
techniques employed, 3
USSR,
call for greater efficiency, 18–20
discussion on use of computers, 35
increased quantitative emphasis, 41–42
overburdening planners, 42–43
terms of 1979 decree, 40–42
Yugoslavia, in first five-year plan
(1947–1952), 282
see also Economic planning
Combines *see* Associations of enterprises
Communist parties,
ages of leaders, 12–13
control in Romania, 256–260
high membership rate in Romania, 256
ideological conservatism, 12
leaderships' fear of loss of control, 10
Computers,
for economic planning in Bulgaria, 238
use in Soviet planning, 35
Construction industry,
Bulgaria,
aim to reduce projects in late 1970s, 222
problems in meeting plans, 220
use of brigade system, 237
German Democratic Republic, problems
in, 73–74
Hungary, failure to achieve quota, 202
Romania, quality control measures, 263

Construction industry (*cont.*)
USSR,
attracting investment, 29–30
indicator of net value of completed
work, 39–40
inefficiencies, 25–26
Consumer goods,
Bulgaria,
estimated consumption (1960–1977), 248
growth rate of consumption fund, 230
increasing import share, 229
means of improving supplies, 229, 230
reported and projected consumption,
228
retail trade plan overfulfilled, 218
Czechoslovakia,
fewer 'final goods' produced, 171
given great importance in 1970s, 143
limited exports to West, 153
panic buying in 1968, 172
restoring market equilibrium, 175
retail price increases, 160–161
German Democratic Republic,
enhancement of sector, 50
improved planning decisions, 74–75
price maintenance, 72
product mix incorrect, 69
Hungary,
linking prices to producer prices, 209
price structure, 183, 184
supplemented by Western markets, 206
Poland,
growth in retail turnover, 94
increasing imbalances, 131
increasing imports, 107–108
longstanding market disequilibrium,
106–107
physical consumption rates, 97
strain on structure of supply, 125
Romania,
functions of 'public control' teams,
261–262
retail price control, 271
USSR,
outstripped by increases in incomes, 39
policy objectives, 22–23
production, 20
Cooperatives,
Albania, agricultural, 330
Romania,
agencies established (1976), 263
in agricultural sector, 274
Corruption,
increasing in Bulgaria, 232
increasing in Poland, 131
Cost planning,
German Democratic Republic, 63–64
Hungary, calculations imperfect, 185

Council for Mutual Economic Aid (CMEA),
    average annual growth rates of national
        income and gross industrial output,
        243
    Comprehensive Programme, 56
    demands on Czechoslovakian industrial
        output, 176
    effect of agreements on Czechoslovakian
        foreign trade, 152
    foreign trade (1950–1976), 249
    German Democratic Republic's problem of
        coordination, 48
    rankings in foreign trade growth rates, 218
    serving Soviet hegemony, 12
Credit operations,
    German Democratic Republic, 68
    Hungary,
        action to limit investment boom, 196
        annual policy guidelines, 196
        differing types for investment, 197
    Poland,
        causing economic tensions, 104
        increasing indebtedness, 131
    Yugoslavia,
        anti-inflation measures, 291
        from Western sources, 298–300
        role of banks, 305, 306
Czechoslovakia, 139–179
    early 1970s economic crisis, 139
    federal state structure, 156
    five-year plans (1971–1980), 140–144
    five-year and annual plan preparation, 158
    limited reform of centralized planning, 9
    loss of economic growth, 1
    methods of implementing economic policy,
        155–167
    standards of living, 172–173
    see also country subheadings under
        principal subjects

Decisionmaking,
    Albania, directors subordinated to
        workers' control, 322–323
    at enterprise level, resisted by central
        administration, 5
    Bulgaria,
        devolution to monopolistic
            organizations, 216
        in large branch managements, 226
    Czechoslovakia,
        at enterprise level, 4
        structure, 156
    devolution from centre, 3
    lack of yardsticks, 6–7
    German Democratic Republic,
        by managers, 77
        effect of industry restructuring, 79
        restrictions, 49

Decisionmaking (*cont.*)
    Hungary, on investment projects, 195, 198
    reform period, 317–318
    Yugoslavia, decentralization, 283
Delivery plans,
    inclusion in Czech planning, 158
    USSR,
        non-fulfilment, 29
        stressed in 1979 decree, 37
        volume targets, 38
Division of labour, international, 4
    utilization in USSR policy, 24
    Yugoslavia's entry, 283

Economic analysis, aggregate and partial, 56
Economic growth,
    Albania, reasons for poor performance, 323
    Bulgaria, 217
        deceleration in 1970s, 215
        major indicators (1965–1976), 242
        of national income, accumulation and
            consumption (1937–1977), 245
        of national income, output and
            investment (1951–1977), 244
    Czechoslovakia, 167–175
        factors facilitating, 175
        problem areas, 144–155
        reduced targets, 140
        up to 1970, 139
    disruptions in 1970s, 7
    Hungary, internal and external influences,
        205–206
    Poland, 92, 95
        developing strains, 104–108
    related to reform of system, 233
    Romania, 217
    Yugoslavia, objectives following
        revolution, 282–284
Economic planning,
    Albania,
        adaptations in 1970, 321–325
        'fundamental principles' Decision (1966),
            316–317
        investigation of mathematical
            techniques, 325
        'moral' incentives for workers, 323
        new methodology introduced (1978),
            324
        plan preparation, 317
        reorganization in 1960s, 318–319
        revolutionary tone of Labour Code,
            319–320
        targets and results, 332
    Bulgaria
        attitudes to change, 238–241
        'new planning technology' announced,
            236

Economic planning (*cont.*)
  Bulgaria (*cont.*)
    reasons for poor performance, 238–239
    system and its management, 232–238
    tendency to monopolies, 240
  Czechoslovakia,
    experiments in decentralization, 166–167
    hierarchial structure, 157
    instruments, 158–164
  evaluation problems, 238
  German Democratic Republic,
    aggregate process, 55–61
    annual plans, 58–60
    construction of plans, 56–57
    problems besetting plan formulation, 57
  Hungary,
    changing attitudes to centralization, 180
    harmonizing centralized and
      decentralized systems, 204
  recentralization, 7–8
  reforms, 1–2
    consideration of central planning
      complexity, 32–33
    effect of world factors, 8
    in Bulgaria, 233; political consequences,
      240–241
    in Czechoslovakia, 142, 144, 165–167
    in German Democratic Republic, 45
    in Hungary, 180–181
    in Poland, 108–122
    in Romania, 254–255
    in USSR, 36–44; failure of movement,
      17–18
    in Yugoslavia, 283–284
    international similarities, 2
    no theory developed, 6
    reasons for limitations, 9–16
    results of experiments, 6
    retreat from, 5–9
  relaxation of target planning, 4
  Romania,
    agencies reorganized, 257
    centralization theme from 1978, 264
    integration of enterprise budgets, 266
    'new economic mechanism', 264–276
    relationship between party and state
      agencies, 259
  Yugoslavia,
    devolution to republican and other
      organs, 286
    five-year plan (1971–1975), 284–286,
      287
    'parametric' system, 283
    role of banks, 305
    social plan (1976–1980), 286–289
  see also Centralized economic planning
Economic policies,
  Albania, disputed areas (1974–1976),
    331–340

Economic policies (*cont.*)
  Czechoslovakia,
    aims in 1970s, 139–155
    methods of implementing, 155–167
  Hungary,
    evidences of income levelling, 194
    revisions for 1980s, 207–212
  Poland, introduction of 'new strategy'
    (1971), 93
  Yugoslavia, regional, 301–303
Efficiency,
  Bulgaria, 215–216
    reforms to improve, 239–240
  Czechoslovakia, 167–175
    adverse long-term trend, 142
    lacking in late 1960s, 140
  German Democratic Republic,
    encouraged by formation of combines,
      78
    plans for improvement, 68–70
  Poland, low capital and labour utilization,
    131
  USSR,
    causes of failure, 25–30
    moves to reduce waste, 39
    need for improvement, 18–20
Employment,
  Bulgaria,
    by sector (1948–1977), 247
    rural-urban migration, 217
  Czechoslovakia, improvement in late
    1960s, 146
  Hungary,
    development in south-west region,
      202–203
    labour made dearer than capital, 190
    link with enterprise profitability, 191
    need to balance with investment, 200
    shortage of workers, 190
  Poland,
    in pilot units, 118–119
    rate of growth, 99
    structure decided by pilot units, 114
  Romania, regulations controlling, 268–269
  Yugoslavia, 310–312
Energy,
  Bulgaria, world situation's effect on
    economy, 223
  costs, effect on prices in German
    Democratic Republic, 65
    see also Oil: price increases
  Czechoslovakia,
    problems for economic growth, 147–148
    production, 147–148
    results of conservation programmes, 148
  Hungary, price increases in 1980s, 209
  Poland, participation in Soviet projects,
    105
  Yugoslavia, internal resources, 281

Eurodollar market, Soviet dealings on, 24
Exchange rates *see* Foreign trade
Exports *see* Foreign trade

Fertilizer industry, Soviet, 42–43
Food prices,
  Bulgaria, 1979 increases, 231, 232
  Czechoslovakia, 1977 increases, 161
  Poland,
    increases forcefully rejected (1976), 123
    rationing substituted for increases, 121
    1970 revolt, 112
    worsening supply situation in early
      1970s, 107
  USSR, official and free market prices, 23
Food supplies,
  effect of Soviet shortages, 23
  Poland, in 1976–1980 plan, 125–126
Foreign policy,
  Albania, desire for ideological purity, 339
  influence on economic planning, 8
  Soviet dominance threatened by reforms,
    12
Foreign trade,
  Albania, 335
    loss of Chinese aid, 329–330
    possibly with West, 336
  Bulgaria,
    by product groups (1960–1977), 250
    composition and efficiency, 217–218
    imports of consumer groups, 229
    mainly with socialist countries, 224
    with the West, 225
  CMEA countries (1950–1976), 249
  Czechoslovakia,
    balance of trade by major country
      groups, 154
    benefit of strong agricultural sector, 175
    factors causing problems, 151
    hierarchical organization, 156
    problems created by trade with West,
      154
    problems of regional structure, 153–154
  Hungary, 209
    deterioration since reform, 206
    doubling of deficit in late 1970s, 207
    price differentials, 185
  no longer state monopoly, 4
  Poland,
    balancing by pilot units, 116; scheme
      withdrawn, 118
    change in policy, 93
    deficit with Western countries, 103
    encouragement in late 1970s, 121
    fluctuations, 101–102
    incentive scheme (1966), 110
    monopoly of specialized corporations
      broken, 112
    plan (1976–1980), 124

Foreign trade (*cont.*)
  Poland (*cont.*)
    tax on export earnings, 118
    trade with West below objectives,
      129–130
  related to strains of economic growth,
    104–105
  Romania,
    establishing 'trading' rate of exchange,
      272
    exchange rate problems, 271–272
    organization, 273
    transferable ruble devalued (1981), 272
  Yugoslavia,
    imports from West and Third World,
      295
    invisible earnings, 298
    shift of exports from EEC to CMEA,
      293–294
    structural changes, 295–296

Gas, production in Siberia, 23
German Democratic Republic (GDR), 45–90
  annual plans, subsequent changes to, 69
  anticipated changes in planning system,
    71–72
  banking and credit, 67–68
  economic development indicators, 53
  'economic levers' ineffective, 47
  effect of greater decentralization, 71
  functions of Council of Ministers, 54,
    56–57
  functions of State Planning Commission,
    54, 56
  likely developments in planning, 80–81
  long-term plans to 2000, 55
  loss of economic growth, 1
  monetary steering policies, 61–68
  more efficient use of capital, 72–74
  move back to centralized planning, 49
  New Economic System (NES), 45, 46
    abandoned, 48–49
    imperfections, 46, 48–49
  recentralization, aims methods and
    instruments, 49–68
    weaknesses of present system, 68–71
  reformed system's lack of success, 45–48
  'socialist rationalization' plan, 73
  tasks of principle management organs,
    53–55
  see also country subheadings under
    principal subjects
Gosplan, aims laid down in 1979 decree, 40

Housing,
  Bulgaria,
    problems in construction, 230
    rural/urban imbalance, 230
  Hungary, 207

Housing (*cont.*)
  Poland, shortages, 97, 126
  Yugoslavia, funding through banks, 289
  see also Construction industry
Hungary, 180–214
  assessment of new economic mechanism, 203–207
  basis of labour unrest, 15
  cautious reforms, 9
  economic reform model, 3–4
  improved standard of living, 206
  markets constrained by limited number of suppliers, 184
  new strategy for 1980s, 207–212
  post-war centralization, 180
  recentralization in 1970s, 181
  shifts between centralization and decentralization, 180
  see also country subheadings under principal subjects

Imports *see* Foreign trade
Incomes, personal *see* Wages
Industrial output,
  Albania,
    structural changes, 333
    targets and results (1971–1975), 323–333
  Bulgaria,
    chaos created by counterplans, 236
    plans overfulfilled, 218
  Czechoslovakia,
    CMEA demands on, 176
    inputs related to national product, 168
    proportion of 'final products', 171
    stockholdings, 170–171
  German Democratic Republic,
    balancing process, 60–61
    policy of enhancement, 50
    problems of setting priorities, 46
  Hungary, product range defects, 201
  Poland, related to wage fund, 114–115
  USSR,
    changes in plan target, 28
    effect of planning by gross value, 26–27
    indicators, 37–38
    inefficiency caused by administrative splits, 27–28
    planning based on negotiated contracts, 41
    waste caused by quantitative targets, 27
Industry,
  Albania,
    capital–labour ratio, 333
    enterprise 'planning commissions', 322
    managed by district councils, 322
  Bulgaria,
    capacity underutilized, 222
    counterplan campaign, 235–236

Industry (*cont.*)
  Bulgaria (*cont.*)
    establishment of combines, 234–235
    failure to achieve plans, 222–223
    insistance on machine-building, 223
    integration with agriculture, 225–226
    investment allocation, 217
    joint ventures with Western firms, 225
    structural change, 216, 223–224
    structure and growth, 246
  Czechoslovakia
    expansion priority in 1960s, 142–143
    growth of capital stock, 149
    increasing equipment imports from West, 152
    problems of investment targets, 149–150
  German Democratic Republic,
    additional 'counterplan' obligations, 60
    cost planning, 63–64
    data preparation for annual plans, 59
    defects in capital planning, 69–70
    'final product' indicator, 76
    functions of industrial ministries, 54–55
    indicators directed towards intensification, 75–76
    modernization, 51
    performance measurement, 75–77
    proposal for more efficient use of capital, 72–74
  Hungary,
    inefficient use of manpower and resources, 200–201
    linking prices with world markets, 208–209
    price structure, 183, 184
    regional structure policy, 202–203
  Poland,
    disequilibrium apparent, 118
    in 1976–1980 plan, 128
    machinery for gradual reforms, 113
    productivity, 99–100
    restructuring under four ministries, 121–122
    return to centralized management, 130
  Romania,
    advice from 'organization offices', 263
    economic and financial self-administration, 264
    external and internal causes of underfulfilment, 256
    organization following 1978 resolution, 265
    self-financing, 265, 266
  USSR, plan indicators, in 1979 decree, 37–40
  Yugoslavia,
    joint enterprises, 300
    modernization, 313

Industry (*cont.*)
  Yugoslavia (*cont.*)
    problems caused by lack of skills, 282
    transport difficulties, 282
    use of foreign capital, 298
    see also Associations of enterprises
Inflation, in Yugoslavia, 289–290
  anti-inflation measures, 290–292
  role of played by wage increases, 308
Investment,
  Albania, bank control, 329
  Bulgaria,
    characteristics in 1970s, 216
    imbalance with consumption policy, 227
    main recipients, 220
  Czechoslovakia, 175
    efficiency in decline, 169–170
    problems in 1970s, 148–151
    productive and non-productive sectors,
      150–151
  German Democratic Republic,
    disruption (1969–1970), 48
    in unplanned projects, 70
    two new decrees promulgated, 73–74
    strict control for planned projects, 62
  Hungary, 194–203
    boom period in late 1960s, 196
    change of responsibility since 1976,
      197–198
    consistency of functions, 195
    dealing with disruptions, 205
    differentiation in decisionmaking, 195
    encouraged from profits, 198
    high share of building, 200
    planned expenditure exceeded, 207, 208
    reasons for delay, 199–200
    structure, planned and actual, 202
    unsatisfactory aspects, 199
  Poland,
    degree of decentralization, 121
    failure to maintain growth, 129
    halted in 1976–1980 plan, 125
    increases (1970–1975), 98
    little for modernization programmes,
      119
    period of optimism, 106
  USSR,
    attracted to construction industry, 29–30
    decline in volume, 26
    faulty planning, 24–25
    in agriculture, 20–21
    increasing trend to centralization, 41
    1979 decree statements, 37
    plan indicator, 39
  Yugoslavia,
    affecting inflation, 288
    cuts to reduce inflation, 291
    funding by bond issues, 307

General Investment Fund, 305
  in underdeveloped areas, 301–302
  joint ventures, 300
  main sources, 289
  role of banks, 306

Labour *see* Workforce
Living standards,
  Bulgaria, 227–232
    targets lowered, 215
  Czechoslovakia, 172–173
  Hungary, 206

Management,
  Albania,
    devolution to slim central
      administration, 318
    subject to workers' control, 320–321
  Bulgaria,
    adopting technocratic approach, 233, 241
    for agricultural sector, 226
    ineffective at association level, 234
    instability of top echelons, 237–238
    sanctions against deficiencies, 236, 237
  complaints against traditional planning
    systems, 14
  Czechoslovakia,
    involvement in plan preparation, 158
    structure, 156–158
  German Democratic Republic,
    need to encourage decisionmaking, 77
    tasks of principal organs, 53–55
  Hungary,
    bonuses from profits, 189, 190
    view of profit motive, 188–189
  Romania,
    constraints on enterprise directors,
      261–263
    under 1967 reform, 261
  USSR, 17
    complex incentive schemes, 34
    deciding rate of technical innovation, 31
    need for freedom from tight control, 43
    stable norms under 1979 decree, 41
  Yugoslavia, 287–288
Market economy, socialist form of, 2
  demands on management, 14
  Hungarian model, 4
    incomes policy, 187–8
  USSR, causing greater problems for, 11
  Yugoslavia, introduction into, 283–284
    tending to favour developed areas, 302
Military expenditure,
  threatened by economic reforms, 11
  USSR, high levels of, 24

Mineral resources, of Yugoslavia, 281
  see also Energy; Oil
Monetary instruments,
  in Czech economic plan, 159–166
  in Yugoslavia, to overcome illiquidity, 306

Oil
  Albania, accusations against ministers,
      335–336, 338
  price increases,
    adding to Soviet earnings, 24
    affecting Czech economy, 147
    affecting Yugoslav economy, 312
    influence on economic reform, 8
    production in Siberia, 23

Poland, 91–138
  balance of payments, 101–102
  basis of labour unrest, 15
  Commission for Modernization of
      Functioning of Economy and State,
      113
  development factors, 98–104
  growth rates, actual and planned
      (1966–1975), 92, 95
  influence of 1970 workers' revolt, 91
  national income, 103–104
    in 1976–1980 plan, 124
  plan for 1976–1980, 122–134
    results and prospects, 128–134
  plan for 1981–1985, 132–133
  problems created by over-expansion, 120
  reasons for deteriorating performance, 7
  reconsideration of economic problems, 5
  see also country subheadings under
      principal subjects
Political stability, threat from market
    economy reforms, 11
Prices,
  Bulgaria,
    arbitrary setting, 239
    increases in 1979, 231
  Czechoslovakia,
    basis of setting unclear, 160
    frozen in 1970, 160
    policy as steering instrument, 160–161
    restoring equilibrium in consumer
        goods, 175
    review of wholesale prices, 161
  decentralization of decisions, 4
  domestic linked with foreign, 4
  German Democratic Republic,
    effects of recentralization, 64–67
    equalization fund, 66
    price setting process, 64–65
    problems of plan formulation, 58
    reforms unlikely, 71–72

Prices (*cont.*)
  German Democratic Republic (*cont.*)
    revisions for industrial inputs, 66–67
    three groups (to 1975), 65
    unsatisfactory structure, 46
  Hungary,
    consumer goods to link with producer
        prices, 209
    domestic/world market link defective,
        185
    effect of near-monopolistic markets, 184
    effect on mid-1970s increases, 185–186
    importance in planning and steering, 182
    in concept of 'unfair profit', 211
    integrated system, 186
    liberal policies affecting income and
        investment policies, 204
    policy changes for 1980s, 208–210
    principle underlying producer price
        increases, 208–209
    varying amounts of central control,
        182–183
  insufficient information for
      decisionmaking, 7
  Poland,
    after 1970 revolt, 91
    changes in 1971–1975 plan, 110–111
    increases (1971–1974), 96
    paid by state for agricultural produce,
        100–101
    rules for determining, 117
  Romania,
    control under 'new economic
        mechanism', 270–271
    Law on Prices and Tariffs (1971), 270
  USSR,
    causing problems for efficiency, 33–35
    cost-plus calculations, 17
    effect of 1965 'Kosygin' reforms, 33–34
    imprecision of Soviet index, 20, 26
  Yugoslavia, 309–310
    anti-inflation measures, 290–291
    basis for setting, 309
    price freeze (1970), 289
    role of federal government, 288
  see also Food prices
Productivity,
  Albania, 329, 333
  Bulgaria, 248
  Czechoslovakia,
    declining trend, 168–169
    in 1970s, 141, 142
    incentive schemes, 164–165
    stimulating 'socialist competition', 165
  German Democratic Republic,
    bonus fund, 47, 62–63
    disappointing results (1971–1975), 52–53
      causing planning problems, 58
    performance fund incentives, 63

Productivity (*cont.*)
Hungary, 190–191, 206
Poland, 99
USSR,
below expectations, 30
plan indicators in 1979 decree, 39
Profits
as measure of enterprise success, 4
Bulgaria,
division by combines, 235
in blueprint for reform, 233
Czechoslovakia,
as measure of efficiency, 159
deduction for bonus fund, 164
profit-sharing schemes, 164; in reform
period, 162
German Democratic Republic,
as plan indicator, 62
effect on any new planning system, 71
utilization of profits, 62
Hungary,
complications in assessing, 191–192
concept of 'unfair profits', 211
manipulation by enterprises, 204
policy orientation, 188
profit-sharing schemes, 189–190,
211–212
simplification of distribution, 193
Poland,
related to wage fund, 114–115, 116
Romania,
distribution and taxation, 266
profit-sharing schemes, 264, 269–270
unsatisfactory basis for reforms, 33
USSR,
disposal outside Soviet enterprises, 18
plan indicator in 1979 decree, 39

Quality control,
measures introduced in Romania, 263
rewards in Soviet plans, 38–39

Reforms of economic planning *see* Economic
planning: reforms
Romania, 253–279
coal miners' strike (1977), 269
constitutions and hierarchy, 256–257, 258
creation of National Council, 263
office of President established, 256
party control, 256–260
studies of economic system, 253–254
see also country subheadings under
principal subjects

Siberia,
economic development, 11
economic policy objectives, 23–24

Social policies,
Bulgaria, 230
Czechoslovakia, deductions from
enterprises to finance, 159
effects of economic reforms, 13
German Democratic Republic, 51
attempted unity with economic policies,
51–52
transfers of income, 50
Poland, 97
Romania, 270
Stockholdings,
in Czechoslovakia, 170–171
in Hungary, 207–208
Subsidies,
Bulgaria, 232
German Democratic Republic, 65, 66
Hungary, 205
for energy, 209
USSR, 21–22

Technological progress,
Bulgaria, 215
foreign-generated innovations, 223
problems of diffusion, 240
Czechoslovakia, unwillingness to innovate,
140
German Democratic Republic,
means of increasing rate, 77
modernization of capital stock, 51
unwillingness to innovate, 69
Hungary, function of investment policy,
195
Poland, 110
poor capacity to absorb, 131
USSR,
deterrent effect of plan target, 31
development seen as too slow, 25
link between industry and research
institutes, 35
reluctance to innovate, 30–32
Yugoslavia, through joint ventures, 300

USSR, 17–44
administration's reasons for opposing
reforms, 10–11
Albania's request for aid refused, 336
close trading links with Bulgaria, 224
economic blockage of Albania, 317
economic policy objectives, 20–24
ninth and tenth five-year plans, 18–20
loss of economic growth, 1
new reforms in 1979 decree, 36–42
assessment, 42–44
possible result of reforms, 12
problems of meeting Czech fuel demands,
147
reasons for poor economic performance,
24–25

USSR (*cont.*)
  work of the planning organs, 40
  see also country subheadings under
    principal subjects

Wages,
  Albania,
    differentiation of mental and physical
      work, 326
    income distribution, 325, 326
    level of supplementary payments, 327
    moves towards equalization, 327–328
    need to introduce incentives, 326–328
  Bulgaria,
    average annual increases, 220
    growth, 248
    increases (1979), 231
    material and non-material incentives, 239
    new system for industry, construction
      and agriculture. 236–237
    relative levelling, 230
  Czechoslovakia,
    central decision on enterprise's total
      wage bill, 164
    graded structure, 162
    incentive schemes, 164–165
    occupational differentials, 162–163
    policy as steering instrument, 161–164
    privileges of officials and directors,
      163–164
    time worked to earn basic commodities,
      173, 174
  Hungary,
    bonuses for management, 189, 190
    bonuses for workforce, 189, 190
    enterprise policy for 1980s, 210
    incentives, 210
    income policy, 187–194; changes for
      1980s, 210–212
    increasing centralization from
      mid-1970s, 192–194
    little affected by profitability, 212
    policy objections on economic grounds,
      204
  Poland, 93
    excess wage funds transferred to
      reserves, 118
    fast increases, 96
    fund dissociated from planning targets,
      115
    increases, (1970–1975), 106
    increases postulated in 1976–1980 plan,
      125
    restructuring related to wage fund, 114
    revival of incentive schemes, 121
  Romania,
    abolition of tax on, 267
    guaranteed in agriculture, 275–276

Wages (*cont.*)
  Romania (*cont.*)
    industry branch differentials, 267–268
    most regulated East European system,
      268
    under 'new economic mechanism',
      267–270
  Stalinist doctrine on income distribution,
    325–326
  USSR,
    increases faster than supply of consumer
      goods, 22–23, 39
    increases for agricultural workers, 21
  Yugoslavia, 307–308
    differentials, 307
    right of state to intervene, 308
    voluntary agreements, 308
West Germany, equipment supplied to
    USSR, 24
Worker participation,
  Albania, 317
    control of enterprise directors, 320–321
  Czechoslovakia, 4–5
  Hungary, 181
  Poland, 120–121
  Romania,
    brought into enterprise management,
      260–261
    control role emphasised in mid-1970s,
      262
    objective of 1978 resolution, 264
    three types of organization, 255
  Yugoslavia, 288
Workforce,
  Albania,
    all workers engaged in some physical
      work, 318–319, 326
    three income groups, 325
  Bulgaria,
    given variety of incentives, 239
    reorganization into brigade system, 237
  Czechoslovakia,
    disparity between skills and occupations,
      147
    exhaustion of potential, 173
    structure in economic sectors, 146–147
  effects of economic reforms, 14–15
  German Democratic Republic,
    bonus fund, neglecting quality
      requirements, 76
    use of incentives, 63, 64
  Hungary,
    mobility, 191, 192
    percentage engaged in moving materials,
      200
    wasted manpower, 200–201
  Poland
    diminishing rate of increase, 123–124
    incentives in 1971–1975 plan, 111–112

Workforce *(cont.)*
  Romania,
    elevating role of foreman, 264
    payroll tax, 267
    regulations controlling, 268–269
  Yugoslavia,
    civic responsibility assumed, 287
    number employed in Western Europe,
        310, 312
    privileges of bank employees, 305
    problems of overcoming cultural
        backgrounds, 282
    rural/urban migration, 31
  see also Productivity
World Bank, loans to Yugoslavia, 298, 299

Yugoslavia, 280–314
  Communists' rise to power, 281

Yugoslavia *(cont.)*
  degree of autonomy for republics and
      provinces, 284–285
  economic objectives of revolution, 282–284
  economic problems after 1918, 280
  economic reform model, 4
  five-year plan (1971–1975), 284–286, 287
  future prospects, 312–313
  high inflation from 1967, 284
  inherited regional inequalities, 301
  involvement in world economic problems,
      287
  nationalist pressures, 284–285
  rupture with East European bloc, 282
  social plan (1976–1980), 286–289
  sources of foreign capital, 298–300
  see also country subheadings under
      principal subjects